Heart Full of Rhythm

Armstrong solos in front of his big band at the Apollo Theater in February 1942.
Photo by Charles Peterson, Courtesy of Don Peterson

Heart Full of Rhythm

The Big Band Years of Louis Armstrong

Ricky Riccardi

OXFORD

UNIVERSITY PRESS

OXFORD
UNIVERSITY PRESS

Oxford University Press is a department of the University of Oxford. It furthers
the University's objective of excellence in research, scholarship, and education
by publishing worldwide. Oxford is a registered trade mark of Oxford University
Press in the UK and certain other countries.

Published in the United States of America by Oxford University Press
198 Madison Avenue, New York, NY 10016, United States of America.

Library of Congress Cataloging-in-Publication Data
Names: Riccardi, Ricky, 1980– author.
Title: Heart full of rhythm : the big band years of Louis Armstrong / Ricky Riccardi.
Description: New York : Oxford University Press, 2020. | Includes bibliographical references and index.
Identifiers: LCCN 2020008383 (print) | LCCN 2020008384 (ebook) |
ISBN 9780190914110 (hardback) | ISBN 9780190914134 (epub)
Subjects: LCSH: Armstrong, Louis, 1901–1971—Criticism and interpretation. |
Jazz—New York (State)—New York—1931–1940—History and criticism. |
Jazz—New York (State)—New York—1941–1950—History and criticism. |
Apollo Theater (New York, N.Y. : 125th Street)
Classification: LCC ML419. A75 R46 2020 (print) | LCC ML419. A75 (ebook) |
DDC 781.65092 [B]—dc23
LC record available at https://lccn.loc.gov/2020008383
LC ebook record available at https://lccn.loc.gov/2020008384

1 3 5 7 9 8 6 4 2

Printed by LSC Communications, United States of America

For my ladies: Margaret, Ella, Melody, and Lily.

You know how we survived? Through humor and manipulation—subterfuge. Most comedians were actually being themselves, reflecting that manipulation. They weren't acting. Louis Armstrong was criticized for Tomming, for instance, but that's the way Pops was off the stage. He was the most entirely natural man I ever met in my life. What you saw onstage was him; he acted the same way in the joints after the show was over. Anyone who calls Pops a Tom has to be among the dumbest individuals alive. It's pathetic that people don't really understand that. I resent all the criticism of those comics, because the critics don't take into consideration the era in which they grew up.

—Honi Coles, 1979[1]

Man, it makes no difference to me who thinks I'm God and who doesn't. All I want to do is blow my horn the way I think is best. I want a public, not a pedestal!

—Louis Armstrong, 1941[2]

Contents

Heart Full of Rhythm

Prologue

Bigger Than Jazz

The Apollo Theater in Harlem is synonymous with some of the greatest names in African American entertainment such as James Brown, Redd Foxx, Ray Charles, Billie Holiday, Michael Jackson—and Louis Armstrong.

Louis Armstrong? A man seemingly vilified by the black press and who lost his black fan base over the years because of his out-of-date stage persona? A hero at the Apollo? And in the black press? The way Armstrong's story is often told, this might be difficult to fathom but it's all true.

Upon his return to the United States in January 1935 after 18 months in Europe, Armstrong's first stop was the brand-new Apollo. Lip troubles prevented him from playing that evening, but his appearance shook up the theater, causing management to put up a placard stating: "Coming Shortly— Louis Armstrong."

On August 30, 1935, Armstrong finally graced the Apollo stage. There was much apprehension before his appearance. It was his first New York engagement in nearly two years. He hadn't recorded in America since April 1933. He spent much of the first half of 1935 physically unable to play his trumpet. What kind of shape would he be in? Could he still hit his famed high notes? Should he retire? The black press whipped itself into a frenzy in previewing his return to Harlem. Armstrong himself knew this was a defining moment and took a snapshot of the marquee, keeping it for his personal collection.

Harlem turned out in full force for the comeback, which brought in over $10,000 for the week, shattering the theater's box-office record. Armstrong opened with "Ain't Misbehavin'," the song that had made him a star on Broadway, immediately proving that he was back and, in the words of Abel Green in *Variety*, "better than ever."[1] Influential columnist Walter Winchell was there and dispensed one of his coveted "New Yorchids" to "Louis Armstrong's horn-tootling at the Apollo."[2] Matters were even more ecstatic in the black press. "Any doubt that may have existed in the minds of people that Louis Armstrong's recent illness has at all impaired his marvelous playing, his distinctive singing, and his magnetic stage personality, is being dispelled

Figure P.1 The marquee for Louis Armstrong's debut at the Apollo Theater in Harlem in August 1935, the first of many such record-breaking engagements at the mecca of black entertainment.
Courtesy of the Louis Armstrong House Museum

by the remarkable performance which he is giving at the Apollo Theatre this week," gushed the *New York Amsterdam News*. "It is indeed safe to say that Armstrong is at the peak of his career and that he has given perfect enjoyment to the record audiences which turned out to see and hear him this week."[3]

The love affair with Armstrong at the Apollo was only just beginning and showed no signs of letting up in ensuing years. When he returned in March 1936, Armstrong not only broke his own box-office record but, according to the *Pittsburgh Courier*, "special police reserves were called out to handle the square-long line of people storming to reach the theatre."[4] A return in September broke his own record for the second time. Armstrong returned in the middle of a history-making run as host of the *Fleischmann's Yeast* radio show in 1937 and broke the box-office record yet again with an appearance at the end of 1938. "Apollo Is Packin 'Em In; Reason!—Louis Armstrong," read a 1939 *Pittsburgh Courier* headline over a review by Isadora Smith. "Injecting the jazz-gay abandonment of his race into his version of modern swing and his own popular form of gyration, the great musician actor holds an entertaining spell over the community," Smith wrote. "In the history of the musical world there have been few men with a more pleasing personality than Armstrong."[5]

Variety agreed when it reviewed Armstrong's 1940 Apollo run, writing, "The showmanship is still there, however, in large doses, his gravel-throated vocals, etc., helping immensely."[6] The impact of Armstrong's showmanship on the Apollo audience was most vividly captured by black writer Peter Suskind in the *New Journal and Guide* in 1942:

> Louis takes a deep breath, shuts his eyes tight and everybody's tense and ready. The drama in the situation pleases the master. In fact, it tickles him pink. He suddenly relaxes completely, destroying the mood and throws himself, his horn and his white handkerchief about in utter abandon. He roars in pleasure and the sweat pours on his shirt. He alternately wipes his horn and his forehead. The audience, in the meantime, is hilarious. Louis shouts back and forth to those in front and to those in the wings. What he says is meaningless, but the manner in which he says it is priceless. All this, and the world's greatest trumpeter has yet to blow a solo note.

When Armstrong finally picked up the trumpet, Suskind assumed the results would be anticlimactic. "To the contrary, the wonder of it is that he is able to take them further and further up to a peak of hysteria and literally set them in the aisles," he wrote.[7]

The pattern continued throughout the 1940s, even with the burgeoning sound of bebop and the explosive popularity of romantic singers like Frank Sinatra and Billy Eckstine. Armstrong played to a standing-room-only crowd in April 1945, *Variety* noting that Armstrong provided "some of the heftiest applause fodder heard at this house in some time."[8]

Two years later, changing winds in the band business and pressure from many in the jazz world led Armstrong to disband his orchestra and form a small group with a traditional trumpet-trombone-clarinet setup. It was the end of an era, an era that needed a proper send-off; only one venue was deemed appropriate. "Indeed, it is rumored about that no stone was left unturned and many out-of-town dates were cancelled so that Armstrong and his band and show could appear at the Apollo," reported the *New York Age*.[9] Armstrong's final big band engagement opened there on July 4, 1947, the day he celebrated his 47th birthday. The old magic was still there. "Many colored bands have played the house but few conjure up so much nostalgia as the ingratiating Armstrong," reported *Variety*.[10] Reviewing Buddy Johnson's Apollo show the following week, *Variety* couldn't help feeling, "Show this stanza is a letdown after Louis Armstrong."[11]

Now at the helm of an integrated small group, the All Stars, Armstrong returned to the Apollo in 1948 and 1949 and again for Christmas week in 1952, receiving much publicity in the black press and doing well each time, according to *Variety*, which remarked on the large crowd in 1952, "House hasn't had as potent a draw in some time." The reviewer made it clear that Armstrong was still a favorite there, writing, "His musical patterns are simply embroidered, and in this Harlem house, he registers a maximum response."[12]

Yet, even though a "potent draw" who received "maximum response," Armstrong never played the Apollo again in the last 19 years of his career.

"Sometimes even a superstar is rejected," Jack Schiffman, son of longtime Apollo owner Frank Schiffman wrote in 1971, the year of Armstrong's death. "Louis Armstrong may be a prime favorite among white audiences, but you could clear the house today in short order by putting on a Dixieland show at the Apollo. . . . Why? My own view is that Dixieland harks back to a day black people would just as soon forget, a day of pickaninnies, Uncle Tom, Marsa Joe, and Yassuh—harks back to Dixie, in short."[13] That opinion is not reflected in the contemporary reviews of the All Stars at the Apollo between 1948 and 1952, but clearly there was no more room for Armstrong's "Dixie" band.

In 2010, the Apollo instituted a Walk of Fame; Armstrong was finally inducted in 2014. Upon his induction, I received an email from a prominent jazz writer and historian stating, "Louis was NOT a major star of the Apollo, he only played there a few times. The Walk of Fame is mainly for stars of the Apollo, it's not the institution for all of black music." Armstrong was a fixture there for 17 years, breaking the box-office record multiple times, but because many jazz people only know his innovative recordings of the 1920s or the later hits of the All Stars era, Armstrong's big band years are taken for granted. But it was in this 1929–1947 period that Armstrong influenced more musicians and listeners than at any other time in his life. He met popular music head-on, adapting the sounds favored by white listeners, and completely transformed them into something new, something exciting, something black, something swinging. Every trumpet solo seemed to contain enough ideas for scores of new compositions and arrangements. Every vocal was a personal statement, blowing up the way singers approached pop tunes forever more. Dozens of songs he recorded in this period became standards. His stagecraft, featuring daring displays of high note prowess and climax-building solos, had audiences screaming and cheering decades before rock 'n' roll. And he was funny, proud of his comic prowess and ability to make anyone, black or white, laugh.

Yet this is the period that is ignored or misrepresented by so many in the jazz world. It was the jazz world that put pressure on Armstrong to break up the big band and form a small group—and then ditched him when the small group didn't reflect the latest trends. But it didn't matter. Armstrong was bigger than jazz.

Louis Armstrong is synonymous with jazz. Jazz is synonymous with Louis Armstrong. No one could argue that, and with good reason as Armstrong is one of the most influential figures in the history of the genre. In the 1920s, he single-handedly changed the way musicians improvised, perfecting the art of the solo and writing the rules on how one should always "tell a story" with one's instrument. Equally as important, he practically invented the concept of jazz singing, liberating singers from the shackles of the written melody, showing them how to interpret a song in an original manner while popularizing scat singing along the way. And everything he did with both trumpet and voice *swung*, establishing the rhythmic feeling that some feel is ultimately his biggest contribution since that swing feeling defined much of the most lasting music of the 20th century.

All these attributes were firmly established by the beginning of 1929, when Armstrong was just 27 years old. If he had tragically died at that point, the preceding paragraph could still be written verbatim and Armstrong would still be a towering influence in jazz.

But he was much more than a jazz musician; he was a popular artist and entertainer who appealed not just to jazz aficionados, but rather to anyone who regularly listened to music and liked to have a good time. If you were hip, you loved Louis Armstrong. If you were square, you loved Louis Armstrong. He ultimately transcended the world of jazz—and for that, the jazz world never truly forgave him.

Armstrong has never received the credit he deserved as a masterful pop artist, though at almost all times in his career, he was more popular with the general public than simply with jazz fans. He was the "King of Pop" before Michael Jackson was even born. Trumpeter Nicholas Payton made this point in a 2012 blogpost, writing, "I'm not saying Pops was more impactful because he was born before Michael, but because of his specific contributions to the interpretation of the American Popular song." Payton created a stir in 2011 when he denounced the word "jazz" in favor of "Black American Music." Because he's not hung up on Armstrong solely as a jazz artist, Payton is able to properly place him in a pop context, calling him "the progenitor of the Black, Pop aesthetic." Payton concluded, "I'm not one for superlatives, but Armstrong's Hot Five recordings are the most influential records in Pop music. More influential than the Beatles or Michael Jackson put together. On those sides, he developed the whole idea of the virtuoso vocal and instrumental soloist in the Pop idiom. It was his voice that shaped what would become the Popular song."[14]

Armstrong's "pop" sensibilities have led to the overall diminishing of his reputation in the jazz community. He's acknowledged as a great innovator, but scant attention is paid to his post-1928 output, the years when he became bigger than jazz. For example, in 1932, pure, hot jazz was found in records by the likes of the Rhythmmakers with Henry "Red" Allen or Sidney Bechet's New Orleans Feetwarmers, small groups that created torrid music. That same year, Armstrong was recording with a big band, aping Guy Lombardo's signature syrupy reed sound and covering Bing Crosby hits like "Love You Funny Thing" and "Lawd You Made the Night Too Long," in addition to appearing in a Betty Boop cartoon. In 1938, when Count Basie was loosening up the feel of the rhythm section and Lester Young's lighter-than-air solos were paving the way for modern jazz, Armstrong was recording spirituals with Lyn Murray's mixed choir for Decca and singing "Jeepers Creepers" to a horse in the film *Going Places*. When Charlie Parker and Dizzy Gillespie exploded onto the scene with the complex sounds of bebop in 1945, Armstrong was scoring a hit with a cover of a recent rhythm and blues ballad, "I Wonder," appearing in the film *Pillow to Post* with Ida Lupino and Sydney Greenstreet and backing up the era's biggest sensation, Frank Sinatra, on a radio broadcast.

Such film appearances and pop efforts have led many to cast a blind eye toward what Armstrong was accomplishing in this period. Few of his vocals reach the levels of sensuality he achieves on "Love You Funny Thing" and "Lawd You Made the Night Too Long," the Lombardo-sound inspiring him to great heights. Instead of being defeated by the racial stereotyping in *Going Places*, Armstrong brought enough natural comedic timing to his role to receive praise in the *New York Times* as "a solid man for comedy." And his sober vocal on "I Wonder" is most affecting, topped by a gorgeous, even "modern"-sounding trumpet solo. These widely varying examples of his different types of artistry might not scream "innovation" but they're all ripe for serious rediscovery, causes for celebration not scorn.

The disparaging of Armstrong's big band years began in his lifetime, with a specific narrative first laid out by Rudi Blesh in his 1946 work *Shining Trumpets*, which argued that Armstrong "inherited" a "responsibility" to what

Blesh referred to as "true jazz." Blesh lamented, "His grasp of what jazz means, the sort of group effort which it must represent, unfortunately failed to match his genius."[15] But Armstrong felt no allegiance to "true jazz," which in Blesh's limited definition solely referred to small group New Orleans polyphonic ensembles. "Oh, we played all kinds of music," he once said of his days of playing on riverboats in his hometown. "We had to play waltzes and rhumbas, fox trots, you know, cause [we played for] all types of people."[16] Even when recording the influential Hot Fives and Sevens, Armstrong was playing the pop songs of the day with large ensembles in his regular gigging life.

Twenty-two years after Blesh, Gunther Schuller penned an influential chapter on Armstrong, "The First Great Soloist," as part of his groundbreaking book *Early Jazz*. Though full of praise for Armstrong's 1920s works, Schuller bemoaned that Armstrong "did succumb to the sheer weight of his success and its attendant commercial pressures."[17] His chapter ends with allusions to some worthy early 1930s works but concludes, "For the rest there is a wasteland of whimpering Lombardo-style saxophones, vibraphones and Hawaiian guitars, saccharine violins, dated Tin Pan Alley tunes and hackneyed arrangements."[18] Everyone is entitled to their own opinion, but it's worth noting that when Armstrong was asked to list his favorite recordings during an interview for the *Record Changer* in 1950, he rattled off a list of his 1930s big band recordings, the same ones Schuller referenced in his quote.[19] He surely didn't feel he succumbed to anything.

When Schuller finally dealt with Armstrong's big band recordings in his 1991 follow-up book, *The Swing Era*, he complained about "the creepy tentacles of commercialism" and admitted to having difficulty evaluating Armstrong in this period. "And yet, linking Armstrong to the thirties and forties, the Swing Era, is not without its perplexities and controversy, for the fact is that he was in a sense not really a part of the swing era," he wrote.[20] This speaks to a very limited view of the Swing Era as being the property of jazz-centric big band leaders like Benny Goodman or Count Basie. In that era, Armstrong was a fixture on radio and in films, published an autobiography, broke box-office records, recorded in numerous different settings, and even starred in a Broadway show. Just as he was bigger than jazz, he was bigger than the Swing Era.

Schuller's second book was published after James Lincoln Collier's 1983 biography, *Louis Armstrong: An American Genius*. Collier's final chapter is spent lamenting "the bitter waste of [Armstrong's] astonishing talent over the last two-thirds of his career. . . . I cannot think of another American artist who so failed his own talent. What went wrong?"[21] Collier insinuated a phoniness in Armstrong's performances, writing of a "desperate need to hang onto the boundless love his audiences offered him explains so much about Armstrong: the show-boating, the tomming, the endless appetite for applause."[22] Armstrong might have wanted a large audience, but he only made music to please one person: himself. "I'm my own audience and no critic in the world can tell me how I should play my horn, and I won't do it anyway," he told an interviewer in 1959.[23]

Each of these writers took Armstrong to task for what they viewed as his abandoning the principles of a relentlessly creative jazz musician artist, choosing to go "commercial" instead and committing unpardonable sings such as "setting" his solos.[24] But there are dozens of examples of him performing a song live before recording it in the studio—especially in his earlier years.[25] If Armstrong was working out his solos and vocals on the road before committing them to wax, then some of his most analyzed and celebrated recordings of the late 1920s and 1930s were not examples of extemporaneous jazz created on the spot but rather perfectly crafted pop performances worked out for months, sometimes years, and then captured for posterity when it achieved something akin to perfection. It's hard to find another major figure in any other art form who wrote all the rules before almost immediately breaking them.

As Armstrong grew more comfortable in his role as a pop artist, he began to lose not only many hardened jazz fans who believed he was selling out but also many African Americans mostly because his stage presence, in the words of African American cultural critic Gerald Early, "made a lot of black people uncomfortable." Early was born in 1952 and thus grew up in the turbulent 1960s when the Armstrong who sang "Hello, Dolly!" might not have been the hippest representation of a black artist in America. But few scholars have remarked on how comfortable many African Americans *were* with Armstrong's persona, especially in the years covered in this book. The black press especially regularly singled out Armstrong's showmanship for praise in the 1930s and 1940s, and those African Americans who made the effort to get to know him offstage were stunned by just how comfortable Armstrong was in his own skin. "As I watched him and talked with him, I felt he was the most *natural* man—playing, talking, singing—he was so perfectly natural the tears came to my eyes," pianist Jaki Byard said of encountering Armstrong at a rehearsal with his big band in the 1940s. "I was very moved to be near the most natural of all living musicians."[26] No less than Miles Davis agreed, telling Bill Boggs and Maurice Hines in 1986, "[Those who see Louis as an Uncle Tom] don't realize that Louis was doing that when he was around his friends. You know he was acting the same way. But when you do it in front of white people, and try to make them enjoy what you feel—that's all he was doing—they call

Figure P.2 Armstrong offstage, "the most natural man" in the words of Jaki Byard, enjoying a beer and a bite to eat between shows backstage at the Paramount Theatre in 1937.
Photo by Charles Peterson, Courtesy of Don Peterson

him Uncle Tom."[27] If Miles Davis was comfortable around Armstrong, he was far from alone.

Early added, "Then too, his music, he had made certain kinds of adaptations in his music for popular taste but not significant adaptations in his music for *black* popular taste."[28] Armstrong is usually called out and criticized for not adapting enough for black popular taste, but what about Ella Fitzgerald recording the Cole Porter songbook? Miles Davis recording "The Surrey with the Fringe on Top"? Oscar Peterson playing Django Reinhardt's "Nuages" at the Stratford Shakespearean Festival? Charlie Parker with strings? Were those artists adapting to "black popular taste"? Fitzgerald, Davis, Peterson, Parker, and much of the rest of the jazz world of the 1950s didn't show any particular concern with adapting to black popular taste, but it was Armstrong whose reputation suffered the most, mostly because of non-musical issues such as his stage persona—which was perfected in front of black audiences in the 1920s and 1930s.[29]

The bigger point is that *jazz* in general didn't adapt to shifts in the kinds of music many African Americans wanted to hear beginning in the 1940s. The standard history of jazz tells us that swing led to bebop and from there, cool jazz, hard bop, modal jazz, free jazz, and avant-garde followed. But in the African American community, swing led to bebop, and most African Americans fled from those sounds to the more danceable rhythm-and-blues (R&B) and eventually rock 'n' roll, supporting the likes of Ray Charles, Chuck Berry, Little Richard, Fats Domino, and Sam Cooke. Armstrong's fingerprints could be detected on each of these artists, even if many might not make an immediate connection: for example, Cooke, the definition of "black popular taste" of his era. When asked to name his favorite singers in 1964, Cooke told soul singer Bobby Womack, "You know who I try to sound like? I know you're going to think I'm crazy: Louie Armstrong. Bobby, he projects, it's not like he's singing a song on the beat. He would just say something [*scat sings*], 'Da da-da da da, be de da de lo,' like he's talking to you. Take his voice away and listen to my voice and you'll hear the same thing."[30] Armstrong's impact on Cooke and other popular black R&B, rock, and soul artists of the 1950s and 1960s—one can even claim that his pop singles paved the way for the success of Motown—is immeasurable, but the prevailing narrative is still that he somehow failed when he chose not to adapt his style to the modern jazz developments of the 1940s and 1950s.

This skewed view of Armstrong's place in the music world was still apparent in a 2018 *New York Times* profile by Giovanni Russonello, who tackled later criticisms of Armstrong, arguing, "With jazz's identity solidifying as an art music in the 1950s, Armstrong became especially unfashionable to the critical establishment. The autumnal hits he scored in the mid-1960s, 'Hello, Dolly!' and 'What a Wonderful World,' seemed only to confirm the media consensus that the times had passed him by."[31] "Hello, Dolly!" knocked the Beatles off the top of the pop charts at the height of Beatlemania. "What a Wonderful World" went to number one in England, again displacing the Beatles and the Rolling Stones. In between, he appeared on the pop charts with "So Long Dearie" and "Mame." A black jazz musician in his 60s, regularly landing on the pop charts alongside some of the most iconic rock and pop acts of all time? That is the very opposite of the times passing Louis Armstrong by. He went along with the times his entire career. His innovations dictated the times.

Because pre-1928 Armstrong is universally acknowledged in the jazz community as Armstrong's most "important" work, this book will not attempt to retell the stories of the Hot Fives or find new ways to wax poetic about "West End Blues" and other masterpieces of that era. The following narrative will start with Armstrong's choice to meet white popular music head-on in 1929, the ways he impacted it with his undeniably and unapologetically black sound, and how he, in turn, catapulted into becoming a multimedia superstar, becoming beloved by white audiences, while remaining a hero in the black community on the same level as Joe Louis.

Just as important as his music, much time will be spent on Armstrong the person. As often as possible, his own words will be used to tell his story. He spent the last several decades of his career carefully curating his own personal archive of writings, tapes, scrapbooks, and more, determined to be allowed to speak for himself after he was gone. He was a joyous figure offstage, viewed as a God by musicians and as a hero to fans of all backgrounds. But he was not infallible, especially when he felt disrespected. In these pages, he feuds with jazz immortals like Coleman Hawkins, Zutty Singleton, and Sidney Bechet, spars with critics, severs ties with loyal friends like Zilner Randolph, and cheats on all of his wives. But Armstrong himself didn't try to censor these sides of his personality and this work will follow his lead. It's possible to still disagree with his choices after reading his words, but at least he will be allowed to speak for himself

The second part of the book will chronicle the changing trends in music in the 1940s and how Armstrong became a lightning rod to the tastemakers who earned a living telling him how he should present his music. He eventually found an ingenious solution that brought him his biggest fame but further served to alienate his standing in the jazz world.

Does it even matter? Was Louis Armstrong even a jazz musician? Armstrong himself would scoff at such a debate. His goals were to play good music, to please himself, and to connect with his audiences. He succeeded on every front. In the process, he became one of the most beloved and recognized men on the planet, experiencing a life and a level of fame no other African American knew before him and one few others have ever known since. While he was a young man with the odds against him, Armstrong's mother, Mayann, told him, "Son, you got a chance. Don't waste it."[32]

He did not.

1

"There's a New King"

March 1929

The Savoy Ballroom was the mecca for jazz in Harlem, but there was an extra buzz surrounding it in early March 1929. Luis Russell's Orchestra was performing, which wasn't unusual, but for two nights only, the band would feature a special guest on trumpet: Louis Armstrong.

Armstrong left Fletcher Henderson's band in New York in November 1925 and hadn't been back—by choice. "Louis was getting bids from New York, but he didn't like New York," Charles Carpenter remembered. "He'd been there before with Fletcher Henderson. 'This ain't for me,' he said, and split, and came on back to Chicago."[1] He was playing with his best friend Zutty Singleton in Carroll Dickerson's band at the Savoy Ballroom and making $100 a week. But the new Regal Theater opened nearby in 1928 and according to Carpenter,

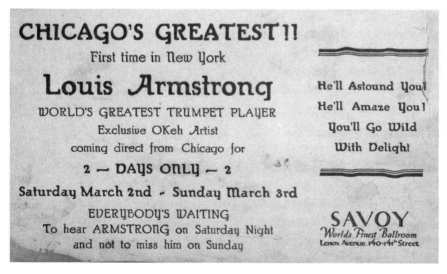

Figure 1.1 New York newspaper advertisement for Armstrong's March 1929 appearance at the Savoy Ballroom in Harlem. This clipping was added to a scrapbook compiled by Louis and his then-wife Lil Hardin Armstrong.
Courtesy of the Louis Armstrong House Museum

Armstrong and Singleton "weren't drawing flies" at the Savoy. It was time to give New York another chance.

Armstrong and Panamanian-born bandleader Russell were no strangers to each other, having first played together in New Orleans in the early 1920s. Russell's big band was one of the hottest in New York and featured many of Armstrong's old homeboys, including bassist Pops Foster and drummer Paul Barbarin. At the time, Russell was the king of the Savoy Ballroom. "He had never lost a battle in the Savoy against *nobody*," recalled Russell's alto saxophonist, Charlie Holmes. "It was an exciting band."[2]

But Russell already had a highly touted trumpet player named Louis in the brash, 24-year-old Louis Metcalf, "just the rave of New York City at that particular time," according to guitarist Lawrence Lucie.[3] Metcalf played his trumpet while seated on a stool in front of the orchestra but that wasn't enough. "Louis Metcalf had a crown," recalled Holmes. "He was the king."[4] Metcalf was not worried about Armstrong's visit. According to guitarist Danny Barker, Metcalf "was cautioned that Louis [Armstrong] was going to appear and that he would look ridiculous with this emblem of supremacy on his highly greased head when Louis mounted the stand. Defiantly he retorted, 'I'll wear this crown if Gabriel comes down from heaven.'"[5] Even Armstrong knew about it. "And he'd wear his crown every night—he had a little paper crown he'd made, that's the way people would signify in those days," he said. "Well, nobody would take it off, because he was *blowing*, see?"[6]

Because of their faith in Metcalf, some of the musicians in Russell's band were wary of Armstrong's visit. "When Louis come, we was ready to pan Louis!" said Holmes. "Somebody asked me once, didn't I get a big thrill when I found out I was going to [be] working with Louis Armstrong. I said, 'Big thrill for what?' We was gettin' ready to pan him! We was gettin' ready to just let him make one little slip or something, and it would have been all over, Louis!"[7]

Armstrong knew he was the subject of much discussion among the other New York musicians. "So, they all commenced debating, now," he remembered. "I hadn't been there in four years. 'I wonder what's he going to play like?' 'Louie Armstrong's going to go play at the Savoy? Well, who's heard him?' 'Well, I don't know.' Well, I was out in Chicago and I was blowing but the cats in New York still were all wondering."[8]

Finally, it was showtime. Charles Buchanan, the manager of the Savoy Ballroom and a man of British West Indies descent, began a long introduction. Metcalf took his place on his stool, unfazed. Armstrong soon appeared. Trumpeter Bill Coleman recalled, "When Satchelmouth came on the stand

I was pleasantly surprised because he was a much better looking man than the few bad photos I had seen and collected of him. . . . His trumpet looked like the most beautiful golden horn that I had ever seen."[9]

It was finally time for him to play.

"I don't remember the opening number," Charlie Holmes said, "but I know on the end of it he played a high F, which in them days, that had never been heard of before. And Louis hit that F, big and broad and loud and clear. And the house *did* come tumblin' down."[10]

"I never heard anything like it," said Lucie.[11]

"His fingers seemed to be flying over the valves and the things that were coming out of his horn were things that I had never heard from any trumpet player before and that's when I realized that Armstrong was the king of all kings of jazz," wrote Coleman.[12]

In all the adulation, it was easy to forget about Louis Metcalf, still sitting on his stool with his crown on his head. One man didn't forget: Russell's alto saxophonist Teddy Hill. "That's when Teddy Hill got up and turned around to Louis Metcalf, with that crown on his head, and snatched the crown off and threw it out in the audience!" said Holmes. "And [Hill] said, 'The King is now dethroned! There's a new King. Long live the King!' He was talkin' about Louis Armstrong."[13] The following set, Metcalf did not return to the stand.

Armstrong continued playing with ferocity the rest of the first night. "Boy, the people were screaming," Holmes added. "Boy, everybody in amazement, you know. Because I mean, other trumpet players would hit them notes, just like they do nowadays. They'd be hitting high notes, but they sound like a flute up there or something. But Louis wasn't playing them like that. Louis was hittin' them notes right on the head and *expanding*. They would be notes. He was hittin' *notes*. He wasn't squeakin'. . . . People were screamin' and carryin' on."[14]

Armstrong might have not even noticed the effect he was having on the younger musicians as he was fixated on his mentor, King Oliver, in the audience, "standing right in front of that trumpet. That was a thrill. Those things he had talked to me about my horn just when I was a kid, running errands for his wife, lessons and things—it was coming right out of that horn. Tears coming right out of his eyes, man. Knocked him out. And I laid the good old good ones on him, Pops and killed him. Knocked him out." Armstrong dedicated a special song to Oliver: "I Can't Give You Anything but Love."[15]

After the first night's performance, many of the musicians in attendance left in a state of disbelief. "And after that night, when I went back on the streets again, all the musicians met at the Rhythm Club," Lucie remembered. "He was the rave of New York City. And if you were the rave of Harlem, you were the rave of New York City as far as jazz is concerned. And from then on, it was all Louie. . . . After that one night when Louie appeared at the Savoy, when I went back to the Rhythm Club—when you go to the Rhythm Club, you have the whole feel of all the jazz musicians, really. And so the feeling I got when I got back there, Louie had changed the whole world."[16]

In the four years since Armstrong last performed in New York, he had recorded dozens of songs with his small studio groups, the Hot Fives and Hot Sevens. Released as "Race Records" by OKeh Records and aimed at the black community, Armstrong's recordings might today be the gold standard for jazz in the 1920s, but at the time, they did not have a tremendous impact on New York musicians. "Louie was great, he had something different and special," reedman Garvin Bushell said about Armstrong's 1924–1925 time in New York, "But he didn't really prove to us that he was God until 'West End Blues' and when he came back to New York the second time."[17] "West End Blues," featuring Armstrong's astounding unaccompanied opening cadenza, was released in the second half of 1928 and reached a larger audience than the Hot Five recordings usually did. Someone at OKeh noticed: the second great architect of Armstrong's career, Tommy Rockwell.

The first great architect was Armstrong's wife, Lil Hardin Armstrong, who pushed him to leave King Oliver in 1924, pushed him to join Fletcher Henderson that same year, pushed him to leave Henderson the next year, pushed him to join her own band in Chicago (billing him as "The World's Greatest Cornetist"), pushed him to write more songs, and pushed OKeh Records to start recording Armstrong as a leader—until eventually, her hypercritical ways pushed him into the arms of young chorus girl Alpha Smith, whom Louis began dating on the side. Lil had pushed him as far as she could.

Rockwell came to OKeh in 1927 and noticed Armstrong was popular with more than just black audiences. Still, with their limited urban marketplace target and with their inherently old-fashioned trumpet-trombone-clarinet-banjo-piano setup, the Hot Fives were not destined to be among the best-selling platters of the period. Rockwell was determined to get him a wider audience and soon started simultaneously releasing his recordings on OKeh's "Race" series and its "Popular" series. *Variety* noticed the trend in a January 16, 1929, Armstrong review, mentioning that OKeh was "aiming for white and colored appeal."[18] Rockwell also replaced the old-fashioned New Orleans instrumentation, which Armstrong didn't even use in public, having him record arrangements by Don Redman and Alex Hill in December 1928. He also took part as a sideman in a date featuring the nasal vocalizing of Lillie Delk Christian on a few popular ballads. Rockwell ramped up the advertising of Armstrong's recordings, proclaiming him as "The Country's Greatest Trumpet Player."[19] It was a good start, but Rockwell wanted more direct control over Armstrong's recordings. He wanted him to come to New York.

After Armstrong's opening triumph at the Savoy, he attended a banquet thrown in his honor featuring many top New York musicians, black and white. Charles Buchanan hosted the banquet and old boss Fletcher Henderson served as master of ceremonies. Some of New York's finest musicians, including trombonist Jimmy Harrison, drummer Chick Webb, and multi-instrumentalist Benny Carter, delivered speeches in tribute to Armstrong. One newspaper account reported, "Never before in the history has New York lauded an individual in the music profession as it did Mr. Armstrong, who well deserves the name 'King of Jazz.'"[20]

Another musician present was banjoist Eddie Condon, a man with many ideas and the nerve and gumption to make them happen. "I looked around the table and shook my head," he said. "I had never seen so many good musicians, white and colored, in one place at the same time."[21] In February 1928, Condon organized a recording date for Victor that was revolutionary for the way it combined black and white jazz musicians in a loose, jam session setting (Jelly Roll Morton recorded with the all-white New Orleans Rhythm Kings in 1924 but as far as interracial recordings went, that was it). Condon now had a similar idea and insisted that Rockwell record Armstrong with an integrated band. Unsure, Rockwell responded, "I don't know about using a mixed group." Condon argued, "If Victor can do it OKeh can do it." Rockwell agreed.

Rockwell might have hesitated about an integrated setup, but to the musicians, this was important. "We were all in contact with each other at that time, and it was a very close brotherly thing with white musicians and black musicians in Harlem," Lucie recalled.[22] Armstrong himself always encouraged the white musicians in Chicago who were interested in his music, jamming with Bix Beiderbecke, hanging out with Muggsy Spanier, and even inviting the New Orleans Rhythm Kings to his apartment so they could rehearse for their record dates.[23] "[T]he mixed band was just a pipedream in those days," wrote clarinetist Mezz Mezzrow, adding, "Louis and I used to talk about it all the time—it was our idea of the millennium."[24]

Rockwell had already booked studio time for Armstrong to record with Russell's band in the morning but decided to push the big band to the afternoon. "Get your boys together and I'll speak to Louis," Rockwell told Condon. Condon went to work and within a few hours, the studio was filled with three black musicians—Armstrong, tenor saxophonist Happy Caldwell, and drummer Kaiser Marshall—and three white musicians, guitarist Eddie Lang, pianist Joe Sullivan, and trombonist Jack Teagarden. The musicians never even went to sleep, having breakfast together in the morning and stopping to get a jug of gin to help keep spirits bright. Nobody was particularly shy about imbibing; Condon apparently got so drunk, he passed out before the recording light went on.

Once assembled, Armstrong immediately became taken with Texas trombonist Teagarden. The two had met once before, years earlier, while Armstrong was still playing on a riverboat with Fate Marable's band. They now had a chance to bond at the session and immediately took to each other like brothers, Armstrong telling Teagarden, "I'm a spade and you an ofay. We got the same soul—so let's blow."[25] Musically speaking, Teagarden proved to be the ideal partner for Armstrong and was often named by the trumpeter as his favorite musician. "Jack, he lives music like I do," Armstrong recalled in 1950."[26] As the engineers got everything in place and Teagarden began to warm up, Armstrong placed his hand on his heart and said, "It moves me. It moves me right through *here*."[27] He became so enamored with the sound of Teagarden's trombone, he found a stepladder and ascended it so he could hear it better, only coming down when the engineer persuaded him to get in place for the recording.

When the light went on, the integrated group lit into a slow blues. There was no theme, just a string of solos, a true jam session that pointed the way to jazz's future, topped off by two choruses by Armstrong in storytelling mode, before hurling himself into a bubbling unaccompanied closing cadenza. Rockwell asked for the name of the song. "I don't know," Armstrong responded before glimpsing the empty jug of gin. "Man, we sure knocked that jug—you can call it 'Knockin' a Jug!' "[28]

"Knockin' a Jug" became one for the history books, but when the band couldn't get through the next song planned, "I'm Gonna Stomp Mister Henry Lee," Rockwell pulled the plug and sent everyone home, ostensibly to sober up. After a few short hours to rest, Armstrong was back in the studio in the afternoon, this time to record the one song that was the main reason for Rockwell bringing him to New York in the first place, "I Can't Give You Anything but Love." Already one of the smash hit songs of 1928, recorded by Paul Whiteman, Seger Ellis, Annette Hanshaw, Red Nichols, and Lillie Delk Christian (the last of which featured trumpet work by Armstrong), Rockwell knew that no one else was going to approach it the way Armstrong did. Since Armstrong remembered performing it and dedicating it to King Oliver at the Savoy the night before, everyone was familiar with the routine.

That doesn't mean everything went down easily in the studio. After the free-wheeling days of recording with the Hot Five, Rockwell's traits as a perfectionist came to the fore, frustrating some of the other musicians in Russell's band. "I know it had taken us the whole session to make one side—'I Can't Give You Anything but Love,'" said Charlie Holmes. Asked why it took so long, Holmes answered, "Everything was Louis. Everything had to be perfect for *him*, according to the technicians. They were the ones back in the room with the stuff on their ears, and this-that-and-the-other, placing him here and placing the horns there."[29] The music itself was not a challenge as the band had to play the simplest arrangement imaginable, just keeping the melody going steadily in the background as a backdrop for Armstrong's daring vocal and trumpet explorations.

The extra effort paid off, though, as the master take is a masterpiece. Over a slow tempo, the saxophones croon the melody in a way reminiscent of Guy Lombardo's famed reed section, as Pops Foster saws away on his bowed bass. If Armstrong was removed from the equation, it could be almost any 1920s dance band, which was most likely Rockwell's point. But instead, he's front and center, using a straight mute, playing lead, respecting the melody but also spinning variations on it as he goes on, another technique that would soon become a hallmark on his future recordings. Midway through, he passes the lead to the brilliant trombonist J. C. Higginbotham, who maintains the somber mood before Armstrong sings.

The vocal alone pushed this recording into the pantheon, Armstrong retaining the sentiment of the original lyrics and infusing it all with a sense of passion not commonly found in pop vocals of the late 1920s. He sings the title phrase on a single pitch, infuses high notes with a vibrato usually reserved for his trumpet, and even finds spots for scatting. American pop singing would never be the same.[30] But the genius of Louis Armstrong is he could follow an earth-shattering vocal such as that one with a trumpet solo that's nearly as striking, building higher and higher—until the end of the record, when he accidentally goes too high. Working on an ascending chromatic motive, he makes his way up to a high concert E♭, but doesn't quite hit it, squeaking out the final note just short of the target. Still, given what just transpired, Rockwell knew he had a winner on his hands and released the recording even with the pinched final note.

Rockwell was done and more than satisfied with the results, but perhaps to commemorate what was happening at the Savoy, Armstrong and the Russell Orchestra teamed up for one more song, "Mahogany Hall Stomp," this one featuring a special guest, New Orleans–born guitarist Lonnie Johnson.[31] The song was credited to Spencer Williams and named in tribute of a famed New Orleans brothel, Lulu White's Mahogany Hall, where Williams was born (his mother, Bessie Williams, was Lulu White's sister and worked at the hall). This must have tickled all the New Orleans musicians in the studio that day, but truthfully, it isn't a very strong composition. After a catchy introduction (devised by Luis Russell, according to Charlie Holmes), Armstrong leads the band through the first strain, which bears more than a passing resemblance to the spiritual "Bye and Bye." Armstrong's lead is strong but there's some sloppiness in the background as the other horns play a semblance of an arrangement, suggesting either poor reading or perhaps some spontaneous creation. Eventually, the song morphs into a 12-bar blues in E♭, but bassist Pops Foster sounds momentary lost with his bow, hitting a few off notes behind Holmes's alto solo.

However, when Armstrong takes his solo after a dazzling unaccompanied chorus by Johnson, the piece zooms ahead from the shaky, 1918-style two-beat of the first section to pulsating, swinging, sweating, modern jazz. Foster ditches the bow and starts walking, Johnson offers a stream of countermelodies, and Armstrong takes over, mute in bell, for three perfectly constructed choruses that would provide fodder for countless big band arrangements that followed.

With that, Rockwell now had three sides ready for release, each one pointing the way toward the future of Armstrong's career—and the future of jazz.

"Knockin' a Jug": a themeless string of solos performed by an integrated band.

"I Can't Give You Anything but Love": a definitive Armstrong reading of a pop song with a vocal that established new rules for singing jazz.

"Mahogany Hall Stomp": a New Orleans–flavored romp with a swinging rhythm section and an influential three-chorus solo that practically became part of the composition.

Rockwell immediately released "I Can't Give You Anything but Love" at the beginning of April 1929 as both a race record and as one of OKeh's pop series. OKeh even devised ads for both, choosing not to use a photo of Armstrong's in the general ad, which included the bland line, "There's a rhythm that glides your steps into an easier grace."[32] But his photo was featured prominently in the race ads, proclaiming "Louis Armstrong is The King of Trumpet Players," and describing "I Can't Give You Anything but Love" as "Dance music that is different. . . . Rhythm that is the most wonderful you have ever heard."[33]

Armstrong clipped out many advertisements for the song, saving them in one of his scrapbooks. He also saved coverage of his two-day stand at the Savoy. "Louis Armstrong Takes New York by Storm," one article stated, while another opined, "Too bad Louis can't stay with us a couple of months. . . . Here's wishing you a world of luck old boy and then some more. You are a prince and we will miss you. So hurry back."[34]

2

"If Louis Did It, It Must Be Right"

April–December 1929

Armstrong returned to Chicago and resumed his role a featured sideman with Carroll Dickerson's Orchestra, but he couldn't shake the thrill of his short jaunt to New York City. "Zutty," he said to Dickerson drummer Zutty Singleton, "Man, they had my name in lights at the Savoy, you know. 'LOUIS ARMSTRONG.'" "And that knocked him out," Singleton recalled.[1]

While Tommy Rockwell worked to get Armstrong back to New York, the trumpeter was invited by *Chicago Defender* columnist Dave Peyton to be featured in one of his all-star "Sparkling Speed Shows" for a full week at the Regal Theater on 47th and Grand Boulevard, the most popular venue for black audiences on Chicago's South Side. Armstrong received three full minutes of applause after taking the stage before "his big jovial smile and dynamic personality" launched into "I Can't Give You Anything but Love," sending the Regal crowd with his tender vocalizing and hot trumpet finish. In the words of one reviewer, "Louis Armstrong certainly had the packed house at his mercy, and after five healthy encores, left the stage wringing wet and triumphantly retaining his crown as the king of jazz."[2]

Days later, Rockwell came through with a sensational opportunity for Armstrong to perform as part of a new Vincent Youmans Broadway show, *Great Day*. Armstrong knew he had to accept, but he was also reluctant to leave the other members of the Dickerson Orchestra behind. He showed Rockwell's telegram to the musicians in the band, who were hit with a wave of bittersweet emotions. "[W]e hated like hell to Break up our Band.—Because it was a good Band," Armstrong later wrote. "And we just couldn't see the idea of Breaking it up. And although Mr. Rockwell only sent for Me—I was one Guy who always stuck with a Bunch of fellows, especially if I liked them."[3]

Armstrong suddenly came up with an idea: would they come to New York with him? "They all jumped up into the air with Joy," he remembered. He knew Rockwell wouldn't be happy to see this, but he also had enough faith in his band that he knew they'd find work quickly in New York. He also knew that he was taking a risk. "Imagine a son-of-a-bitch sacrificing all I did in

Chicago at the Savoy, about to lose my home, Lil, everybody, to stick with that band," Armstrong recalled years later. "Rockwell was booking me, sent for me to come join *Great Day* when that show was going in. I had a helluva spot in that show. But I brought the whole fucking band, split money, put gas in all our raggedy cars."[4]

The band piled into four "raggedy" cars and headed to New York, passing through Toledo, Cleveland, Detroit, and Buffalo and going 40 miles out of their way to see Niagara Falls.[5] It was not an easy trip. The musicians eschewed hotel rooms and instead slept in their cars and took turns driving. Singleton brought along a set of vibraphones, which rusted. A generator blew out. A gas line in Armstrong's Hupmobile kept leaking. Dickerson wrecked his car and was lucky no one died in the accident. But there was something that made the grueling trip much more bearable: the reaction of the people they met in each city who were big fans of the band. "And every big town we'd come to, we'd hear Louis records being played on loudspeakers and stuff," Singleton wrote. "Louis was surprised—he didn't know he was so popular. If we'd known that, we would have had an agent line us up one-niters all the way to New York."

At last, they hobbled into New York in a scene that would have been appropriate in a Laurel and Hardy two-reeler: "[T]he minute we were Crossing '42nd and Broadway," Armstrong wrote, "My Radiator Cap Blew off—And Steam was going every place—And were we Embarrassed." This got the attention of a police officer who, noticing their Illinois license plates and familiar with all the gangland murders then emanating from Chicago, asked, "Hey there, have you boys any shotguns in that car?" Armstrong, fearful, answered "No Suh Boss." The officer just smiled and left them alone, allowing Armstrong to fix the car one more time and limp up to Harlem. Having spent their money, the men in Armstrong's band relied on the kindness of other musicians in New York to put them up until they got settled. Armstrong and Singleton sought out another hometown boy from New Orleans, Duke Ellington's bassist Wellman Braud, and moved in with him, leaving their wives behind in Chicago.

Now it was time for Armstrong to meet with Rockwell. To Rockwell, it was a simple meeting: he had a contract prepared for him to begin exclusively representing Armstrong—and Armstrong alone—and they would work out the details for *Great Day*. The contract was dated for May 18, 1929, and assured Armstrong $175 a week, with Rockwell getting $75 and the two men splitting the balance of the profits 50–50.[6] "Oh fine, Mr. Rockwell," Armstrong said upon looking over the contract, before stuttering, "But—'er, wer—I brought my Band with me and you'll have to Book us Some place." Rockwell was not pleased and "hit the ceiling," in Armstrong's words.[7]

"What the fuck you bring that band for?" he demanded.[8]

Armstrong remained calm. "Just the same Mr. Rockwell, we're here now," he said. "I just couldn't leave my Boys 'that's all—I know you can Book us 'Some place.'"[9] Armstrong knew his band was suffering without work and made another demand. "I even borrowed money for them to put in their pockets, to keep their heads up, to keep their laundry," he recounted in 1954. "I borrowed $5,000, divided it through all them cats."[10]

Rockwell found a quick opportunity to have Armstrong and Dickerson's orchestra fill in for Duke Ellington for one show at the Audubon Theater. The pit band wasn't expecting to see Armstrong's crew and looked them over with suspicion. "But then Louis played the 'St. Louis Blues' and I saw something I'll never forget as long as I live," Singleton said. "When he finished, even the band in the pit stood up and applauded for him. It was a wonderful, wonderful reception."[11]

In late May, Armstrong traveled to Philadelphia to rehearse *Great Day* as previews were to begin on June 3 at the Garrick Theater. He was to be reunited with Fletcher Henderson, but the reunion ended almost as soon as it began, though the reasons remained mysterious. "Louis Armstrong was supposed to be first cornetist in the orchestra, and Russell Smith, second cornetist," Percival Outram reported in the *New York Age*. "In fact, it is alleged they were so seated at a rehearsal, and after a number had been played, either Dr. Felix, who is said to have arranged or composed the music, or the conductor, is alleged to have told Armstrong to change chairs with Smith. This placed Russell as first trumpet, Armstrong second. The number was replayed and the decision was made that Armstrong was not adapted to the show business and his seat was declared vacant. Russell was retained as first trumpet."[12] What exactly happened? Could Armstrong not cut the part? Kaiser Marshall also quit the show and told the press that Armstrong was given only one feature in the entire show and according to Outram, "figured the limitation might seriously affect his maintaining his capabilities."

Rockwell now found himself starting from scratch, looking for an opportunity to book not only his new prized client, but also the entire Carroll Dickerson Orchestra. He managed to squeeze them into the Savoy Ballroom in Harlem for two nights, June 1 and 2, where Armstrong topped his March appearance in front of a record-breaking crowd that included musicians ranging from black clarinetist Fess Williams to white cornetist Red Nichols. Outram was there and noted that Armstrong's trumpet playing inspired "wild outbursts of applause from the crowd," who "often demanded encores for Armstrong's features." (Outram didn't know what to make of the natural "hoarseness" of Armstrong's voice, assuming "the crowd must have worked him pretty hard.") Trumpeter Cootie Williams had Duke Ellington time his sets at the Cotton Club so he could walk down to the Savoy and witness Armstrong in person. "Well, I would stand up there and listen to him blow," Williams remembered. "And there would be this amazement out of me that he could blow that trumpet like that. Wait till he got off. And I was asking him was he going home, could I walk home with him. Then he'd tell me yes, and I'd walk home with him. He was a wonderful man."[13]

Outram also singled out the saxophone section for special praise. "Louis' three saxos were a distinct pleasure to hear, even blowing and phrasing alike— in fact, unanimity was their watchword," he wrote. That unanimity came from one direct inspiration: Guy Lombardo's Royal Canadians, Armstrong's favorite band. In 1950, Bill Grauer of the *Record Changer* asked him, "Why are you fond of Guy Lombardo?" "Why?" Armstrong shot back, almost incredulously. "Because they play music. Good music. Everything they play is perfect. They can play anything." He was quick to point out that in 1928, the same year he was changing jazz history with records like "West End Blues," he and the other musicians in the Dickerson band were obsessed with Lombardo. "Every Sunday night, we'd catch that Owl Club with Guy Lombardo," he continued. "As long as he played, we'd sit right there, Zutty, Carroll Dickerson and all the band, we don't go nowhere until Guy Lombardo signed off. That went on for months."[14] Armstrong was far from alone in his appreciation for Lombardo. White clarinetist Mezz Mezzrow moved to Harlem around this time and later recalled, "When I first hit The Stroll, Guy Lombardo was head man on the juke boxes—the girls liked him especially, because his sax section had such a lyrical quality and played the sentimental tunes so pretty."[15] It made sense for Armstrong's band to mimic such a popular sound and according to Outram's review, they were succeeding.

Two days after the Savoy engagement, Rockwell recorded Armstrong for OKeh, but not as a leader. Perhaps now proud of the success of the integrated "Knockin' a Jug" date, Rockwell added Armstrong to an assemblage of all-star white musicians to back one of OKeh's most popular singers of the era, Seger Ellis. Ellis had a simple style, singing the pop hits of the day exactly as they were written, delivering the lyrics in a quiet, almost nasal voice, but always in tune. Reviewing his latest records in January 1929, *Variety* wrote, "Okeh is out to 'make' this tenor its star seller. Individually, Ellis is probably the best thing the company has."[16] Armstrong backed Ellis on "S'posin'" and "To Be in Love," playing quiet obbligatos and short, explosive solos. It was smart of Rockwell to introduce the sounds of Armstrong's trumpet playing on the recordings of his label's star artist, getting the general public more acclimated to what was still to come.

Finally, Rockwell came through with a major opportunity. *Connie's Hot Chocolates* was a revue due to open at the Hudson Theater on Broadway on June 20. The "Connie" came from Connie Immerman, who, along with his brother George, had turned Connie's Inn into the second most popular nightclub in Harlem, behind only the Cotton Club. The Immermans' new revue, "Hot Chocolates," featured music written by Fats Waller and Andy Razaf, and proved so popular, they decided to stage it simultaneously on Broadway with Leroy Smith's Green Dragon Orchestra supplying

Figure 2.1 This publicity photo from 1929—which Armstrong referred to as his "movie star pose"—was inscribed from Louis to Lil, "To my Dear wife, whom I'll love until I die. From Hubby, Louis Armstrong. 9/23/29."
The Lil Hardin Armstrong–Chris Albertson Collection, Louis Armstrong House Museum

the music. This left an opening an Connie's, which Rockwell filled with the Dickerson Orchestra. Armstrong would double each night, first playing the revue on Broadway, and then heading uptown to play with his band in Harlem.[17]

Rockwell had found work for everyone but now there was a change: instead of being billed as Carroll Dickerson's Orchestra, the unit would now be presented under Armstrong's name. He even had new publicity photos made up, one with the band and one of himself that he referred to as his "movie star pose." He signed one photo to best friend Singleton, inscribing it, "May we never part," and another for Lil, "To my Dear wife, whom I'll love until I die."[18]

Soon after, Armstrong made his Broadway debut. He only had one song to perform in *Connie's Hot Chocolates*, Waller and Razaf's "Ain't Misbehavin'," but with that one song—more than "I Can't Give You Anything but Love"— Armstrong "crossed over." "From the first time I heard it, that song used to 'send' me," Armstrong wrote. "I wood-shedded it until I could play all around it. . . . When we opened, I was all ready with it and it would bring down the house, believe me!"[19]

Indeed it did. A reporter from the *New York Times* took note, writing "A synthetic but entirely pleasant jazz ballad called 'Ain't Misbehavin'" stands out and its rendition between the acts by an unnamed member of the orchestra was a highlight of the premier." Soon enough, those in the audience had no choice but to know the name of this "unnamed member of the orchestra"; due to the popularity of the performance in the Entr'acte, Armstrong was moved from pit to the stage and given a featured billing in the program. He was officially a Broadway star.

On July 19, almost a month to the day after the show's debut, Armstrong recorded his star-making performance for OKeh. His was one of many recordings of the song that were made at the time, competing with versions by the likes of Leo Reisman, Gene Austin, Ruth Etting, and many others. In comparison to those, Armstrong's stands out as sounding like it was from another planet. Not only is it a completely unique interpretation, but by the time he got in the studio, he had a full month to "woodshed" it every night in front of live audiences on Broadway, which practically guaranteed his recording to be a crowd pleaser.

After the almost violently swinging Luis Russell band on "Mahogany Hall Stomp," in March, it takes a second to adjust to the more two-beat-styled dance-band bounce of Dickerson's band, still using banjo and tuba, as well as violin. None of it hinders Armstrong, especially in his revolutionary vocal. He barely touches the written melody, barking out the opening lines, and infusing it all with the blues, especially on two raw, yearning breaks. On the second one, he moans, "Oh *baby*, my love for you," and practically invents soul singing in the process, pointing the way toward the more emotive stylings of Ray Charles, James Brown, Aretha Franklin, Sam Cooke, and others that would follow. Back on trumpet, Armstrong humorously quotes "Rhapsody in Blue" in his first break; a few years earlier, it appeared that Gershwin's opus represented the direction jazz was heading but now he was using Gershwin's exact choice of notes to illustrate the true shape of jazz to come.

Armstrong now had a song that was beloved by both his Broadway and Harlem audiences, and one that would push him another huge step forward toward pop stardom. The record was a big seller as Rockwell had it simultaneously released on both OKeh's Race and Popular series to target the largest audience possible. Rockwell even called on Armstrong again to liven up a recording of the tune by Seger Ellis the following month. Listening to Ellis's flat and emotionless reading, it's hard to believe that it was recorded in the same summer in the same year for the same label as Armstrong's. Almost overnight, Ellis, OKeh's "star seller," was out-of-date, eventually dropped by the label in 1931.

Of "Ain't Misbehavin'," Armstrong wrote in 1936, "I believe that great song, and the chance I got to play it, did a lot to make me better known all over the country." He was the toast of New York in the summer of 1929, a hit with white and black audiences and with white and black musicians. The white musicians on Broadway made their appreciation felt one Sunday when a contingent led by drummer Ben Pollack threw Armstrong a party at Connie's Inn and presented him with a gold wristwatch inscribed "To Louis Armstrong, the World's Greatest Cornetist, from the Musicians of New York."[20]

Rockwell's vision of Armstrong as genuine pop star was coming to fruition but for his next recording session, Armstrong chose to make a statement by recording "(What Did I Do to Be So) Black and Blue." Andy Razaf was coerced into writing the song by the notorious mobster Dutch Schultz. Schultz had helped the Immerman brothers finance *Hot Chocolates* and now he wanted to have a say on the type of material that would be featured in the show. According to Razaf's biographer, Barry Singer, Schultz requested "a funny number" about "a little 'colored girl' singing how tough it is being 'colored.' Razaf grinningly pointed out that he couldn't possibly write a song like that. Schultz responded in characteristic raging fashion by pinning Razaf to the nearest wall with a gun. You'll write it, he more or less rasped, or you'll never write anything again."[21]

Razaf and Waller went to work and wrote the song quickly. Director Leonard Harper gave it to one of the show's stars, Edith Wilson, and placed her in an all-white set. Razaf contributed a verse to drive home the point that the dark-skinned Wilson was singing about how hard it was to always lose out to lighter-skinned women when it came to finding a man. The verse and the early lyrics of the chorus drew waves of laughter from the white audience, including a pleased Schultz. But when Wilson got to the more damning lines, culminating in "My only sin is in my skin," the audience grew silent. Razaf feared for his life but the hush preceded a standing ovation—and a pat on the back from Schultz.

Armstrong was affected by watching Wilson perform the number every night. On July 22, he selected "Black and Blue" to be the flip side of "Ain't Misbehavin." Not only that, but he made the decision to not sing the verse and even tweaked a line or two so any feminine connotations were erased.[22] In his hands, it was now a protest song.

One can only imagine what Rockwell thought about choosing this moment for Armstrong to record such a dramatic statement about race, since "Ain't Misbehavin'" was guaranteed to increase his visibility. The result was the most solemn Armstrong recording had made to date. The first half was a plaintive reading of Waller's minor-keyed lament, but the vocal was positively chilling. Armstrong, one of the most joyous figures of the 20th century, sounds like he's in mourning, thinking about all the dehumanizing treatment he had experienced in his 28 years of living in the United States. Even his scatting, which usually exuded bubbling joy, is infused with pain.

OKeh didn't give "Black and Blue" much publicity, but for the next several years, Armstrong often included it in his live performances, telling Richard Meryman in 1965, "I used to sing it serious—like shame on you for this and that."[23] And as the flip side to his biggest hit to date, people got the message, none more so than Ralph Ellison, who later made Armstrong's recording such an integral part of his novel *Invisible Man*. Early on in *Invisible Man*, the protagonist writes about his desire to "hear five recordings of Louis Armstrong playing and singing 'What Did I Do to Be so Black and Blue'—all at the time," and wonders, "Perhaps I like Louis Armstrong because he's made poetry out of being invisible. I think it must be because he's unaware that he *is* invisible."[24] Records like "Ain't Misbehavin'" and "Black and Blue" ensured that Armstrong would never be invisible again.

After the flurry of recording activity, Armstrong settled into his regular routine of doubling on Broadway and at Connie's Inn, which he would continue into the fall. Dave Peyton visited from Chicago in late July and noted of Armstrong and his band, "They have taken the city by storm."[25] Mezz Mezzrow grew particularly close to Armstrong in the summer of 1929—the two were so sharply dressed, they became known as the "Esquires of Harlem"—and later wrote about Armstrong's effect on the young people of Harlem:

> Louis always held a handkerchief in his hand because he perspired so much, on-stage and off, and that started a real fad—before long all the kids on The Avenue were running up to him with white handkerchiefs in their hands too, to show how much they loved him. Louis always stood with his hands clasped in front of him, in a kind of easy slouch. Pretty soon all the kids were lounging around The Corner with their hands locked in front of them, one foot a little in front of the other, and a white handkerchief always peeking out from between their fingers. All the raggedy kids, especially those who became vipers, were so inspired with self-respect after digging how neat and natty Louis was, they started to dress up real good, and took pride in it too, because if Louis did it, it must be right.[26]

While Armstrong remained the king of Harlem, he took his time in the studio, recording two more songs in September and one in November. For the first time, Rockwell recorded vocal and non-vocal versions of each songs. There are multiple reasons as to why he might have done it but the most logical was to appeal to foreign markets that might not have been interested in an American singing in English. Interestingly, he would release Armstrong's vocal versions on OKeh's Popular series, while reserving the instrumentals for the Race series.

First up was "Some of These Days," written by Shelton Brooks and the property of Sophie Tucker since 1911. It was already in Armstrong's repertoire as newspaper articles mentioned him performing it with Dickerson's band at the Savoy in 1928.[27] He had most likely worked out a set routine for his solo by this point, but that doesn't mean it was easy to execute. Rockwell invited singer Victoria Spivey to the session, and she wrote about it in 1963:

> I never saw anything like it. He took off on "Some of These Days." Man! He was blowing! He was at the last 6 bars and he and the band were really laying it down. I saw or heard no mistakes when all of a sudden Louie took his trumpet from his mouth and never said a word. He just walked over to a window, put his leg on the radiator and looked out over the city. I just looked at all the boys, as good as to say, "What's wrong with that guy." Apparently Pops did hear something that he didn't like. Well, everybody was quiet including the recording engineers. Finally, Pops walked back to the recording mike. He and the band took off again on "Some of These Days" and when he finished little me took a deep breath. You never heard nothing like it. I still think that it was one of the finest recordings that he ever made.[28]

Armstrong's concluding solo featured something new in his second chorus: playing the melody an octave higher than expected. He had heard trumpet virtuoso B. A. Rolfe do this on a song called "Shadowland" back in 1924, which inspired him to try it out on "Pickin' on Your Baby" just days later. But after five years of hard blowing, he had expanded his range until he could now pull off such a daring feat and make it sound effortless.

The next day, he repeated the act on what would become one of his most closely identified songs, "When You're Smiling." Armstrong sensed a melancholy tinge to the optimistic lyrics and chose to record it at an unusually slow tempo while letting his reeds carry the melody in their best Guy Lombardo fashion. "And that first chorus of 'When You're Smiling' reminds you of Guy Lombardo if you listen to it," he proudly said in 1950. "I mean [alto saxophonist] Crawford Wethington, he was the nearest thing to Carmen [Lombardo]. Music that's good, you just want to hear it again, that's all."[29] After his delicious vocal—truly warmth personified—he begins his trumpet climb into the stratosphere. He barely improvises and instead, relies on his love of opera and of melody to pull off the 73-second test of endurance. Armstrong's "When You're Smiling" became a sensation with trumpet players. Ensuing records of the tune by King Oliver, Duke Ellington, and Cab Calloway included Armstrong-inspired trumpet playing, but without the same impact as the original.

"When You're Smiling" and "Some of These Days" were issued on a 78 at the end of October—when Armstrong once again began tripling with the addition of a week at the Lafayette—and immediately took off, leading Rockwell to book more studio time in November to record another familiar song, "After You've Gone." Bessie Smith and Sophie Tucker added a bluesy touch to their 1927 recordings, leading publisher Joe Davis to advertise it as "The Greatest Singing Blues Song Ever Written." But no one before—and very few, if any, after—sang it as Armstrong did, taking all sorts of rhythmic chances in the second half that would be unthinkable from any other singer in the jazz and pop world of that era. Davis's Triangle Music Pub. Co. Inc. issued new sheet music featuring the image of 44 artists who had performed "After You've Gone," including Guy Lombardo, B. A. Rolfe, Ted Fio Rito, Ben Bernie, Abe Lyman, Red Nichols, and many more—and Armstrong, the only African American of the musicians depicted. He was bringing a totally black sensibility to the lily-white world of pop music and his impact could not be denied.[30]

By the time of the recording of "After You've Gone," the world was in a different place. Wall Street laid an egg on October 23, heralding the Great Depression. That didn't have any immediate effect on Armstrong, but perhaps

Figure 2.2 After Armstrong's November 1929 recording of "After You've Gone," he was featured on the cover of the published sheet music, the only African American among the 44 artists depicted. Others included Paul Whiteman, Rudy Vallee, B. A. Rolfe, Ted Lewis, Red Nichols, and Guy Lombardo.
Courtesy of the Louis Armstrong House Museum

led to the closing of *Connie's Hot Chocolates* on December 14, after 214 performances. Right to the end, Armstrong was still mentioned in all the publicity for the show, including his very first mention in a column written by Walter Winchell, who simply listed among his favorite things at the moment, "Louis Armstrong's horn-tooting and warbling of 'Ain't Misbehavin'" from the pit during the *Hot Chocolates* intermission." Armstrong clipped it out and saved it in one of his scrapbooks.[31]

Not only was *Connie's Hot Chocolates* closing, but Connie's Inn also fired Armstrong's band, giving them two weeks' notice. Armstrong had grown to be disappointed with the band he had fought to bring to New York and later complained that certain members began showing up late and "Abused the Job." At the end of the two weeks, many of the musicians returned to Chicago, except Armstrong and Singleton, who stayed in New York.[32]

What happened next was subject to Rashomon-like tellings from all parties involved for the next several decades. The undeniable fact is that Connie Immerman let Armstrong's band go and replaced them with Ally Ross's orchestra. Ross asked Singleton to join his band at Connie's the very next day and Singleton accepted. "Of course Zuttie consulted me before he accepted the job," Armstrong wrote in 1944. "I told him to take the job. Because I did not have any work in sight for an Orchestra."[33]

But Singleton's decision hurt Armstrong. Venting to a friend on one of his privately recorded reel-to-reel tapes in 1954, Armstrong retold the story of how Singleton—a "low son-of-a-bitch"—went back to Connie's Inn in much harsher terms:

> We weren't out one night, he come to my house, he say, "What's up?" I say, "What's up? Shit, you just come out of a job. I mean, why don't you get a little elbow room?" "Well, I got another job." I say, "Well, that's fine, that's nice." I'm thinking it's anywhere but Connie's Inn. Now you figure that out. And when that sonofabitch opened up at Connie's Inn, all the cats, shit, they were onto Zutty from then on. Because they could see the sacrifice. I even borrowed money for them to put in their pockets, to keep their heads up, to keep their laundry. . . . He broke a truce that you're supposed to stick together, especially in hardships. And he wasn't interested in nobody. He's a selfish man."[34]

Mezzrow felt the same way about the situation and wrote about what he knew of it in his 1946 book, *Really the Blues*. According to Mezzrow, Singleton told Armstrong he was staying at Connie's Inn and said, "Well Pops, you know friendship is one thing and business is another." "Louis swore from that day on Zutty would never play with him again, even though he was the only drummer in the world that could hold him up every inch of the way," Mezzrow continued. "That split-up hurt me more than either one of them, because it was such a great loss to the music. To this day those two wonderful artists don't realize how important it is for them to be together."[35]

Mezzrow's book upset Singleton, as Armstrong related: "Zutty even asked Mezz to take that scene, that part out there, where he told, you know, what I'm talking about, where he doubled back on the same job after we was fired off it."[36] Singleton was upset because he remembered it very differently from Armstrong and Mezzrow. In a 1975 interview, Singleton and his wife Marge insisted that they went to Louis to see about his plans; Lil Armstrong was there, too. "I asked Louis did he want me to stay with him?" Zutty recalled. "Because if not, I've got a job to stay in Connie's Inn." Armstrong responded by telling Zutty how much money he had a chance to make as a single, saying, "You know, I'm going to become commercial. I can make some money." "And that's when I told Louis, I said, 'Well Louis, friendship is one thing and business is another.' See, but Mezz put it in his book that I was cutting out from Louis."[37]

The rest of Dickerson's band took it hard "because Louis chucked them," as Marge Singleton put it. "They just had to get back to Chicago and get jobs. They just, Louis just left the band flat. . . . Jimmy Strong, he was up to our house crying because he hardly had fare to get back to Chicago." Originally best friends, Armstrong and Singleton became mere acquaintances who worked together only sporadically before Armstrong began viewing Singleton as something of an enemy by the 1950s. Marge Singleton placed the blame on Lil. "And Lil was a big influence," she said. "She would commercialize Louis, too, you know. She loved Zutty, Lil did. But I know when Rockwell told him how much money he could make, and I know Lil was for that, you know. Naturally, because when we went down there that night, Lil didn't look like she was too happy to see us when we walked in. Because Zutty was going to make Louis tell him."

Armstrong himself never mentioned Lil and instead said going out as a single was Rockwell's doing. About becoming a bandleader, Armstrong said in 1950, "I was forced into it, after all. Right here [in New York], Rockwell told me, said, 'Now, you take it or leave it. Do a single or forget it. Your band done broke up.'"[38] Rockwell finally had Armstrong where he wanted him, a single artist that he could book and record instead of worrying about the entire Dickerson band. Armstrong was now about to embark on a life on the road that, for the most part, wouldn't end for the next 40 years.

3

"I Break It Up Everywhere I Play"

December 1929–May 1930

Rockwell's first move with the newly liberated Armstrong was to re-team him with Luis Russell's Orchestra, which boasted a significant addition since the last time Armstrong played with them in the guise of trumpeter Henry "Red" Allen. Born in 1908 in Algiers, Louisiana, Allen had been mimicking Armstrong's career path for years, having been raised to play in brass bands (his father was a leader) followed by a stint on the riverboats with Fate Marable and even a call-up to Chicago by King Oliver in 1927.

In July 1929, he came to New York where he was signed to be RCA Victor's "answer to Louis Armstrong." Allen immediately recorded with members of Russell's band and though the records didn't come anywhere near the sales of Armstrong's, they announced him as a formidable rival. One day, Louis came home to find his wife Lil listening to one of Allen's sides. "He just stood there for a minute, with an angry expression on his face," Lil recalled. "Then after a bit, he smiled and said, 'Yeah, he's blowing.'"[1]

Allen had planned to join Duke Ellington, but decided to join Russell instead, replacing Louis Metcalf. "It had brotherly love going," Allen said of the band. "It was also the most swinging band in New York. It put the audiences in an uproar. One of the reasons was rhythm."[2] Indeed, the Russell outfit swung more than any other band at the time because of its thumping rhythm section anchored by Pops Foster's bass and featuring Paul Barbarin on drums, Will Johnson on guitar and leader Russell on piano. "Oh, I loved it," alto saxophonist Charlie Holmes said about playing over it. "You're not supposed to hear the rhythm section. You're supposed to *feel* it. You're supposed to *feel* that rhythm."[3]

Rockwell was still recording the Russell band for OKeh, so it made sense to team Armstrong and Russell up for some more records, cutting two sides on December 10 and two more on December 13. In the case of the first three—"I Ain't Got Nobody," "Dallas Blues," and "St. Louis Blues"—vocal and non-vocal versions were once again recorded for each song but this time, Rockwell realized that people wanted to hear Armstrong sing; the non-vocal versions remained unissued until 1991.

Like "After You've Gone" and "Some of These Days," Rockwell reached into the past for his selections; "I Ain't Got Nobody" was from 1915, "Dallas Blues" from 1912, and "St. Louis Blues" from 1914. From the opening seconds, the powerful rhythm section makes its presence immediately felt, beautifully captured by the OKeh engineers. On "I Ain't Got Nobody," Armstrong trades so seamlessly with Red Allen's trumpet, many seasoned listeners believed it was one trumpet playing instead of two! "St. Louis Blues" is highlighted by the almost visceral way the Russell band pushes Armstrong during his perfectly constructed, final four-chorus outing. The last riff chorus would even reappear seven years later as the shout chorus on Count Basie's "Swingin' the Blues." Musicians were listening.

With three exciting versions of three very old songs in the can, it was time to record something brand new: Hoagy Carmichael's "Rockin' Chair." According to Charlie Holmes, Carmichael was already in the studio as a guest and after "St. Louis Blues," came up to Armstrong with only a lead sheet for his new song. "Louis, I want you to do this," Carmichael said. "Can you record this for me?" "Yeah, man," Armstrong responded. Carmichael quickly played it on the piano and Armstrong said to Russell, "Yeah, we can make this, can't we, Pops?" Russell said, "Mmmm, yeah, I'll make a little arrangement for it."[4] Indeed, a rare alternate survives that is very sloppy, with the band sounding like they're reading the verse for the first time, but they got it together for the master take, which featured another bit of history: with Carmichael sharing the vocal with Armstrong, "Rockin' Chair" represented the first recorded interracial vocal duet. Armstrong immediately began singing it as a duet in live performances and it would remain in his act until his very last live shows in 1971.

As the new year—and new decade—began, Armstrong and Russell embarked on a series of theater performances, including stops at the Standard Theater in Philadelphia, the Howard Theater in Washington, DC, and the New Albert Auditorium in Baltimore. Armstrong was an especially popular attraction with young audiences in this period. Sixteen-year-old Billy Eckstine was still in high school when he heard Armstrong at the Howard in January and later said of seeing him, "[A]t that particular time, Louie was the guiding light to so many of the younger guys. Because I guess Louie was more of the—we had an adulation for Louie because he was the first one that I think we identified as being one of the hip guys around. Playing good things and playing things with feelings. Unlike with Ellington, which was also an idol, but Ellington was the epitome of class, you know. Louie was more down to earth and more like somebody you could identify with."[5]

On January 24, Armstrong and Russell recorded "Song of the Islands," a breezy Hawaiian number that featured a small string section playing the melody, a glee club vocal episode, and some atmospheric vibraphone playing. To later musicologists like the revered Gunther Schuller, this was the beginning of the end. Schuller wrote of "Song of the Islands," "A painful mélange of non-jazz elements intrude upon Armstrong, and he himself does not escape entirely unscathed. And how could he?"[6] Schuller missed the point. Though he found much to admire in the early jazz music of Jelly Roll Morton, King Oliver, and Duke Ellington, Schuller doesn't seem to have been very interested in the dance band aesthetic of this era, making it impossible for him to appreciate anything with "non-jazz elements." The first chorus does sound like an anonymous period dance band, but the simple, pretty tune and the spare, commercial arrangement undoubtedly inspired Armstrong to great new heights instead of sending him into despair. In fact, Armstrong loved his new record so much, he invited his friend Charlie Carpenter to his house to hear it when it came out and according to Carpenter, "he was just ecstatic about 'Song of the Islands.'" As they listened, Armstrong asked, "You don't hear nothing on there?" "Yeah, I hear some people humming," Carpenter responded. "Those cats are *real* Hawaiians," Armstrong responded. "I had real Hawaiians and violins on that record!"[7] Armstrong loved his record, he loved the pop tune, he loved the strings, he loved the real Hawaiians. He was approaching the pop music scene on his own terms and infusing it with relentless creativity and swing.

Mezz Mezzrow capitalized on the popularity of Armstrong's records during this period. He went up to Harlem, where Guy Lombardo was the most popular performer on jukeboxes, and demanded various venues start playing Armstrong, suggesting "Ain't Misbehavin'," "Black and Blue," "Some of These Days," "After You've Gone," "St. Louis Blues," "Rockin' Chair," and "Song of the Islands." "They all hit the juke boxes fast, and they rocked all Harlem," Mezzrow wrote. "Everywhere we went we got the proprietor to install more boxes, and they all blared out Louis, Louis, and more Louis. The Armstrong craze spilled over from Harlem right after that, and before long there wasn't a juke box in the country that Louis wasn't scatting on."[8]

The same day "Song of the Islands" was recorded, Armstrong and the Russell Orchestra debuted as part of a true vaudeville bill at the Loew's State Theater in New York City. Armstrong was no stranger to revues, but this was an actual vaudeville house and he'd be the only African American act on the bill. Talking pictures and radio had begun to take a bite out of vaudeville's decades-long popularity in the late 1920s and the impending Great Depression would not help matters, but a vaudeville bill was still a popular way to get a variety of entertainment at a price the entire family could afford.

Armstrong had about 20 minutes at the Loew's State and put together a fast-paced set. Jazz fans nostalgic for a world they never experienced sometimes romanticize this as the era of pure, no-frills jamming and spontaneous improvising. Those days were over for Armstrong, if they ever existed; this was show business and Armstrong had to quickly learn how to build a perfect show. One reviewer pointed out that Armstrong's "Act carries elaborate scenery, costumes and special lighting" so it was visually appealing from the start.[9] The Russell Orchestra would begin the proceedings in a semicircle, letting Pops Foster shine on the opener, "Do That Thing." As the band played the intro to "Ain't Misbehavin'," Armstrong made his entrance and did his big Broadway hit. He then brought in female entertainer Bobby DeLeon to sing and dance on "Turn on the Heat." Armstrong followed with two of his fall OKeh hits, "Some of These Days" and "When You're Smiling," before bringing on the 22-year-old, one-legged tap dancer Peg Leg Bates, who had perfected his routine since breaking into vaudeville at the age of 15. Armstrong and the Russell Orchestra would close the set with the rocking "St. Louis Blues," making for a powerful finish.

Variety reviewed Armstrong twice in a week, treating it as a "New Act" and listing the leader as "Lewis Armstrong," with critic Conde G. Brewer writing that Armstrong "Bowed off to a show-stopping reception."[10] But *Zit's Theatrical Newspaper* complained that Armstrong "leaves an impression that he is trying to 'hog' things, in that he insists on either warbling each number or playing his trumpet to solo. . . . Maybe they like Armstrong and his band at Connie's Inn, but Mr. and Mrs. State were rather cool to him at this show." The Zit's reviewer rated Armstrong third on the bill, giving first place honors to headliner, Georgie Price, who was praised for his comic stories "that left everybody in good humor" and the way he put over his songs "in his own inimitable style."[11] Torrid trumpeting would always succeed with a certain segment of the audience but Armstrong was learning that he might need to unleash a little more of his personality if he was going to really succeed in vaudeville with "Mr. and Mrs. State."

The Russell Orchestra went back to the Saratoga Club in February and Armstrong returned to Chicago for the first time since he left in May 1929, booked to do a week at the Regal Theater. Chicago papers—especially the black *Chicago Defender*—really publicized the return. Now, many of the blurbs mentioned Armstrong's ability to hit "high C" and referred to him as "Broadway's biggest hit of 1929." "When Louis Armstrong stepped on the stage at the Regal Wednesday afternoon the capacity crowd started a reception that

Figure 3.1 An advertisement for Armstrong's week at the Pearle Theatre in Philadelphia in April 1930, offering $5,000 "to any person who can hit as high a note as [Armstrong] can and hold same."
Courtesy of the Louis Armstrong House Museum

lasted several minutes, and after the one and only 'Louie' got through singing and blowing that torrid cornet—well, it was just too bad!" read a *Chicago Defender* review. "Such an ovation as was given him has not been seen in these parts for a long time, and certainly never at the theater—anyone of them."[12]

While in Chicago, Armstrong also headlined his old friend Dave Peyton's Theatrical Ball at the Savoy Ballroom; did multiple newspaper endorsements ("Louis Armstrong Is At The Regal This Week—Ask Him About Max's Suits and Overcoats"[13] and "Louis Armstrong, World's Greatest Feature Cornetist, Says: 'In Music It's Harmony, In Hair Pomades, It's Porter's Premier"[14]); appeared at a Bud Billiken party for children with Farina of the "Our Gang" comedies and blackface comedian, "Sweet Papa Garbage" (Marshall Rogers)[15]; and was one of the guests of honor at a banquet given by James Pleasure.[16] Armstrong appreciated the warmth, writing to Luis Russell on February 17, "The people here are crazy about me. Gee they are about to banquet me to death. Ha Ha." But he wasn't happy with the musical backing of the "Regal Symphonists," telling Russell, "I sure miss you all. Of course I break it up everywhere I play but still I miss my old background. These cats here in this town Can't swing." Armstrong looked forward to reuniting with Russell the following week in New York, writing, "Tell my boys how I miss them And will be Oh so glad to be back to them."[17]

However, when Armstrong got back to New York on February 26, the Russell band was no longer in the mix. Instead, Rockwell booked Armstrong to open a new Harlem nightclub, the Cocoanut Grove, fronting a newly formed orchestra led by drummer Willie Lynch. Lynch's band featured some excellent musicians in reedman Castor McCord, pianist Joe Turner, and guitarist Bernard Addison, and would eventually morph into the popular Mills Blue Rhythm Band, but the reliance on Lavert Hutchinson's tuba in the rhythm section at the time Armstrong fronted it gave it a more two-beat, old-time feel after Russell's brand of forward-moving swing.

The Cocoanut Grove—called by one writer "the swank boo-boo-de-doo place on 125th Street"[18]—is where Armstrong really caught the eye of columnist Walter Winchell, who began mentioning the trumpeter almost every week, recommending "pashy platters" "After You've Gone" and "Song of the Islands" in addition to his "endless routine of terrifically-tempoed tunes" in Harlem.[19] Winchell was one of the most widely read columnists at the time and would continue serving as an important advocate for Armstrong in the years to come.

After five weeks of working together at the Cocoanut Grove, Armstrong and Lynch's band recorded on April 5, heard in inspired form on two pop tunes, Jimmy McHugh and Clarence Gaskill's excellent "I Can't Believe That You're in Love with Me" from 1926 and Hoagy Carmichael and Stu Gorrell's somewhat mysterious "My Sweet." Armstrong transformed both into something quite original, improving what was on the written page in each case.[20]

That same day, Armstrong recorded something completely different, a somber rendition of "Dear Old Southland" backed solely by the piano of Buck Washington of Buck and Bubbles, who had just sat in on "My Sweet." In 1928, Armstrong recorded a dazzling duet with Earl Hines on "Weather Bird" but Rockwell didn't have anything similar to pair it, so it remained unissued. Washington was no Hines but didn't need to be as this would be purely a trumpet showcase. It's a dramatic, serious performance, featuring Armstrong at his most operatic, but also with enough humor to refer to Washington as "Satchelmouth," the first time he uttered that descriptor on record. Armstrong masterfully builds toward a big high-note ending, holding a high G for nine seconds, infusing it with the vibrato of his hero, Enrico Caruso, before resolving it to the final high A. Such endings would become common in just a few years, but it was still a novel way for Armstrong to conclude a recording in 1930.

Bob Landry of *Variety* approved of the "Dear Old Southland"/"Weather Bird" coupling, writing, "Both are remarkable demonstrations of his superior management of the three-finger clarion. As novelties and for the study and delight of his numerous followers it's certain to be a popular release."[21] But to some, the record represented something of a great divide in Armstrong's discography. Analyzing Armstrong's recorded output decades later, John Chilton referred to Armstrong's "immense sensitivity and versatility" on "Weather Bird" before complaining that " 'Dear Old Southland' has none of that magic because "there's a quasi-dramatic feel about the whole performance."[22] But at the time, when "Dear Old Southland" was released in England, influential musician and composer Spike Hughes declared it "Armstrong's Best Ever" in *Melody Maker,* and compared Armstrong's "free" playing" to "the way Hungarian fiddlers ramble in the first part of a 'czardas.' "[23] The truth is, comparing "Dear Old Southland" to "Weather Bird" is comparing apples and oranges. "Weather Bird" is all about lightning-fast reflexes and virtuosity, while "Dear Old Southland" is aimed squarely at the heartstrings. Both approaches were valid, so far as Armstrong was concerned.

Armstrong with Lynch toured the east coast for dates in Philadelphia and Baltimore before recording four more sides—"Indian Cradle Song," "Exactly Like You," "Dinah," and "Tiger Rag"—on May 4. A review of the band in Baltimore mentioned the band's performance of "Tiger Rag" and Armstrong himself later wrote about "Indian Cradle Song" being one of his most popular numbers back at Connie's Inn making this yet another session made to immortalize what Armstrong was dishing out to live audiences night after night.[24] The faux-exotic "Indian Cradle Song" has some jaunty trumpet moments, but the song remained a product of its time; "Exactly Like You," on the other hand, was transformed by Armstrong from a new pop tune into a future standard. The vocal brims with desire, punctuated with a closing "Sweet mama," a phrase not commonly found in pop singing of the period. The last chorus also features an early instance of what would become a regular device on Armstrong's records in the next few years: the band urgently playing notes on only the first and third beats of a bar. Musicians referred to this as "fucking rhythm" and, combined with the rhythm section's natural tendency to accent the second and fourth beats, it added up to a push-and-pull feel that inspired Armstrong to float freely on top.[25]

Armstrong's trumpet playing was just warming up as he closed the date with his popular showcases on "Dinah" and "Tiger Rag." There's everything one now would expect from an Armstrong trumpet feature: virtuosity, swing, unpredictable rhythm, a brilliant, yet logical build to a climax, faultless upper register playing, etc., but both solos also feature something a little different: an abundance of quotes from other songs.

This wasn't entirely new, as Armstrong had been doing it sporadically for years, beginning with a quote from Franz Drdla's "Souvenir" in his accompaniment to Clara Smith's "Court House Blues" in 1925 and continuing through "Rhapsody in Blue" on "Ain't Misbehavin'." On "Dinah," he quotes "Oh, Lady Be Good," "My Hero" (from Oscar Strauss's *The Chocolate Soldier*), the "National Emblem March," the bridge to "Lover Come Back to Me," and finally, two repeats from his past, the *Rigoletto* quartet and the "Streets of Cairo" "hoochie-coochie" song. On "Tiger Rag," he enters with a paraphrase of "The Irish Washerwoman" and follows with "Singin' in the Rain," another bit of the "National Emblem March," and finally, more opera with "Pagliacci." Between these two songs, this session had more quotations than an edition of *Bartlett's*.

Later critics such as Gunther Schuller lambasted this use of quotes, claiming Armstrong was simply playing for "audience titters." It's true that Armstrong's use of quotes was a sort of musical showmanship, a way of getting a laugh with horn, which makes sense when one considers his drive to simply entertain his audiences no matter the method. (It also punctures theories that Armstrong clowned around but then got deadly serious when he picked up his horn; there's nothing deadly serious about quoting the "National Emblem March," better known as "Oh the Monkey Wrapped His Tale around the Flagpole.") But it became something musicians really picked up on, not just the laypeople in the audience. "It was a fun thing for trumpet players," trumpeter Taft Jordan said of Armstrong's use of quotes. "How the hell does he figure to put that there, in that spot? No one else had done this sort of thing until he started it."[26] It should be no surprise that later musicians who admired Armstrong, such as Charlie Parker and Dexter Gordon, became quite proficient at the game of musical quotes but like most matters, Armstrong did it first.

Armstrong bade the Lynch band adieu and headed back out on the road as a single, playing with whatever appropriate band he could find in city after city. When he got to Ohio in early May, he performed with Zack Whyte's territory band, featuring 20-year-old trumpeter Sy Oliver, who became so overwhelmed by hearing Armstrong simply warm up, he couldn't play. "Just listening to Louie back there noodling as we played, I was so excited, I didn't know what to do," he said. Oliver was once asked if other trumpet players knew just how special Armstrong was at the time. "Oh no, not only trumpet players; every musician in the business copied Louie's style," he replied, adding, "saxophones, trombones, piano, *everybody* tried to play like Louie. He was unique. There had never been anything like it before. In fact, to this day,

I don't know of any other individual who so completely captured the imagination and the attention of all the other musicians."[27]

Sometime in the first half of 1930, Armstrong passed through Norfolk, Virginia, where a teenaged Taft Jordan begged his parents for 50 cents so he could see "the world's greatest trumpet player." The dance was crowded with trumpet players, each with their own instruments, waiting to see Armstrong perform "When You're Smiling" so they could examine if he was playing a trick instrument. Armstrong agreed to play it after intermission and upon sounding the opening notes, "the house was in an uproar," according to Jordan. "And just as suddenly it quieted down, because everybody wanted to hear this. . . . He had a great big Turkish towel around his neck, and perspiration was coming out like rain water. When he got to the last eight bars, he was getting stronger and stronger. Then he hit that top note and completed the tune." Afterward, a trumpet player asked if he could see Armstrong's trumpet. Armstrong agreed. The trumpeter asked if he could blow it; Armstrong let him. "So the guy put his mouthpiece in and sounded C on Pops's horn and C on his own," Jordan said. "He ran the scale on his, and he ran the scale on Pops's. It was all the same. It was no trick horn. It was just the man, the difference of the man."[28]

Armstrong's tour brought him back to Chicago, where he spent the rest of May performing as part of a vaudeville revue titled "Ace High" at multiple theaters owned by Paramount's Publix Theatre Corporation. But according to the trades, he was now being booked by the William Morris office, not Tommy Rockwell.[29] On May 14, *Variety* featured a huge half-page ad billing Armstrong as "Master of Modernism" and "Creator of his Song Style," quoting positive press from *Variety* reviews and Walter Winchell's columns and listing his latest OKeh releases. For contact information, though, Rockwell wasn't listed but instead all communications were directed to "Miller & Miller."[30] Something was up.

Armstrong's business affairs are hard to untangle in this period. His one-year contract with Rockwell was due to expire on May 18. According to Rockwell, "on or about April 1, 1930," he extended the contract for three years, from May 18, 1930, through May 18, 1933.[31] In an affidavit the following year, Armstrong said "the contract was not renewed in accordance with the terms thereof" and judging by his press in May, Rockwell was clearly no longer booking Armstrong. Armstrong also mentioned that any dates Rockwell booked "were to be subject to the approval" of Louis and Lil.[32] Clearly, they were no longer approving his bookings.

Armstrong visited his old stomping grounds with multiple performances at the Savoy Ballroom on May 18 and a "farewell dance party" a week later before traveling with the "Ace High" revue to Minnesota and Wisconsin. Newspapers reported that "they are calling for him back in New York" and Armstrong had to "return to Broadway."[33] Only he didn't. "I 'Cooled' (*laid off*) for about 'Nine Days,' Having a Little Fun—*etc.*," he recalled.[34]

He had conquered Chicago. He had conquered New York. But now he was getting wind that he was quite popular in California. San Francisco radio station KYA had a request hour each night and Armstrong came in second only to white entertainer Ted Lewis.[35] "I had a friend who ran on the road from New York to California," Armstrong later wrote. "And would always tell me he could GET a Pass for me any time I should see fit to go out there. And always I would ask him, 'what's out there? . . . Not knowing that I was as popular as I actually was in California . . . With the White People of course—mostly." Armstrong knew that "the minute a colored man gets off of a train anywhere West or South," if he didn't have a white man to vouch for him, they "would have my head whipped worst than a kettle drum."[36] Armstrong was ready to conquer California but he needed such a white man. That was a job for Johnny Collins.

4

"He Would Just Amaze You"

June–November 1930

Very little has been written about Johnny Collins. He seemed to mysteriously arrive in Louis Armstrong's life in 1930 and, just as mysteriously, left it in a chaotic state three years later. He never gave interviews after his association with the trumpeter. Most writers hung the moniker "gangster" on him without evidence. Nobody had much good to say about him but it's undeniable that he helped guide the trumpeter to international stardom, and when he was through, Armstrong was a best-selling popular recording artist, a fixture on radio, and a movie star. He was also partially responsible for numerous threats to his star client's life in their short time together, resulting in Armstrong living in fear and traveling with police escorts and bodyguards for protection. This would be a bumpy ride, but not one without merit.

Collins was born in 1876 in Chicago, the son of a police sergeant. He first turns up in *Variety* in 1909 in conjunction with booking acts for Orpheum-owned amusement parks in the Midwest.[1] By December 1910, he had picked up theater bookings on the Orpheum circuit in Cincinnati, Louisville, Indianapolis, Memphis, and New Orleans.[2] In 1912, he began booking the Palace Theater in Chicago, but after a divorce, unexpectedly quit the Orpheum circuit and sailed to England in July 1912, spending the summer booking acts in London. All of these destinations would come back into play during his years with Armstrong.[3]

Collins spent much of the 1910s building up his reputation through his work booking Midwest vaudeville houses for the United Booking Offices, as well as the Keith's Agency. Yet, the 1920s were a roller coaster for him as each step forward was usually followed by two self-inflicted steps back, such as having a nervous breakdown and getting arrested for drunk driving. He rose from the ashes, forming his own independent agency and getting his very own Loew's franchise in February 1928, only to lose it by November because of his "conduct."[4] In 1953, Armstrong summed up Collins's early up-and-down career by saying, "He was an office boy in the RKO . . . and then he worked up to be a big booker but he's an asshole and he fucked up every time."[5] Collins

ended up rejoining Keith in 1929 just as the Radio, Keith, and Orpheum theater chains merged to form RKO, but ill health scuttled this latest opportunity,
sidelining him into 1930.

And that's where the mystery really begins. Sometime in May 1930, most
likely when he drifted out of Rockwell's grasp and played that string of vaudeville dates in Chicago and the Midwest, Louis Armstrong came onto Johnny
Collins's radar. Either they met in Chicago or perhaps Collins learned of him
through Rockwell, as it has long been surmised that Rockwell chose Collins to
watch over Armstrong. Either way, Collins must have sensed an opportunity
and a game plan was hatched to head to California.

Collins went first, as *Variety* reported in a June 4 column, "Johnny Collins on
Coast," adding, "Long a vaude booker and later an agent in New York, Collins
will go into the agency end."[6] According to Armstrong himself, Collins—
whom Armstrong referred to as "my manager"—was waiting for him when
he got to California.[7] An article from 1931 told the story of Armstrong's west
coast move, saying, "After a long and tedious journey across the country he
arrived in the city of stars, where he was met at the train by Johnny Collins,
former Radio-Keith-Orpheum executive, and booking manager of the R-.K.-
O. New York theaters, and having the distinction of discovering and creating
more stars than any other manager on Broadway."[8] When Armstrong arrived
in California, Collins was trying to sell the trumpeter's services for a salary
of $150 a week to drummer Curtis Mosby, in Armstrong's words "a big time
Colored Cabaret owner," who ran the Club Alabam on Central Avenue.

Armstrong immediately met a new friend in California, Luther Gafford, an
African American "record fan personified" who was better known as "Soldier
Boy." Soldier Boy helped Armstrong settle into the Dunbar Hotel on Central
Avenue in Los Angeles, the center of the city's black life. "I checked into my
room. With nothin in perticular to look for or forward to either," Armstrong
wrote. "But, I had my right Loot (means (money.) So I'm Straight enough not
to have to Cop A Beg—or have to blow—my horn right away, unless I actually
WAS satisfied and willing . . . I did'nt have anyone to depend up on me at the
time . . . So, with a few real new Vines, and a nice weight, and young, blowing
my ass OFF—I felt pretty ready."[9]

Soldier Boy took Armstrong to a barber shop on Central Avenue to meet
Mosby, who, Armstrong recalled, "laughed at" Collins for asking for $150 a
week for his services. As the barber removed a hot towel from Mosby's face,
Soldier Boy said, "Meet Louis Armstrong, the great Trumpet Man, who just
arrived from the East. The Trumpet man who Mr. Collins is trying to sell to
you. He's Hot and I know he can build up your business at the club Alabam."
According to Armstrong, "This Colored owner looked me up and down,

sort of sarcastically and said to Soldier Boy, 'Take him next door and give him something to eat.'" Armstrong remained quiet but Soldier Boy "jumped salty"[10] and yelled, "Man, this man don't need no free meal! He has his own loot. He just thought since he's making his first appearance out on the Coast, and you being a man of his Race, he just wanted to give you the first preference to present him. He's already a star. And get all the work anywhere he choose. And here you come with that old signifying shit. Not only did you insult him, but you have insulted me." Mosby apologized, but the damage was done. "We all said later that Curtis Mosby missed the boat by not hiring me," Armstrong recalled.[11]

Finally, an opportunity arose: "The following week Mr. Collins called me at my Hotel and told me, 'Louis Armstrong, I have just booked you out in Culver City at Sebastian's Cotton Club, for the salary of three hundred and fifty dollars per week.'"[12] "Sebastian" was Frank Sebastian, a tall Italian fellow who loved being the center of attention. "He always had that good ole welcome smile, and a very nice little chat for all of his help," Armstrong wrote of Sebastian. "No matter who it was, whether it was the dish washer, gents room boy, the star of the show, musician etc. He always made you feel relaxed and make you want to give everything that's in you. He and his big long white beautiful sixteen cylinder Cadillac was the talk of all Hollywood. I'd say it was the talk of the Nation. He was a real tall good looking sharp cat. Wore the best vines (clothes) and would strut like a 'peacock' I always did admire him."[13]

The band at Sebastian's Cotton Club was run by an older trumpeter, Vernon Elkins, and featured two 22-year-old future legends, drummer Lionel Hampton and trombonist Lawrence Brown.[14] Armstrong decided to perform a reconnaissance mission, going to hear the band without letting anyone know. Upon first hearing, Armstrong was unimpressed, describing them as "nothing but a mediocre band in this place."[15] But when Elkins turned them loose on a romping number, Armstrong "almost jumped out of my skin."[16] "I went out there two nights to hear them," he recalled, "I hung around with them cats and dug what they were playing and the ability they had. That's the first thing I dig about a musician. . . . Frank Sebastian don't even know me, I ain't even been introduced to him yet! But I want to see that band. I'm not thinking about Frank or nobody else. They booked me, I know what I'm supposed to do."[17]

The talent of Brown and Hampton immediately stood out. "I discovered the 'greatness of those 'Two youngsters the very first day I went to 'Rehearsal," Armstrong wrote in 1944. "And 'Lionel was so 'young and 'vivacious (still is) on those 'Drums. And he had taken to 'like me (personally) so well and I felt the 'same way about him. And he was one of the Swinginest Drummers

I had ever seen and heard in my life."[18] Hampton, who stuttered when he got excited, greeted Armstrong with, "Wha-a-t you say, Pops?" That "floored" Armstrong, who responded, "Wha-a-t you say, Gates!" A fast friendship was born. Sebastian's Cotton Club was a 35-minute drive from Armstrong's room at the Dunbar Hotel, but Hampton came through, lending Armstrong a "little Ford" to help him make the commute.[19]

Louis came to California by himself but was soon joined by Lil Armstrong—and a mysterious man she claimed she needed around to massage her hips to keep her in shape. "UMP," Armstrong declared. "She sure must have thought I was a *Damn fool 'Sho Nuff.'* As if I didn't know her 'Hips are sure to 'Ignite' from the 'Friction.'—later on, I found out that this 'Guy' and 'Lil had been "Going together and 'he'd been 'Spending my 'money for years."[20] Not that Louis was innocent himself. He later told how he had to turn down an engagement because he had "some Fish to Fry myself—And I just could'nt change the date. Nay nay—not in California-God no. As bad as those wolves are on Central Avenue—Why they would have Chewed my Back-up! (TAKEN MY GAL)."[21] Chicago-based mistress Alpha Smith even showed up to confess her love for him. "The 'Lord Must have sent her out there to me," Armstrong wrote.[22] Louis found a room for Alpha and began juggling life with Lil and Alpha, each of whom kept a scrapbook chronicling their sweetheart's success—sometimes including the same clippings in their respective books.

On July 16, the day before he was due to open at Sebastian's Cotton Club, Louis found himself back in the recording studio with Lil on piano, but it wasn't for OKeh. Instead, they were recording for Victor on a session led by Jimmie Rodgers, "The Singing Brakeman." It's assumed this was the brainchild of Ralph Peer, as Peer knew the Armstrongs when he was the head of OKeh records in the mid-1920s and was now recording country music for Victor. Rodgers borrowed some lyrics from "The Bridewell Blues," an already obscure 1926 Armstrong record featuring blues singer Nolan Walsh, and together with Louis and Lil's offerings, created "Blue Yodel Number 9," perhaps the most "American" recording of all time. One can discuss the roots and African and European influences of popular music all day long but in the end, the United States has produced three distinct styles of music: jazz, country, and the blues. On "Blue Yodel Number 9," all three intersected as "The Father of Country Music" and "The Father of Jazz" met on the common ground of a 12-bar blues—or at least approximately 12 bars. Rodgers was from the I'll-change-chords-when-I-feel-like-it school of playing; one can hear Louis and Lil listening hard to anticipate his changes. In talking about this record to Irwin Johnson in 1953, Louis didn't hide from discussing the challenge, saying, "And we never did end up on the bar, you know, so I had to get with him. I just made it wrong with him! It turned out fine."[23]

The following night, Armstrong made his debut at Sebastian's Cotton Club as part of an elaborate floor show, "Sebastian's Brown Skin Vamps," staged by the New York–based team of LeRoy Bloomfield and Aurora Greeley and featuring over 40 dancers and lavish costume changes. Armstrong was an instant sensation. According to press accounts, Armstrong played all of his recent OKeh hits, including "When You're Smiling," "Exactly Like You," "Song of the Islands" and "St. Louis Blues."[24] Advertisements originally featured only photos of the ubiquitous Sebastian but by July 19—two days after the first show—new ads were run with photos of both Sebastian and Armstrong. Hollywood caught on immediately, too; reporter W. E. Oliver spotted five celebrities in attendance "with big parties" on Saturday, July 19, in awe of "the most extraordinary trumpeter I have ever heard" and "one of the best showmen I have seen at the head of an orchestra."[25]

Johnny Collins's fingerprints were now starting to show up in the press, too. When Walter Brooks was hired in late July to begin putting together a new revue for Armstrong at the Cotton Club, *Variety* reported, "Deal with Brooks and Armstrong was handled through Johnny Collins."[26] Around the same time, Armstrong found himself doubling at the Cotton Club and appearing in a "Wild and Woolly" vaudeville bill at Loew's State in Los Angeles, vaudeville really being Collins's bread-and-butter. Armstrong "stopped the show," according to the *Los Angeles Evening Herald*.[27] His $500 a week salary, negotiated by Collins, even made the papers.[28]

Collins might have been handling Armstrong's day-to-day bookings, but Tommy Rockwell was still in charge of Armstrong's recordings. The coupling of "Dinah" and "Tiger Rag" in May was the last strict Race record Armstrong would ever make. After a year of experimenting with Race and Pop releases, Rockwell made Armstrong a full-time pop artist starting with a California session on July 21. Now that Armstrong was fully on the pop side—and had already recorded many of his live specialties—Rockwell would begin choosing the hottest songs of the moment, sure that Armstrong would contribute something unique compared to all other recordings of the same tunes at the same time.

First was "I'm a Ding Dong Daddy from Dumas," a 16-bar song that was tailor-made for Armstrong with its built-in breaks to allow him to take off with his trumpet and vocals. His four-chorus trumpet exploration could be dubbed "Storytelling 101" as Hampton and the riffing band inspire Armstrong to take more chances with each passing chorus. The solo was quickly gobbled up by musicians. Bill Coleman mentioned playing it in three-part harmony with Charlie Johnson's orchestra in 1931.[29] A few years later, Count Basie included the repeated, three-note descending motif from the fourth chorus in his band's arrangement of "Limehouse Blues." Trumpeter Dizzy Gillespie used the first phrase Armstrong plays in his final break as the basis for half the melody of "Salt Peanuts" in the bebop era. Trumpeter Jonah Jones quoted the solo in his recording of the same tune with Sidney Bechet in 1953. Used as the basis for arrangements, for compositions, and even for improvised solos, Armstrong's improvisations were quickly becoming the language of jazz.

Armstrong got to stretch out for four full choruses, but apparently that was only warming up compared to live performances. "We were on the air one night," Hampton recalled, "and he said, 'Look out, man, we're gonna open up with "Dumas." I feel good tonight, and if I'm going well, Hamp, you sit on those cowbells with me, and I'll play another chorus.' Well, man, I was sitting on those cowbells, and Louis played about ninety-nine choruses on 'I'm a Ding Dong Daddy from Dumas.'"[30] Trumpeter George Orendorff, who joined the band later that year, remembered a 15-minute radio broadcast that featured "Ding Dong Daddy" for the entire 15-minute duration. "Oh, Louis, he was something else," Orendorff said.[31]

After the intense heat of "Ding Dong Daddy" at the July 21 session, Armstrong settled down with a ballad as the flip side, "I'm in the Market for You," a love song from the film *High Society Blues* that must have taken on a different meaning after the stock market crash of 1929. Aside from some high-quality, lyrical trumpet playing, the highlight is Armstrong's sincere vocal, with little ad-libbed asides such as "oh, you sweet little you" that add a personal flair. Multiple other vocals of "I'm in the Market for You" survive from early 1930 but none of the other bland vocalists of the time could match Armstrong's sincerity and passion.

Except perhaps for one. Bing Crosby was also situated in California at the time and his mutual appreciation society with Armstrong was hitting new heights. Crosby was the toast of Hollywood, performing with the Rhythm Boys and Gus Arnheim's Orchestra at the Cocoanut Grove nightclub in the Ambassador Hotel. "After Bing—the band—Mr. Arnheim and boys would finished work at the Grove, they would Haul Ashes over to the Cotton Club where we were playing and Swing with us until Home Sweet Home was played," Armstrong recalled. As popular as Armstrong's OKeh records were, it's conceivable that more people heard him in this period on radio than on records since he broadcast every single night from Sebastian's Cotton Club at 11 P.M. on KFVD. Crosby broadcast just before Armstrong came on the air and together, the back-to-back live shows established the direction of jazz and popular music was heading. "When Gus went off the air, we went on behind him putting down all that good barrel house music," Armstrong said. "We were so popular that every house had the same program on."[32]

Crosby's calling card at the time was his way with a ballad, exhibiting more intimacy than his other white contemporary crooners such as Seger Ellis, Gene Austin, and Rudy Vallee, while borrowing Armstrong's relaxed ideas of phrasing. Armstrong noticed the impact Crosby was having even on his own race. "There were just as many colored people buying an' Raving over Bing's recordings—as much as anybody else," he wrote. "The chicks (GALS) were justa Swooning and Screaming when Bing would sing."[33] Back in Harlem, Mezz Mezzrow wrote, "Around The Corner there was only one record we'd allow on the boxes with Louis, Bing Crosby's 'When the Blue of the Night.' That was a concession to the sentimental chicks too, because they were starved for sweet romance and they sure didn't get much of it from Louis' recordings."[34]

That was about to change. On August 19, Armstrong recorded two tender love songs, "I'm Confessin' (That I Love You)" and "If I Could Be with You (One Hour Tonight)." He instilled both with a sense of sexuality and eroticism not previously found on record by any African American artist. African Americans could declare their love in a blues setting and with double-entendres but there had never been anything quite like this: a 29-year-old black man recording for OKeh's popular series, coming right out and singing lyrics like "I'm Confessin' that I love you, tell me that you love me too" and "If I could be with you, I'd love you strong / If I could be with you, I'd love you long." It was black sexuality on record and nothing quite so intimate and passionate would come around again until the 1940s and the advent of Billy Eckstine. Audiences responded. Many writers have painted Armstrong as simply a harmless, grinning performer who made white audiences feel safe, but truthfully, his ways with a ballad made him a special favorite with female fans—white and black—many of whom who made their feelings known for him onstage and off. "I've seen women faint when he was singing," Buck Clayton said of Armstrong's vocals in this period.[35]

Alongside such groundbreaking vocals, Armstrong's trumpet work was particularly influential, one break on "Confessin'" forming the basis of Benny Goodman's composition "Pick-a-Rib." Armstrong was no longer going for the quick-fingered virtuosity of "West End Blues" but instead a soaring, operatic bravura with fewer notes and more concentration on tone, upper-register playing, and storytelling. "I happened to be walking down the street and heard a record being played that he had just made, 'I'm Confessin','" Clayton said. "And I just stopped right there and listened. I wouldn't walk any further. I listened to this record because it was such a beautiful interpretation.

I just admired that record so much. Not so much for the execution and all that, which he was famous for, but just for the beauty of it."[36]

Armstrong was inspiring everybody, including the members of Elkins's band. Lawrence Brown takes two of his finest solos on the ballads, completely infatuated by Armstrong, or as he called him, "The only man that ever made me enjoy coming to work. Believe me, he was terrific."[37] Hampton agreed, saying later in life, "I've never heard anyone play the stuff that he played on trumpet there."[38] Hampton added, "Every musician that could get to the Cotton Club in Culver City was there. They were walking off their jobs to hear Louis play, and the place was packed. Musicians were pushing people off the dance floor, so they could get close to hear him, and he was making breaks from high C up to high G." Hampton had two prime seats next to his drums and musicians began offering him money to sit there. Armstrong was already utilizing what would become his trademark handkerchief and kept extras on Hampton's drums. "And do you know, cats used to take his old handkerchiefs away as souvenirs," Hampton said.[39]

To those who lived through it, there seemed to be a consensus that this was truly Armstrong's greatest period. "When Louie first came out to California," said trumpeter Teddy Buckner, "that's when Louie was in his prime. No trumpet player in the world could take him."[40] Buckner was playing in San Diego in Sonny Clay's band but remembered making it a point to catch Armstrong's 2 A.M. broadcast, saying, "And we used to rush to get through our last show, the floor show and everything, in San Diego so I could catch Louie on the radio."[41] It was the same with Duke Ellington and his Orchestra, who were in California filming the Amos 'n' Andy movie *Check and Double Check*. The Ellington band used to play miniature golf on the roof of the Dunbar Hotel and, according to Cootie Williams, "when it was time for Louis to come on the air, we'd drop those clubs and run and get the radio." Williams added, "I think he played the greatest . . . in California."[42]

But those listening on the radio only were getting to experience a fraction of Armstrong's stage presentation at the Cotton Club. By the time of the August 19 session, he was featured in a new revue, "Hitting the High Spots with Louis Armstrong," featuring arrangements by Charles Lawrence, more choreography by Broomfield and Greely, and a talented African American cast including Baby Mack, Aurora Greeley, Evelyn Preer, tap dancers Rutledge and Taylor, and the Anderson Brothers (one of whom was Eddie "Rochester" Anderson).[43] After all of the other acts—dancing, comedy, choreography, love songs—Armstrong finally appeared and did four songs: "Ain't Misbehavin'," "Rockin' Chair," "St. Louis Blues," and "Black and Blue." "This boy will wreck any show that puts him in the right spot, for he had the customers clapping, stamping, whistling and yelling requests simultaneously," according to one reviewer.[44]

This was not the jazz world; this was the world of black show business, a world Armstrong had been firmly entrenched in since the mid-1920s. Comedy was one of his specialties beloved by the black audiences at the Vendome Theater and now it would endear him to the white audiences at the Cotton Club. "Black and Blue" was still a daring choice to make the patrons think about race, but "Rockin' Chair" was carefully chosen to balance it. "Hamp and I did 'Ol' Rockin' Chair' and we mugged and we used to have them holding their stomach," Armstrong said. "And when I looked around, I'm doing comedy—Evelyn Preer was out there, who was a big actress. We used to do 'Poolroom Papa and Schoolroom Mama.' I'll never forget it. That was the big laugh we used to do!"[45] Collins extended Armstrong's contract at the Cotton Club for six more weeks.[46]

In September, Collins pulled off his biggest coup to date by getting Armstrong his first movie role. He'd play a bandleader in a Liberty films

Figure 4.1 Lobby card for the now-lost movie *Ex-Flame* filmed in California in 1930 and featuring Armstrong alongside trombonist Lawrence Brown, pianist Henry Prince, saxophonist Les Hite, and 22-year-old drummer Lionel Hampton.
The Jack Bradley Collection, Louis Armstrong House Museum

production of *Ex-Flame*, a modernized retelling of Ellen Wood's popular British novel from 1861, *East Lynne*. Armstrong filmed his scenes at Metropolitan Studios in mid-September and though Liberty was a smaller operation, part of what is often described as "Poverty Row," it was important for Armstrong to get his foot in the door in Hollywood.

To Armstrong, this was also a sign that Collins was doing a better job as his manager than Rockwell. Rockwell had continued doing his own work as Armstrong's representative, sending him a contract on July 25, 1930, to come back and perform at Connie's Inn "to commence not sooner than January 1st 1931, and no later than May 1st, 1931."[47] Armstrong and Collins ignored the contract and "on or about" September 10, Armstrong, most likely through Collins, "terminated" his arrangement with Rockwell and informed him "that he was not to act as his agent, or manager, or attorney, or representative in the future."[48] Armstrong, who never wanted to be bothered with the business end of the music world, most likely didn't know the full story of what was going on behind the scenes. Years later, he wrote, "Mr. 'Johnny Collins whom was my 'Manager in California through 'some 'Deal he made with Mr. 'Tommy Rockwell my other 'manager—'*Damn*—Come to think of it—I sure had a 'manager's 'Fit."[49] News of *Ex-Flame* hit the press three days after Rockwell received word that Armstrong was terminating his contract with him.[50]

Rockwell didn't put up a fight—yet—but he still had Armstrong's recording contract and set up two dates for OKeh in October. By this point, Armstrong's backing band had undergone some serious changes. Vernon Elkins grew ill at the end of the summer, leading Sebastian to bring in a new band led by alto saxophonist Les Hite—with the stipulation that Lionel Hampton and Lawrence Brown remain. They did, except Brown left by the time of the October sessions to perform with Curtis Mosby.

Armstrong would record three new songs in October that, mostly due to his efforts, would become future standards: "Body and Soul," "Memories of You," and "You're Lucky to Me." Armstrong's peerless way with a ballad were in evidence on the first two numbers, with Armstrong's treatment of "Memories of You" resulting in an especially emotional experience. That song also served as one of the pivotal moments in Hampton's life. Though a drummer first and foremost, he had already been playing a set of orchestra bells with Armstrong at the Cotton Club. The session was held at an NBC radio studio and in the corner, Armstrong spotted a vibraphone. He asked Hampton, "Can you play some at that instrument over there?" Hampton responded, "I'll try!" "By me knowing the percussion, I thought of playing jazz, right there on the keyboard," Hampton recalled, adding, "That was how I came to be the first to play jazz on vibes. Then I made an introduction with Louis on the vibraharp, and that was the first time that four hammers were ever played."[51] Hampton's opening and closing statements made for a winning novelty effect, but Armstrong's somber, hurting vocal and climactic trumpet solo—topping out on a high concert E♭—made it clear to see why he often named this as one of his favorite recordings. On the following "You're Lucky to Me," he aimed even higher, glissing up to a final high F. It came out as a bit of a squeak, but he would eventually grow quite comfortable with that note in a short period of time.

Armstrong continued ruling the Cotton Club through the fall. The radio broadcasts on KFVD were showing no signs of slowing down, his records were selling well, he was popular with many big movie stars, and he had just finished working on his first Hollywood film. He hadn't left California since arriving in early June and didn't have any plans to leave anytime soon. Armstrong was happy. Johnny Collins was happy.

And at this new height of fame, Armstrong got arrested.

5

"Just One of the Cats"

November 1930–May 1931

Armstrong was introduced to marijuana by the white musicians of Chicago, but he soon became something of an ambassador for the drug, naming his 1928 composition "Muggles" in tribute to it and popularizing it in Harlem alongside his friend—and dealer—Mezz Mezzrow. He continued smoking regularly in California; Les Hite's trumpeter McLure "Red Mack" Morris remembered, "That marijuana, Pops smoked so much of that stuff."[1] "We always looked at pot as a kind of a medicine, ya know," Armstrong said in 1970. "Any time we discussed it, anything, I mean, [it was] no enemy or drastic shit. Marijuana was a kind of medicine—and a cheap drunk."[2]

Figure 5.1 Rare Charles Peterson photo of Armstrong getting high with friends, including pianist Nick Aldrich, left, at the Braddock Hotel in Harlem in the early 1940s. The unidentified woman on the right is holding a roach, while Armstrong is spraying the room to mask the smell.

Photo by Charles Peterson, courtesy of Don Peterson

In late November, Armstrong was visited at the Cotton Club by Vic Berton, whom Armstrong called "the greatest drummer of all at that time."[3] During intermission, Berton "came over for a few drags" and the two men began smoking up right outside on the street, "having lots of laughs and feelin' good, enjoying each other's fine company."[4] Armstrong didn't feel like they should be doing it there—and he was right.

"We'll take the roach boys."

It was the voice of one of two detectives who snuck up on Armstrong and Berton from behind. They said nothing. Finally, Armstrong explained he had to go back in and finish off his last show. "They didn't bother Louis right then; they didn't take him down," recalled trumpeter George Orendorff. "When Frank [Sebastian] came back, he was madder 'n hell, 'cause Frank was almost like Al Capone out there; he run the town, but he couldn't fool with them guys. We didn't know what happened because we were still on the bandstand. Louis was mad, I know that."[5]

After the show, the detectives took Armstrong and Berton to the police station. It turned out the detectives were fans of Armstrong's and listened to him every night on the radio. Armstrong had one very important favor to ask: "Since you and your dear family are my fans, they'd be awfully sad, awfully sad, if anything drastic would happen to me, the same as the other thousands of my fans," he said. "So *please* don't hit me in my chops." The detective responded, "Why, I wouldn't think of anything like that." Armstrong calmed down and said, "Okay—ride me," meaning, "let's ride."[6]

Armstrong and Berton were released on bail within 24 hours with a potentially longer sentence pending a future hearing. Still, the arrest made headlines, especially in the black press. "Louis Armstrong Arrested in Big Dope Scandal" screamed the front page of the *Pittsburgh Courier* on December 6. The accompanying article by Chappy Gardner noted that Armstrong was arrested "and arraigned on charges of possessing dope, the kind used in cigarets. . . . In California the charge against the two men is a felony, punishable by not less than six months and not more than six years, if the accused are found guilty."[7] Armstrong went back to work while he awaited trial—and went right back to his old habits, as evidenced by his irreverent recording of "You're Driving Me Crazy!" on December 23.

By this point, Armstrong's natural comic stylings were becoming a big part of his popularity at the Cotton Club. It was now time to bring a taste of the fun to the recording studio as Armstrong and Hampton opened the record with a little comedy sketch, playing up Hampton's nervous stutter. It might be politically incorrect today, but Armstrong later said of the routine, "That was some funny stuff. A nice little record. That Chinese talk really gasses me."[8] Armstrong and Hampton also unleashed a torrent of slang—"cats," "muggin' lightly," "chop suey," "Satchelmouth," "Pops," "we're gone"—basically teaching hip listeners across the country how to speak like a proper jazz musician.[9] But the most important word he utters comes after a particularly wild vocal: "Swing, swing," he insists, somewhat ominously. This is December 1930, 14 months before Duke Ellington wrote "It Don't Mean a Thing (If It Ain't Got That Swing)" and five years before what most historians cite as the start of "The Swing Era." While Hite solos, Armstrong's on fire, shouting the song's title phrase, scatting, accenting Hite's phrases and dropping phrases like "Oh you dog," "Lawd today," and "Yessir!" He's tearing down the studio walls and giving listeners a glimpse of the entertainer packing them in at the Cotton Club, a force of nature—and almost assuredly high as a kite.

Armstrong contributed a solo for the ages that same day with his take on Guy Lombardo's 1928 hit "Sweethearts on Parade." He tones down the comedy here and offers a very heartfelt vocal, in love with the tune he had been performing since 1928. But as much as he admired Lombardo's command of melody, Armstrong leaves it in the dust, uncorking multiple double-timed breaks that contain more seeds for the eventual flowering of bebop, including a quote from the famous piccolo part of the march "High Society" that would crop up 15 years later in Charlie Parker's solo on "Ko-Ko."

Armstrong finished out the December 23 session by recording a new specialty out of Cuba, "El Manisero." Outfitted with English lyrics and renamed "The Peanut Vendor," it was recorded by a slew of bands in late 1930 and 1931. Armstrong caught the wave at its height and his unique interpretation inadvertently helped to popularize what would become known as Latin Jazz. "The Peanut Vendor" became a fixture of Armstrong's live performances for several years and one of his most publicized songs of the era. "His treatment of 'Peanut Vender' [sic] is one of the most novel in the country," said one critic at the time."[10]

Armstrong's run of California records was remarkable. Producer and writer John Hammond gave a lot of the credit to Tommy Rockwell. "Tommy Rockwell did wonderful things with Louie at OKeh, because Tommy Rockwell would record Louie on commercial tunes like 'You're Driving Me Crazy,' 'Sweethearts on Parade,' 'Body and Soul,' and most black artists didn't have a chance to do this kind of thing."[11] But was Rockwell still overseeing Armstrong's recordings at this point? It seems doubtful. According to Rockwell's son, Malcolm, Rockwell left OKeh to become general manager of rival ARC, the American Recording Corporation, sometime in 1930 and then worked for Jack Kapp at Brunswick Records beginning in 1931.[12] The music trades don't seem to mention a move to ARC but Rockwell is listed as "Brunswick's recording man" in the fall of 1931 so he most likely left OKeh while Armstrong was in California.[13] Rockwell might no longer have been overseeing Armstrong's recordings, but he wasn't out of his life just yet.

Armstrong officially became a movie star with the release of *Ex-Flame* in February 1931. Critical reception was lukewarm and the film soon disappeared—literally. It has been lost ever since it left theaters, robbing history from properly judging Armstrong's film debut. Because the appearance doesn't survive and because he wasn't mentioned in the *New York Times* review of the film, many critics and historians have downplayed this entry in the Armstrong filmography. But it's clear that the film's advertising campaign leaned heavily on Armstrong's rising star power, often giving him featured billing and sometimes even printing his picture instead of the film's white stars, Neil Hamilton and Marion Dixon. "The famous cornetist and his silver trumpet gave a performance which will rouse the spectator from his seat," reported African American newspaper the *New York Age* in a review.[14]

As his star grew, so did his repertoire. There were more pop songs such as "How Am I to Know" and "Little White Lies," as well three songs that would eventually become the basis for some of his best-known records, "When It's Sleepy Time Down South," "Star Dust," and "I'll Be Glad When You're Dead, You Rascal You." The latter even made the news on February 7, over two months before Armstrong recorded it. "Louie Armstrong is singing this week before the 'mike' at Sebastian's Cotton Club, 'I'll Be Glad When You're Dead, You Rascal, You,'" wrote Harry Lovette for the Associated Negro Press. "It has some pretty risqué lines, but the censors are not kicking."[15]

Armstrong also had a new trumpet specialty, though it was on a very old song: "Shine," written in 1910 by African American composers Cecil Mack and Ford Dabney. Though the term "Shine" was—and still is—a derogatory epithet aimed at blacks, Armstrong's racial pride allowed him to deliver the lyrics with a joyous self-assurance, listing his positive attributes with a strong sense of self-confidence and not a trace of pity. But the most appealing attribute of "Shine" was its excellent set of chord changes to blow on. He soon began featuring it at the Cotton Club, building up to a big finale where, backed only by Hampton's drums, he would start hitting high C's in an almost ludicrous feat of strength and endurance. With the band counting along, Armstrong routinely would hit 100 high C's—sometimes more—and top it off with a high F, cementing his status as a God among musicians, as well as with the Hollywood crowd. "When we used to make all those high C's, it was at the end of 'Shine,'" he said in 1960. "And I was playing out at the Cotton Club one night in Culver City, California, George Raft—I'll never forget him and his chick come by one night, you know how he could really dance anyhow—he come to me, I was standing out there leading the big band, and he say, 'Daddy, lay a little "Shine" on me. Give me 400 high C's tonight.' I say, 'Okay, Daddy.' Just that easy—400 he got!"[16]

On March 9, Armstrong recorded an exciting version of "Shine," but with the three-minute time limit, there was no room for the parade of high C's at the end. For the flip side, Armstrong performed the sentimental ballad "Just a Gigolo," infusing it with plenty of heart, vocally and instrumentally—until about the final minute when his irrepressible spirit took over, causing him to change "Just a Gigolo" to "Just another jig I know." Walter Winchell found it all very funny and raved, "Recommended to diversion seekers: the very comical record by Louie Armstrong, horntooting and singing, 'Ah'm a Jigaloooo!'"[17] Trumpeter Buck Clayton though, remembered, "It kind of stirred up some people, especially the NAACP back home. Well, you know the word 'jig' often means a coloured person, which isn't too bad a word really; we use 'em, words like 'spook' and 'jig,' or at least we used to use them in those days, not so much now. But that's just the way Louis was; he put his own little version in there."[18] Indeed, Armstrong continued slipping in off-color words in recordings over the ensuing decades, a nod to the juvenile leanings of his own sense of humor. The damage was minimal at the time but foreshadowed Armstrong's later problems with his own race, many of whom no longer found any humor in the use of such epithets.

Just days later, Armstrong's trial for his marijuana arrest took place and he was sentenced to one month in jail for violating California's "poison act." The news made Armstrong a poster child for the drug, with *Variety* calling him "the king of reefers."[19] A follow-up report on marijuana in the *Baltimore Afro-American* stated, "The craze was allegedly imported into Harlem by Louis Armstrong, famous cornetist, who spent some time on the coast."[20]

After nine days in prison, Armstrong was sent back to see the judge. As the other prisoners noticed him walking down the corridor with a deputy sheriff, some started calling to him, one yelling, "Hey, Louis Armstrong! Sing 'Old Rocking Chair'!" Armstrong smiled and said, "Fellas, I don't have time right now for nothing but to concentrate on what I'm going to tell that judge." The other prisoners began laughing and cheering, as some shouted, "Good luck, Louis!" A sheriff looked at Armstrong incredulously and asked, "Who in the hell are you?" "Oh daddy, just one of the cats," came the reply. "Let's go."[21]

At the trial, Armstrong was relieved to see Frank Sebastian, Johnny Collins, "and a whole gang of lawyers." "I'm straight," he said to himself. "The judge gave me a suspended sentence and I went to work that night and wailed just like nothing happened." Armstrong might have performed at the Cotton Club the night he was released but it would be one of his last nights in California as he was paroled with the understanding that he would immediately leave town.[22]

California had been Armstrong's home for nearly 10 straight months and his west coast friends threw him a big going-away celebration after his closing night. Louis left Lil behind and headed directly to Chicago, arriving on Sunday, March 22, and catching his old hometown by surprise because of reports in the black press that he had been sentenced to six months in prison. Johnny Collins immediately booked Armstrong into the Regal Theater, but after the trip and all the chaos, Armstrong was exhausted and slept into the afternoon. He only awoke when four young men with guitars and ukuleles showed up to his apartment to serenade him—and to get high. "That moment alone helped me to forget a lot of ungodly, unnecessary—you know, all that shit that happened out on the coast," Armstrong said. "It wasn't bad, but I don't know. It could've been avoided but you got so many dog ass people in the world. I wasn't surprised, I threw it out of my mind."[23]

The Regal was "packed to the rafters" for Armstrong's return and he was greeted with several minutes of applause. "It made my heart flutter with happiness," he recalled. "So, when they quieted down, I said 'Yeah, you thought I was—but I wasn't!' And that did it."[24] Armstrong was back, doing three shows a day with the house band at the Regal, while Collins was working frantically to not only get him more work but also to form a steady backing band. Pianist Charlie Alexander was hired and started the process of recruiting musicians from all over Chicago to join the band. Armstrong always enjoyed being around New Orleans musicians and was happy to have some hometown boys in his new band, including drummer Tubby Hall and trombonist Preston Jackson. The band was filled out with the reeds of Lester Boone, George James, and Albert Washington, guitarist Mike McKendrick, and a bassist whose identity remains unknown to this day.

Armstrong rehearsed his new band while Collins worked out an engagement beginning April 1 at the Showboat, a nightclub formerly known as My Cellar and located at Clark and Lake. The club also had a radio hookup, allowing Armstrong to broadcast nightly on WIBO, one 15-minute set at 12:15 five nights a week and a half-hour set at 1 A.M. on Saturday and Sunday. He was performing some of his California specialties, such as "You're Driving Me Crazy" (with pianist Alexander handling the comedy) and "The Peanut Vendor," but also new material he was preparing to record like "I Surrender Dear," "Little Joe," "When It's Sleepy Time Down South," and an ode to his fellow marijuana smokers, "The Cry of the Vipers" (later recorded as "Song of the Vipers").

The Roaring Twenties were over, but Chicago was still a haven for gangland activity, some of which unfurled at the Showboat. Trombonist Jackson remembered a night when members of two rival gangs got into a skirmish "and out came the guns. I've never seen so many guns!"[25] Such scenes must have made Armstrong recall his days of blowing in New Orleans when he became somewhat desensitized to bullets flying past him. "One of the 'Gangsters took a chair and 'hit a 'woman over the 'head with it—And the 'Chair "Crumbled up all in a lot of little 'pieces," he wrote. "Some of the 'pieces 'hit my 'horn. But 'even '*that could not* make me 'leave the 'Bandstand—you know? The 'Captain must go 'down with the 'Ship."—Then too, things like that never 'frightens. I've seen so much of that Bullshit 'during my days of 'playing music."[26]

Armstrong could deal with such gangster action in which he was just an innocent bystander but he did admit, "Ain't but one *incident* at the 'Show Boat' that *kind of* 'got me."[27] The gangsters of Chicago were about to play a bigger role in his personal life than he ever could have imagined.

Armstrong admitted that he knew Rockwell and Collins were having a "feud (fuss over my contract)," but added, "Why—And for 'what'—I've 'never 'found out 'until this day." However, he did know one thing: he had zero desire to ever play for Connie and George Immerman again after the way they fired him in 1929. "If you 'Kick my 'Ass' 'Once you can 'bet I won't come back if I can 'help it, so you can 'Kick it Again," Armstrong wrote. "And "*Connie's Inn*" was 'going 'Down, by the 'degrees. And at 'that time I was the 'Rage of the 'Nation (U.S.A). But 'Nay Nay—'Never no 'Connie's Inn."[28]

As 1931 began, Rockwell and the Immerman brothers grew offended by Armstrong's and Collins's refusal to come to New York, so they decided to come to them. On April 11, Rockwell arrived at the Showboat with a group of men including songwriter Milton Weil, who was part owner of Coffee Dan's, a rival nightclub that was losing business since Armstrong came to town; Joe Fiore, former bodyguard of murdered *Chicago Tribune* reporter Jake Lingle; and Robert Emmet Ryan, simply described in the press as a "hoodlum."

Weil later testified, "A certain Mr. Rockwell, a former manager of Armstrong, had been threatened by Mr. Collins because of an honest debt owed Rockwell by Collins over Armstrong's contract. I felt obligated to Mr. Rockwell as a friend and volunteered to go over and straighten the matter out with Mr. Collins." On the way to the Showboat, Weil met Ryan and Fiore. Once there, Rockwell and his henchmen went to a table to talk the matter over with Collins. It did not go well. Rockwell demanded Collins pay them $6,000 without giving a reason. Collins refused. The demand was reduced to $3,000, Rockwell stating he needed the money immediately because he planned to take the 20th Century Limited Train back to New York in the morning. Armstrong was also there and called their bluff. "Armstrong's lack of fear is said to have caused the gangsters to drop their initial demand, a thousand dollars at the time, until they stated that one thousand dollars would keep Louis alive and tooting his cornet," according to one report. "But Louie wasn't to be bluffed. 'Not a dime!' he is reported to have told the men."[29] With the demand down to $1,000, Collins later testified, "Fiore pushed me to a table and made me sit down. He threatened to burn my mustache off."[30] Collins's wife, Mary, called the police and Rockwell, Weil, Fiore, and Ryan left without their money. The police provided an escort home to Collins and his wife, as well as to Armstrong, while Collins filed a complaint against Weil, Fiore, and Ryan charging them with extortion.[31] Collins was not a full-fledged gangster but he was close with "Big" Bill Duffy, a boxing promoter connected to mobster Owney Madden. That might have been enough to put a scare into Rockwell. According to Rockwell's future partner, Cork O'Keefe, when Rockwell got back to his room at the Morrison Hotel, there was a heavy pounding at his door. "Is this the room Mr. Tom Rockwell is in?" said the voice on the other side. Rockwell answered in the affirmative. "Well buddy, let me tell you something," said the voice. "The 20th Century leaves town tomorrow morning. You make sure that you get on that train and don't come back to this town again. And stop fooling around with other people's artists."[32]

Rockwell's first attempt to extort money from Armstrong and Collins was unsuccessful. It was now time to break out the literal big guns. On Tuesday, April 14, two more gangsters visited the Showboat. Armstrong was blowing on stage with his eyes closed when one of them touched him and said, "Somebody wants you in the Dressing Room." Armstrong agreed to go as soon as he finished playing his dance set, figuring it must be "one of the cats." Instead, he was greeted by a "White 'Guy with a 'Beard on his 'Face—'Thicker than one of those 'Boys from the 'House of 'David."

"Hello," spoke the man with a sarcastic tone.

"Hello," answered Armstrong pleasantly.

"Do you know who I am?"

"Why, uh, no, no I don't."

"I am Frankie Foster."[33]

At first the name didn't mean anything to Armstrong but a year earlier, Foster had been indicted in the killing of Jake Lingle, before being let go. "Well, I didn't know this Frankie Foster, he's a killer, man," Armstrong said later. "I don't have no idea. See, he's supposed to bump you off."[34]

"Well, it was nice knowing you, ol' boy!" Armstrong said, still clueless as to Foster's intentions.

"Well, you're going to New York tomorrow," Foster said.

"I didn't know nothing about that," replied Armstrong. "I thought I was to play here for weeks. Excuse me, I'm going to go back on the stand."

"Wait a minute," said Foster. "You're going to New York to work at Connie's Inn. And you're leaving tomorrow morning." With that, Foster pulled out a .45 pistol and aimed it straight at Armstrong.

"Well, uh, maybe I *am* going to New York," Armstrong said, his eyes "as big as 'Saucers' and 'frightened too.'"

Foster kept his pistol in Armstrong's ribcage and marched him to a nearby telephone booth. The receiver was already down and waiting for Armstrong. He picked it up and heard the voice of one of the Immerman brothers asking, "When are you gonna open here?" Armstrong turned and looked into Foster's eyes and said, "Tomorrow A.M."[35]

That's how Armstrong always told the story in his later years but in an affidavit he gave later in 1931, he told a slightly different version, mentioning that the voice on the phone told him that a show was being built around him in New York and he had to be there as soon as possible. Foster then "attempted to force" Armstrong to send a telegram to Connie Immerman saying he would be on an airplane to New York that evening. But according to the affidavit, Armstrong "stated over the telephone to the person purporting to be Connie Immerman, that he would not come to New York; nor did [Armstrong] send a telegram as requested."[36] Perhaps Armstrong knew he was too valuable to kill. Telling this story in 1967, he said, "They never wanted me dead, [they] wanted me blowing so they could rake in my bread."[37]

Still, he wasn't going to take any chances. The phone call ended and Foster left, but Armstrong, fearing for his life, didn't leave the phone booth, ducking down to hide below the glass and putting up an "Out of Order" sign. The rest of the band didn't know what was going on. "I think they've kidnapped Pops," guitarist Mike McKendrick told the other musicians. "I know for sure that the mob from New York is in town, I don't know whether they've got Pops or not."[38] Saxophonist George James remembered, "We got backstage and everybody was excited and whispering and upset, because we didn't know where Louie was."[39] Eventually, Armstrong was found in the phone booth "on his hands and knees." Armstrong told McKendrick, "You go out and tell Johnny Collins what happened."[40]

Collins sprung to action. "And that son-of-a-bitch," Armstrong said of Collins, "if there's one thing, he was on the ball because he was a gangster himself, you know, he knew all them little tricks. In a half hours' time, he had every gangster in Chicago rounded up. Every one of them. Including Frankie Foster."[41] Collins might have had some gangland connections but as his father was once chief of police in Chicago, it's safer to assume that Collins felt more comfortable turning to the law instead of turning to crime. Armstrong now had bodyguards at the Showboat and a police escort taking him to and from work every night. "The whole time of my engagement, I had two squires to take me home," Armstrong said. "I had a little yellow Ford; I'll never forget it. And one would be in the front and he kept, I think, six of them, big Cadillacs—big, big Cadillac cars—and one in the front and one in the back and me and my gang, we'd be in the middle blasting!" "Blasting" was one of the many ways Armstrong referred to smoking marijuana.[42]

Collins immediately got the story covered in all the major papers, using it to build up publicity for Armstrong. "Gang Threats Make Cornet Player Tremble in Rhythm!" screamed one headline. "One way to make a good cornetist better is to scare him half to death," it opened. Collins was quoted as saying, "Louis thinks he might get bumped off. . . . Louis has been receiving threats. Hoodlums dog his footsteps. One of them, who looked like Frank Foster of the Lingle case, followed him right into a telephone booth. . . . But the more they scare him, the better he plays the cornet—gets those shivery, shakery, tremolo effects, you know, like the girls love."[43] By April 19, Weil, Fiore, and Ryan were arrested for extortion, leading to another round of publicity.

One day later, with all of this drama surrounding him, Armstrong began a series of recording sessions for OKeh with his new Chicago band. He somehow sounded unperturbed, swinging lustily on "Walkin' My Baby Back Home" and contributing a knockout opening cadenza on "Blue Again" that brought back memories of "West End Blues." He also tackled "I Surrender Dear," Bing Crosby's first major solo hit from earlier in the year. He displays some of the tips he picked up from Crosby on how to handle a ballad, especially his use of what's known as an upper mordent, the little catch in his voice heard when he sings the titular "I Surrender De-ear." Of course, Armstrong's interpretation is also very much his own with some mumbling, some repeated phrases ("I may act gay, I may act gay"), an "oh baby," a yearning "ohhhh" before the bridge, some tumbling scat asides, and simply an overall mood of burning intensity.

Other singers were paying attention. Rudy Vallee was one of the most popular singers of the day and though he'd have a career lasting several decades, his genteel style of crooning was about to be overtaken by the lessons of Armstrong and Crosby. Vallee could not quite believe what he heard on "I Surrender Dear." "Perhaps one of the most unusual renditions of it on phonograph records is that of the negro orchestra leader, Louis Armstrong,"

Vallee wrote in his *Radio Digest* column. "He is little known except to musical faddists and a few of the elite who have run across him either in a night club or on one of his phonograph records. He is a mixture of a hot trumpet player and a vocalist who bellows his lyrics out in much the same fashion as he plays his hot chorus on the trumpet, so that his rendition of 'I Surrender, Dear' is one of the most fascinating things I have ever listened to."[44]

The fourth song recorded on April 20 would go on to become the most oft-performed number of Armstrong's career, his current and future theme song, "When It's Sleepy Time Down South." It was written by three African American songwriters, the New Orleans–born Rene brothers, Leon and Otis, and multi-talented actor Clarence Muse. The latter introduced it onstage as the character of "Jackson, the Negro servant" in a Los Angeles theatrical production of *Under a Virginia Moon* that opened in June 1930, as well as on a radio show hosted by Bill Sharples.[45]

While still performing at Sebastian's Cotton Club in the fall of 1930, the Rene brothers invited Armstrong, Lionel Hampton, and Les Hite to have dinner with their mother in Pasadena, listening to Guy Lombardo as they dined. Afterward, Leon Rene started to play "When It's Sleepy Time Down South" on the piano while Otis Rene sang. Armstrong listened and when they finished, said, "That's my song, give me that copy, I'm going to feature it every night at the 'Cotton Club' and record it in my next recording session."[46] Vallee called it "one of Louis' masterpieces" and now noticed the influence Armstrong was having on his contemporaries. "The Brunswick record of Mildred Bailey would seem to show that she was not averse to the Armstrong influence," Vallee wrote. "And I suppose Messrs. Crosby and [Russ] Colombo will do it a la Armstrong."[47]

For some, it was—and still is—problematic that Armstrong could find so much to love in a song about the racist south, especially one that used the epithet "darkies" not once, but twice. But Armstrong truly loved it for a variety of reasons. First, there's the actual melody, based on a series of repeated major sevenths, an interval that was always a favorite with him ("Struttin' with Some Barbecue" also revolves around the major seventh). He was also sentimental about his days in New Orleans, having not been back home since 1922. Every word spoke to something he experienced in his time there. "Well, it's a tradition of the south, you know," he said in 1952. "Everybody's lazy down there in that hot sun and I can see it so plain, a cat lazy under that tree, too lazy to even go and get his meal, man. Just, 'Bring it over here.' And I know all about dear old Mammy. It's the life of the song. It just fits my music, I think. It's the Armstrong theme. And [if] I make a million tunes, that'll still be the number one tune in my files."[48]

Armstrong was especially proud that the song was written by three African Americans, two of them from his hometown. Even with the problematic "darkies," Armstrong admired on some level that it was written by black people about black people. Armstrong had fierce pride in his race but in private conversations, often referred to his people as "spades" and had just recorded "Shine," as well as sneaking "jig" into "Just a Gigolo." "Darkies" was not exactly uncommon at that time, with "That's Why Darkies Were Born" being published in 1931 (the title phrase was quoted in "Underneath the Harlem Moon" in 1932). Thus, from a melodic standpoint, from a nostalgic standpoint, and even from a standpoint of racial pride, "When It's Sleepy Time Down South" was indeed "the Armstrong theme."[49]

On April 28, Armstrong finally recorded the number that made the censors nervous in Culver City, "I'll Be Glad When You're Dead You Rascal You." Armstrong's personality almost explodes through the speakers, repeating "Oh, you dog" enough times, it became his catchphrase. He even got to reference his recent troubles with the law, singing, "I'll be standing on the corner high, when they bring your body by," a line decidedly not in African American actor and comedian Sam Theard's original composition.

Armstrong closed a busy month of recording on April 29 by transforming two more pop tunes—"Them There Eyes" and "When Your Lover Has Gone—into future standards before closing at the Showboat on May 12. He and Collins no longer felt safe in Chicago. Collins reached back into his old days as a vaudeville booker and looked toward one of the cities he used to book, Louisville, Kentucky, getting Armstrong a gig on May 15 at Club Madrid.[50] On May 14, Armstrong once again said farewell to Chicago with a performance at the Savoy Ballroom in front of 2,700. One reporter couldn't get backstage to see Armstrong. "A squadron of police with sawed-off shotguns were patrolling the rear entrance," he wrote. "Louis' gangster trouble necessitated the precaution."[51]

All the goodwill of the Savoy farewell came crashing down the same day with a telegram from Joseph N. Weber, president of the American Federation of Musicians. Tommy Rockwell always maintained that he never had anything to do with sending Frankie Foster to Armstrong's dressing room; that was all the Immerman Brothers (and possibly Dutch Schultz). But Rockwell was still miffed after his visit to Chicago ended with his three associates being arrested for extortion and with Rockwell himself being threatened in his hotel room. Rockwell sent Weber the contract from July 25, 1930, stipulating that Armstrong perform at Connie's Inn in 1931. That was enough for Weber, who sent a telegram to Armstrong on May 14 demanding he honor the contracts "or submit reasons why you should not be held in violation of said contracts."

Armstrong and Collins immediately answered with a telegram of their own to Weber claiming Armstrong canceled his contract with Rockwell in September 1930. "[Rockwell] has no authority to act for me and I personally made no agreement to appear at Connie's at any time," the telegram read. "Rockwell using improper methods to embarrass me."[52]

With police escorts getting him to the Savoy and sawed-off shotguns patrolling the backstage area and with the president of the American Federation of Musicians demanding he fulfill a contract he never signed to appear at Connie's Inn, Armstrong, his band, and Collins packed up and headed down south—toward New Orleans.

6

"I Done Got Northern-fied"

May–August 1931

About to embark on a southern tour for the first time, Armstrong was leaving behind the comfort of the police escort that kept him safe in Chicago. He needed a bodyguard and decided to hire a friend from his past, drummer "Little" Joe Lindsey. Armstrong was once the cornetist in Lindsey's Brown Skin Jazz Band, one of his first professional experiences as a musician.[1] He also invited his down-on-his-luck New Orleans friend—and "one of the all-around gamblers of that period"—"Professor" Sherman Cook to be his valet and serve as something of a personal secretary. New Orleans was his eventual destination and it would help to have two homeboys to keep him safe in the south.

Kentucky was the first stop for what was billed as "Louis Armstrong of Screen, Stage and Record Fame and His Okeh Recording Orchestra"; multiple advertisements played up Armstrong's appearance in *Ex-Flame*, further proof of the importance of this film at this point in his career.[2] They played a dance date on May 15 at the Club Madrid, the night before the Kentucky Derby, and followed that with a "Kentucky Derby Ball" in Louisville. "We were the first colored band ever to play that, and that was some engagement," saxophonist George James recalled.[3] Collins had to take gigs wherever he could find them, which meant following the Kentucky sojourn by traveling back up north to Detroit to play opposite McKinney's Cotton Pickers at the Graystone Ballroom and Jean Goldkette's Orchestra at the Blue Lantern.

Armstrong's reed-heavy band cooked on stage, and in guitarist Mike McKendrick they had a good "straw boss" to discipline the members and make sure they were always ready when they needed to be. Bassist John Lindsay of New Orleans (no relation to Joe) joined in Detroit, a solid addition who locked in with drummer Tubby Hall to form a potent rhythm team. But what the band really needed was a music director and in Detroit, they found one in trumpeter Zilner T. Randolph. Randolph was born in Durham, Arkansas, on January 28, 1899, and like many musicians of his generation, fell under the spell of Armstrong after hearing him in the 1920s, saying to himself,

"That's the kind of horn I want to play, I want to play that."[4] When Armstrong returned from California, Lil Armstrong began studying arranging with Randolph, which put him on Louis's radar. One time at the Regal, Randolph went backstage with a song he had written, "I Don't Care What You Do," and showed it to Armstrong. Randolph said, "I didn't know too much about Louie and everybody had told me that Louie couldn't read music." Armstrong took one look at it, started scatting the melody and "took me off my feet," according to Randolph. "He was singing all those intervals." Randolph went back and told his wife, "They say Louie can't read music. Louie took that song and solfèged that song off. He solfèged that song off direct from sight."

Though Lindsay and Randolph were regulars in Chicago, they didn't join Armstrong until opening night at the Graystone. Armstrong must have been impressed because after the first intermission, he said to Randolph, "Hey Randy, pick you out a set and take it down. Now, this is your band." This caught the rest of the band off guard. "When he said that, why, they all looked at one another," Randolph said. "But I didn't think nothing of it, you know." Though some of the other members resented the immediate promotion for the new man, Armstrong was satisfied. With Randolph handling the music, McKendrick handling the band business, and Collins doing the booking, Armstrong was free to just concentrate on his trumpet playing and singing and not worry about anything else. He would later refer to this as his "happiest" group, writing of them, "Now there's a Band that really deserved a *whole lot of credit* that they *didn't* get."[5]

Armstrong started for New Orleans, playing one-nighters in Minneapolis, Ohio (including a college date at Ohio University), and another swing through Kentucky, again, all territories Collins used to book in his vaudeville days. Professor Sherman Cook had already left Armstrong to head to New Orleans—by taxicab—to begin working on a grand reception for the trumpeter's arrival. Armstrong had not been back at all since July 1922 and might not have expected much of a welcome, but Cook's handiwork promised a "monster reception" and a "gigantic parade."[6] It was not hyperbole.

The Armstrong band traveled to New Orleans by private rail car, arriving on Friday, June 5. "When we arrived at the station there, Cook had spread the news, and the L & N station out by the Canal Street Ferry were packed and jammed with people who I was raised with, played with, and lots of spectators waiting for our train to come in," Armstrong wrote. "We took Canal Street for ourselves, stopped all the traffic; all the cops gave us the right of way when they found out it was their home town boy Louis 'Satch' Armstrong, returning home after nine years."[7] The police helped guide Armstrong through the crowd of thousands of people—including five bands—but many in the crowd did not emerge unscathed. The parade ended at the Astoria Hotel, where Armstrong and his band were guests of honor at a special banquet. The huge crowd gathered outside the hotel to get a glimpse of the conquering hero, but soon grew restless. "Arguments ensued and then fights, and complaints began pouring into the First Precinct police station," reported the *New Orleans Times Picayune*. "Captain George Reed and seven patrolmen responded, and when the street was finally cleared about midnight 29 negroes had been booked on charges of loitering, disturbing the peace and numerous other minor offenses."[8]

While that was happening outside the Astoria Hotel, Armstrong was being honored inside, sharing his table with Captain Joseph Jones and Peter Davis, the two men who were the most vital in changing his life at the Colored Waif's Home in 1913. Because they had an exclusive contract with the Suburban Gardens, Armstrong's band didn't perform at the Astoria but when he sensed the crowd's disappointment, he offered a vocal version of "The Peanut Vendor." But it soon appeared that might be the only song he'd perform in his hometown: Armstrong and his band had been expelled from the National Federation Union of Musicians.

Matters with the union had deteriorated while Armstrong was in Detroit on May 25, when American Federation of Musicians president Joseph Weber responded to Armstrong and Collins's telegram by calling it "unsatisfactory," arguing that Armstrong's "attempt to dismiss" Rockwell as his agent "does not absolve you from filling all contracts he entered into on your behalf during that time it cannot be disputed that he was your agent." Weber demanded an answer if Armstrong was going to play Connie's Inn after all and threatened to "place [his] membership in jeopardy" if he did not.[9]

A meeting was scheduled at the office of the American Federation of Musicians in New York City on May 28. Rockwell was there, along with Johnny Collins and his wife Mary representing Armstrong, their attorney Henry A. Friedman, and F. W. Birnbach, a representative of the A.F.M.'s Executive Committee. Upon examining the July 25, 1930, Connie's Inn contract, it was discovered that Rockwell's signature was the only one on the document. Birnbach claimed it was Connie Immerman's copy and a copy signed by Immerman was in Rockwell's safe deposit box. After several days of delays (Rockwell claimed he misplaced the key), Rockwell eventually produced the signed contract. Collins's lawyer claimed Immerman only recently signed it, and even brought in a handwriting expert to confirm that "the signature had been affixed only recently." Weber refused to back down and now delivered swift punishment to Armstrong on June 4:

YOU HAVE BEEN EXPELLED BY THE INTERNATIONAL EXECUTIVE BOARD FOR
FAILURE TO OBEY THE FEDERATIONS ORDER STOP I AM NOTIFYING LOCALS
TWO HUNDRED EIGHT AND EIGHT HUNDRED TWO ERASE YOUR NAME FROM
MEMBERSHIP—JOE N WEBER.

Armstrong and Collins were shocked, claiming the Musicians' Union was "ev-
idently engaged in a conspiracy with" Rockwell and the Immerman Brothers,
and sent a telegram to Weber demanding a trial, Armstrong wiring, "I AM
CONVINCED THAT I COULD PROVE THAT THE CONNIE CONTRACT
WAS SIGNED WITHIN THE LAST THREE WEEKS AND FURTHER
THAT IT WAS NOT ENTERED INTO IN GOOD FAITH."

This all came as a great shock to the owners of the Suburban Gardens, the
establishment where Armstrong was signed to perform for the next six weeks.
The venue was owned by Mark Boasberg—better known as Jack Sheehan, a
bootlegger during Prohibition—and was managed by Earl Dalton, who would
later have ties to the "Southland Syndicate" when it controlled gambling in
Dallas.[10] Boasberg and Dalton didn't care about the union and planned to have
Armstrong perform anyway. After getting word that Armstrong was expelled,
the management of the Suburban Gardens argued that they "changed its entire policy of entertainment, cancelled its contract with extensive and popular
acts that it had heretofore had, and further expended large sums of money on
newspapers, billboard, handbill and radio advertisements, as well as other extensive publicity in connection with its engagement of [Armstrong] and his
orchestra."[11] This plea bought the Suburban Gardens one week of Armstrong
instead of six, but at least he was free to perform.

Meanwhile, matters were getting more dangerous by the minute for
Armstrong and his band. "[W]e were followed every night by a car with three
or four guys in it," Preston Jackson said.[12] This was nothing new. "Ever since
we had left Chicago, we had been followed by two or three men—that was
right through Ohio, Michigan and Kentucky and right down to New Orleans,
but those guys, I'm sure they were gangsters, never did do anything to us—
not directly," Jackson added.[13] Armstrong left Chicago to avoid harassment
and now was dealing with "personal threats" in his hometown. Armstrong
and Collins called upon the authorities of Jefferson Parish, who sent police
protection to the Suburban Gardens but even they admitted it was still "in-
adequate" given the number of musicians in the band and their daily individual travels around the city.[14] According to George James, Earl Dalton did
his part to protect the musicians. "[A]ll that summer this man had arranged
for us to be collected every day from our hotel and taken to his club under
police escort," James said. Some of the musicians in Armstrong's band took

matters into their own hands. "Big Mike [McKendrick] always had a gun, a luger pistol, which he took everywhere, even on to the band stand, because you never knew what sort of trouble there might be," James said, adding, "If we had been a white band, there would have been no harassment, but we were the first colored band to do these things, and that meant trouble."[15]

Armstrong never discussed the details about the musician's union and the harassment during this time; he was just happy to be back in New Orleans and playing music for his hometown—or at least part of his hometown. The Suburban Gardens was something of a strange choice for Armstrong's return home and one might assume that Collins picked it because of his history of booking vaudeville acts in the region. It was located ten miles outside of New Orleans on the levee of the Mississippi River, featured gambling, and catered to whites only. Armstrong, who complained later in life about his "disgustingly segregated" hometown, wasn't surprised, but did see a silver lining, writing, "In fact we were the first Colored Attraction, at the time, who ever played there. So opening night there were twenty thousand Negroes on the levee listening to us play."[16]

Armstrong later referred to the managers of the Suburban Gardens as the "Dalton Boys," inferencing that Earl Dalton and Mark Boasberg had some gangland connections themselves, especially with the amount of gambling at the club. "The Dalton Boys and a lots of their associates were a little skeptical about us appearing there, wondering what reaction the customers would take, etc.," Armstrong wrote. "Of course we did not know all of this because we had been playing everywhere in the North and a lots of places in the South without any trouble at all and they loved us and our music. So we felt real at ease as to say it's just another place, with another opening." Armstrong would at least be able to reach more folks of his race through broadcasting, as the Suburban Gardens was set up to broadcast on WSMB each night. That, too, created a buzz, resulting in even more African Americans showing up on the levee to witness something they couldn't quite believe. "Since they too had never in the history of New Orleans witnessed a Colored Band and a Colored musician rated so high as to do his own show and broadcast, they too thought that somebody was 'goofing,' by booking us out there," Armstrong wrote. "But to me I felt so at home until there wasn't a fear in my whole body."[17]

Armstrong had been making his own announcements on the radio for years but at the Suburban Gardens, he would have to turn over that role to a white announcer, Charles Nelson. "Radio was just about five years in, and you never heard of no spade playing on no radio in those days," he said. "And you know what the life was: all strictly ofay. . . . See, now, I had been away about

Figure 6.1 Armstrong onstage with his orchestra directed by Zilner Randolph (second from right) at the Suburban Gardens in New Orleans in the summer of 1931.
Photo by Villard Padio, Courtesy of the Louis Armstrong House Museum

nine or 10 years and I done got 'northern-fied' and forgot about a whole lot of that foolishness down there, you know?"[18]

Just before the broadcast, Earl Dalton pulled Nelson aside and told him, "This is a big deal now, you bring on Louis Armstrong, he's a New Orleans boy."[19] But just before the broadcast was to begin, the announcer looked over at Armstrong and told Dalton and Johnny Collins, "You know? This is a situation that I have never had to fight in my life before. I just can't introduce that 'Nigger.'" Dalton was angry, but Armstrong was unfazed. "I did not hear the conversation," he wrote. "If I had, it wouldn't have made any difference because I knew my abilities as a trumpet player and I had been in the game long enough to know, long as I give my public what they expect of me I was straight with the world." Collins approached Armstrong and said, "Why, er, that guy has refused to introduce you."[20] Armstrong said, "Well, don't worry about it," turned to his band and said, "Give me a chord, boys." They did and Armstrong stepped out onstage.

"And the minute that I stepped on the floor from the stand the house came down with thunderous applause and it was over ten minutes before I could say a word," he recalled. "Dig that big ovation!" he exclaimed to his band. "While the people were applauding so heavily I had a chance to dig a few facial expressions, such as my band, my manager and the Dalton Boys, who were all smiling real broadly and the radio announcer, well he was so flabbergasted, and so surprised over it all until you could read a million thoughts on his mind. Of course, he was fired the minute the show was over."[21]

Armstrong could see only white people from the stage, but he felt the warmth from them because "the majority of those people who were at the opening were White boys who I grew up with during my childhood days around New Orleans." Armstrong did his theme song, "When It's Sleepy Time Down South"—an appropriate choice—and after some announcing, went into "I Can't Give You Anything but Love." Each number that followed was "a show stopper," he said. "The place was jumping and when we went into some jumping blues, the whole levee with all of those Negroes started rocking and they rocked to everything that we played. Oh they had a rocking good time. The reaction from the radio broadcast was so tremendous until the Dalton Boys immediately appointed me to announce my own radio shows every night that we appeared there."[22]

Backstage after his first show, Armstrong found a gangster waiting for him, but unlike in Chicago, this was not a fearful occasion. "A New Orleans Gangster who remembered me from the early days came into my dressing room, shook my hand and gave me a large roll of money, saying, 'You went up North and *got good*, here's a present for you,' " he remembered. "That thrilled me."[23]

The press agreed with the assessment of the gangster. Mel Washburn caught Armstrong live on Monday, June 8, two days after his opening, and gave readers a vivid glimpse of what was happening each night at the Suburban Gardens. "As a special number Armstrong played more than 20 chorus of 'Tiger Rag' from the center of the dance floor," Washburn wrote. "His playing beggars description. He also sang a number of choruses during the dance numbers. There has long been a complaint among New Orleans dancers that this particular kind of dance music had passed from our dance floors. There should be no further lament."[24] Armstrong's sleek big band arrangements were a far cry from the old-fashioned brand of New Orleans jazz he played as a teenager with elders like Kid Ory and King Oliver (Oliver was recording for RCA Victor at this point, also fronting a bigger orchestra and playing many pop songs). But New Orleans was loving it, especially "The Peanut Vendor" and an updated version of the old march "High Society."

However, the Suburban Garden gig ended almost as soon as it began when Weber sent a telegram to the New Orleans Local 174 notifying them that Armstrong had been expelled from the union.[25] Under President John De Droit, a white trumpeter who had recorded in the 1920s, the New Orleans Local 174 responded by expelling Armstrong and his musicians, too, and demanding they go before the board of directors. Before Armstrong's band met the union board, Dalton told them, "Don't give those people any excuse for arresting you, don't do anything rash, and you won't get hurt. Just don't answer any questions. You came down here to work at my place, and you're gonna stay here all summer." "We just didn't answer any of their questions, and so they got us for contempt of the Union and black-listed us," said George James. "This meant we were no longer Union members and they figured that they could get this man to get rid of us." Dalton didn't budge. "But he was a pretty powerful guy," James said of Dalton, "had a lot of influence, and he didn't take any notice, and we didn't either, and we worked there the whole of that summer although we stayed out of the Union which, really was a pretty dangerous thing for us."[26] The union troubles soon spilled out on the radio and in the press. Jackson said, "The daily papers, both the *New Orleans Item* and the *Times Picayune* said it was a shame that the niggers had come down from Chicago and taken the white musician's jobs."[27]

During Armstrong's first week back home, he made a very special pilgrimage back to the Colored Waif's Home, now known as the Municipal Boys' Home, where he reunited with both Peter Davis and Captain Joseph Jones, the men most responsible for his becoming a musician. Armstrong was also met by Judge John D. Nix of the Juvenile Court bench, Superintendent Robert McAlree, educational supervisor Reverend H. H. Dunn, and a crowd of "hero worshipping delinquent colored boys."[28] Armstrong, though admittedly "northern-fied," made his love for New Orleans crystal clear. Asked, "Your home is in Chicago now?" he instantly replied, "No indeed, sir. I only live in Chicago. My home's New Orleans."[29]

Eventually, the Boys Home's 25-piece band played for Armstrong and on "Auld Lang Syne," he joined in on the original cornet he first learned on in 1913, presented to him by Captain Jones. He followed it up with a "hot and high" version of "When You're Smiling" and then surprised them with a gift: a $150 radio. Armstrong had it installed within an hour, so the "enthralled youngsters could hear his broadcast from the night club that very evening," according to the *New Orleans Item*. "The cheering ovation the broadcast from this radio set received in Gentilly might have been heard in Shrewsbury, where the broadcast originated, too."

Soon after, Superintendent McElree wrote a touching letter thanking Armstrong for the radios:

Dear Louis:

Childhood is the period of hero worship. You are, and rightfully so, the hero of many boys of our City, and especially boys of the Municipal Boy's Home. One of them has appropriated your name, and is making an effort to follow in your path.

It is indeed a fine trait of character to recognize so humble a beginning as you had, now that you have won distinction, and to give so much credit to your old friends, Peter Davis and Joseph Jones, whose influence undoubtedly started you on the road to success. Your recognition of them has made them happy.

On behalf of the boys of this institution I am taking this occasion to thank you for the fine radio set you sent them. They heard your program last night, enjoyed it very much, and acknowledge the dedication of a number to them.

Respectfully

R. B. McElree, Sup't.[30]

Lil Armstrong was there for the visit to the Waif's Home, but New Orleans is where the relationship between Louis and Lil officially came to an end. "Because Lil, my second wife and I wasn't getting along none too well," he wrote. "So she and I agreed to disagree; so we finally got a divorce."[31] They did find time for one last musical collaboration, according to Zilner Randolph. On June 13, Armstrong played two shows at the Lincoln Theater, finally given a chance to play for an African American audience. "Well, Louis and Lil put on an act, honest to goodness, I had never seen such a superb act," Randolph said. "That act was immaculate. Those two people *performed*. I didn't know—they looked like they could just breathe together."[32] It was a fitting end to one of the great romances in jazz. Soon after, Lil told Louis, "You don't need me now you're earning a thousand dollars a week [$16,930 in 2019 dollars]. We'll call it a day."[33] Louis had already been spending most of his time with Alpha Smith and her mother when he was in Chicago (they also took care of his adopted son Clarence). "Don't know when or how long Louis had an affair with Alpha," Lil later said. "I can assure you she was not the only one, so I didn't worry too much about it."[34]

Lil referenced Louis's salary and she wasn't exaggerating. Johnny Collins has always had a reputation as something of a crook, but the truth is for the first time in his career, Armstrong was doing quite well financially thanks to his arrangement with Collins. "And being on percentage, I made a lot of

Figure 6.2 Louis and Lil Armstrong visit Peter Davis and Capt. Joseph Jones at the Municipal Boy's Home (the old Colored Waif's Home) during Armstrong's return home in 1931. Louis and Lil separated soon afterward.
Photo by Villard Padio, Courtesy of the Louis Armstrong House Museum

money," he later wrote of their deal.[35] Earl Dalton also helped the situation. "We really drew in the crowds, and that guy was very fair—the more money he made, the more we made," George James said of Dalton. "He raised our salaries about three times while we were there."[36]

It must have been surreal for Armstrong to visit the same neighborhoods he used to roam as a poor, barefoot child, now returning as a hero to his race, sharply dressed and armed with more money than he knew what to do with. He soon discovered what he could do with it: give it away. "Louis had had a hard time in his earlier days, but he gave a million dollars away," Preston Jackson said. "It was a common sight just about six o'clock in the evening to see two lines form in the lobby of the hotel where he was staying, and then Louis would walk out and start distributing money like it was going out of style. He just didn't know how to say 'No.'"[37]

Armstrong's generosity even affected the deceased. On July 4, the day Armstrong celebrated his birthday, he learned that cornetist Buddy Petit died.

Petit had been an inspiration for the young Armstrong and now Armstrong wanted to do something for his old friend and sometimes rival. "He buried Buddy Petit," said New Orleans–based clarinetist Joe Darensbourg, "and a lot of those old-time guys like that, Louis put up the money for 'em." To Darensbourg, it was another sign of the generous spirit he flaunted in his hometown, giving money to anyone who asked for some. Darensbourg remembered Armstrong justifying it, saying, "Maybe that cat was hungry." Friends would respond, "You crazy, Louis, giving that guy money all the time, guy's just hustlin' ya." But Armstrong wouldn't hear of it. "Well maybe he was, I don't know; but maybe he wasn't, I ain't taking no chance on turning the guy away and him being hungry," Armstrong would say. "Cause when I was a little boy I went to bed too many times hungry myself, I know what it feels like to be hungry, and there's no worse feeling in the world to my idea."[38]

Armstrong's men enjoyed working for their boss that summer, George James saying, "Louis was terrific, just unbelievable!"[39] He managed to feature them individually during his nightly broadcasts. One night he let tenor saxophonist Al Washington, a master of circular breathing, solo on "St. Louis Blues," and according to Armstrong, "Al held that note for thirteen minutes. The radio people did not cut us off thinking that we would stop any minute, of course we could only do that number one time on the air."[40] Preston Jackson also was featured regularly, including singing on "Rockin' Chair" with Armstrong, which made him popular with the ladies, but unpopular with his bandmates. "[W]e began to argue and then the reed section turned on me and stopped talking to me, and then Randolph stopped talking to me too," he said. Mike McKendrick took matters into his own hands and told Jackson that Johnny Collins had told him to fire him. Jackson visited Armstrong and told him what had happened. "What!" Armstrong exploded, uttering a string of expletives and finally stating definitively, "This is *my* band, not John Collins's band!" Jackson said, "Louis had given me the job in the first place, and now he was keeping me in the job, and you can't help but look up to a man like that and take him as a friend. Louis was very good to me in lots of other ways—I loved that man!"[41]

Armstrong's generosity showed no signs of slowing up as the Suburban Gardens engagement was extended into August. "I even made up a Ball Team with the kids whom their fathers were my school mates etc.," he wrote. "The team was called 'The Louis Armstrong's Secret 9.' They whipped everything that they played in the Sand Lots."[42] Indeed, the "Secret 9" was a glorified sandlot team but because of the publicity over Armstrong's sponsorship and armed with sharp new uniforms, they were given a big showcase game against the New Orleans Black Pelicans of the Southern Negro League. The game took place at Heinemann Park, which Armstrong described as "A White Folks park with the bleachers for the Negroes. This day Negroes and the White Folks all sat together, and had a ball."[43] The good times didn't last long for Armstrong's team. "Louis Armstrong's Secret Nine was sure dyked up Monday," read one newspaper report. "The team is outfitted with just about everything a good ball club needs, from their baseball caps down to the mascot's water bucket—cause didn't no less a personage than the renowned Louis Armstrong, the 'Emperor of the Trumpet' himself, dress 'em up?—but they couldn't make the grade against 'Lucky' Welsh's Black Pelicans, and Welsh and his crew got right out there in Heineman Park, under the very eyes of the Secret Nine's Santa Claus and administered a coat of whitewash to the mysterious order with 4–0 as the score."[44] Armstrong later surmised the reason for the loss. "Of course they lost, but I still say they wouldn't have been beatened so badly if they hadn't been too proudly to slide into the plate," he wrote. "Just because they had on their first baseball suits, and brand new ones, at that, but it was all in fun, and a good time was had by all I know. I had myself a ball."[45]

Many were surprised Armstrong was still at the Suburban Gardens in August as it was announced at one point that he was due to end on July 27. At that time, Joseph Weber and the American Federation of Musicians were confident that Armstrong would finally head to New York to fulfill the Connie's Inn contract; stories were even planted that he was already back at Connie's performing nightly. "Louis Armstrong, familiarly known as the king of the trumpet, is back in New York giving the patrons of Connie's Inn a nightly mélange of incomparable music," the *Pittsburgh Courier* wrote. "He had to play 20 choruses of 'Tiger Rag' the other night to satisfy his enthusiastic admirers."[46]

But Armstrong wasn't going anywhere, as Dalton extended his engagement through the end of August. At least one unnamed Louisiana reporter was feeling a little burned out, writing, "We understand that Armstrong was re-engaged for four more weeks . . . and nothing is in view so far to follow him . . . in the meanwhile he is tiring the listeners with his vocal efforts on the air and the attendance drops off."[47] Even with the occasionally dwindling business at the Suburban Gardens, Armstrong made the most of his final month in New Orleans, throwing out the first pitch (and indulging in a little comedy with Professor Sherman Cook and Joe Lindsay) before a baseball game, judging the Page Hotel's "Popular Lady" Contest and being the guest of honor at a dinner thrown by the Zulu Social Aid and Pleasure Club at the Silver Slipper Cafe on August 23. Armstrong was a great admirer of the Zulus since he was a kid and was honored to receive a lifetime membership card and "a belt of alligator skin with a gold initialed buckle."[48] A. J. Piron, a popular bandleader in New Orleans when Armstrong was a young man, even helped launch a "Louis Armstrong Special" cigar, advertised as the "Best 5c Hand Made Cigar on the Market."[49]

Armstrong managed to squeeze in one more trip to the old Colored Waif's Home in August, bringing along his entire band and a representative from the Unity Life Insurance Company, who donated new instruments for the Home's band. "I take this opportunity to thank you for the instruments given the boys at the Municipal Home," Armstrong wrote to C. C. Dejoie of Unity. "I know that your gift will do much to instill in some boy's mind the desire to emulate me. More power to you." Armstrong addressed the youngsters currently living at the Home and, according to one report, "told them that success was waiting for all of them if they but availed themselves of the opportunities to make good of their chances."[50]

Armstrong's eventful summer back home was to end with a dance at the Army Supply Base on Dauphine and Poland Streets on August 31, aimed strictly at African American fans who had been shut out of the Suburban Gardens all summer. Johnny Collins went all out, placing full-page ads emphasizing that this event would feature "Dancing for Colored Only" and all proceeds would go toward the "Benefit of Hospitalization Work for Colored."[51] The *Louisiana Weekly* reported that Armstrong would entertain "his people" and was "looking forward with much pleasure to his performance here and wants to see all his old friends there."[52]

Armstrong's old friends—and many more—showed up from all over the region. "To show you how famous we were, the night that the dance was in New Orleans people coming into New Orleans from those little towns had dump carts, some had Oxen hitched up to their carts, to dig the dance, me and my band," he said. "All night long they kept coming. The whole town was flooded with folks out of town."[53]

But on the afternoon of the dance, something went wrong. "When we reached the gate of the Army Base it seemed as if there were a whole regiment of soldiers motioning with their hands to all cars to keep moving because the dance had been called off because there was a clause in the government Contract, that the U.S. Army Base is for Red Cross purposes and not for dancing," Armstrong said.[54] "In all kinds of automobiles, by street car, and on foot the negroes went to the party, their tickets, for which they paid good money, held fast in their hands," according to one news report. "But the place was closed. They couldn't get in."[55] No one quite bought the official reason the venue was padlocked. "As to me until this day, I have never gotten the real truth about it all," Armstrong wrote in the mid-1950s. "All I know is it caused a lot of upset, because we had been plugging this farewell dance for a long time on the air during our broadcasts from the Suburban Gardens."[56]

Zilner Randolph blamed it on Armstrong's still unresolved issues with the musician's union, feeling that union officials "got together and they wouldn't let us have it."[57] Preston Jackson had another theory, saying it was "probably a political move" to cancel the dance "as it would have hurt the Astoria and Pythian Temple which were close by."[58] For a moment, Collins attempted to get Armstrong into the Pythian Temple, but A. J Piron and His Orchestra were already booked there and Piron refused to sacrifice his gig.[59] Finally, a distraught Armstrong gave up. The story spread across the black press for the next month, as the Associated Negro Press published it as a wire story in multiple newspapers across the country. The *Louisiana Weekly* found the promoter who originally signed a contract authorizing the dance and couldn't get him to talk. "We have tried every way possible to locate the reasons [that] led to the postponement of the dance, but as yet we have met with no success," the paper concluded.[60]

Armstrong ended up back at the Patterson Hotel, where he had been living since the beginning of June, vowing to come back to make it up to his loyal African American fans. The next night he was due to play in Houston so he asked some New Orleans friends to help him pack and headed to Texas. When he got there, Armstrong made a discovery. "My friends was helping me to pack. They stole a $200 watch and brand-new patent leather shoes. They're *helping* me now! And when I got to Houston, Texas, I had about $300 worth of stuff lost."[61] In some ways, this story summed up and foreshadowed the complex relationship Louis Armstrong would have with New Orleans for the rest of his life.

7

"They Admit You with a Smile"

September–November 1931

Though raised as a southerner, Louis Armstrong didn't embark on his first full tour of the Deep South until he left New Orleans in 1931. This was a time when it was not easy for any African American to emerge unscathed in that region of the country—and even Armstrong wouldn't—but in Houston, he quickly realized how popular he was there with both black and white audiences. "That night we played to a crowd of eight thousand people," he said. "And the next night we played to the same amount. Since we were the first big name to tour the South, all of our crowds were sell outs. We played every city and the Big towns in Texas."[1] The *Houston Chronicle* estimated the crowd size at 5,000 but agreed with Armstrong's assessment, writing, "For the first time in the writer's recollection, the high and the low, the rich and poor, white and black, learned and unlearned all, all turned out under one roof to such an occasion in Houston."[2]

Texas was a hit, as were following stops in Tulsa and Oklahoma City. In the latter city, Armstrong was asked by the African American newspaper *Black Dispatch* about his views on prejudice. "Race prejudice is no trouble," Armstrong said. "When they find out that you have what they want and can't get it elsewhere, they admit you with a smile."[3] Sometimes, they admitted him with more than a smile. Ralph Ellison saw Armstrong in Oklahoma City and remembered, "[T]he bandstand in our segregated dance hall was suddenly filled with white women. They were wild for his music and nothing like that had every happened in our town before. His music was our music but they saw it as theirs too, and were willing to break the law to get to it. So you could see that Armstrong's music was affecting attitudes and values that had no immediate relationship to it."[4]

However, not every response to Armstrong in the south was positive. In Wichita, Preston Jackson remembered, the musicians were invited by a woman to stop at her 15-room house. When her husband arrived, he told his wife "to get those dirty musicians out of his house" and then threatened to shoot the first one he caught hanging around outside.[5] After a record-breaking

Figure 7.1 Southern tours were not always easy for Armstrong and his band, but he did manage to make friends with black and white fans of all ages, as seen in this snapshot taken on the road in Houston in 1933. Armstrong's then-girlfriend Alpha Smith is in the center.
Courtesy of the Louis Armstrong House Museum

appearance in Dallas—over a thousand people had to be turned away— matters didn't improve in Tyler, Texas, where the band couldn't get a bus and had to travel in a large truck. With adequate lodging difficult to find, the band began staying with musicians they could trust, such as pianist Little Brother Montgomery, who put them up in Jackson, Mississippi. This would become a regular part of Armstrong's touring life for much of his career and though he didn't like to dwell on it, occasionally anger came bubbling over when he discussed it, such as this striking passage from a profile by Larry L. King in 1967:

> When I was coming along, a black man had hell. On the road he couldn't find no decent place to eat, sleep, or use the toilet—service-station cats see a bus of colored bandsmen drive up and they would sprint to lock their restroom doors. White places wouldn't let you in and the black places all run-down and funky because there wasn't any money behind 'em. We Negro entertainers back then tried to stay in private homes—where at least we wouldn't have to fight bedbugs for sleep and

cockroaches for breakfast. . . . I knew some cats was blowing one-nighters in little sawmill stops down in Mississippi, and one time these white boys—who had been dancing all night to the colored cats' sounds—chased 'em out on the highway and whipped 'em with chains and cut their poor asses with *knives*! Called it "nigger knocking." No reason—except they was so goddamn miserable they had to mess everybody else up, ya dig? *Peckerwoods*![6]

With its specific reference to Mississippi, one wonders if Armstrong had this 1931 tour in mind during that 1967 rant; of course, he would return to this territory frequently over the years and it would take some time before matters started to improve. But he had to be aware of the impact he was having on white southerners during this tour. A most striking example occurred in Austin, Texas, in late September when Armstrong played a dance at the University of Texas. Sixteen-year-old Charles Black was one of many in attendance, later admitting that he wasn't even there for the music, but rather to meet girls. Black was on the prowl when Armstrong began to play; his life changed right then and there. "He was the first genius I had ever seen," he wrote. "The moment of first being, and knowing oneself to be, in the presence of genius, is a solemn moment; it is perhaps the moment of final and indelible perception of man's utter transcendence of all else created. It is impossible to overstate the significance of a sixteen-year-old Southern boy's seeing genius, for the first time, in a black."[7] Black had been around some African Americans, who "were honored and venerated, in that paradoxical white-Southern way." This was different. "But genius—fine control over total power, all height and depth, forever and ever? It had simply never entered my mind, for confirming or denying in conjecture, that I would see this for the first time in a black man. You don't get over that. You stay young awhile longer, with the hesitations, the incertitudes, the half-obediences to crowd-pressure, of the young. But you don't forget." One of Black's friends—"a good old boy"—could only look at Armstrong, shake his head, and say, "After all, he's nothing but a God damn nigger!" Black and his friend parted ways. "Every person of decency in the South of those days must have had some doubts about racism, and I had mine even then—perhaps more than most others," he wrote. "But Louis opened my eyes wide, and put to me a choice. Blacks, the saying went, were 'all right in their place.' What was the 'place' of such a man, and of the people from which he sprung?"[8]

His mind wide open, Black's course in life changed after hearing Armstrong. He became a famed professor of constitutional law and, in 1954, helped Thurgood Marshall write the legal briefs in the case of *Brown v. Board of Education*, which helped bring an end to segregation in schools. Armstrong's tour of the south, and similar ones he would undertake in ensuing years, must have made many white southerners question their own feelings on race, as, when confronted with genius in a black man for the first time, they, too, could not help but admit him with a smile.

Johnny Collins doesn't seem to have been part of the September tour of the south as he was busy planning his client's next move into vaudeville. For black entertainers, breaking into vaudeville was a surefire way to guarantee steady work at decent money, as well as the opportunity to hone one's craft on a nightly basis, even if accommodations were far from ideal. There had always been the black TOBA circuit—Theatre Owners Booking Association but known to performers as "Tough on Black Asses"—but now, African American performers were breaking into mainstream vaudeville, starting with RKO's *Hot from Harlem*. Described as the "first all-colored bill ever routed by a major vaudeville circuit," it opened in St. Louis on September 18 with Bill "Bojangles" Robinson as its star.[9] Collins knew what he had to do. "Armstrong Goes Vaude," the headline in *Variety* read, announcing appearances in St. Louis, Chicago, Cleveland, Cincinnati, and Columbus—all of Collins's old territories—to commence on October 19.[10]

Collins was also busy with a team of lawyers getting ready to go to court. In the summer, after matters hit rock bottom with Rockwell, the Immermans, and Joseph Weber, Armstrong sued them all, delivering a powerful affidavit while still in New Orleans. His lawyers crafted a sprawling complaint with 27 allegations, detailing the incidents with gangsters in Chicago, including all the telegrams with Weber and ending with a plea that Armstrong "has ever since on or about April 11th, 1931, been suffering, is now suffering and will continue to suffer irreparable injury from and as a result of the acts and omissions hereinabove."[11] The Immermans countersued for $10,000 while Rockwell filed an injunction, saying that he was owed a percentage of Armstrong's earnings considering how Armstrong had been especially thriving in the past year. Rockwell reached out to numerous figures in the music business and "asked them to prepare affidavits to the effect that Armstrong's method of leading a band was special, unique and extraordinary."[12]

Those who spoke to Armstrong's talents included Jack Kapp of Brunswick Records, Duke Ellington's manager Irving Mills, and none other than the "King of Jazz" himself, Paul Whiteman. "[Armstrong] is a creator, his style of phrasing unique and he is the one and only exponent of that type of phrasing," Whiteman said. "It is entirely original, individualistic, and impossible of duplication. His services are most definitely and decidedly extraordinary. I know of no colored performer who could replace him."[13]

Rockwell brought his evidence to court on October 6 but a Judge Bondy denied Rockwell's injunction and instead called for a "quick trial of all the issues" to be held in December or January. Rockwell would have to continue stewing for a few more months but now with copies of all the affidavits in his possession, Collins went to work. "The big laugh is that Armstrong will use the affidavits filed against him to ADVERTISE the band," Ed Sullivan reported on October 9. "The extravagant praise of Whiteman and the others will be reprinted in full and placarded prominently wherever Armstrong plays."[14]

Collins might have enjoyed outsmarting Rockwell up north, but he was quickly needed down south when his prized client found himself behind bars for the second time in a year.

The southern tour had been a major success and though they had suffered some indignities along the way, all that was stopping Armstrong's outfit from beginning their prestigious RKO vaudeville tour would be stops in Little Rock and Memphis in early October. In Jackson, Mississippi, Mary Collins, Johnny's wife, chartered a deluxe new bus from the Dixie-Greyhound Lines to travel to Little Rock so, as Mezz Mezzrow later wrote, "they could get through the Murder Belt without riding in dirty spine-cracking Jim-Crow coaches."[15] In Memphis they would have to change drivers, a simple-sounding task that ended up being anything but.

They arrived at Union bus terminal in Memphis, where station master Felix Barron "asked them to transfer to another bus to continue the trip," according to a press account.[16] The musicians remembered it much differently. "Well, get them niggers out of here because I'll have to put them in another bus," was the way Preston Jackson remembered being "asked." Seeing a brand-new bus filled with black men and one white woman—who was sitting next to guitarist Mike McKendrick—was too much for the Memphis officials to handle. "When that bus pulled into Memphis the pecks all crowded around goggle-eyed, staring at the well-dressed colored boys in this stream-lined buggy, and especially at the one colored boy up front who was, God forbid, sitting there actually talking to a white woman cool as pie, just like he was human," Mezzrow wrote.[17]

According to Armstrong, the new driver in Memphis took one look at the situation and said, "I'm not driving you anywhere." Mary Collins got out the contract and said, "Look here, it says so-and-so to drive Louis Armstrong and his Orchestra from this date and so on." "I didn't know it was going to be like this," came the reply. "Remember, this was the Old South," Armstrong said when recalling the situation. He noticed the man was fixated on one of the musicians "smoking a cigarette in a long fancy holder" and "he kept looking at my trumpet man Zilner Randolph who had some sort of French beret on.

Zilner began to make it pretty clear that he wasn't standing for any of this shit." Armstrong saw what was about to go down and told McKendrick, "Go off and phone Mr. Collins and he'll sort this mess out." "I'd seen this kind of scene before," he said.[18]

Mary Collins held her ground, stating, "Well, I paid $50 difference in these buses so the boys could enjoy themselves." The new bus she selected had reclining seats so everyone could sleep comfortably; they were now offered a much smaller bus with seats that did not recline. Armstrong's musicians refused to leave the bigger bus. After about 10 minutes of back and forth, the police showed up. "All right you niggers, get out of there," one officer barked. "You're in Memphis now—and we need some cotton pickers, too!"[19] Naturally, press accounts put the blame on the musicians. "The negroes refused to leave the bus and exhibited some pistols—six to be exact," according to one report.[20] George James said the police lifted up the seats of the bus and found all the guns, which had been purchased in New Orleans. "Everybody on that bus had a gun that he could get to as quickly as possible, because we figured if there was any trouble down there we might as well fight back," James said. "So when they found the guns, they arrested us for that too. But when they questioned us, nobody knew anything about any guns!"[21]

A squad full of detectives showed up but the musicians stayed put. Finally, they were handcuffed and according to the press, "the driver started his motor and drove the party in style to headquarters."[22] However, as the police were handcuffing the musicians, Armstrong saw a peculiar sight: Mike McKendrick running for his life, heading straight to a Western Union to notify Johnny Collins. "I can see him now his coat all flapping," Armstrong said. "He was quick, but so were the rest of the band, nobody waved or shouted or did anything, and Big Mike kept on running just like all he wanted to do was catch a train and at least we had somebody on the outside."[23] On the inside, the musicians arrived in jail and gave their names to the desk sergeant. While standing around, one officer alerted them, "I'm going to tell you right now, you niggers, you ain't gonna come down to Memphis and try to run Memphis—we'll kill all you niggers."[24] The talk continued as they entered their cells, Jackson remembering, "While we were held in jail they kept talking about how they were getting short of cotton pickers, how they needed cotton pickers, and how they needed this and needed that."[25] Zilner Randolph later recalled the officers still unable to get over the way McKendrick was talking to Mary Collins on the bus. "This big, burly blankety-blankety-blank was sitting on the arm of the seat that this white woman was sitting," one officer said. A captain responded, "Why didn't you shoot him in the leg?"[26]

The musicians were put behind bars, two to a cell. Armstrong shared his with Professor Sherman Cook, who was nervous, but not for the usual reasons. He turned to Armstrong and said, "Now look Louis I've got something in my pocket that could mean trouble." With that, he pulled out "a great big joint all neatly wrapped." "Hey man," Armstrong said, "we can't be in any more trouble than we are in right now." "So we lit-up and smoked our way out of trouble," he said. "Now when the other cats in their cells caught the smell of the stuff they all started shouting out about passing around, but old Cook and myself we demolished the evidence."[27]

While the rest of his bandmates were in jail, McKendrick managed to contact Johnny Collins up north. "So Collins wired the man who was booking the band and told him if he wanted a show down there he'd better get the boys out of jail," according to James, "otherwise he could forget about the contract, and he wouldn't get his advance back either. Anyway, after we'd been in the cells for about two hours, the man from the theatre came and bailed us out."[28] Armstrong carefully observed the situation and realized that the advice he had received in New Orleans—"Always keep a white man behind you that'll put his hand on you and say, 'That's my nigger'"—was sadly true. "If you didn't have a white captain to back you in the old days—to put his hand on your shoulder—you was just a damn sad nigger," he said in 1967. "If a Negro had the proper white man to reach the law and say, 'What the hell you mean locking up *my* nigger?' then—quite naturally—the law would walk him free. Get in that jail *without* your white boss, and yonder comes the chain gang! Oh, danger was dancing all around you back then."[29]

The band now had to get to Little Rock to play their engagement, but Armstrong was understandably upset. "Louis was so mad at first that he wanted to go straight back to Chicago, but he calmed down, and we made the date after all," James said.[30] There was no way they'd make it on time and there was no time to haggle over buses, so the band took a train. "We were late getting to Little Rock, but the crowd was still there," Randolph recalled.[31] Armstrong performed from 11 until two in the morning and then boarded another train—heading straight back to Memphis.

After being treated as less than human the day before, Armstrong and his band now had to come back and perform, arriving at 6 A.M. with a full slate of activities planned. On October 8, there would be a broadcast from the Peabody Hotel at 10 A.M., shows at the Palace Theatre at 3:30, 7:15, and 9:30, a dance at the Palace at 10 P.M., and a "Breakfast Dance" at 12:30 A.M. at the Appomattox Club. The next day would include three more shows at the Palace, including a "Midnight Ramble" "for white patrons." The Ritz Cafe at

322 Beale Street even offered a special "Louis Armstrong Dinner" with each meal named for a member of the band.[32]

None of the press mentioned Armstrong's arrest the day before but it was still on his mind. The first engagement on his docket was the broadcast at the Peabody Hotel and what happened there soon became the stuff of legend. While on the radio, Armstrong announced a dedication to the Memphis Chief of Police: "I'll Be Glad When You're Dead You Rascal You." George James later relayed the title of the song and added, "and he really meant it!"[33] "[T]hat was when I really thought that Louis had lost his marbles and when it came to my solo, I was all confused because all I could think of was cotton," Preston Jackson said. "After we were through there was a rush towards the band stand which frightened us after the experience of the previous day. But they were appreciative as they did not understand what he meant."[34] Jackson added that at the Midnight Ramble the following night, "the first five rows of seats were filled by policemen and their families." "The place was so crowded I had to climb over the floor to get to where I had to play," Armstrong said, "and do you know some of those crackers who'd given us all the trouble were sitting down there on the floor applauding louder than anyone, strange."[35] As Armstrong himself was fond to say, "Ain't that a bitch?"

Having survived Memphis, Armstrong and his orchestra were finally able to leave the Deep South and begin the tour Johnny Collins had set up of prestigious RKO theaters along the Midwest vaudeville circuit, opening in St. Louis on October 10. Surprisingly, Armstrong was not an easy sell. Before St. Louis agreed to take him, the theater manager called New Orleans writers and critics for their opinion on whether Armstrong could turn a profit. "The unanimous opinion was that 'for one week he would be a riot,'" according to one writer, who added, "Funny that a man, whose style of singing and trumpet playing is more imitated at the present time than any other person on the American stage, should find it so hard to get even a week's work."[36] However, Collins, relying on his years of experience, convinced enough theater owners to book Armstrong on what would be quite a lucrative tour, receiving an astronomical Great Depression sum of $2,250 a week ($39,000 in 2020 dollars).[37]

Armstrong opened up at the RKO St. Louis as part of a bill that included other acts such as Jim McWilliams ("The Pianutist"), the Yacopi Troupe ("Argentine Gymnasts"), the 3 Brox Sisters, and Martha Morton ("Darling of the 4 Mortons") in tandem with "the Slick Soap Salesman," Eddie Parks. These were professional vaudevillians, each of whom honed their act onstage after years of experience and knew they had something that worked, so they didn't feel the need to change it. For example, in the case of McWilliams, "a skilled monologist," multiple reviews praised his "comedy piano offering" and mentioned that for an encore, he performed his "familiar political speech." This would now be Armstrong's challenge, to pick his best-received specialties and create a surefire act that could stand alongside the vaudeville pros.

The tour got off to a bumpy start, through no fault of the trumpeter. "The first three shows we were booed," Preston Jackson wrote. "It seemed to come from a certain area of the theater. I don't know if the fellows that were following us had been hired by Louis Armstrong's previous manager to cause trouble, but at each show they just booed us and didn't give us any peace. Finally, one of the big shots—I think he was the vice president of RKO—flew down from New York and straightened things out and the booing stopped as quickly as it had started."[38] Perhaps it was the gangsters making their presence felt as Armstrong's injunction against Rockwell and the Immerman Brothers went public in mid-October, filling up newspapers with stories of Armstrong being "repeatedly threatened and intimidated by gangsters."[39]

Vaudeville critics caught up with Armstrong in Columbus and began reviewing his nightly 20-minute spot, which included showpieces like "Shine," "Rockin' Chair," "You Rascal You," and "Tiger Rag." Critic Tod Raper felt that Armstrong had "no voice or personality to speak of," but admitted "he is likeable in the songs he sings for the extreme effort and body he puts into them."[40] Even those who didn't exactly enjoy Armstrong had to admit his effect on his audiences. "Armstrong completely stopped the show Sunday afternoon, receiving an enthusiastic ovation from the audience," "W. S. C." wrote in the *Columbus Citizen.* "Apparently this reporter was the only person in the theater not particularly entertained by Armstrong's trick solos, so I bow to an overwhelming majority."[41]

That writer was not alone in feeling that Armstrong played "trick solos." Harry "Sweets" Edison was a high school student excited by the prospect of Armstrong coming to his hometown of Columbus. Edison's music teacher at school told him the range of a trumpet was from low C to a high C, saying "that's as high as a trumpet player can play." When Armstrong started playing higher than that, Edison recalled "the symphony musicians, they indicated he had a trick mouthpiece, he had a trick horn because there's no horn made and there's no mouthpiece made that a trumpet player can play that high— and that long. His endurance was just, oh, the man could just play all night and still never miss a note." African Americans were not allowed to attend the Palace Theatre in Columbus, but Edison and some friends waited for Armstrong to come out of the backstage door. The symphony musicians had come by to analyze Armstrong's equipment and were shocked to find that he was using a regular trumpet and mouthpiece. Armstrong told them, "Well, since you're so curious about my mouthpiece and my horn today, I'm going to hit 200 high C's and I'm going to end on a high F!" Armstrong made good on his promise, Edison saying, "And when he had 200 C's—the mouthpiece never left his mouth—and he ended up on a high F that would just shatter the lights. Oh, it was such a fantastic performance until, you know, you would get *chills* really."[42]

At his next stop in Cincinnati, Armstrong also had what Preston Jackson referred to as "a spot of bother" when Lil showed up for one last chance at reconciliation. "It seems he was caught in a hotel with Alpha Smith . . . and Lil had him arrested," Jackson remembered.[43] This didn't make the press— or Louis and Alpha's scrapbook—but Johnny Collins himself later alluded to "court action in Cincinnati" that resulted in Armstrong agreeing to pay Lil $100 every week that he was employed.[44] There would be no further attempts at reconciliation.

Armstrong's RKO tour continued in November at the Palace in Chicago, his first trip back since being chased out by gangsters in May. He didn't have to worry about anyone walking out in the Windy City as he remained a tremendously popular act. Walter Barnes Jr. detailed Armstrong's vaudeville set of this period at the Palace:

> Louie opens his act with "Sleepy Time Down South," nicely done, and comes back with a clever arrangement of "Dinah," played as only he can play it. And did it go over? While it is openly admitted that from a very critical musical standpoint, Louis has no voice, still the way he gets himself into "Confessing," his vocal offering, puts him down as a wonder man in front of an audience. His modulation into "Shine," where he continues to hit F and E with ease, clinches for him his title as the ace of trumpeters. The act finishes with a hot rendition of "Tiger Rag," played in a purely Armstrong style, and running the course of 10 complete choruses. At the curtain the thunderous applause from the audience honored Louie back with an encore.[45]

While in Chicago, OKeh records capitalized on the attention being paid to Armstrong and had him record eight songs in November, recording two songs a day each day from November 3 through November 6. With Rockwell out of OKeh's picture, it is not known who was supervising the dates from the label's standpoint; it's quite possible Armstrong and Collins knew what they wanted to record and OKeh was simply happy to have him doing anything he pleased—well, almost anything. Armstrong was intent on recording a jazzed-up version of the spiritual "When the Saints Go Marching In," even though he didn't have an arrangement. According to his friend Charles Carpenter, he decided to do it right then and there for the OKeh executives, singing it and "playing ten of the most inventive choruses I ever heard in my life." When it was over, Armstrong asked OKeh's A&R man, "How was that?" "Louis, I hate to say this, but I think you're a little ahead of your time with that song," came the reply. Armstrong wasn't buying it. "What do you mean?" he asked. "The Holy Rollers and everybody else do it in that tempo." "Yeah, Louis, but the masses are not too much aware of the Holy Rollers," OKeh responded. "I think they'd take my head off in New York if I sent this in."[46]

The "Saints" was off the docket—for now—but Armstrong had a full slate ready for recording. Taken as a whole, his November 1931 recordings constitute an almost overwhelming display of every tool in Armstrong's arsenal: roof-shaking trumpet solos, transformative vocals, comedy, crooning, scatting, glissing, even heavy doses of slang.

"Lazy River" was up first and the results were so powerful, Armstrong had a showpiece he would continually perform in much the same way into the 1960s, complete with a proto-bebop double-timed scat chorus and a climactic gliss, an effortless slide up to a high note that wowed trumpeters around the world and soon became another important hallmark of Armstrong's style. The tempo is much more manic on "Chinatown, My Chinatown," but Armstrong sounds supremely relaxed, as a stream of singable phrases float out of the bell of his horn. Ever so gradually he builds higher and higher, tossing in glisses, riffs, and held notes, sometimes spending an entire chorus just working over a pitch or two. The endurance needed to get through such a solo is unimaginable, but Armstrong's stamina never flags, and he hits the final high C right on the nose. This was the song he called after "When the Saints Go Marching In" was axed, and Carpenter offered a visual, saying Armstrong "did it the same way, sitting on the table, swinging his legs."[47]

The next day, he recorded his versions of two Bing Crosby hits, "Wrap Your Troubles in Dreams" and "Star Dust." Intonation problems plague the horns on both sides (and even the voices of the musicians providing Armstrong's favored "glee club" backing behind his vocal on "Wrap Your Troubles in Dreams"), but they're mostly just there to hold chords and occasionally provide their patented "fucking rhythm" with emphasis on beats one and three. From a vocal standpoint, "Wrap Your Troubles" is definitely Crosby-esque at times (Armstrong seems to replace Crosby's trademark "boo-boo-boo" with his own "bay-bay-bay"), but he takes many more chances with "Star Dust," in this writer's opinion, Armstrong's single greatest recording. He had been playing it since his California days the previous year so he evidently had a routine worked out, though two surviving takes contain some differences in the "Satchmofication" of one of the great songs of the 20th century.

The opening and closing trumpet solos are pure opera, Armstrong belting out Hoagy Carmichael's melody, playing with it, teasing it, making love to it, all at a medium tempo that can best be described as insistent. For the trumpet playing alone, "Star Dust" belongs in the Armstrong canon but nothing he ever did before or after quite compares with his thrilling vocal deconstruction of both Carmichael's melody and Mitchell Parish's poetic lyrics. It's all there: the repeated notes (listen to his almost rushed, breathless entrance), the dramatic rephrasing of the melody, eliminating words ("Melody, memory"), all the mumbled asides, and just the pure joy and passion infused in every syllable and sound. On one take, he sings Parish's last line, "the memory of love's refrain," and repeats it, adding a "Mama" for good measure. But on the more famous take, he takes Parish's poetry and finds the essence in two words: "Oh memory, oh memory, oh memory," repeated three times with a swinging phrasing that would crop up several years later in Count Basie's "One O'Clock Jump." Three stunning choruses in three and a half minutes.

The next day, Armstrong did his young friend Charles Carpenter a solid by recording his and Louis Dunlap's new composition, "You Can Depend on Me."[48] Randolph's arrangement and Armstrong's crooning vocal helped make "You Can Depend on Me" one of Armstrong's most popular recordings of the early 1930s, especially "a hit among black people," Carpenter proudly stated. Just like the popularity of Guy Lombardo in Harlem, there were clear signs that Armstrong was not alone in the African American community in his love of pretty melodies. He followed with "Georgia on My Mind," the third Hoagy Carmichael composition in three days. It was well received, especially overseas where young trumpeter Nat Gonella became enamored of it, recorded his own version, and renamed his band "Nat Gonella and His Georgians." The popularity of Gonella's version only created more buzz for Armstrong in England.

On November 6, Armstrong and his band concluded their busy week of recording (and performing at the Palace) with two fun performances, "The Lonesome Road" and "I Got Rhythm." With "Lonesome Road," Armstrong decided to put his mock sermon bit, something he had been doing since the mid-1920s with Fletcher Henderson and Erskine Tate, on record for the first time, with hilarious results. Armstrong and the other members of his group obviously indulged in a little bit of "gage" before the recording began; the record even ends with a send-off, "Bye bye, you vipers!"

Armstrong continues in his role as master of ceremonies on "I Got Rhythm," introducing each member of the band for a round of swinging solos. Finally, he leads the way out for two exciting choruses, taking the song's title as a challenge, playing nothing but concert B♭'s for an entire half-chorus, dropping them like bombs out of a B-19, some landing on the beat, others in between, some dropped in pairs, others with long gaps between them. In the bridge, he enters with a string of repeated D's; 18 bars into a 34-bar song and Armstrong has only played two different pitches but his rhythmic placing of them keeps it from ever getting predictable. He continues floating into a second chorus, surrounded by New Orleans polyphony, but stops on a dime at the end to allow the band to get in one more laugh, imitating a car horn as a coda.

OKeh now had eight songs in the can, which they would release slowly into 1932. With each release, American pop culture changed. Yes, Armstrong's trumpet playing and singing were revolutionary but now there was also the comedy, the allusions to marijuana, and perhaps most abundantly, the popularizing of African American slang that is still in use today. Almost every song has something: "Way down, way down," "Oh, you dog," "Swing out on those ivories, boy," "Before we riff, we're going to chirp a few for you this time," "Look at them cats getting away," "I'm ready, I'm ready, so help me I'm ready" (code for Armstrong being high), "More power to ya, boys," "Bye, bye, you vipers," "Every tub," and more, not to mention various utterances of "Oh baby," "Oh babe," and "Now, Mama" in his vocals. Armstrong was unapologetically black, taking the same songs being performed by all the white bands and infusing them with a combination of swing and sex and slang and smoke (of the marijuana variety), changing the sound of music and the shape of culture for eternity.

8

"An Artist of Eminence"

December 1931–June 1932

In addition to the groundbreaking trumpet playing and vocalizing, Armstrong's live performances at the end of 1931 were also pointing the way toward the future spectacle of entertainment in America, almost predicting the screaming excitement of rock 'n' roll to come. Young trumpeter Ray Nance attended an Armstrong performance at the Savoy in Chicago in November. His description of the closing "Tiger Rag" and the effect it had on the Savoy audience is one of the most exciting eyewitness accounts we have of Armstrong in this period:

> And he used to play these choruses on "Tiger Rag" and make these hundred high C's! Had a cat in the wings and he's counting them, you know? And this mother-fucker, when he get to 99, boy, when he get to 99, he'd hit this C, you know, and rattle it [imitates a high note with vibrato], yeee-yeee-yeee-yeee, you know, rattle it, and man, people about to *piss* on themselves! Me right with them, man, I'm sitting there thinking, "If this motherfucker don't make it, boy!" This motherfucker reared back, rolling his eyes and take a breath—and *BAM!* Hit that note, boy, and the whole motherfucking place—pandemonium, boy! I tell you, that was the greatest thrill I ever had in my whole life. In fact, it's one of the greatest thrills that I've ever witnessed.[1]

Armstrong's theatricality also sold his performances of numbers like "Tiger Rag" and "Shine." Not content to just stand in one place, he stalked up and down the stage as he hit each note and feigned tiredness before rallying to hit that last high F. Erskine Hawkins was a young trumpeter who was inspired by Armstrong to become proficient in the upper register, even using his routines while making a name for himself at the University of Alabama. Eventually Armstrong heard him and gave him some advice to make it look "like it was hard for me. That's what Louis explained for me. He said, 'Now you made your point. Now, let them think it's a little hard for you to do it.'"[2] It was pure show business, lessons Armstrong was learning from the vaudeville stage and out of his desire to impress other musicians. Some writers sensed this change in popular entertainment brewing. "Here seems to be quite the climax of high temperature in rhythm," Archie Bell wrote of Armstrong's next stop in Cleveland. "We've been moving in that direction for months, if not for years, and it takes a novelty nowadays to stir the pulse."[3]

Armstrong completed his five weeks as a vaudeville headliner and had enough money to enjoy a week off in New York with Alpha. Still, he did not quite have peace of mind. In Cleveland, reports noted that "Louis Armstrong, ace trumpeter, enters Palace thru front door accompanied by local detectives, and leaves the same way."[4] With Armstrong in New York, the Immermans planted an item in Walter Winchell's column that "Louis Armstrong returns to town in a fortnight at Connie's."[5] But there was no way he was returning to Connie's until his trial was over.

Collins next booked Armstrong as part of an all-black revue on what African American entertainers referred to as an "Around the World Tour" featuring stops in Philadelphia, Washington, DC, Baltimore, and New York. In Philadelphia, Armstrong met someone who would become one of his closest friends, black actor and comedian Slim Thompson. The two men immediately bonded over their shared sense of humor, Armstrong calling Thompson "the muggingest man in the world!" They worked up a running gag that involved mumbling the word "motherfucker" until it came out "mother fuyer" and wrote little comedy sketches solely to amuse themselves. On one of Armstrong's private reel-to-reel tapes made in the 1950s, Armstrong and Thompson re-created one of their routines, the "pork chop gag." Thompson played a chef and Armstrong played his friend who would come by his window and ask for food. Armstrong would gesture frantically, saying, "Well, you're my buddy and I'm hungry, what in the world, let me have one of them pork chops, man! I'm your boy!" Thompson would reply incredulously, "Man, I couldn't give you none of them pork chops! The man had them counted!" Armstrong replied, "Yeah, yeah, but them beans wasn't counted!" Armstrong's punchline drew uproarious laughter on his tape, but Thompson saw a way to improve it. "You know, the good way to say that son-of-a-bitch is, 'Yeah, but you could give me some of them damn beans, you didn't have *them* counted!'" Thompson then mugged broadly to much laughter and said, "See that?" "We used to mug!" Armstrong said. "And we'd mug on it, too!" Thompson agreed. They did the routine again from the start, Thompson alerting everyone in the room, "Now watch this mugging! We used to do this all the time." After delivering the proper "mug" with proper timing and eliciting more hysterical laughter, Armstrong exclaimed, "Yeah, look at that son-of-a-bitch mug! Ahhhhhh!" "See, we used to go through all the gestures," Thompson said proudly. With Thompson in his corner, Armstrong's natural comedic ability improved even more as he perfected the art of communicating with his eyes and facial gestures.[6]

After breaking the box-office record and being extended into a second week at the Pearl Theatre in Philadelphia, Armstrong headed to the Howard Theatre in Washington, DC. While there, Armstrong looked ahead to his next engagement at the Royal Theatre in Baltimore, and, in the midst of the most lucrative year of his career, decided to give back to his people. The Royal was located in "a poor Negro neighborhood" and the weather was brutally cold that December. Armstrong recounted:

> It was freezing, and when I heard about those poor people who couldn't afford to buy hard coal so that they and their kids could keep warm—I bought it for them. Yes I did. I went to the coal yard, ordered a ton of coal and had the company deliver it to the lobby of the Royal Theater. And then, all the folks who needed coal to help themselves, which made them very happy. They made it their business to come backstage and thank me personally. Of course, it all made me stick out my chest with pride. I came up through life the hard way, just like those folks.[7]

Armstrong's gesture was selfless and from the heart, but Johnny Collins knew a good story when he saw it and immediately rushed to the press with tales of Armstrong's generosity. "Louis Armstrong to Give Away Coal," read the headline in the *Baltimore Afro-American* on December 12. Collins even went as far as having each bag of coal personally adorned with an advertisement: "KEEP THE HOME FIRE BURNING SAYS LOUIS ARMSTRONG NOW AT THE ROYAL THEATRE." Photographers were on hand to capture the moment, with Collins even getting into one of the photos, a stubby cigar protruding from his closed mouth. But Armstrong wasn't doing this for publicity and even reached into his own pocket when the coal ran out. "Armstrong arrived here a few minutes after the distribution of the bags of coal had begun, and finding the 300 bags insufficient to take care of the crowd of approximately 500 men and women, he gave away real cash," the *Afro-American* reported, adding, "This means to aid the needy was Armstrong's own idea, and the coal and cash were from his own pocket."[8]

After finishing his engagement in Washington, DC, Armstrong returned to the Royal a hero. Before his first morning show, he was waiting in the wings ready to go onstage when he was approached by a young, 16-year-old kid, who "seemed a little down in the dumps, although he was very glad to see me because I was his idol," Armstrong recalled. "And to my surprise, this kid had so much confidence in me, loved my music so well, he personally felt that I could

Figure 8.1 In December 1931, Armstrong offered free bags of coal to citizens of Baltimore in front of the Royal Theatre. Manager Johnny Collins, far right, never one to miss a marketing opportunity, used each bag to advertise Armstrong's engagement at the Royal.
Courtesy of the University Library of Southern Denmark, Timme Rosenkrantz Collection

do most anything, you know." Armstrong asked the kid what was wrong. "Pops, my grandmother, here of late, has had trouble sleeping nights," he said, "And it's almost driving me out of my mind. What shall I tell her to do?" Just then, Armstrong heard a stage manager call "All on!" and the band went into "When It's Sleepy Time Down South." Armstrong rushed to the stage, turned to the kid and said, "Son, tell your grandmother to take a good physic and light up one of them big sticks of gage and sleep peacefully." The next day, the same young man walked into Armstrong's dressing room and simply said, "Pops, it worked!" Armstrong said to himself, "Well, I'll be damned."[9]

While Armstrong was in Baltimore, Johnny Collins was making deals behind the scenes. The music industry did not publish numbers of record sales because sheet music sales were viewed as the more important figure. But at the end of 1931, *Variety* published a stunning chart of "Disc Leaders in 1931." For Columbia Records, of which OKeh was a subsidiary, there were most of the usual suspects: Guy Lombardo, Ted Lewis, Paul Whiteman, Ben Selvin, and so on. But leading the pack was Louis Armstrong, the number one best-selling dance artist on Columbia's entire roster.[10] Armed with this information, Collins began negotiating behind-the-scenes with RCA, signing a contract on December 23, 1931, that would go into effect on May 8, 1932.[11] Collins must have been pleased but still had to tell OKeh that their number one seller was leaving the label, news they were bound to not take lying down.

Collins was also busy preparing for the upcoming trial with Rockwell, as newspapers were filled with juicy details. "Lawyers, gangsters, gunmen, producers, and musicians will be involved in a legal battle scheduled for the United States' court here, when a showdown to determine who is the rightful manager of Louis Armstrong, is adjudicated sometime this week," the *Baltimore Afro-American* reported on its front page with headlines "Ace Trumpeter Lived in Fear of Gangsters" and "Louis Armstrong Made Pawn of Chicago and N.Y. Racketeers."[12] With all these articles mounting up (many of which were saved by Armstrong and Alpha Smith), the trumpeter still had to concentrate on performing. His revue, now titled "Dixiana," opened at the Lincoln Theatre in Philadelphia in early 1932 to good reviews and excellent box-office returns. In the audience was a 21-year-old man who would have quite an influence over the music industry for the next 50 years: John Hammond. In his inaugural *Melody Maker* column on "the great Louis," Hammond wrote, "He is still full of vitality, but looks far from well, works too hard, and has shaved his hair off leaving just a tuft over his forehead."[13] Hammond correctly guessed that "perhaps his recent lawsuit has caused him concern."[14]

A few things had changed before the trial. The Immermans withdrew their $10,000 counterclaim against Armstrong and Armstrong dropped his suit against the American Federation of Musicians since they allowed him to be reinstated. Armstrong was still suing Rockwell to forfeit all claims he had on him as an agent, while Rockwell was countersuing that Armstrong broke his contract and therefore should be reinstated as his representative. Rockwell claimed that because of Armstrong's "unique and extraordinary" talent, he was worth $250,000 a year—of which a percentage was owed to Rockwell. To counter this, Armstrong, Collins, and their lawyer, Henry Hechheimer, enacted a somewhat unusual strategy: to prove that Armstrong was *not* unique and extraordinary!

Collins called on a parade of witnesses from his past including Marty Forkins, Bill Robinson's manager who came up together with Collins in their early days; Nat Nazarro, manager of Armstrong's friends, Buck and Bubbles; Aaron Kesseler of RKO; and Joseph E. Shea, a successful vaudeville producer. One by one, each man took the witness stand and did everything in their power to diminish Armstrong's talent right in front of him, delivering "a terrible wallop to his ego," in the words of one reporter.[15]

Rockwell pulled a cagey move in calling Eli Oberstein to the stand. Oberstein was the head artists and repertoire man for RCA Victor and would be supervising Armstrong's future recordings. Oberstein was honest about the erratic nature of Armstrong's appeal, saying he was "particularly interesting to musicians" and "college students," but added "the average layman does not understand this type of work." Still, Oberstein was proud to announce that he had signed Armstrong to begin recording for RCA Victor in May and did not discredit Armstrong's phenomenal record sales, as gleaned from this exchange:

KLEIN: Can you give us a comparison of the sale of the Armstrong records as compared with other colored cornetists?
OBERSTEIN: Armstrong is the largest selling artist on records today, bar none.
KLEIN: Of all classes of records?
OBERSTEIN: Yes, sir.[16]

Hechheimer cross-examined Oberstein, immediately asking him if Armstrong "is extraordinary and cannot be replaced?" Oberstein responded, "No man cannot be replaced in the record business."[17] When asked about Armstrong's main rivals, Duke Ellington and Cab Calloway, Oberstein admitted that Ellington was a superior bandleader and that Calloway made more money and was regarded in "a class superior to Armstrong" from the public's point of view. But asked if Calloway could take Armstrong's place on a planned record date, Oberstein responded, "No, sir."

Elsewhere, Hechheimer argued that Rockwell never told Armstrong he was exercising his option and "neglected the duties of managership over so long a period as to invalidate whatever contract may have originally been made, and that the threats and duress which he is alleged to have exercised against Armstrong destroyed the last vestige of his obligations as a manager." Rockwell's lawyer, David Klein, answered by saying that Rockwell "made" Armstrong, transforming him from a trumpeter making $100 a week as a sideman to a leader making $15,000 a year. Armstrong finally got on the witness stand and told the judge that he was already "an artist of eminence" recording for OKeh when he met Rockwell; that even with Rockwell as his manager, he never made more than $350 a week; he never really knew the terms of the original contract from 1929; and he never received any notice of a renewal. Armstrong said that with Johnny Collins, he was now making $500 to $2,000 per week but needed police escorts and bodyguards because of the trouble caused by Rockwell and the Immermans.[18]

After three days of testimonies, Armstrong was declared the victor and was freed of Rockwell and allowed to remain under Collins's stewardship—but at a price. He and Collins would pay Rockwell $150 a week for every week Armstrong worked, adding up to $30,000 over the next three years and 10 months ($542,681 in 2020 money).[19] Armstrong also couldn't relax entirely, retaining his bodyguards after his planned first appearance in New York in nearly two years fell through because Collins wouldn't make a deal with the mob. "[W]e went down to the Paramount to claim our dressing rooms," George James recalled. "But when we got there, they didn't know anything about Louis Armstrong playing at the Paramount Theater. People had actually seen Louis's name up outside the theatre on the previous Thursday night or Friday morning, but when we arrived, nobody knew nothing!"[20]

Through Armstrong's ordeal, OKeh had been steadily issuing his November output, garnering more top record sales and now set up two more record dates for January 25 and 27.[21] During the trial, the name of Cab Calloway kept getting thrown in Armstrong's face for his greater popularity, even though Armstrong sold more records. Armstrong and Calloway met in Chicago when Calloway was the house singer at the Sunset Cafe where Armstrong performed in 1926 and 1927. "I dug his singing; it always got to me," Calloway said of Armstrong at the Sunset. "I have often wondered how one man could have so many talents and still have his feet on the ground."[22]

Armstrong was even responsible for one of Calloway's big breaks, getting him the juvenile lead part in *Hot Chocolates* on Broadway in 1929. Calloway built up his reputation, recording for Brunswick and becoming the second house band along with Duke Ellington's at the famed Cotton Club. While Armstrong was touring the Midwest and the Deep South to avoid gangsters, Calloway was entrenched in New York City and broadcasting twice a week on NBC, elevating his stature. Calloway began having hit records with scat escapades such as "Minnie the Moocher," but he gave credit where it was due. "I subsequently put [Armstrong's] scat material in my own act when I started to work at the Cotton Club a year or so later, with all the hi-de-hoing," Calloway said. "It was Louis Armstrong's creative scat-singing that freed us all from straight lyrics."[23]

Armstrong had been scatting on record since 1926, but Calloway's explosion of popularity led the media to finally pick up on the trend with a series of stories in early 1932. "A new lunacy is on the air," wrote one columnist. "It is called 'scat' singing. Radio listeners of average sound mind and understanding who have heard it declare that it is worse than crooning, worse than 'torch' singing, worse than anything in the way of singing and so-called singing that has ever come out of a loudspeaker."[24] "At the moment chief contenders for such honors are Cab Calloway, band maestro of the Cotton Club, and Louis Armstrong," Gilbert Swann wrote, adding, "Calloway appears to be the most closely identified with its spread, whether or not he was the originator."[25]

With Calloway getting the exposure, OKeh decided to go the if-you-can't-beat-them-join-them route and have Armstrong record two songs first introduced by Calloway in a Cotton Club revue, "Between the Devil and the Deep Blue Sea" and "Kickin' the Gong Around" on January 25. Comparing Armstrong's recordings with Calloway, Calloway remained the master at such drug-themed craziness as "Kickin' the Gong Around," a reference to smoking opium that even caused Armstrong to blush, "Ohhhh, lord," at one point. But there's no comparison when it comes to "Between the Devil and the Deep Blue Sea," which Calloway treated as a straight ballad, singing it stiffly like the types of crooners Armstrong and Bing Crosby were routinely displacing. Armstrong contributed a masterful trumpet solo on the latter, experimenting with a new technique: using a mute to explore rapid-fire double-timed lines reminiscent of his 1920s work (and in certain instances, once again projecting the future of bebop) before removing the mute mid-solo to play longer, held high notes with the golden sound of his open horn.

He repeated the device on "All of Me," recorded two days later, but the highlight here was his effervescent vocal. A month earlier, Russ Columbo recorded a slow, sensual version of the song, helping to fuel the craze for crooners. The public was now picking up on the more sexually charged singing of the day but as with scatting, not everyone was pleased. On January 10, 1932, William Cardinal O'Connor attacked crooners as "whiners and bleaters defiling the air . . . crying vapid words to impossible tunes."[26] Though the tempo is bouncy on "All of Me," Armstrong inflicts his vocal with enough growls, moans, and "babes" to make it into an intensely personal and intimate vocal. The result would become the biggest hit of his career to this point.

Collins now focused on getting his client back into the movies, something he hadn't been able to do since *Ex-Flame* in 1930. Armstrong and his entire band were brought out to Paramount's Astoria studios to film two showcases in February 1932, a 10-minute short called *A Rhapsody in Black and Blue* and an appearance in a Betty Boop cartoon named after his big hit, *I'll Be Glad When You're Dead You Rascal You.*

A Rhapsody in Black and Blue features a threadbare plot where a lazy, Armstrong-loving man played by Sidney Easton gets conked on the head by his loud, angry wife, Fanny Belle DeKnight. Easton dreams he is the "King of Jazzmania" and, allowed to make any wish he desires, asks for Louis Armstrong to appear. And so he does—wearing leopard skin and standing amid a studio filled with soap bubbles. Within that demeaning setting,

Armstrong does "You Rascal You"—with more exaggerated mugging than usual—and "Shine," the minstrel song based on an epithet for African Americans. For decades, the short has served as a lightning rod for discussion: there's the racist stereotypes prevalent throughout, including Easton's and DeKnight's characters; Armstrong's dehumanizing wardrobe; his minstrel song choice; his sexuality (the leopard skin does show off his impressive 30-year-old physique); Armstrong being defeated by it all; Armstrong transcending it all; and more.

Armstrong probably dealt with similarly conflicting notions of how to feel about the experience. He most likely enjoyed a lot of it: he was performing "You Rascal You" and "Shine" nightly so he felt comfortable showcasing those on film; he loved comedy, especially black comedy, and would have found Easton and DeKnight's bickering funny; and the one time he was asked point blank about the film, he warmly recounted the plot, praised Easton's comedic ability, and summed it up by saying, "I liked it!"[27] But even he must have felt ridiculous in the costume. As he begins his vocal on "Shine," Armstrong points to himself—with an extended middle finger. He leaves the gesture out in the open for a number of seconds, but then continues communicating with his hands as he sings about liking "to dress up in the latest style" while holding up part of the leopard skin and rolling his eyes, a way for the always fashionable Armstrong to signify to his black audience, "*This* is the latest style?"

Armstrong and his band were at least allowed to wear their customary suits for the Betty Boop cartoon—if only in the beginning. It's a tantalizing but too brief glimpse of the onstage Armstrong of the period, playing "High Society" and "Chinatown, My Chinatown" brilliantly, leading the band, stalking around the stage, even uttering his secret signal to the vipers, "I'm ready, I'm ready, so help me, I'm ready." Everything goes well—until the scene of the cartoon turns to Africa and Armstrong and his band are turned into cannibals, chasing Betty Boop and her cohorts Koko the Clown and Bimbo through the jungle, singing "I'll Be Glad When You're Dead You Rascal You." "Cast as a primitive among primitives, he nevertheless appears, too, as the highly polished leader of a band for which he is the conductor, singer, and principle [*sic*] soloist," Robert G. O'Meally has written in trying to make sense of the contradictions in the film. "And his song, despite its 'fried chicken' lyrics and foolishness, is unmistakable in its aggressive declarations that its singer will be glad when '*you*'—the whites in the cartoon? Betty? the producers? the audience?—are all dead." Like "Shine," Armstrong gets one over on the censors by uttering a hard-to-decipher "You a motherfucker, boy" while cheering on the trombone solo. Armstrong follows that with "Chinatown," each high note visually aided by a spear flung from one of the savages. O'Meally correctly argued

Figure 8.2 On the set of the Paramount short, *I'll Be Glad When You're Dead You Rascal You*, the earliest surviving footage of Armstrong on film. Mike McKendrick is in the background on guitar.
Courtesy of the Louis Armstrong House Museum

that Armstrong doesn't simply transcend the material and the stereotypes; the effect is much more complicated.

> No, rather it seems to me that Armstrong's is an indivisibly double or triple role—genius, clown, and aggressive warrior, salesman in the racial marketplace, actor, and revolutionary giving no quarter when the moment for war arrives. *I'll Be Glad* has its transcendent and aggressive sides. With this said, it is also important to admit the embarrassing foolishness of this cartoon, the racial travesty in which Mr. Armstrong is complicit. With this admission freely made, the history told here is that much richer, for it does not lie about American racism and the roles to which even our most brilliant black artists have been consigned.[28]

Paramount threw its most demeaning portrayal of African Americans at Armstrong in both shorts, but he still managed to light up the screen by the sheer force of personality and musicality, finally capturing on film a touch of what made him so irresistible—and impossible to follow—on stage. A short tour of New England followed, climaxing with a battle of the bands at the Crystal Ballroom in Shawsheen Village, Massachusetts, featuring Armstrong's group locking horns with his old boss, Fletcher Henderson and His Orchestra, as well as the popular white group the Casa Loma Orchestra.[29] Both Henderson and Casa Loma were better bands with better arrangements and better soloists (Henderson still had Coleman Hawkins and J. C. Higginbotham)—but they didn't have Armstrong. Jackson remembered the other bands "fought well," but after 10 choruses of "Tiger Rag" and a version "Shine" with 300 high C's topped with a high F, "they lost. Armstrong would sometimes play fifty choruses of 'Tiger Rag' and when he finished, there wasn't anything for the other fellow to do."[30]

Not everyone was as enamored with Armstrong's routine of hitting hundreds of high notes on "Shine." In February, Armstrong finally came back to New York to play the Lafayette Theatre in Harlem. John Hammond was there and wrote, "Unfortunately, he is almost killing himself by hitting high C about two hundred times in succession at the conclusion of 'Shine,' all for no reason whatsoever. Sometimes he does this three and four times a day, and then drops dead."[31] But Hammond aside, Harlem was thrilled to have Armstrong back, the *New York Age* reporting that "audiences go wild over him."[32] In one of those audiences was a 21-year-old trumpeter from Pittsburgh named Roy Eldridge. He hadn't recorded yet, but he was making a name for himself in banjoist Elmer Snowden's band with his speed and flashy high notes. Eldridge had some familiarity with Armstrong's records, but was more heavily influenced by the fast fingers and deep harmonic knowledge of tenor saxophonist Coleman Hawkins. Even with his speed, though, Eldridge lacked substance, later admitting, "I had lots of technique, but no heart."[33] Eldridge was in New York playing with Snowden's band at Small's Paradise when he decided to check Armstrong out at the Lafayette. He wasn't impressed by Armstrong's first show and almost left, before deciding to give Armstrong a chance to warm up a bit more. Eldridge admitted Armstrong improved during his second show but he wasn't quite prepared for what happened next:

The next show is when he played this "Chinatown." The rhythm section was chuggin' on him, baby, and it just kept building. He started down here and went to F, up there, then to A out of the staff, then to the C and the D, and those cats was whippin' him, didn't let up one bit! They got just as intense as he did. See, that's what's supposed to be! When he hit that note on the end, everybody jumped up, and I looked, and *I* was standing up! I said, "Shit, what's going on? I got to stay for another show!"[34]

Eldridge came out of the Lafayette Theatre a changed man. "I started to feel that if I could combine speed with melodic development while continuing to build, to tell a story, I could create something musical of my own."[35] Armstrong, for his part, returned the favor and went to Small's Paradise to hear Eldridge. Impressed, he told him, "Little Jazz, you gonna be all right."[36]

While in New York, OKeh had Armstrong record four more songs over two sessions on March 2 and March 11, opening with "The New Tiger Rag," a turbocharged version to reflect what he was now doing onstage. Because of time constraints, it was still impossible for him to replicate his full routine, but he still managed to take eight choruses over a ludicrous tempo, throwing in plenty of musical quotes for good measure. Armstrong's lyrical side comes across better on a new Fats Waller–Andy Razaf tune, "Keepin' out of Mischief Now," but he really shines on two songs already recorded by Bing Crosby, "Love You Funny Thing" and "Lawd You Made the Night Too Long." Both men undeniably admired each other, but Crosby always made it clear that it was Armstrong who was his number one influence. On February 11, 1932, Crosby recorded a version of "St. Louis Blues" with Duke Ellington, complete with a scat chorus. Playing the record on a Voice of America broadcast with Willis Conover in 1958, Crosby asked Conover, "Sound a little like Louis Armstrong? I like to think so, because that was what I was trying to do. Yessir, much of my early 'buh-buh-boo-ing' was inspired by what I heard Louis Armstrong doing." Crosby then played his scat chorus on "St. Louis Blues" and followed it with Armstrong's scat chorus on "Lazy River," remarking, "The thievery is unmistakable. . . . He was my idol, there's no denying it."[37]

Armstrong and his band must have felt pretty good after the run at the Lafayette, the short films for Paramount, and the latest recordings for OKeh but the good times hit a brick wall quickly. Armstrong might have been a hit at the Lafayette, but the New York mob didn't make it easy for him. Max Jones wrote, "A New York musician recalls that all the posters advertising these appearances were torn down, which suggests that business disagreements had not been settled."[38] The *Afro-American* put up a headline, "Extortion Continues," reporting, "After throwing scares into Louis Armstrong, the trumpeter, and the Immermans of Connie's Inn, three white gangsters turned their efforts to extorting $500 from the manager of the Lafayette. [Lafayette manager Bernard] Burtt called the law and grabbed off one of the boys."[39] According to George James, " 'Pops' Collins decided it was too hot for Louis and [had] to get him out of harm's way."[40]

Collins held the band up for two weeks while he plotted his next move. Armstrong's musicians were running out of money and were still owed their share for the Paramount shorts and the latest OKeh sessions. Armstrong had no knowledge of the band's finances and assumed they had gotten paid, telling Mike McKendrick, "I know you boys are really sticking fat," meaning they had plenty of money—but they didn't. "We were due a nice piece of money for the recordings and the pictures," Jackson said. "Eventually, Collins showed up and paid us. But I was surprised because it was a lot less money than I had anticipated."[41] "Anyway, it wasn't enough to write home about," Randolph said about the money. "And, see . . . that was the manager's doings. The manager did that. He gypped me out of that money."[42] Collins used this as an opportunity to break up Armstrong's band. George James remained despondent over the breakup of the band for the rest of his life, saying in 1979, "There was so much we could have done—all the vaudeville theatres, all those shows and places, we could have made so much money, believe me! He sure messed us up. It was ridiculous!"[43]

While the musicians in his band were furious with Collins, Armstrong had no complaints. "After paying off the band and other expenses, I was really 'sticking' with money when we went back up North and layed off in Chicago," he wrote.[44] Armstrong was happy to be back in Chicago but he was burned out; the *Chicago Defender* even hinted that his friends thought he might retire.[45] After a short time off, though, Collins decided to return to Sebastian's Cotton Club. Armstrong was greeted by hundreds of friends and fans, as well as Frank Sebastian, and the entire Les Hite band—with Lionel Hampton still on drums and Lawrence Brown back on trombone—playing "California, Here We Come" for him.[46]

To prove that he had money to burn, one of Armstrong's first orders of business in California was to go to downtown Los Angeles to buy a new Buick. Bringing Hampton and his friend Soldier Boy along with him, the men were greeted by a salesman. "I could tell from the way he approached us, that he wasn't expecting to sell no car at all," Armstrong recounted. "We must have looked like three 'squares' to him and was just going to take up his time, and nothing happening." Armstrong told the man he'd like to see a new Buick and was brought over to a little six-cylinder convertible. "To me," Armstrong wrote, "it was a dinky looking thing, especially since I had almost five thousand dollars in my pocket." Armstrong said to the salesman, "Aw man, show me some car." The salesman laughed and brought him over to an eight-cylinder convertible with whitewall tires, a radio, and a rumble seat. Armstrong's eyes "lit up" and he asked the price. The salesman still seemed skeptical but finally told him it was $2,800. Armstrong said, "I reached down into one pocket and came out with all of this money and said 'wrap it up.' "[47]

Armstrong was proud to show off his new Buick to the Hollywood elite, writing "the Movie Stars were very happy for me."[48] The night the Buick was delivered to the Cotton Club, Tallulah Bankhead was in attendance. "That's when Tallulah told me how popular I was out to her home," Armstrong said of meeting the Alabama-born actress. "She said that all of her Colored help just raved about me, and I should come out to her home, and meet them, first chance that I get."[49] Armstrong was used to hearing such stories and though he and Bankhead grew close, he quickly got tired of it coming from other celebrities. "In the early days of Hollywood I socialized a little with the film crowd," he later wrote in *Ebony*. "The few parties I did go to left a sour taste in my mouth. Somebody would always come up with a few drinks in him and say, 'Y'know, I once had a colored mammy.' I would explode inside and say: 'Is that necessary?'"[50]

Armstrong remained a hit with the Hite band, broadcasting nightly from the Cotton Club and scaring the rival nightclub owners who quickly began losing business after Armstrong's arrival. When the Frolics Garden brought in Ted Fio Rita from Chicago and billed him as "Ted Fio Rita—the sweetest music this side of Heaven," Sebastian's responded by billing, "Louis Armstrong—the hottest music this side of hell."[51]

While in California, Armstrong received some welcome news: his latest recordings were selling better than ever. "Louis Armstrong tops the Columbia record sales with 'Home' and 'All of Me,' greatest hits of the season," the *Pittsburgh Courier* reported in April.[52] *Variety* started running a monthly chart of the best-selling Columbia records by city. On the March chart, the coupling of "Love You Funny Thing" and "New Tiger Rag" was number one in New York, beating out pop records by Kate Smith, Eddy Duchin, Ben Selvin, and Ruth Etting. "All of Me" was number one in Chicago, followed by "Between the Devil and the Deep Blue Sea" at number two and "You Can Depend on Me" at number four. And in Los Angeles, "All of Me" was number one, "Kicking the Gong Around" was number three, and "You Can Depend On Me" was number six.[53] The results were even more impressive in the "April Music Survey," with "Love You Funny Thing" charting in New York; "All of Me," "You Can Depend on Me," and "Keeping out of Mischief Now" dominating in Chicago; and "Love You Funny Thing," "Kicking the Gong Around," and "I Got Rhythm" selling heavily in California.[54]

Armstrong's RCA Victor contract was due to start on May 8, but as the label's number one seller, OKeh was not going to let him go easily. In late May, they sued RCA, claiming the final option on their contract with Armstrong didn't expire until May 6, 1933. Naturally, RCA was upset—published reports stated that they had signed Armstrong to replace Rudy Vallee—and prepared for a battle in court.[55] Both labels must have salivated when *Variety* published its "May Music Survey," now with more Armstrong selections than ever.[56]

Armstrong was now getting noticed by major media outlets and became the subject of a profile in *Time* magazine on June 13. The article painted him out to be a "bad boy" of sorts, much like mainstream profiles of rap and hip-hop artists in the latter part of the century. Titled "Black Rascal," it mentioned his "jail sentence in his past for using drugs," described an "enraging" Armstrong smashing his trumpet after being accused of playing a trick horn, offered images of Armstrong smoking "Muggles" and swigging from a phial with mysterious contents ("said to be dope") onstage, and ended with stories of radio being "a little wary of his improvisations," adding, "Several times he has been switched quickly off the air for getting profane or slipping in sly remarks about his friends' extra-marital escapades." The lawsuit between Victor and OKeh was even mentioned, *Time* accurately observing, "In Depression not many phonograph artists are worth fighting over but Victor and Okeh are both aware that more than 100,000 Louis Armstrong records sold during the past year." In the middle of all the vague scare tactics, the profile did at least acknowledge Armstrong's work ethic. "Louis Armstrong may have developed a fancy man's taste for clothes, travelling with 20 trunks full of them," it read. "But no black man works harder than he does."[57]

Armstrong closed at Sebastian's Cotton Club on June 22 and headed back east for a short rest. Two days later, England's *Melody Maker* held up its printing press for 24 hours so it could publish some exciting breaking news: "LOUIS ARMSTRONG COMING TO LONDON."[58]

9

"The Real Test Is Entertainment"

July–November 1932

Between 1929 and 1932, three British magazines, *Melody Maker*, the *Gramophone*, and *Rhythm*, regularly featured breathless reviews of Armstrong's OKeh discs, issued overseas by Parlophone. "Whew! What a trumpet player!" *Rhythm* gushed in its review of "Shine" and "If I Could Be with You."[1] Edgar Jackson reviewed Armstrong records monthly in the *Gramophone*, praising "The extraordinary versatility of both Louis Armstrong and his orchestra! It is really amazing."[2] Jackson didn't mind the "commercial" stuff, calling a pairing of "Confessin'" and "Song of the Islands" "two of the very best records"[3] Armstrong made, and he found the trumpet pyrotechnics on "Tiger Rag" "amazing," summing it up by calling Armstrong "a natural genius."[4] The *Melody Maker* used silly pseudonyms for its reviewers with "Needlepoint" being Jackson and "Mike" being bandleader Spike Hughes. They could be a little tougher at times on Armstrong, but often were still full of praise, sometimes to the point of not knowing what to say. "It really becomes increasingly difficult to say anything intelligent about Louis Armstrong, and I am almost tempted to think that I have done my duty by the Parlophone Company if I just mention the records and leave it at that," Hughes wrote of "Dinah" and "Chinatown," adding, "But honestly what can one say about the Great Fun-Man of music?"[5]

In addition to Armstrong's popularity there, Johnny Collins had experience working in England during his vaudeville days and though nearly 20 years had gone by, he must have been confident enough in the territory to book Armstrong, getting him a plum engagement at the Palladium. On July 8, Armstrong, Collins, and Alpha Smith climbed aboard the RMS *Majestic* ship and set sail for England.[6] *Rhythm* magazine reached out to Armstrong on his second day at sea and commissioned him to write a column. The resulting article, "Greetings to Britain!," was at least partially ghostwritten, but still conveyed much of Armstrong's actual feelings. "I believe that my style of playing is unique, but I am not so swollen-headed as to suppose that everyone likes it," he wrote. "I only count myself fortunate that there are sufficient people who find it interesting or amusing enough to fill the house." He also addressed musicians who relied on novelty, writing, "Some people are tempted to perform certain 'stunts' or novelties just because they are novel. But the real test is entertainment. Does it interest your audience? Of course, you can gradually teach them to appreciate new styles and absorb new ideas, but it must be gradual and they must have no idea that you are 'teaching.'"[7]

The buzz surrounding Armstrong's arrival was tremendous. The *Melody Maker* prepared a reception and dinner in his honor at the Ambassador Hotel, sending Technical Editor Dan S. Ingram to meet him when he docked at Southampton. But when Johnny Collins followed up with a radiogram stating that the *Majestic* was going to arrive in Plymouth instead, Ingman could only exclaim, "Consternation!"[8] Armstrong's arrival in Plymouth served as the setting for the most oft-told story of his lifetime, how he got the nickname "Satchmo." In 1960, this is how he told it to John McClellan and Herman Chittison on the television show, *Dateline Boston: The Jazz Scene*:

> The *Melody Maker* met me in Plymouth. And my name was "Satchelmouth" at that time, see? And he grabbed my hand and said, "Hello, Satchmo!" You remember Percy Brooks, strictly English? I say, "Well, uh, whatcha say, Daddy?" But I waited until I got to my trombone player who was with me in the band then—no, the trumpet player, what's the trumpet player that speaks French fluently? And he just died. He used to run on the boats. He was my second trumpet man. He was very good. Charlie something. I asked him, "Why in the hell he call me 'Satchmo' when my name is 'Satchelmouth'?" So he say, "Cause the man thought you had mo' mouth!"[9]

It's a great story, though definitely problematic. The "Charlie" Armstrong refers to is most likely Charlie Johnson, who played trumpet with him at the Palladium, but Johnson had not arrived in England yet—could the "Satchmo" incident have happened later? Other times, he said it was his "trombone man," but again, Armstrong didn't travel with a band so it's not likely he had a musician nearby in Plymouth. There's also the fact that because of the Southampton confusion, the *Melody Maker* didn't have anyone in Plymouth. And as Dan Ingman said of Percy Brooks, "He certainly did not meet Louis at Plymouth and say, 'Hello Satchmo.'"[10] Brooks and Ingman *were* on hand for his arrival at Paddington Station from Plymouth—could it have happened there? The fact is someone said it somewhere because when *Melody Maker* published a two-page spread about his arrival in their August 1932 cartoon, they included a little cartoon drawing of Armstrong addressing his trumpet and saying, "Speak to 'em, Satch 'mo." And in the accompanying article, Ingman wrote, "His technique, tone and mastery over his instrument (which he calls 'Satchmo' a contraction, I am told, of 'Satchel Mouth') is uncanny." Thus, it might not have been Brooks in Plymouth but *someone* early in the trip heard Armstrong refer to his trumpet as "Satchelmouth," shortened it to "Satchmo," put it in the *Melody Maker*, and gave him his most famous nickname.

At the train station, Ingman saw a "small, slight fellow with an enormous white cap and a long biscuit-coloured blanket coat" and asked, "Where was Louis?" Collins responded, "This is Mr. and Mrs. Armstrong." "I nearly collapsed!" Ingman wrote. "From his photograph I had been expecting a six-footer, broad in proportion, with a moustache, and at least thirty-five years of age. And this boy—! I hardly believed it. That is, not until he spoke: there was absolutely no chance of mistaking that voice!"[11]

Collins never booked a hotel for Armstrong, so Ingman quickly began phoning around London for a room. He quickly encountered the same discriminatory practices that were common in the United States. "When Mr. Armstrong arrived in London the other night, it took his friends nearly an hour to find an hotel that would put him up," future Parliament member Tom Driberg reported in the *Daily Express*. "Had his skin been brown instead of black, had he been idle and wealthy and a maharajah, instead of merely one of the world's greatest exponents of his particular art, the snob-hotels of Mayfair would, of course, have laid down red carpets."[12] They finally found accommodations at the Howard Hotel, a small establishment just off the Strand. Ingman got Armstrong to his room, promised to return in the morning, and finally fell asleep at 5 A.M.

The next day, Ingman helped get Armstrong's horn to Boosey and Hawkes for repair. Word got around, eventually reaching trumpeter Nat Gonella. Gonella was in awe, but also was immodest enough to know that he had a little something to do with Armstrong being in England. "Because it was with me, pumping out Armstrong, doing impressions of him in my little way that sort of got the public interested in Armstrong to a certain degree, made it possible for him to come to England," he said.[13] Gonella went down to Boosey and Hawkes and talked his way to delivering it to Armstrong personally. "I think they got Louie out of bed, got him respectable looking, and I met him for the first time," he said. "I didn't bow to him as I thought I would have done, but I gave him the trumpet, told him where it come from and broke the ice quietly about what I was doing, I was a trumpet player. Of course, naturally, he was very interested. And from that moment, we were great pals."[14]

Once at the reception at the Ambassador Hotel, Armstrong was greeted by a telegram from popular bandleader Jack Hylton, offering "a hearty welcome to England and all my best wishes for a terrific success at the Palladium on

Monday." The reception was packed with musicians and writers, all of whom enjoyed being in Armstrong's company. "Louis Armstrong surely had the best send-off which any Monarch, etc., etc., could wish for," Gibson Young wrote in the *Daily Express*. "He charmed us all with that enormously dentiferous smile and his modest politeness."[15] The program for the event also listed a seven-course dinner, something Armstrong was not accustomed to—and something that quickly frustrated him. "So I'm straight, sitting there, sharp," he said. "And I noticed these waiters, you know, they'll bring you this one course and one course and something like this. 'Motherfucker, put that back!' Every time I look for my plate, it's gone! So we named them 'the snatchers!'"[16]

Armstrong's backing band arrived from Paris on Saturday afternoon. There had been rumors that Armstrong would use one of the British bands, perhaps Spike Hughes's organization, but as Edgar Jackson reported, "the powers that be decided that the public would expect a coloured band, and so there had been a hunt round for Negro musicians." Paris had more black musicians than England, but as Jackson observed, "The quantity was obtained, but the quality was dire."[17] Still, the rehearsals became an event, with musicians hanging outside the doors, listening through the cracks to what was happening inside. Armstrong himself remembered that though the band was black, they were from different parts of the world and not all of them were as fluent in African American slang as their leader. "When we were first rehearsing in London, you know, [with] all these different nations," he remembered, "like we say in America, when a band is jumping, we say, 'Swing, you cats!' And I did that and all of them ran off the stage! They thought I was mad!"[18]

Finally, Armstrong's Palladium debut arrived on Monday, July 18. Nat Gonella and his brother Bruts purchased first-row seats for every show and were nervous with anticipation. "You were just wondering if you were going to be impressed as much as you were with the records," Nat Gonella said."[19] For all of its prestige, the Palladium was another vaudeville house, offering a variety bill featuring acts such as the Three Swifts, a "club-juggling" act; the team of Harold and Lola, who did a "snake dance"; and the "Joyful Jovers," a combination of "eccentric musicians" and "straight acrobats."[20] Armstrong closed the first half of the bill. On opening night, he received an enthusiastic introduction from singer George Chisholm, who called him a "great artist." "Before he could mention Armstrong's name, there went up a roar of welcome that culminated in pandemonium as soon as Armstrong stuck his head through the curtains," according to one report.[21]

In the audience was 17-year-old Leonard Feather, who had his life changed when he heard Armstrong's recording of "West End Blues." Feather was in Paris in July 1932 but took his first ever trip in an airplane to be there for

Armstrong's opening. "The Palladium curtains parted, and Louie was fronting this makeshift band, which was composed mainly of black musicians that he recruited on the continent, and he launched into 'Sleepy Time Down South,'" Feather remembered. "The legend became flesh and blood."[22]

With all of that buildup, Armstrong only had time for four full numbers: "Them There Eyes," "When You're Smiling," "Chinatown, My Chinatown" (this one "dedicated to the musicians"), and "I'll Be Glad When You're Dead You Rascal You." "Each one was received with tumult," Ingman wrote. "The packed house absolutely rose to it. There is no doubt, of course, that musicians preponderated the house—familiar faces were everywhere—but members of the lay public, once they had got over their astonishment, were equally enthusiastic."

In his second show that night, Armstrong, sufficiently warmed up, swapped in "Confessin'" and "Tiger Rag." "Oh, that was madhouse, yes," Gonella said of "Tiger Rag." "He'd do it so fast, you could hardly keep up with him. That was a show-off, of course. . . . For a man to have a lip like that, you know, was ridiculous. After playing for, say, 12 choruses and then doing all these top notes at the end, I mean, it was ridiculous really, wasn't it?"[23]

Indeed, musicians like Gonella made up the most enthusiastic fans that first night. "Cause it was so overpowering, it was so much *more* Armstrong, so much *more* thrilling than every record could be," Gonella said. "And to see the man in the flesh and his funny little antics, and his perspiring, etc., really was—well, they use the word fantastic a lot now, don't they? Well, it really was fantastic. A dream coming true."[24] Spike Hughes, who admitted to "suffering from a growing indifference to Armstrong's records," called his appearance "Heaven's gift." "For the benefit of those who were unable to see the Great Fun-Man of Music let me say that Armstrong is all, and a hundred per cent more than, he impresses you as being when recorded," Hughes wrote.[25]

The jazz writers were impressed, too. Ingman wrote of Armstrong's eight choruses on "Tiger Rag" ("all different!") and praised his range ("Top F's bubble about all over the place, and never once does he miss one"), his singing ("It's like it is on the records, only a thousand times more so!") and what he described as "the most amazing thing": Armstrong's personality. "He positively sparkles with showmanship and good humour the whole time."[26] Jackson agreed about Armstrong's personality, writing, "The grotesque dynamic little spark was everywhere at once. Those high F's tumbled out of his trumpet one after another, and, with the amazing expressions which rapidly chased each other across his face, to appropriate antics from his lithe body, his crazy singing became a thing of even greater wonder and entertainment."[27] But Armstrong's future biographer Max Jones, only 15 at the time, remembered a

Figure 9.1 Jack Hylton (to the right of Armstrong) and members of his popular British dance band meet Armstrong in his dressing room at the London Palladium in the summer of 1932.
Courtesy of the Louis Armstrong House Museum

"smallish but power-packed figure prowling the stage restlessly, menacingly almost, and growling and gesticulating when he was not playing, singing or talking into the microphone. . . . I remember doubting if he was in full control of himself."[28]

Jones was not alone. Some folks were aghast at Armstrong's antics and walked out of his initial performances, angering Gonella. "And we really got mad at this, my brother and I," he said, "We couldn't believe these people that left the two evenings previously. As they came out, we were so mad, we were tripping them over! We sat down in the aisle . . . and as they went down either side, my brother was tripping them on one side, and I was tripping them up the other side."[29]

Judging by the reviews he received, some of those walking out might have been critics. Tom Driberg described his vocalizing by writing, " 'Singing,' indeed, is hardly an adequate description of those incoherent, ecstatic, rhythmical jungle noises which none of Armstrong's imitators have yet succeeded in rivaling. This savage growling is as far removed from English as we speak or sing it—and as modern—as James Joyce."[30] Some critics became obsessed with his handkerchiefs, his sweating, and his neck. "He can't help the fact that his neck bulges like a gorged python when he is playing, though they say he wears a low-cut collar in New York night clubs so that people can get a good look at the swelling," reported the *Sunday Mail* in Glasgow. "Nor can he control the perspiration that drips off him like water on to the stage, forcing him to change into a new suit after every house, because the one he has been wearing is wringing wet. His jungle antics are a very necessary frenzy, I should imagine, to achieve notes beyond the compass of the piano."[31] In a column titled "Storm over Negro Trumpeter," Hannen Swaffer described people leaving early, as well as a woman with her hands over her ears, and quoted a theater manager, "determined to hear it through," saying, "I wanted to know what he was going to do next. I have never seen such a thing. I thought he might play the trumpet before he was through. Besides, I could not understand one word he said. It sounded to me like . . . no, I cannot spell it and I cannot say it."[32]

A follow-up column by Swaffer in the *Daily Herald* produced one of the most negative, racist, and horrifying reviews Armstrong ever received. After admitting that Armstrong "is the most amazing performer the stage has seen for months," Swaffer dug in:

> Armstrong is the ugliest man I have ever seen on the music-hall stage. He looks, and behaves, like an untrained gorilla. He might have come straight from some African jungle and then, after being taken to a slop tailor's for a ready made dress-suit, been put straight on the stage and told to "sing." His singing is dreadful, babyish, uncouth. Yet, while he makes animal noises into the microphone which sends the sound to a loud-speaker at the side, he makes love to the instrument as though it were a dusky belle![33]

Swaffer's columns went off like a bomb. Multiple articles referred to the controversy, with headlines like "The Armstrong War." Swaffer attempted to defend himself by claiming Armstrong wasn't offended. "Armstrong himself is by no means angry with my reference to his looks," he wrote. "After all, he has seen himself in the glass several times and he has got used to it." Swaffer claimed that Armstrong was only bothered by one section: the part about the "slop tailor"; Armstrong defended his wardrobe consisting of 139 suits made from the finest tailors in the United States.[34]

Swaffer might have been right about Armstrong's overall reaction to his column. Nat Gonella remembered all the comparisons to a gorilla and said, "Of course, this wasn't averse for Armstrong; it publicized him much more.

Everybody wanted to see who the 'gorilla' was!"[35] Sure enough, Armstrong and Collins worked on compiling a scrapbook of all of Armstrong's press in England and Swaffer's articles, along with other negative columns, were peppered throughout.

Apparently, Armstrong toned it down a little as his Palladium run continued. "Louis Armstrong in his second week, worked a little more piano than last week and was, consequently, more acceptable to English audiences," wrote one critic. "His music is far too hot for a mere Wagnerian-Straussian-Beethovenian like myself to give a just verdict upon. The audience thought him sublime."[36]

One evening at the Palladium, Armstrong was visited backstage by Ben Davis, a British saxophonist who established the Selmer Company in London in 1928 with the blessing of Henri Selmer, founder of Selmer instruments in France. Davis brought along a new Selmer "Challenger" trumpet. "That Ben Davis came down with this nice new horn and asked if I thought I could use it," Armstrong recalled in 1968. "I told him if he was giving it to me I could play it all right. Up to that time, back home, I'd paid for all my new horns. So I took it straight out on stage that night and played my show on it, and I been using one like it ever since."[37] On July 26, he wrote a handwritten letter to Selmer, stating, "I specialize in the top register and beyond it. A Climax finish on a high F or even high G is frequently vital and these notes come easier on the Selmer than on any other trumpet I have ever used. . . . And as for its tone and timing I find it faultless. You sell a wonderful instrument and I was lucky to have discovered it during my visit to London." That was all Davis needed. He published the entire letter in an advertisement in the September issue of *Rhythm* announcing that Armstrong's famed "Satch'—Mo'" trumpet was now a Selmer. It was the start of a relationship that would last until the end of Armstrong's life.[38]

Armstrong was also thrilled to find the Prince of Wales in the audience three times in a single week, calling him "a grand fella." News trickled out that the rest of the Royal Family showed up, but Armstrong put an end to such talk, telling one reporter, "Say, put in this article that all crap about the King and Queen coming to see me, etc., is just a lot of hooey. They never did get around to it, although one of their high-grand guards all done up in feathers, brought me a card which would have gotten me into seeing the palace. . . . But, shucks, I said. If they were too busy to see me at the theatre, then, I wouldn't bother them at home."[39]

After his two weeks at the Palladium, Armstrong rested for about 10 days before going back to work with a professional British outfit made up of white musicians, Billy Mason's Hot Rhythm Recording Band. After a pair of concerts in Nottingham and York for the *Melody Maker*, Armstrong did a week at the Glasgow Empire in Scotland, once again dividing the opinions of the audience. "To some he was the last word in syncopation and rhythm—to others something akin to musical savagery," read one report. "To everybody he was something new and very forceful."[40] The anonymous "Bass Clef" was not amused, writing, "I would advise the thousands of players who are taking the *Daily Record* Theory Course not to accept Armstrong as a musical model, despite the applause which his turn invariably receives."[41]

After a full month playing all over London, Armstrong spent the rest of September performing one week each at the Liverpool Empire, the Birmingham Empire, and the Sheffield Empire. "Here we are in dear ole Liverpoole and everything's just lovely as usual," Armstrong wrote to female trumpeter Mabel "Hixie" Hicks on September 17. "I am still swinging with my English orchestra and pal, we are still Stopping All Shows." Armstrong sent Hicks reviews from *Rhythm* and *Melody Maker*, but didn't harp on any ugliness, instead accentuating the positive aspects of each one. "I merely (only) sent them because I thought you would appreciate reading about how

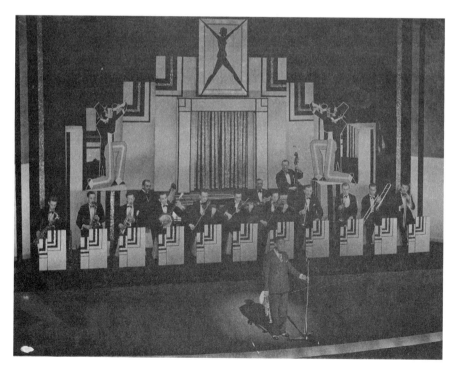

Figure 9.2 Armstrong onstage at the Trocadero in Elephant and Castle, London, in August 1932, backed by the orchestra of Debroy Somers.
Courtesy of the Louis Armstrong House Museum

wonderful and plain spoken these Critics were, etc.," he wrote. "What really amuses me is—no matter what the Critics said, they'd always wound up by saying something partaining [*sic*] to 'Marvelous Trumpet player,' etc. Oh I Think they're interesting."[42]

Hicks had written to Armstrong first, worrying about the quality of the bands backing him up in England. Armstrong had no complaints, regardless of what the critics were saying. "All the boys had to do was Swing as I told 'em to do—and they did," he said. "I explains to these musicians—in fact all musicians I work with—just what I want behind me. And it is honestly so simple until any musician that's halfway up with the times will grasp understand? No pal—never no trouble. And you can take it from me—The musicians over here are just as hot or hotter than most musicians in America."

Armstrong ended his letter with an early iteration of what would become his philosophy of life. "Oh girl you sho said a mouthful when you said you bet I was the happiest man in the world—Well I am—Everything and Everybody's marvelous to me," he said. "Even the world is marvelous. A man can't help but be happy especially when he feels good and in the very best of health. What more does he needs—'eh? No more."[43]

The very next day, writing from Birmingham, England, Armstrong shared some breaking news with his friend Mezz Mezzrow. "The Victor Record Co. has just won the case from the Okeh Record Co. and wired Mr. Collins that all's well and I can start on my new Victor contract which replaces the Rudy Vallee anytime. Gee, Gate, what a victory that is to win from our boy Rockwell. Looka heah, Looka heah. Now just watch those good royalties—dividends—shares—'n' everything else. Ha. Ha. And the contract Pop's (MR. COLLINS) made with these people for me, why you've never heard of one like it before. And that includes the ole King of Jazz himself Paul Whiteman. Nice, eh?"[44]

Armstrong also had a favor to ask of Mezzrow. Collins had booked Armstrong for another month of performances, followed by two weeks off in Paris and then they would sail home, taking "the round about way," which would extend his journey. "I'd like for you to start right in and pack me enough orchestrations to last me the whole trip," Armstrong stated. "Will ya? Now you must look into this matter and give it your best attention, hear Gate? If you ever done anything at all for your Boy, do it now, then our troubles are over." Mezzrow was a clarinetist and bandleader so to some reading this letter, it made sense that "orchestrations" would mean musical arrangements—and that's just what Armstrong wanted people to think. In reality, this was Armstrong's secret way of asking for enough marijuana to last him until he got home![45]

Armstrong had already wired Mezzrow the money and told him to ship the stash to the American Express Company in Paris, France. Armstrong then made small talk, asking about friends in Harlem, mentioning plans to go on a tour of Paramount Theaters, as well as another trip down south ("THAT'S WHERE THE MONEY LIES," he wrote) and even told Mezzrow to make sure he was taking a laxative, in this case, Abilene Water. But just in case Mezzrow missed the code, Armstrong grew a little more explicit: "What we want to keep in mind now is the orchestrations (MUTA) in Paris," "muta" being slang for marijuana.

Armstrong was full of praise for Johnny Collins in his letters home but Collins was rubbing many in England the wrong way. "Well, he was a typical Yank that you would see in these gangster films, you know, with a big cigar out of the corner of his mouth," Gonella remembered. "He'd never take the cigar out of his mouth. Tough guy, gangster I should think."[46] Collins wasn't, but liked to act like one. Right before Armstrong was about to perform one evening, Collins suddenly barked, "Where's the dough? If I don't get the dough, Louis don't play." Dan Ingman witnessed this and kept his eye on Armstrong. "It must have been humiliating for Louis, though he showed no sign of it," Ingman said. "He just looked at the floor and went on swinging his trumpet in his hand until such time as matters were settled. He seemed utterly detached as this pasty-faced man with the cigar in his mouth demanded the money there and then, or no show." After receiving bags of silver, a satisfied Collins turned to Armstrong and said, "Okay, Louis." "I felt that he was telling his 'boy' to go on," Ingman said. "And of course Louis went on and did his stuff, as he always did, magnificently. Two things impressed me about his attitude. He was docile, this world-famous musician, subservient in the presence of Collins. And he was the one in the party who behaved himself best. The grandson of a slave, as he used to tell me, and he was the gentleman. Everything he did was right in an embarrassing situation for which we were all responsible to a degree."[47] Collins had no regrets about his behavior and actually thrived on it. "The management of artists in America is a much more serious matter over there than here," Angus Scott wrote. "In fact, it is not too much to say that when an American artist has assigned his business by contract to a manager, he is no longer his own master, but immediately acquires a boss. Louis Armstrong, for instance, does just what he is told by Johnny Collins in all matters, evidently being satisfied that he is under an all-wise direction." That blurb was cut out and affixed into a scrapbook by Collins—who circled the last sentence with a red pencil.[48]

The end of Armstrong's British tour inspired lots of reflection. "Louis Armstrong is a charming personality," wrote a columnist in Leeds, who concluded, "Personally, I prefer to hear him on a gramophone record. On the stage he mixes 'showmanship' with his playing. A more restrained show would appeal better to his audiences who are apt to judge his playing by his fantastic gestures and vocal effects."[49] As Armstrong's time in England came to an end, it was indeed his showmanship that left a bad taste in the mouths of many of his admirers. "The sweating, strutting figure in the spotlight hitting endless high notes had only a tenuous and intermittent connection with the creator of the intensely moving music of 'West End Blues' and 'Muggles,'" said Iain Lang.[50]

This was an issue. His onstage persona hadn't changed but some critics had a certain image in mind based on his recordings—especially the ones from the 1920s—and seeing him live shattered that image. One British critic wrote, "Coming to Armstrong's records, however, I am now confronted with another little aesthetic and critical problem, for I cannot reconcile the electric, incessant energetics of the entirely delightful personal Armstrong, both on the stage and off, with the lazy and charming person I had conceived in my mind's eye as the Armstrong of the records."[51] "The main trouble is to reconcile the Armstrong of the stage with the Armstrong of the records *before* his appearance over here," Spike Hughes and Dan Ingman wrote. "It is all very difficult and worrying, for it means revising one's whole attitude towards his records, an attitude which is the result of several years' listening and study. So sad."[52] They didn't want to admit it at the time, but the opinions of most of the original British worshippers would change gradually but dramatically after his visit.

After some time off in Paris, where he first met 20-year-old French jazz authority Hugues Panassie, Armstrong returned to the United States on the *Majestic* on November 2. British musicians remained divided in their opinions of his worth after he left the country. *Melody Maker* published a "What I Think of Armstrong" piece that featured quotes that ran the gamut from Britain's leading musicians. There was much praise, but also a common refrain. "I would rather enjoy his records than hear the man in the flesh, however," reedman Joe Crossman stated, adding, "His actual presence gave me, in a sense, a shock, and I much regret to have to admit to finding something of the barbaric in his violent stage mannerisms." Composer Reginald King regarded Armstrong's show "as an insult to any musician," while bandleader Percy Bush called it "A disgusting and abortive exhibition, likely to nauseate all decent men." Even after describing Armstrong as "Marvellous!," drummer Billy Harty quickly added, "But very certainly not for the public."[53]

Perhaps the best summary of Armstrong's impact on England came early on in his stay when Dudley Leslie caught one of his first shows at the Palladium and addressed the naysayers, writing, "Adore it, or deplore it—do whatever comes natural—but at least try to realise you are criticising the music of to-morrow, not the polkas of Victoria. . . . The music you hate so fervently is less the invention of Mr. Louis Armstrong than the rage of 1935." He concluded his eloquent editorial:

> Look at the facts: Matisse was criticised, Wagner slaughtered, Van Gogh despised, John Ignored, Epstein tarred and feathered. What more proof of genius do you need than the lashings of adverse criticism? It is the same old story, through the ages and through the arts. Interpret anything unusually new, and it will live in glory the moment you are dead.[54]

10
"Always a Way, Man"

November 1932–June 1933

Armstrong's return to America didn't get any mainstream press coverage in outlets such as the *New York Times* or *Time*, leading Leonard Feather to later assume "the American press didn't carry a single word about Louie's conquest that he had made in Europe because jazz just wasn't news, wasn't even recognized as an important art form in America at that time."[1] But Feather forgot about an important outlet in the United States: the black press had been following Armstrong's British journey every step of the way.[2] The *Afro-American* even published an interview with Armstrong about the tour when he got back. "Er—well, London's all right in spots," he said, calling it a "big, old dirty town. Reminded me of the warehouses in South Philly—you know 'em. The people are kind of funny. Hard to understand. But, that first week they wowed me with, 'Ohh, Mr. Armstrong, cawn't you play those dwipping Sawnt Louis Blues, et?' Now, you know, pal—I had to go some to get around stuff like that! But they seemed to like me, anyway."[3]

Armstrong's huge African American fan base was aware of what he accomplished overseas and couldn't wait to welcome him home. He arrived in New York on November 9 and made a beeline to Harlem. His destination of choice might have surprised some: Connie's Inn. Since the trial ended in January and with Rockwell now out of the picture (though still receiving his $150 a week), Collins felt comfortable dealing with the Immerman brothers again, negotiating to have Armstrong star in a new revue, "Hot Chocolates of 1932," that would begin in late November and would be co-produced by Collins and George Immerman.

After receiving a "tremendous ovation" at Connie's, Armstrong headed to see famed barkeep Big John, bringing along Paddy Harlow, a trumpet player who played on the *Majestic*.[4] Harlow begged Armstrong to show him Harlem and was now experiencing the real thing as Armstrong opened the door to Big John's and started trading greetings and nicknames with those present.

"Whattaya say, Gate!"

"Whatcha say, Douchebag!"

"Hey, Gizzard!"

Harlow got all excited and yelled, "Oh my God! What is my moniker?"

"And Alpha stood right up," Armstrong recalled, "and said, 'Majestic Face!' And killed that son-of-a-bitch!"[5]

Melody Maker writer Bill Mather was also along for the ride and described Armstrong's welcome at Big John's as "absolutely unheralded," saying Armstrong "was penned in his corner by a crowd of musician friends about six feet thick!"[6] The party continued at Mike's, where Slim Thompson, noticing a coin-operated jukebox, put a nickel in and selected Armstrong's recording of "All of Me." Armstrong fondly recalled the memory 20 years later as Thompson "led about 40 cats all singing just like the record! You talking about beautiful! I wish I had a mike that night. . . . It was just like a glee club. Yeah, everybody in that place!"[7]

Armstrong and his crew left at 6 A.M. and finished the day with breakfast at the Sunset Restaurant before doing it all over again the next night with a stop at Small's Paradise and more late-night hangs. He was a king in Harlem, but he soon returned with Alpha to their home in Chicago, where he rested for a few weeks. Meanwhile, Collins formalized the contract with the victorious Eli Oberstein of RCA Victor, now re-dated to cover the period of November 15, 1932, to November 14, 1933.[8] Armstrong was due to start the new "Hot Chocolates" revue on November 26 but he didn't have a band and there wasn't enough time to assemble one from scratch. Collins solved that by hiring Chick Webb's Orchestra to back Armstrong for the time being.

"Hot Chocolates of 1932" was to have tryout performances before black audiences at the Lafayette Theatre in Harlem and the Pearl Theatre in Philadelphia before opening on Broadway. "The general idea, according to Johnny Collins and George Immerman, producers of the show, is to keep the entire proceeding entirely Negroid, and the only way to know that it is Negroid is to exhibit to colored audiences, say the producers," reported the *Philadelphia Inquirer*.[9] The *New York Age* caught a performance at the Lafayette and praised Armstrong's showmanship: "He is a musical clown but a lovable one and puts his whole soul into his work, which is something few of our artists do—they are far too busy thinking of the money they are going to draw."[10]

While in Philadelphia, Eli Oberstein booked Armstrong and the Webb Orchestra to record at RCA's famous church studio in Camden, New Jersey, on December 8. Armstrong personally invited Mezz Mezzrow to the session, wanting to spend more time with his friend who helped him out with the "orchestrations" in Paris. Mezzrow said that Armstrong had done five "Hot Chocolates" shows and two broadcasts and showed up to the session exhausted and with a new problem: a sore lip. "I didn't see how poor old Pops was going to blow note one," Mezzrow wrote.[11] Armstrong overcame the pain to play magnificently on the first two numbers, a soaring "That's My Home" (a sequel to "When It's Sleepy Time Down South" by the Rene Brothers) and an exciting "Hobo, You Can't Ride This Train," his tone brilliantly captured by the Victor engineers. But by the third tune, Fats Waller's "I Hate to Leave You Now," he was showing signs of duress. In his climactic solo, he sounds like a boxer in the final round, a little out of gas but with enough smarts and pure power to flurry when it counts, emptying the tank with a series of bone-chilling high A's before resolving to a high C at the final bell. The finale was "You'll Wish You'd Never Been Born," a complete rip-off of "I'll Be Glad When You're Dead You Rascal You." He opens with one of his patented unaccompanied cadenzas but takes his time, creating something dramatic out of the pain, unable or unwilling to play it safe. Armstrong's chops were not about to heal quickly.

After more performances of "Hot Chocolates of 1932" at the Howard Theater in Washington DC—where he began featuring Jimmy McHugh and Dorothy Fields's new song, "On the Sunny Side of the Street"—Armstrong went back to Philadelphia by himself to do a week at the Lincoln Theatre, accompanied by a pit band led by trumpeter Charlie Gaines. The band included 24-year-old alto saxophonist Louis Jordan, who called Armstrong "the greatest." and said the experience was "a lot of fun because he's always happy. . . . Most of the time, if he was with the fellows, he was always carrying on some foolishness."[12] Armstrong recorded two "Medleys of Armstrong Hits" with this band on December 21, an attempt to beat OKeh by having fresh versions of some of his best-known numbers, such as "You Rascal You," "When You're Smiling," and "Dinah." The playing of the backing band was rough going at times, but Armstrong played and sang well, especially on one of his finest renditions of "Sleepy Time Down South." Though "darkies" was still prevalent in the lyrics, he ended with a much more pointed characterization of the Deep South, undoubtedly colored by his 1931 experiences on tour, singing, "When it's slavery time down south"! But on an unreleased alternate take of the second part of the medley, Armstrong's chops troubles came to the fore during the transition to "Dinah," as he attempted a note and produced nothing but the sound of air. He was now struggling in the studio as he never had before.

Armstrong's chops hit rock bottom on Christmas Eve at a dance with Webb's band at Lehmann Hall in Baltimore, vividly described by Mezz Mezzrow, who was still traveling with the band, and who remembered what happened as "one of the most dramatic and pathetic scenes of Louis' career."[13] Already picking at a sore with a needle beforehand, Armstrong came onstage and called "Them There Eyes." "This was the real drama of Louis life, taking place before all those people who thought they were just seeing another good show," Mezzrow said.

> He started to blow his chorus, tearing his heart out, and the tones that came vibrating out of those poor agonized lips of his sounded like a weary soul plodding down the lonesome road, the weight of the world's woe on his bent shoulders, crying for relief to all his people. He was fighting all the way, aiming to see it through and be understood by all, right down to the last heartrending wail of his plea. All the lament and heartache of life, of the colored man's life, came throbbing out through that horn. That wasn't any horn blowing this night. It was the conscience of the whole aching world, shouting damnation at the sins and evil. There were tears in all the eyes around me, tears for what Louis was preaching on that horn, tears for wonderful, overworked, sick and suffering Louis himself, the hero of his race.

As Armstrong approached his final chorus, he headed to the upper register of his horn as everyone backstage "shook with fear." Webb's trombonist, Charlie Green, started crying and left the stage; the entire band was "sobbing," according to Mezzrow. Armstrong somehow climbed up to a final high F, making it on his knees, as the whole place erupted. "Louis stood there holding his horn and panting, his mangled lip oozing blood that he licked, and he managed to smile and bow and smile again, making pretty for the people," Mezzrow recalled. Backstage, Armstrong just grinned and said, "Tough scuffle Mezzie, but that's all in life. Ha!"

It was clear that Armstrong needed to rest. He left the "Connie's Hot Chocolates" tour and went back to Chicago, barely even leaving his home for several weeks. During this time, he met with *Chicago Defender* reporter Hilda See, who caught him in a testy mood. Asked about his plans, Armstrong responded, "Sure, I am going back to work as soon as I rest up a bit, but why bring that up? You know, I never have the chance to forget my work as others do. Whenever I stop in with friends or admirers they persist in talking of music and trumpeting." Armstrong also talked about Europe, See reporting, "He thinks the foreigners are much more human than are we Americans."[14]

Armstrong couldn't rest for long. Collins was getting offers and RCA Victor wanted to make more recordings, especially since the first single of "That's My Home" and "Hobo, You Can't Ride This Train" had been warmly received, Walter Winchell giving it an "orchid" and calling it "a hot plate" and John Edgar Weir calling it "a knockout."[15] It was time to go back to work, and once again Armstrong wanted a regular band behind him. He always referred to his 1931–1932 band as his "happiest band" so it wasn't a surprise that he reached back out to Zilner Randolph to be music director and to Mike McKendrick to return as guitarist and straw boss. Because of the clique-ish nature of that band, though, Randolph did not bring anyone else back and instead filled it with youngsters, including the Oldham brothers, George on reeds and Bill on bass; the Johnson brothers, tenor saxophonist Budd and trombonist Keg; trumpeter Ellis "Stumpy" Whitlock; reedman Scoville Brown; drummer Yank Porter; and a young pianist recommended by the Johnsons, Teddy Wilson. Wilson studied piano and violin at the Tuskegee Institute, which is when he first heard Armstrong's records with Earl Hines and was inspired to become a jazz musician; now, just a few years later, he was in Armstrong's band. "Well, that was really something for me to play with Louis Armstrong, because I had idolized this man so much, and he was as influential in developing music as the piano players that I used to listen to, I would say," Wilson said.[16]

Sufficiently rested, Armstrong went back to work with a vengeance, recording six songs in one session on January 26, three more on January 27, and a final three on January 28. He would follow that with 11 more over a series of sessions in April. Some of the RCA songs are dogs, some of the arrangements are poor, and some of the section-playing from Armstrong's band is woeful but none of it matters; on track after track, Armstrong flies around his horn like Superman, totally in command and able to pull off any and every idea in his mind. He has one foot in his 1920s style, full of flash and playing with joyous abandon. At the same time, he was continuing to mature, using more space in his solos and loving the big, dramatic high-note endings. He was also singing beautifully with that tenor voice of his before the gravel settled. In all, the 1933 RCA recordings are a priceless snapshot of a genius in transition.

The January 26 session stands out as one of Armstrong's finest days in the studio, opening with standout performances of two new Harold Arlen–Ted Koehler songs, "I've Got the World on a String" and "I Gotta Right to Sing the Blues." Each one opens with Armstrong's voice, unleashing his prodigious personality and swinging while simply counting off the band. Other than some impressive Wilson cameos, showing how he ingested the style of Earl Hines, Armstrong is the entire show and loving it, shouting with joy in the background while the band plays. "I Gotta Right to Sing the Blues" is a good illustration of Armstrong's impact on songwriters of the era, as Arlen's melody, based on strings of repeated pitches, sounds like something Armstrong would have improvised. Readying himself for his concluding trumpet solo, he makes one of his most memorable entrances: a single held D. Perhaps the Armstrong of 1928 would have played something flashy and jaw-dropping in this two-bar break, but the Armstrong of 1933 knew he could convey just as much drama and feeling with a perfectly placed held note. How do you make one held note swing? It's all in the placement; Armstrong hits it a shade after the beat and with that special vibrato of his, the whole thing pulsates. The rest of the solo is a masterpiece of storytelling, climaxed by a soul-stirring glissando from a low F to a huge high D during the bridge.

Armstrong's high batting average continued throughout the day, especially on "Sittin' in the Dark," when he indulges in a bit of the grandstanding that was an integral part of his live shows, hitting a series of relentless high C's. It's one of the only examples that survive of Armstrong's exhibitionistic side and though many critics found it appalling, it did impress young Herman Blount—the future Sun Ra. "I was traveling on the road with a band some place in Kentucky or thereabouts," he remembered in 1970. "I heard a recording by Louis in a tavern. The name of it was 'Sittin' in the Dark.' I haven't heard it since, but I still remember the sound-image impression it gave me. His contribution to jazz is immeasurable and his contribution to music is a world thing not fully evaluated yet."[17]

Armstrong also dipped into the past, recording Randolph's up-to-date arrangement of "High Society"—with the band hanging on for dear life—as well as sterling remakes of two OKeh classics, "Basin Street Blues" and "Mahogany Hall Stomp," flexing his muscles on each with his mind-bending use of glisses. Only the band's sloppiness mars Randolph's "Swing You Cats," causing the composer to later lament, "It really wasn't played right. I wish it could have been just really played."[18]

Teddy Wilson admitted that the band had some rough nights, but he was inspired by how Armstrong didn't rely on them. "The band could be terrible, and he just went right straight ahead and played in that world of his own and was never at the mercy of the band," he said.[19] Part of that might have been Armstrong's ability to tune out the other musicians in his group. Drummer Harry Dial joined in March and found the band to be "really putrid" but remembered Armstrong telling him, "I'm only playing by the bass, drums and piano. I ain't paying those other guys no mind." Dial also remembered Armstrong telling Wilson, "I don't want any of that fancy stuff on the piano, I want to hear those changes."[20] Armstrong also was able to tune out the band onstage because he had another band playing in his head. "He told me once that when you play there are always two bands—the one you hire, and yourself," Ruby Braff recalled. "When the hired one is good, you turn them up mentally and dig them. But when they're not, you turn them off and YOU become the band. 'If you spend your life depending on other musicians,' he'd say, 'it's too bad for you.'"[21]

Indeed, there were nights when Armstrong practically was the entire band. In St. Louis, he shared the bill with another group, the Crackerjacks. Before Armstrong took the stage, the Crackerjacks played "Shine" and their trumpeter, Harold "Shorty" Baker, imitated Armstrong. "Well, this kind of upset Pops," Budd Johnson remembered. "He says, 'Can you imagine that? What is he trying to do?'"[22] But Johnson pointed out that Baker was hitting G's, ending on high C, a fourth lower than Armstrong. The Crackerjacks left the stage, Armstrong took over—and immediately called "Shine"! "And that night—I never heard it before and won't ever hear it again—Louis hit about 250 high C's, just *tch, tch, tch*, which will tear a man's chops to pieces," Johnson said. "Man! Then he hit that high F, and held it, and made the walls tremble! The people just looked up at the roof. He wasn't going to take Shorty doing his number and getting a big hand on it!"[23]

St. Louis was just one stop on a tour that included performances in places such as Louisville, Kentucky; Oklahoma; Nebraska; Mississippi; and Texas. Armstrong's reputation as a viper spread to wherever he went, especially in St. Louis when the band showed up to play a dance and noticed each music stand was "filled with reefers" according to Budd Johnson. Six guys walked up to Armstrong and said, "We want to present you with this." "And they held their arms out like that," Johnson continued, "and it was a great big joint rolled in the form of a baseball bat. It must have been about a foot long. And they had taken, like, a fountain pen and punched holes in it to read, 'To the king of the vipers from the vipers club of St. Louis, Missouri.'"[24]

Armstrong's love of marijuana might have helped to save his life in this period. While making a private reel-to-reel tape with some friends in 1953, Armstrong talked about how the effects of marijuana were much better than the effects of alcohol. To illustrate, he told a story from the 1933 tour. As many photos illustrate, Armstrong had a band bus but often preferred to drive in his new Buick in this period. One night, at around 1:30 in the morning, Armstrong was driving into Gary, Indiana, with Alpha and his adopted, developmentally disabled 17-year-old son Clarence, smoking marijuana and "having a ball." They stopped to get some coffee and noticed some "raggedy niggers" in a nearby car. Louis didn't pay attention and instead focused on Clarence, who was "so glad" to be with him. "We'd wrestle, we'd spar, and little things like that," he recalled.

While fooling around with Clarence, he heard one of the men say, "Why don't you kiss him?" Alpha and Clarence didn't hear it, but Louis knew there'd be trouble. "You all get the car," he told them. As the man started to approach them, Louis heard it again.

"Why don't you kiss him?"

Louis turned on his smile and said, "Well, you know, these little cats, man, they think they young, you know, they give us old cats, you know, shit, we're better men anyway, it ain't nothing."

He turned to Clarence and said, "Hey, get in there, little old boy!" and shoved him in. "Then that leaves me," Louis remembered. "I got to go into this nigger almost to get to this steering wheel." Louis continued smiling and talking. "Yeah, these little summitchs think they can wrestle and they think they can win, you know?" He started the car. "But we're better men than them! Ain't that right, Gate? We'd teach those little kids, anytime!"

"And when I pulled off, the nigger pulled out a .45, say, 'See what you missed?' Clarence say, 'Oh, Pops, look out!'" Alpha screamed, too, but Louis remained calm. "He ain't gonna shoot it," he said. "You can't pay him to shoot it. Don't worry. The nigger's in good humor now." This was the major lesson of the story. "All I had to tell him was, 'Nigger, tend to your business and go fuck yourself,' and we all would have been dead," he said. "He just wanted to shoot that pistol, that's all. And nobody out there except us and this nigger and the pistol. And he put the pistol back and goes all the way around the corner. I says, 'Don't worry about it. Light up, that's all. Fuck it.'" Armstrong ended his story simply by saying, "Always a way, man."[25]

The aroma of marijuana could be detected on Armstrong's next series of RCA Victor recordings, 11 more songs recorded at the end of April at the Merchandise Mart in Chicago. Budd Johnson had written an arrangement on "Sweet Sue" with an Armstrong vocal but after singing it in the studio, Armstrong announced, "Now I want my little tenor player to come up here and sing it in the viper's language." "This was a little language that we made up on the road and that we all used to talk," Johnson remembered. "And it took me by surprise, you know, as I wasn't prepared for anything like this. Anyway, I got up and I tried to sing it in the viper language. . . . And Louie said, 'Yeah!' So anyway, do you know—do you know that was picked as the record of the month? That thing was picked as the record of the month and it was very funny."[26]

But the other big marijuana-scented number recorded in April was deemed too far out to even release at the time: "Laughin' Louie." "Louie used to get up there and we wouldn't allow anybody on the recording sessions, you know, unless they were real personal friends, because Louie would like to get high, and he'd like for the band to get high," Johnson said. "So he says, 'We going to record "Laughing Louie" today, gentlemen.' And he says, 'I want everybody to smoke a joint.' So, we all got high and made this 'Laughing Louie.'"[27] Getting everyone high was only part of Armstrong's plan; the other goal was to re-create one of the biggest selling novelty records of the 1920s, "The OKeh Laughing Record," which consisted of nothing more than the sound of an unaccompanied trumpet player practicing, while people start giggling and laughing louder and louder in the background.[28]

Figure 10.1 Snapshot of Louis and his beloved adopted son, Clarence Hatfield Armstrong, in Chicago, 1933.
Courtesy of the Louis Armstrong House Museum

After a corny, almost theatrical introduction, Armstrong steps up to the mike and introduces his vocal, announcing he's going to play his new Selmer trumpet ("bless its little heart"). With everyone obviously feeling high and happy, Armstrong begins to "chirp" the inane lyrics, laughing after every line. After a swinging chorus by the Johnson brothers and another humorous monologue, the "OKeh Laughing Record" parody commences, with cameos by Joe Lindsey of New Orleans, trumpeter Ellis "Stumpy" Whitlock, and Clarence, the last of whom shouting, "Look out there, Pops!"

It's all very silly until the 2:18 mark, when Armstrong begins playing more seriously, unleashing some blistering proto-bebop double-timed lines. With extra time remaining on the disc, Armstrong announces, "Here comes the beautiful part" and starts playing an unaccompanied reading of Minnie T. Wright's sentimental melody, "Love Song," from 1920. Armstrong himself couldn't even remember the title—bandleader Vince Giordano identified it in the 1990s—but he remembered where he learned it, saying on tape, "Of course, that classical number that came at the ending there, I just dubbed that in because we didn't have anything else to put in to close the record, but it came from Erskine Tate's symphony orchestra when I used to play with them at the Vendome in Chicago in 1925."[29] As Armstrong plays "Love Song," the laughter ceases. He lovingly caresses the melody before straining a bit to push out a pained, but glorious high F. The band hits a corny "ta-da" kind of static chord and the record suddenly ends.

RCA Victor didn't know what to make of it and shelved it, eventually issuing it years later on their cheaper Bluebird label. But to this writer, it remains the quintessential recording of Armstrong's career. It contains all his formidable weapons: there's singing, there's scatting, there's double-timed trumpet playing, there's operatic trumpet playing, there's high notes, there's pain, there's laughter, there's slang, there's marijuana. If one were to boil "The Louis Armstrong Experience" down to 210 seconds, then "Laughin' Louie" gives you everything.

The rest of Armstrong's April output was a mixed bag, though, especially regarding the performance of the band. For reasons never explained, bassist Bill Oldham switched to tuba on these sessions, setting the rhythm section back a little bit in terms of drive. Also, Teddy Wilson had left the band, though even his few months with Armstrong were enough for him to later declare, "I think Louis is the greatest musician that's ever been."[30] A number of alternate takes surfaced in the 1990s, really demonstrating the slipshod nature of the band: there are missed cues (as well as miscues), wrong notes, muddy harmonies, and even some trumpet cracks, mostly due to sore chops. But Armstrong still makes each selection worth listening to. For example, on "Dusky Stevedore," the band is very shaky, but Armstrong is so on fire from the opening double-timed cadenza to the closing high notes that the result is still overwhelming (Dan Morgenstern once named it one of his "ten best" Armstrong records, flaws and all[31]). Armstrong's 1932–1933 Victor output features plenty of stunning moments but just as quickly as they began, they ended. Armstrong could not have known it when he walked out of that Chicago studio on April 26, but he wouldn't record again for the label for 13 more years.

On March 26, Armstrong was dealt a blow by the death of his friend, guitarist Eddie Lang, who passed away at the age of 30 due to complications from a tonsillectomy. Lang's death made headlines but not as many as did the death of Louis Armstrong—in April 1933! "Louis Armstrong, known as 'the man with the iron lips,' and the most famous 'hot' trumpeter in the world, has died suddenly in a nursing home in New York, a victim to the terrific strain which his art put on him," came a report out of London, originally in the *Daily Express*, adding "Armstrong gave himself no rest. He was always carried away by his own enthusiasm. He spared himself nothing. . . . It is a great loss to the world of modern music and rhythm that those 'iron lips' will blow no more."[32] The result was pandemonium. "From early morning the telephone rang incessantly," Edgar Jackson wrote. "People of all sorts, from classical musicians to young girls literally in hysterics, were coming through begging to be told that it wasn't true." Jackson concluded "that few pioneers of anything in the nature of a new form of Art are appreciated by the majority until they are dead, or believed to be."[33]

There was no cause of death at first but eventually it was reported that it was from a dog bite. Further reports revealed that no, Armstrong hadn't died, but yes, he was bitten by a dog and was now in critical condition.[34] Rumors continued to spread, with Johnny Collins inundated with telegrams and phone calls. Collins finally fired off a telegram to Walter Winchell to clear up matters, writing, "Armstrong was bitten by a dog, so what?"[35] Armstrong took to setting the record straight himself, writing to Henry "Red" Allen in New York, "Tell 'all the 'Folks in Deah (Dear) 'ol' Harlem—THE TREE— that (I) heard of my—FALSE RUMORS—Death. Tell 'Em (THEM) I ain't fixin to 'leave this good ol' world as good as My 'Little 'Darling 'Alpha Can Cook those good ol' Red Beans + Rice—etc. 'Yeah man."[36] He also sent a telegram to *Rhythm* magazine in England to say, "Thank all the folks for the nice free publicity."[37]

Armstrong left Chicago and embarked on another quiet tour of the Midwest and the south, doing six more days in Memphis—this time without incident—and then playing places like Paducah, Kentucky, and Evansville, Indiana.[38] It was far cry from the Lafayette Theatre in Harlem. Collins no longer seemed capable of getting Armstrong out of the Midwest and southern territories he knew best. Armstrong's band was growing disgusted with Collins, too, and took to going on strike in the middle of May because of money issues. Armstrong didn't want to get involved in any business matters and let Collins and McKendrick handle it. "Louis never would have anything to do with the band," Johnson said. "He always had somebody else handling it, and would never come to our defense."[39] Collins finally gave in and paid the band what they wanted, but the writing was on the wall and the band broke up in late May.

Collins turned his attention back to England, as Armstrong's previous tour was still in the news. "They tell it about Louis Armstrong, gayest of the blackbirds, who with his sizzling orchestra played a command performance before Brit's King and Queen," Walter Winchell reported in May. "To the amazement of everyone, except the King, who laughed, Armstrong turned to him between numbers and flipped: 'Ah'm gonna swing the nex' one fer you—Rex!' "[40] Never mind that it wasn't true and that Armstrong had already told a reporter, "Say, put in this article that all crap about the King and Queen coming to see me, etc., is just a lot of hooey."[41] It was such a good line that Armstrong adopted it and would tell this story until the end of his life (further embellishing it by adding that he dedicated "You Rascal You" to "Rex").

But all (printed) jokes aside, England was on Armstrong's mind. He wrote a letter to a British musician on April 5, reminiscing about his 1932 tour. "Alpha 'n I talks about those days all the time," he wrote. "Maybe some day we'll Come over there again. *Who knows? Eh? Gate* that really would *break it up*, especially the way I understand London n it's people and it's everything. *Gee*, that would be real swell." He sent regards from Johnny Collins and his wife and added praise for Collins's tactics, "Papa (Mr.) Collins sure did believe in protecting us didn't he?"[42]

Armstrong was still resting in Chicago in June, Collins telling the press that it was due to "Armstrong's health," perhaps a reference to chops trouble.[43] While he was convalescing, Duke Ellington made his first tour to England, which probably only increased Armstrong's yearning to return.[44] Finally, on July 1, news broke that Armstrong would be heading back to England, opening at the Holborn Empire on July 31. He once again boarded the *Majestic*, accompanied by Johnny Collins, Mary Collins, and Alpha (listed on the passenger list as Armstrong's "maid"). Coincidentally, John Hammond was also on the voyage, a last-minute decision made to flee the oppressive heat wave in New York. "Louis Armstrong's presence on the *Majestic* was about the most agreeable surprise one could hope for," Hammond wrote in his *Melody Maker* column. "It more than compensated for all the mishaps of the voyage, for we played records and talked every morning until at least six o'clock."[45]

Hammond didn't elaborate further on the "mishaps" at the time but what he was referring to was the end of the relationship between Armstrong and Johnny Collins.

Armstrong told the story to George Avakian and other friends gathered at his home in 1953. With a tape recorder running, Armstrong used the tale to once again advocate for why marijuana was better than alcohol. "Cause I'll get on a soapbox and tell them all they're assholes, trying to down marijuana," he said. "It's the greatest fucking medicine in the world."[46]

The story began on the *Majestic*, where Armstrong was having dinner with Alpha, Hammond, Collins, his wife, and his mother-in-law. Armstrong was admittedly high, but Collins was drinking heavily. "[L]iquor brings out your fucking thoughts sometimes," Armstrong said. "He waited till he got drunk to argue with me about my program." Armstrong said that Collins was "jealous of John Hammond" and wanted to show that he was an expert, too, and could tell Armstrong what to do.

"Well, you know, Mr. Collins, I've been in show business a long time," Armstrong responded. "I'm an old hustler [from] way back. I know that horn better than I know my wife. We play this number, that number, you know, all of them are hand whackers so what the fuck's the difference?"

Collins barked, "Now I want you to play *this!*"

All eyes turned toward Armstrong's table, but he remained calm and cool. "I'm sitting there and I'm mellow, God damn, just *fine*. Motherfucker, [I] say,

Figure 10.2 Armstrong poses with Johnny Collins and one of his first Selmer trumpets in this photograph from c. 1933. Note Armstrong's later annotation describing Collins as his "Ex Manager."
Courtesy of the Louis Armstrong House Museum

'Man, you can't drag me, I feel too good so fuck you.' So I ain't going to get mad about nothing—I hope."

Armstrong controlled his anger as he addressed Collins, explaining why he played the songs he did. Collins interrupted him.

"You'll play—"

"Listen, cocksucker!" Armstrong snapped. "You might be my manager and you might be the biggest shit and book me in the biggest places in the world. But when I get on that fucking stage with that horn and get in trouble, you can't save me. So we'll just as soon play this, that—"

"Take that nigger off the boat!" Collins shouted, banging the table, sending silverware flying.

Everyone was "excited" but Armstrong. He looked at Alpha and told her, "Don't worry about a thing, honey, I've got this shit under control." He stared at a bottle of red wine on the table ("They call them van rouge and vin whatever-the-fuck—it was wine"). "All I had to do was take that and the bald-headed motherfucker had his head down when he said it, I could have just tapped him like a pansy and killed the motherfucker." Armstrong thought better. "But the first thing I thought, all the black cocksuckers in Harlem would say, 'I knew he would blow his top someday!'"

After Collins's outburst, security descended on the table and removed Collins from the dining room in handcuffs. As they escorted him out, Armstrong noticed everyone on the boat giving Collins dirty looks. "You know, I'm a Southern boy," Armstrong whispered to Alpha. "Now, everybody on this boat is against Johnny Collins, the rotten motherfucker, acting like an asshole, you know. They're mad at him. Okay. I'm mad at him too. Now, I hit this motherfucker and bash his fucking brains out, see what I mean? Then it's a different story. They say, 'Wait a minute, it's a white man after all,' see? So I don't fuck with Johnny."

After everything calmed down, Armstrong and Alpha went back downstairs to listen to records with Hammond, the occasion fueled by friendly disagreement over musical opinions. The mood was broken by Collins, who wandered in, looked at Hammond, and snarled, "What the fuck are you doing, you little punk?" Hammond, startled, responded, "What the hell?" Collins only got angrier, yelling, "Get out of here!"[47]

According to Armstrong, Collins "swung at John Hammond, that little young son-of-a-bitch ducked just enough to miss that drunken swing and hit him with a sharp, *hard* jab right on his fucking chops, Pops. Zoom! And I'm standing right behind him. See? He's falling, all I had to do was just catch him with a finger." Armstrong watched this unfurl and did some quick thinking. "I said, 'I can't hit this motherfucker myself—but I sure could let him fall and bash his fucking brains out!' Boom! . . . Let him make an ass out of himself. And he did. All I did was step aside. And that was the same as if I hit him with a fucking right myself."

Collins eventually sobered up and came to Armstrong to apologize. Armstrong wouldn't hear of it. "You're a rotten son-of-a-bitch anyway," he told him. "I've always respected you. You lost my fucking respect for you when you did that. Not that I haven't been called a 'nigger' before. But from you?"

Almost three years to the day that Armstrong started performing at Sebastian's Cotton Club, his relationship with Johnny Collins was over.

11

"What the Hell Is Wrong with Louie Armstrong?"

July 1933–June 1935

When Armstrong came to England in 1932, there was palpable excitement, writers and musicians unable to believe that they were about to witness their hero in the flesh. It was different in 1933; the worshippers no longer worshipped. "I cannot deny that I am apprehensive about it," Edgar Jackson wrote of Armstrong's visit, speaking for many. "Armstrong is still the world's greatest hot trumpet player and an unique singer, but there are unhealthy signs that this 'commercialisation' of his art will ruin him unless he pauses seriously to take stock of where it is leading him."[1]

The apprehension became realized when Armstrong opened at the Holborn Empire in London on July 31. The *Melody Maker*'s headline spoke volumes:

AMAZING RECEPTION FOR ARMSTRONG
FRENZIED APPLAUSE FOR MEANINGLESS PERFORMANCE
LOUIS DELIBERATELY ALL COMMERCIAL

Armstrong was pleasing the majority of the crowd, but the *Melody Maker* said the audience "cheered, wildly, unreasoningly, unjustifiably—out of sheer loyalty." The unidentified author—most likely Percy Brooks—complained, "His act was fifty per cent showmanship, fifty per cent instrumental cleverness, but about naught per cent music. He seems to have come to the conclusion that a variety artist's only mission in life is to be sensational, to pander to the baser emotions, to sacrifice all art to crude showmanship; this from the most admired and outstanding individual dance musician in the world! . . . What a dreadful shame, and what a wicked waste."[2] John Hammond, who found Duke Ellington's recent concert in Paris "astonishing," agreed, writing that he was "terribly disappointed" with Armstrong's second show at the Holborn Empire. "He is now a super-salesman and a marvellous actor—but not enough of a musician," Hammond wrote. "There is no line to his playing, no phrasing, and little sincerity. A few notes, then a pause in preparation for some high ones, and so on."[3]

The *Melody Maker* believed Armstrong toned it a down in his second week, winning him their praise, but they also admitted that "75 percent" of the audience would enjoy whatever he did. "Louis, therefore, was leaving only one small section dissatisfied—the dance music critics." The critics blamed it on the American public, whom they described as "even more dumb than the great B.P." and were just after "cheap sensation and belly-laughs." The *Melody Maker* saw Armstrong five more times and reported "By the end of the week, Louis was almost his old supreme self."[4]

But the next *Melody Maker* headline might have explained Armstrong's erratic nature: "Armstrong's Iron Lips Let Him Down." At the Palladium, Armstrong was "in great pain" and compensated by hardly playing the trumpet and indulging in more singing and showmanship. "He winced with pain when he put the instrument to his lips," the magazine reported.[5] Armstrong took a week off to recuperate in September and returned to the Holborn Empire in top form, *Melody Maker* reporting, "There was no meaningless virtuosity, and not one soul walked out during the set at Monday's first show."[6] Even Selmer got into the act, running a new ad with Armstrong kissing one of their "Louis Armstrong Special" Challenger trumpets, claiming, "Now that Louis has got over his lip trouble, he promises to give of his very best."[7]

Johnny Collins was still hanging around as he booked the first part of the tour and was going to collect his share, even if Armstrong wasn't talking to him. *Variety* published a one-line blurb on September 5, "Johnny Collins admitting plenty of trouble with Louis Armstrong." Soon after, he was gone, leaving Armstrong "in London with no bookings and without telling the musician when or where he was going."[8] "I woke up one morning and he'd sailed unbeknownst to me, and taken my passport with him," Armstrong said. "I was a man without a country then."[9] Back home, Collins sneakily renewed Armstrong's contract with RCA Victor, extending it to November 1934 and increasing the royalty rate from $.02 to $.03. All royalties would be paid directly to Collins; Armstrong remained oblivious to this exchange.[10]

Armstrong needed a new manager and found just the right man in Jack Hylton. One of the most successful dance band leaders in England—*Melody Maker* called him "the grandest hustler and impresario in the country"— Hylton had just handled Duke Ellington's successful European tour.[11] He soon worked his magic to book Armstrong on a Scandinavian jaunt. Armstrong and his band arrived in Denmark on October 19 and were shocked to see 5,000 people waiting for them outside Copenhagen's Central Station. Erik Tuxen's orchestra was on hand but according to Gösta Hägglöf, they "were so over-come with emotion they couldn't play." Armstrong received "enough flowers to fill half a dozen cars," according to Ivan H. Browning of the black press, who also reported that crowds gathered every morning at the Hotel Palace just to get an autograph or at minimum, a glimpse of Armstrong.[12]

Armstrong performed seven shows in three days at Tivoli Hall, playing more than he was allowed on the British vaudeville stage, his chops holding out for roughly 13 numbers each performance.[13] "The musical battle was over, and when the audience had stomped and cried the concert hall into pieces, Louis came forward in a bathrobe and a handkerchief and shook his hands like a boxer—and it was over," wrote a Danish critic. "But there was applause for another ten minutes. Hot! Very hot!"[14]

While in Copenhagen, Armstrong filmed three songs for a Danish movie, *København, Kalundborg og—?* Without any of stereotyped trappings of the Paramount shorts, Armstrong and his band could be themselves, performing as they did them night after night throughout Europe. The footage is especially important given the amount of controversial reviews from this period, allowing modern-day viewers to see what Armstrong did to make critics love him or hate him. He commands the stage; it's impossible to take your eyes off him, even as he hunches over to conduct the band, a curious sight. His singing is spectacular, swinging physically with every inch of his body on "I Cover the Waterfront" and "Dinah" and there's no signs of chops trouble either, giving a taste of the high-note fireworks on "Tiger Rag" (though choosing not to do the "100 high C's" bit). Priceless footage of Armstrong at such an important, yet polarizing, moment in his career.

From Copenhagen, Armstrong headed to Stockholm, once again greeted by a huge number of admiring fans. Unlike the Danes, though, the Swedish press wasn't as kind when it came to Armstrong's stage persona, echoing the racist descriptions of Hannen Swaffer that blotted his first tour of England. Gösta Nystroem, a classical music composer, wrote, "Mr. King of Jazz and man-eater offspring, Louis Armstrong, shows his clean shaven hippopot-amus physiognomy. Flapping with an ordinary trumpet and a giant handker-chief, he splashes up to the tribune, shows his teeth, snuffles, raises one of his wild negro african ancestor's primitive cries . . . alternating with a gra-velly gorilla roar . . . Physically he probably comes from ancestors of gorillas." Another critic added, "This settles the old dispute about apes having a lan-guage."[15] It's almost no wonder that when Armstrong was asked, "Did you enjoy Stockholm?" he answered, "Liked Copenhagen better."[16]

At least both the Danish and Swedish press made time to interview Armstrong, something that had rarely happened to this point in his career.

Asked by the Danes if jazz music was dying, Armstrong presciently responded, "On the contrary, jazz is growing and living. It has its own tone that will always remain. And some of the jazz songs will live eternally. . . . But a lot will of course fade away, and there will turn up new forms."[17] In Sweden, he was eloquent on his feelings about the origins of music. "Us negros have created jazz," he said. "White musicians have followed us, but they haven't reached us yet and I think they never will. Because this music is namely an expression for something that lives within us and that white men never fully will understand. The liberation from slavery explains how the jazz was born. The negro has created two kinds of music. First there are these melancholic spirituals, the folk songs from the time of the slavery. And now jazz, which is a reaction, because now we dare to laugh and smile—we got human dignity."[18] Armstrong realized that his laugh and his smile were powerful tools that reflected his confidence and his dignity and if they made critics uncomfortable, that was their problem, not his.

On December 18, Armstrong began a week of three shows a day at the Ambassadors cinema in Hendon, North London. He had now been playing for about two months straight without a rest. His lip started betraying him in Hendon, *Melody Maker* reporting "the mere contact of the mouthpiece with his lip was causing him great pain."[19] Armstrong's lip woes were only made worse by the salt air in Brighton, where he spent Christmas day. On December 26, he began a full week at the Holborn Empire. He only made it through the first two shows.

"In England, on the stage of the [Holborn] Empire," Armstrong remembered, "my lip split, blood all down my tuxedo shirt, nobody knew it."[20] Because nobody knew it, audiences were confused when Armstrong stopped playing and carried on the rest of the day by just singing and clowning. The results were two "unconvincing" shows, which *Melody Maker* dubbed a "disaster."[21] Even back home, *Variety* carried a short mention of the debacle, writing, "Louis Armstrong was razzed at both shows at Holborn Empire on Boxing Day. Management canceled him and substituted Billy Cotton's local band."[22] A doctor was brought in and after examining Armstrong, insisted that he had to rest for a full month.

Armstrong spent much of that month in the company of *Melody Maker*'s newest hire, 19-year-old Leonard Feather, who wrote multiple columns based on his visits with the trumpeter (one under the pseudonym "Bettie Edwards"; yes, *Melody Maker*'s first major female writer was a man). "In sketching a personality one is always tempted to announce the discovery of 'the *Real* So-and-So,' but there is no part of Louis which is unreal," Feather wrote. "Earnest observers in personal contact with him can discern a lustrous and decorative intelligence, a vessel of character chartered by Independence, an ego at once ironic, sentimental and too much neglected by journalists exasperatingly engrossed in discussion of his work."[23]

Of course, that didn't stop Feather from being engrossed in discussing Armstrong's work himself (it also didn't stop him from penning a *Downbeat* cover story in 1962, "Who Is the Real Louis Armstrong?"). Feather had begun collecting Armstrong's American records from the 1920s and was determined to educate his readers about the glories of Armstrong's partnership with Earl Hines, as only three of their sides were available in England in 1934. He knocked the early Hot Fives ("all very much the same and hardly worth listing in full") and the most recent RCA recordings (with their "booming, pretentious orchestrations of 1933"[24]) and instead wrote, "Personally, I'd a thousand times sooner hear anything from the grand old Hines-Redman days, 'Muggles,' 'Save It, Pretty Mama,' and all those were just superb."[25]

But as with John Hammond, Feather found himself mostly disagreeing about music when discussing it with Armstrong himself. Feather did an article in February where he asked top musicians and writers for a list of records they would bring to the South Pole. Armstrong chose Duke Ellington's "Ducky Wucky," Fletcher Henderson's "Queer Notions," Don Redman's "Nagasaki," and Jack Hylton's "Ellingtonia!" Feather called the choices "somewhat bizarre" and asked him "if he were positive that these would be his final decision." "Boy," Armstrong said, "I never let my mouth say nothin' my head can't stand."[26] Sixteen years later, Armstrong still remembered the moment—and his line—as he vented to editors of the *Record Changer* on critics:

> See, years ago, just because a man had a lot of money—you know, filthy rich or something—then he could write something about a cat and get away with it. That don't make him right. I told John Hammond in London, I say, "With all you have, Daddy, you don't tell me how to blow that trumpet. Cause you don't know my horn. Now you can say what you want about it, as long as you're talking about music, but you don't tell me how to blow that horn." There's a whole lot of people write articles about musicians just to be sarcastic, to get back at certain musicians. They're not writing from what they know. . . . So you take a fellow like Hammond or Leonard Feather, some of those boys—take Leonard, he come to me in London and asked me to pick ten records that I liked. You know? So I gave him the list, and he asked me, "Are you sure?" I said, "What the hell you ask me for? Cause I don't let my mouth say *nothing* my head can't stand!" See what I mean? I don't put them bands that *he* want in there. That's what I'm talking about.[27]

In another conversation with Feather at this time, Armstrong said, "Progress in music, as in everything, is a motion-picture, not a still-life study. Something new comes along, and everyone breaks his neck to follow."[28] Feather would have no shortage of opinion about progress in music in the future.

Armstrong went back to work on January 29, staying out of the major halls and pacing himself a bit more. Johnny Collins sent a telegram out of the blue, stating, "Still all for you." He added, "Telegraph time of your arrival" in hopes that Armstrong would sail back to the United States. Armstrong "crumpled it up angrily," according to those present, threw the telegram to the ground, and said "Never, never, never!" Armstrong was happy with Hylton whom, the *Melody Maker* reported, had "a sensational plan germinating to present Louis in an entirely new way, but one which is a deep secret not yet due for disclosure."[29] The new plan involved the next big American musician due in England: Coleman Hawkins.

The true nature of the relationship between Armstrong and tenor saxophonist Hawkins remains a mystery. Of their time together in Fletcher Henderson's Orchestra in 1924 and 1925, Hawkins once said he often asked himself "if I would ever be able to attain a small part of Louis Armstrong's greatness," while Dan Morgenstern remembered the two titans sharing a joint in a bus during the Newport Jazz Festival in the 1950s.[30] However, some, such as Scott DeVeaux, have speculated that Hawkins's over-the-top praise could have been "disingenuous," while trumpeter Cootie Williams, who played with Hawkins in Henderson's band in 1929, stated, "Coleman hated Louis," adding that "Hawkins seemed to think he ought to have had the recognition Louis had—a bit jealous, I think."[31] Hawkins was the opposite of Armstrong in many ways. Though both men were geniuses at improvising, Hawkins had no use for singing or showmanship or any of the other "show business" stage tactics Armstrong had perfected over the years. Hawkins also didn't "set" his solos like Armstrong, preferring to improvise as often as possible. As he got older, Hawkins became petrified of being thought of as old-fashioned, leading him to record with the likes of Thelonious Monk, John Coltrane, and Sonny Rollins without ever giving an inch. In many ways, he represented the stereotypical image and ideals of a true "jazz" musician more than Armstrong ever did.

Of course, none of this was known to the many promoters and writers of jazz in England. Hylton quickly teamed with the *Melody Maker* to announce a special concert at the London Hippodrome on April 22 that would pair Hawkins with Armstrong and his band—though they hadn't told either man.[32] Armstrong, for his part, sent Hawkins a telegram upon his arrival in late March reading, "WELCOME TO OUR COUNTRY—LOUIS."[33] *Melody*

Maker continued breathlessly promoting the April 22 concert, but the good feelings did not last long.

"Louis Quits: Concert Wrecked" cried the following week's front-page headline, noting that Armstrong, "seized with an acute attack of artistic 'temperament,' has walked out in the best traditional manner of the 'great' artists. Louis Armstrong, *who had already acquiesced in the programme arrangements*, suddenly and deliberately threw a wrench into the works by declining flatly to go on with the show."[34] *Melody Maker* editor Percy Mathison Brooks went on the record with a nearly 2,000-word story of his side of what went wrong. "[Armstrong's] amazing conduct hurt me then, hurts me now, and is still genuinely inexplicable," Brooks wrote. He said Armstrong never protested the idea and as late as an April 6 meeting with Hawkins, Dan Ingman, and others, he "professed to be keen to get on with it."[35] But on April 9, Armstrong backed out, simply saying, "I've figured it out, and it seems it ain't going to do me any good." He said he didn't want to "risk his reputation" by having his band embarrassed in front of an audience of mostly musicians, an explanation Brooks found "incoherent." "Finally, he made it quite clear that he would not budge, neither for me nor Hawk or Hylton, not even for all the fans in the world," Brooks said. He did admit that Hawkins responded "diffidently" to Armstrong's attempts to plan a rehearsal, but defended Hawkins, writing "the truth is that Armstrong had set his face against any association with Hawkins, and Louis himself alone knows what was in his own mind to cause this attitude."[36]

However, British *Tune Times* magazine asked Armstrong for his side and concluded, "It is very different from that which appeared in the *Melody Maker*."[37] *Tune Times* reported that Armstrong was not only willing to play the concert, but he had tenor saxophonist Fletcher Allen transcribe some Fletcher Henderson arrangements so Hawkins could be properly featured. But as the *Melody Maker* admitted, Hawkins didn't know he was playing with Armstrong's band when he arrived and showed no signs of wanting to play with him once in town. When Armstrong approached him to discuss what they were going to perform, Hawkins gave him vague answers, wouldn't commit to any rehearsal times, and wouldn't even tell Allen what keys he wanted for the Henderson arrangements. "It was at this stage that Louis began to get a little bit fed up; and who can blame him?" *Tune Times* asked.[38] Armstrong told the *Chicago Defender*, "I know the musicians were coming to the concert with critical tongues to wag and I wanted to be right for the performance, which was impossible without proper rehearsals or proper musical arrangements."[39] "The editors of *The Melody Maker* thought their readers would swallow the stupid story that Louis refused point blank, without any reason, to play this concert," Hugues Panassie wrote. "They did nevertheless succeed in somewhat hurting his reputation."[40]

Armstrong continued to stick to his story less than a year before he died, telling Max Jones, "Hawkins didn't think I was big enough to share a concert, or top billing equal with me and some funky shit" and summing it up as "bullshit from the start."[41] Regardless, knowing the way Hawkins felt about Armstrong, he must have enjoyed being the darling of the *Melody Maker* in the aftermath of the concert debacle. When he played the Palladium, the magazine wrote of his "Triumph," adding in capital letters, "A TRUE ARTIST ALWAYS LAUGHINGLY OVERCOMES DIFFICULTIES, MAJOR AND MINOR."[42]

Brooks reported that Armstrong was packing his trunk to return to the United States but that wasn't going to happen. Not only was Johnny Collins still waiting for him, but Armstrong also had to contact his lawyers back in Chicago after an irate Lil Hardin let it be known that Collins stopped paying the $100 a week they had agreed to in Cincinnati in 1931. Lil was now touring as "Mrs. Louis Armstrong," the leader of an all-female band, featuring Armstrong disciple Valaida Snow on trumpet. It was the closest Louis got to regular coverage in the mainstream American press, which was quickly forgetting about him. Pianist Fats Waller, with his new series of "Fats Waller and His Rhythm" records, was now the darling of Walter Winchell's column. Armstrong's influence could be heard on the Waller records, as well as on most jazz output of the period; Chick Webb even recorded "On the Sunny Side of the Street" with Taft Jordan not only contributing a "Satchelmouth" vocal, but playing Armstrong's solo before Armstrong had the chance to record it.[43] But even if he was in danger of being forgotten, he wasn't planning on going back to the United States anytime soon. "They don't know how to treat a fellow over there if he happens to be black," he told reporter Cleveland Allen at the end of April.[44]

On top of all of this, Armstrong's chops gave out on him again in May, causing him to cancel an engagement at the Coventry Hippodrome because he was "indisposed through a swollen lip."[45] He soldiered on into July, mostly playing smaller theaters in the provinces, as "he had ceased to be of much valuable as a bookable head-liner."[46] Armstrong's British stay was stumbling to its conclusion, but at some point in July, Armstrong had a special fan in the audience: King George V. Not only did Armstrong play a command performance (perhaps he remembered Winchell's joke and used, "This one's for you, Rex" here?), but he was presented with a gift from the king: a gold-plated Selmer trumpet with the inscription, "Property of Louis Armstrong."

Armstrong left England and sailed to France in late July, bringing his band with him since most of them came from Paris in the first place. Still, he was in no shape to perform. Trumpeter Arthur Briggs was living in Paris and remembered, "Louie, at the time he was having a little lip trouble, too, 'cause they worked him to death. . . . I don't know what happened, but there was pus coming out of his upper lip."[47] "When I left London that summer and went to Paris I needed a rest," Armstrong recalled. "My bookings were finished in England so I just lazied around Paris for three or four months, had lots of fun with musicians from the States—French cats too."[48] One of the French cats was gypsy guitarist Django Reinhardt, who looked upon Armstrong as a god. Armstrong sang with accompaniment by Reinhardt at a party and later said of him, "He knocked me out! Ooh, boy! That cat sure could play, couldn't he?"[49]

In September, Armstrong was approached by Jacques "N. J." Canetti, *Melody Maker*'s France correspondent, who expressed interest in booking him and recording him for Brunswick Records. Briggs described Canetti as "a very intelligent person" but when asked if Canetti was reliable, Briggs responded, "I don't think so."[50] Armstrong didn't care and hired Canetti; he needed a manager to handle the booking and business end since he had a full-time job getting his lip back in shape.

Canetti sprang to action, getting Armstrong to sign an affidavit on September 4 entrusting Canetti with "the care and representation of all his interests relative to phonographic matters." The next day, he sent the affidavit to RCA Victor and asked for a royalty statement showing the number of records Armstrong had sold for the label and insisting Collins "has no longer the right to represent his interests."[51] RCA Victor was confused and not swayed by Canetti's plea. "Our contract specifically states that all monies are to be paid to Collins and this contract was signed by Armstrong as well as Collins," stated an inter-office memo.[52] RCA wrote to Canetti on September 24, stating their contract with Armstrong and Collins was "perfectly legal."[53] Canetti continued pleading his case, but RCA not only ignored him, they sent a letter to Collins in Chicago, notifying him that the label was exercising the option and extending Armstrong's contract another year to November 14, 1935. Collins received the contract and returned it immediately, singing his name and forging Armstrong's signature.[54]

Once Armstrong's lip healed, Canetti decided to go ahead and record him on the French Brunswick label on November 7. He enlisted New Orleans–born reedman Peter DuCongé to form a band, keeping some holdovers from the Hot Harlem Band such as drummer Oliver Tines and reedman Harry Tyree, but adding some excellent new players, most notably pianist Herman Chittison, an outstanding talent from America who came to Europe with

Figure 11.1 Armstrong spent the second half of 1934 living in France, taking time here to pose in front of a Metro station in Paris.
Courtesy of the Louis Armstrong House Museum

Willie Lewis's band in 1933 and stayed. Armstrong called Chittison "One of my favorites—this cat can blow a lot of piano, man."[55]

Armstrong opened the Brunswick session with two demanding trumpet features, "St. Louis Blues" and "Super Tiger Rag," ending the latter with 30 high C's in the last chorus. After taking it somewhat easy on "Will You, Won't You Be My Baby," a song that Armstrong had been playing since his days with Les Hite, he finally recorded his special rendition of "On the Sunny Side of the Street," utilizing both sides of a 78 for his six-minute magnum opus,

Armstrong's personal favorite of his many renditions of the tune. Feeling stronger as the session went on, Armstrong remade "St. Louis Blues" in even more command than earlier and closed with the hauntingly beautiful "Song of the Vipers." Unfortunately, very few people heard these sides at the time because RCA intervened and forced Brunswick to them off the market. They wouldn't get a wider release for 13 more years.

Two days later, Armstrong gave his first of two concerts at the Salle Pleyel in Paris. There was much trepidation beforehand; would his lip hold out? Was his band any good? How would he compare to the other American artists who played Paris? Duke Ellington was a sensation, but Cab Calloway didn't click. Hugues Panassie was "somewhat concerned" as he had heard from John Hammond that Armstrong's "inspiration had declined."[56]

As the band played the opening strains of "When It's Sleepy Time Down South" Armstrong ran onstage "like a brilliant meteor flourishing his trumpet," Panassie said, mumbled some pleasantries, and performed "Them There Eyes" to tremendous applause. Writing for the black press, Edgar Wiggins reported, "In those few brief moments Armstrong had won the admiration of the entire audience, composed of men and women of all nations and from all walks of life; his success was inevitable; and so for the two hours duration of the concert Louis with his instrument sparkling like a rare gem, held the assemblage under the spell of his art."[57]

Armstrong had learned to pace himself better, calling on German chanteuse Arita Day to sing a few numbers, letting the band play a special arrangement of "Rhapsody in Blue" without him and featuring Chittison on three piano solos. But he still pushed himself on demanding numbers "St. Louis Blues," "I Got Rhythm," "Chinatown," and "Tiger Rag," in addition to doing comedy on "Rockin' Chair" and wowing the audience with his solo on "On the Sunny Side of the Street." After the closing "You Rascal You," the applause did not stop for seven full minutes until Armstrong finally emerged in his bathrobe and with a towel around his neck. He did some shadowboxing and raised his arms like a heavyweight champion, much to the thrill of the crowd.

The next night, he "let go even more than the evening before," according to Panassie, adding "Dinah," "Confessin'," and a dramatic "Dear Old Southland" to his program. Wiggins agreed that the following night's concert was even better, concluding that Armstrong's success in Paris "marks the pinnacle of his achievements. He cannot climb higher; there is no loftier height to reach. He can only repeat himself."[58] In some ways, Wiggins was right. Armstrong had now perfected a mixture of trumpet showpieces, pop songs, ballads, comedy, female vocals, and sideman features that would form the template for his concert work for the rest of his career.

Armstrong continued to be a hit in Antwerp, Gaude, Liège, and Strasbourg, but in Switzerland, he hit a snag with Canetti. Armstrong and the band had a verbal agreement to perform four concerts a week for 16,000 francs (about $1,060 USD per week). When Canetti's wife booked a last-minute return engagement in Bern—a fifth concert in the week—the band asked for more money, but Mrs. Canetti didn't want to pay them. Canetti returned and told them he could book them for two weeks at the Moulin Rouge theater in Paris, but their salary would remain the same 16,000 francs a week, though now for four shows a day instead of four shows a week. The band refused and the Moulin Rouge engagement fell through, angering Canetti.

Things went from bad to worse at the start of 1935 as Armstrong's lip once again failed him and two concerts had to be canceled in Geneva, Switzerland. The Swiss promoters threatened to sue Canetti, asking him to pay 12,000 francs immediately for the cancellation. Canetti panicked and asked Armstrong, then performing in Turin, Italy, to leave his band behind and go play two concerts with a Swiss orchestra in Geneva. According to Edgar Wiggins, "Armstrong, characteristic of his nature, was loyal to his musicians and emphatically refused to go with [the Swiss Orchestra]."[59]

While Armstrong was in Turin, Canetti told him that he would next perform two weeks in Nice, France, opening on January 20, but at a reduced rate. Instead of Armstrong's 16,000 francs-per-week salary, Canetti was going to pay him 4,000 francs for the entire two-week duration. Wiggins reported, "Armstrong was never so insulted in his life and he made no effort to conceal his feelings." After the blow-up, Canetti approached Wiggins and explained why Armstrong was a "bad fellow" for not being okay with the reduced salary. "Why should Armstrong be insulted by my offering him 2,000 Frs. per week," Canetti asked. "The way he and his wife live they don't spend one thousand francs a week." Wiggins was shocked, addressing the readers of the black press (his story was picked up by multiple papers), "[Y]ou will be able to judge for yourself the mentality of the man who has exploited practically every Negro artist that has resided in Paris."[60]

Incensed, Canetti ran back to the *Melody Maker* and had them run a huge front-page story about his threatening legal action, claiming Armstrong might be incarcerated for his behavior. The article ended in capital letters: "APPARENTLY LOUIS HAD ALREADY MADE IT KNOWN THAT HE WAS RETURNING TO AMERICA FROM PARIS, BUT CANETTI IS SAID TO HAVE PREVENTED IT."[61]

Canetti might have thought he prevented it, but he was wrong; Louis and Alpha boarded the SS *Champlain* on January 23 and sailed for New York City. Wiggins and valet Joe Henderson were the only people Armstrong told before he left; he even left his entire trunk of music arrangements behind as a decoy to fool Canetti. "Before sailing, Armstrong began to regard the matter as a joke and now he laughs about it," Wiggins wrote. "You are right, Louis. It is funny, but bravo to you for upholding your standard and proving to your ex-manager that all American Negroes that come to France will not submit themselves to everything and anything just to remain there in preference of returning to America."[62]

Canetti was livid and once again returned to the front page of the *Melody Maker*. This time, it was personal. He wrote of Armstrong's "many managerial troubles," and how, when it came time to assembling a backing band, "he would not tolerate having near him any musician of fame," resulting in resentment of Herman Chittison and Arita Day. Canetti closed with one more swipe: "Always it appears that the supremacy of his art has been undermined by ineradicable streaks of weakness in his character. Not for the first time he has left his best friends and admirers in the lurch, even when more money was being poured into his pocket than he had ever possessed before."[63]

Canetti was definitely right about one thing: the United States didn't represent the end of Armstrong's troubles but in many ways, the beginning. Louis was being sued by Lil for the failure to pay the court-ordered $100 a week, Canetti was threatening a lawsuit of his own, his Brunswick records were pulled, he didn't have a band, he didn't have any performances lined up, Johnny Collins would be waiting for him, and worst of all, his lip was mangled beyond repair. He was officially at rock bottom.

He and Alpha docked on Wednesday, January 30, and headed straight for Harlem and the new Apollo Theater, shocking those in attendance and listening to the broadcast on the radio. Rumors started spreading about Armstrong performing there, but he was not ready to perform just yet.[64]

Before he could book anything, Armstrong turned to Mezz Mezzrow for help, as according to Canetti, Mezzrow wrote Armstrong a letter in Turin "offering himself as the stage manager for this comeback."[65] But it was Mezzrow, broke and suffering from opium addiction, who needed the help. "When I got off the boat I had three thousand dollars with me, even though I did not know where or when I would work again, I divided the money with Mez," Armstrong wrote. "I wanted to make him happy as he had often made me. . . . I wanted to help him get started again and straightened out."[66] Armstrong even wrote a letter to the Local 802 of the Associated Musicians of Greater New York announcing that Mezzrow was his manager and musical director. Mezzrow was overcome with emotion. "Mezz, stop cryin'," Armstrong said, "Don't worry, I'll go back to Chi and rest my chops for a while, and you go to work on some arrangements for me and we'll start out together."[67]

Louis and Alpha returned to their Chicago apartment for the first time since July 1933. He hadn't been back a couple of days before the Harlem Opera House, rival to the Apollo, announced that Armstrong would be performing that week. But Harlem Opera house manager Frank Schiffman had to cancel his plans as soon as he announced them when he received a call from Johnny Collins. Schiffman said that he was originally contacted by Armstrong himself and even produced a letter that Armstrong wrote him from Paris back in August 1934, saying, "I will keep in touch with you and I won't accept any other proposition in America but yours, I promise. Of course, you realize the trouble you are liable to have with that fellow Collins, who used to manage me, but never will again, so long as I can keep my right mind. So, any one of your good old propositions you have in mind, write me with the details, because now I am free, single and disengaged."[68]

But he wasn't. When Collins got word of his return, he immediately negotiated with the Apollo for Armstrong to perform the week of February 15, insisting to the press that Armstrong "would have to fill the engagement at the Apollo whether he likes it or not."[69] Armstrong did not like it and would not fulfill it, much to the disappointment of his Harlem fans. He admitted to the press that Collins never contacted him about the booking, but he couldn't have played it if he wanted to: his lip was in tatters. To avoid trouble with the union, Armstrong went to Chicago doctor A. N. Gordon Jr. and had him write a note stating that "the reason Louis had failed to appear was due to the fact that his lips were in such a condition that they bled every time he attempted to play his trumpet." Apollo management enlarged a photostatic copy of the letter and affixed it to a sign in front of the lobby.[70]

There was nothing Armstrong could do. His lip was beyond repair and he was no longer getting paid. "Everything was in hock," he remembered of this period. "Had a 32-hundred dollar Buick—which was a bitch way back then. Sold it for $390."[71] The April–May 1935 issue of *Down Beat* ran a front-page story, "Louie Armstrong Lays Down His Trumpet," insinuating perhaps that the end was near.

In actuality, he was secretly plotting his comeback. He reached out to Zilner Randolph to see about getting a band together for him and to help him assemble arrangements since he left his music trunk with Canetti. On March 12, he checked in with Mezzrow to tell him that his lips were improving, and that Randolph was hard at work building up his library of arrangements. "You see 'Gate,'" he wrote, "I figure with you and Randolph handling the Arrangement department I can't go wrong. Eh?" What Armstrong didn't know was Mezzrow was incapable of providing anything for Armstrong because of his addiction. "I couldn't keep my attention on the notes, couldn't even stay awake," Mezzrow wrote. "I wasn't breaking the habit. It was breaking me."[72] Embarrassed, Mezzrow avoided contact with Armstrong for over a year and received a frosty reception when they did cross paths, creating a rift that lasted several years.

Randolph, though, was providing Armstrong with something more important than just arrangements: he was giving him trumpet lessons. One day, a friend stopped by Randolph's house to see him and noticed that Randolph was giving Armstrong exercises to help strengthen his lip. "Randolph, if I hadn't seen this with my eyes, I never would have believed it," he said. "You sitting down there, giving Louis a lesson."[73] Speaking privately in 1953, Armstrong said, "But I stayed off my trumpet six months. I had to get a beginner's method. Start with whole notes, damn near a whole month. Laaaaa, laaaaa, laaaaa [sings scale in long whole notes]. You'd think I'd never played before."[74] Meanwhile, speculation only grew in the press. The *Afro-American* ran a photo of him on April 20 with the heading "Is He Through?" The caption stated that Armstrong "is reported washed up due to an infection of the lip, which it is feared may develop into cancer if he attempts to play again."[75]

Armstrong was "washed up" in the press, but he was still in demand from managers. Collins insisted he still represented Armstrong and prevented anyone else from handling him, which continued to burn Armstrong nearly 20 years later. "Kept me out of work four to five months at a time," he vented in 1953. "In Chicago there, the papers, 'What the hell is wrong with Louie Armstrong? He ain't working or anything.' "[76] Meanwhile Canetti reached out to Edgar Wiggins in Paris in April and said he planned to sail to America on May 28 "to re-engage Armstrong for one year and pay him $52,000," Wiggins reported.[77] Even Tommy Rockwell reappeared from the past, having started a new booking agency with Cork O'Keefe and now wanting Armstrong back in his fold.

One day, Budd Johnson visited and was curious about Armstrong's game plan.

"What you gonna do, Pops?" Johnson asked.

"Well, there's a lot of cats want me to sign up with them," Armstrong answered. "Rockwell want me to re-sign with him. He offered me $5,000.00 to sign a contract. But I'm not going to sign with him."

"I think I'm going to get with old Joe Glaser, because he ain't got nothin' and I can tell him what I want."[78]

12

"A Much Improved Salesman"

June–December 1935

On February 25, 1942, syndicated columnist George Tucker turned over part of his "Manhattan" column to a special guest for a game of "What's My Name." "I'll give you some hints," the mystery man started. "In fact, I'll tell you everything I know about myself. Ready to go?"

> I was born in Chicago. My dad was a doctor. I'm the guy who started the Rent-a-Ford Plan. Later I sold it to another company and they made it into the Drive-ur-Yourself plan.
>
> I became a promoter, and a prize fight manager. . . . I had some good boys under my wing. . . . I managed Dave Shade, Art Lasky and Jack Roper. . . . I managed Eddie Anderson, Eddie Shea and Tommy Grogan. . . . I managed Ray Miller.
>
> Not only did I manage fighters, I became a night club operator on a big scale, and I managed dance bands. . . . I'm Les Brown's manager . . . . I manage Louis Armstrong, Lionel Hampton, Glenn Garr. I manage Don Bestor, Andy Kirk, and Buck and Bubbles. . . . Among the names I have helped to stardom are Noble Sissle, Lucky Millinder, and Jack Benny's Rochester. . . . I once lifted Stepin Fetchit from $35 to $3,500 a week. . . .
>
> But my real love is dogs. . . . I like white collies, Bostons, poms and Pekes, but I guess I like Bostons most of all. . . . I keep six ribbon-winning Bostons in my apartment. . . . I live in a pent-house and each of these Bostons has a specially built kennel. . . . Some people say I'm something of a dandy, that I like to wear expensive clothes. . . . That's true.
>
> Now. What's my name?[1]

His name was Joe Glaser. And the above did not quite represent "everything" Glaser knew about himself.

Glaser was born in 1897, the son of Bertha Glaser and Dr. George M. Glaser. The Glasers were patrons of the arts, even regularly attending the opera, where Dr. Glaser was a boxholder.[2] The family wanted young Joseph to be a doctor and as the story goes, he got as far as medical school, but quit because "He couldn't stand the sight of blood."[3] But early on, Glaser did find some use for his father's practice, resulting in his first mention in print—and his first arrest. "Diploma Mill for Physicians Laid to Doctors," read the *Chicago Tribune* story of April 19, 1916, about several physicians being arrested for selling fraudulent diplomas to medical students fearful of failing their exams. "All the men accused are Italian physicians with large practices, except one, who is the son of a well known south side physician," the article stated.[4] Bertha Glaser put up the $1,500 bond to release her son but it was clear that he had an appetite for action that was only going to keep getting him in trouble. "Joe Glaser, who drove a 'speedster,' and said he lived at 3149 Morgan street, Chicago, got tired bumping the bumps on Sixteenth street last Sunday, so he took to the sidewalk between Center avenue and Hanover street," came a report in August. "Officer Ross saw him and arrested him."[5] Once again, bond was paid.

Glaser was driving a "speedster" because he now worked as a used car salesman. On August 20, 1916, he put in his first small ad in the *Chicago Tribune*, advertising a "practically new" 1915 Cadillac 8 Touring Car. As he made a name for himself, the ads grew more frequent, as Glaser honed his skills as a salesman in the press:

> June 23, 1918:
> BEFORE YOU SELL YOUR CAR
> See. Me. I pay cash and pay more for any late model car than any one in town. Quick action. Don't delay. Bring car and take home money. No red tape.
> JOSEPH G. GLASER[6]

Glaser concurrently developed what would later become a famous interest in breeding dogs, his hobby also appearing in the want-ads section of the *Chicago Tribune* on December 19, 1918:

> FOR SALE—BEAUTIFUL, FEMALE PEDIGREED Boston terrier; perfectly marked; will sell reasonable to good home. No dealer. Jos. Glaser.[7]

On June 26, 1922, Dr. George M. Glaser died at the age of 53, leaving Bertha Glaser as the head of the house. Bertha was successful enough in real estate to not have to struggle; in December 1923, she sold 19 apartments for $120,000, just one of many of her transactions from this period.[8] One of her properties was the notorious Sunset Cafe, located on the corner of 35th and Calumet, one of the "menaces to good citizenship in the black belt," in the words of Rep.

Figure 12.1 An early 1920s photo of Joe Glaser's used car dealership in the 1920s, with Glaser standing in front, on the left wearing the cap. The lessons he learned selling used cars would come back to play when he became an agent.
Courtesy of the Louis Armstrong House Museum

Adelbert H. Roberts, who would become the first African American senator in Illinois. Roberts also pointed out that within the Sunset's neighborhood "were three houses of prostitution, running wide open and with solicitors stationed in front as policemen sauntered by."[9] Those were most likely Joe Glaser's, too.

Once, when asked how he got into show business, Glaser responded, "On account of the whorehouses." In the late teens, one of Glaser's top car salesmen was Roger Touhy. As Prohibition began in January 1920, Touhy began working as a bootlegger, soon getting bigger aspirations. "I want to join the mob, and I need your help," Touhy told Glaser. Glaser continued paying Touhy's salary for years to come, regardless of whether he worked. Finally, Touhy returned one day and said, "OK, Joe, I got it made. I'm in the mob, solid. What can I do for you?" They talked it over and Touhy helped supply Glaser with a chain of brothels. "Hell," Glaser said, "I was practically a kid and I had the biggest chain of whore houses on the South Side of Chicago."[10]

Each brothel had a parlor where the customers were entertained by various musicians. Glaser called this his first experience with show business, but he soon began spending more time at the Sunset Cafe, eventually becoming its manager for co-owner Ed Fox. By 1924, Glaser was still placing his used car ads in the *Chicago Tribune* but now he left his name out, instead pointing people toward his chauffeur, "Mr. Smiley."[11] "Mr. Smiley" was Robert Smiley, an African American man who became not only Glaser's chauffeur but also a confidant and sometimes, a spy. The Sunset also became a frequent hangout of Al Capone and his crew. Earl Hines remembered Capone saying, "I've got to have a playground." "That's all he wanted it for, just a place to bring some of his people and have fun," Hines said. "He only took 25 percent. He said to Ed Fox, 'You need protection.'"[12]

In 1926, Louis Armstrong came into Glaser's orbit for the first time when he joined Carroll Dickerson's band at the Sunset Cafe. Armstrong remembered Glaser as "a sharp young 'Cat' [who] would stand at the front door of the 'Sunset' greeting the people as they entered especially the chicks (most of them - his' - 'ha ha')."[13] One night Armstrong came to work and saw the marquee of the Sunset reading, "Carroll Dickerson's Orchestra featuring Louis Armstrong, the 'World's Greatest Cornetist.'" "Surprised I was," Armstrong said, "But that's the way Mr. Glaser wanted it." Armstrong never forgot the night "one of those tough Ass Gangsters" approached Glaser and said, "Listen, this is a wide world. Why do you keep Louis Armstrong's name up there as the 'World Greatest?'" Glaser looked him in the eye and responded, "Listen: I think he is and this is my place—and I defy anybody to take it down."[14] Armstrong would not forget Glaser's act.

Armstrong knew everything Glaser was involved with, too, as evidenced by his joke about Glaser's "chicks." On Christmas Day in 1926, two of Bertha Glaser's properties, the Sunset Cafe and the Plantation Cafe, were raided by eight squads of detectives, who arrested 19 people for violating Prohibition laws, including Glaser at the Sunset and Fox at the Plantation.[15] In court, Capt. William Schoemaker provided evidence "that girls of 17 were brought to the cafe by escorts and carried off the dance floor drunk." That was enough for Judge John P. Haas to fine Glaser $200 and declare the Sunset "a public nuisance."[16] Glaser paid the fine but his problems with underage girls were just beginning.

One day in February 1927, Glaser was at the Sunset when a young girl caught his eye. "She wore make-up and seemed to be in her twenties," he later told a friend, adding, "In fact, it was her mother who pointed her out to me and encouraged my interest in her."[17] He invited her in. The girl was Dolores Wheeler. She was 14 years old.

On February 25, 1927, Glaser was arrested for sexually "attacking" Wheeler. Glaser spent a year using the legal system to his advantage, obtaining "numerous continuances" and making "every effort . . . to block the progress of justice." Finally, in February 1928, Glaser was tried for the rape of Dolores Wheeler. It took the judge 45 minutes to declare Glaser guilty, sentencing him to 10 years in prison.[18] It was an open and shut case—or so it seemed.

Just days after testifying on February 8, Wheeler retracted her entire story. She and her stepfather sent in new affidavits and disappeared.[19] Judge Harry B. Miller found it too "suspicious" and denied Glaser's motion for a new trial.[20] Just days later, another incredible twist: Dorothy Wheeler finally turned up—and married Joe Glaser in Lexington, Kentucky. Glaser showed up beaming as his attorney asked for time to argue his case—but was denied and Glaser's sentence to the penitentiary held. "Too many unusual things have happened so far," Judge Miller said. "I am going to dispose of this motion now and you can appeal to the Supreme court." Glaser's face "was flushed to a deep red" when he was led back to the jail, according to the *Chicago Tribune*.[21] Glaser was released on a $15,000 bond but his freedom didn't last very long. Literally four days later, he was arrested again, this time for "attacking" 17-year-old Virginia Sherman.[22] This time Glaser was released on a $7,000 bond but it was front-page news across the region.

But in June 1929, Glaser scored a seemingly unthinkable victory in the Wheeler case when the Illinois Supreme Court reversed the original decision "on the grounds that the evidence was of an unsatisfactory character and that the girl's story was not corroborated."[23] Two years after the initial charge, Glaser was now a free man. But instead of learning his lesson, he fell right back to his old ways, allegedly raping 18-year-old Helen P. Parmley of Des Moines in August. The following January, Parmley sued Glaser for $10,000 in damages.[24]

But newspapers never followed up on the suit of Helen P. Parmley, nor was there any follow-up to his arrest for raping Virginia Sherman. It can only be deduced that these were settled out of court.[25] In 1931, Wheeler sued Glaser for divorce, leading him to start paying her $15 a week alimony.[26] It wasn't a lot but the alimony, the assumed settlements to his other victims, and the closing of the Sunset Cafe (which became the Grand Terrace Cafe, run by Ed Fox), combined with the onset of the Great Depression and the eventual end of Prohibition in 1933, sent Glaser's finances into a tailspin. He disappeared from the newspapers in the early 1930s, only appearing sporadically in relation to one of his boxers, none of whom became a champion.

There seemed to be only one way out for Glaser: the world of black show business, the one avenue of his life that hadn't resulted in scandal or failure. In March 1934, Glaser was named as the new manager of the Frolics cafe, hiring Percy Venable to stage the floor show. The *Chicago Defender* approved, writing, "When Glaser moves into the cafe next month he will be accompanied by the first Race floor show ever to play the cafe. Likewise the presence of Southsiders in the cafe as patrons will set some new sort of precedent [as] in the past it has been patronized by whites exclusively. Thus Joe Glaser opens another cafe to give employment to hundreds of our Race."[27] Glaser soon realized the black press was very kind toward him. "Joseph Glaser has been responsible for many little unknown colored stars soaring to great heights," the *Pittsburgh Courier* reported in June 1934. "Space at this time will not permit us to point out successful stars created by Glaser." There was also an early published glimpse into Glaser's clout in relation to Armstrong's friends Buck and Bubbles when Glaser was able to get the incarcerated John Bubbles out of jail to play a benefit at the Apollo.[28]

In July 1934, Glaser went so far as reopening the old Sunset Cafe at a new location and started producing all-black shows such as the "Cotton Club Revue" and "Dixie to Harlem" throughout Chicago.[29] But just as he got a little ahead, he was once again caught by the law: the new Sunset Cafe was stocked with $2,500 of stolen liquor delivered by a group of criminals, some with ties to the late Jack Zuta's vice syndicate. The *Chicago Tribune* reported on April 9, 1935, that the police were still looking for Glaser.[30] Once again, Glaser snaked his way out of trouble, heading down to Louisville, Kentucky, where he began booking a show at The Brown. The *Courier-Journal* caught him there and for the first time in print, referred to Glaser as a "booking agent."[31]

By June, Armstrong was ready to go back to work. His lip was getting stronger and Randolph was in the process of assembling a new orchestra. It was now time for Armstrong to approach Glaser. Glaser described Armstrong as "broke and very sick" and practically begging, "Please Mr. Glaser, just you and I. You understand me, I understand you." Glaser responded, "Louis, you're me and I'm you."[32] But in his telling of the story, Glaser left out his own present financial condition. "And Joe Glaser was broke," Armstrong told Ernie Anderson. "And I said, 'I want you to come and take care of me and all you have to do is pay me a certain amount of money every week and you take anything beyond that that you can get.' . . . Joe said, 'Well, I haven't got a dime, I couldn't give you anything!' And [I] said, 'Don't worry about it, I'll make the money. But you just make sure I get *that* much and you get the rest."[33] The men shook hands and a partnership was formed.

Armstrong never regretted his decision to hire Glaser. "I look around, I was hung up with gangsters and everything else," he recounted in 1951. "So you get a gangster to play ball with a gangster, you're straight. I could relax and blow the horn like I want." Armstrong knew other managers were interested in him, mentioning one who was "a millionaire" but Armstrong wasn't impressed.

"He could give me a hundred thousand dollars on my contract and it wouldn't have done as good as telling one of those bad sonofabitches, 'Well, Joe Glaser is my manager.'" Armstrong audibly winced as he mimicked the reaction such a declaration inspired: "'Ohh, Jesus Christ!' See what I mean?" Glaser provided him with something more than money: "Peace of mind." Armstrong added, "Money ain't all of it. And then eventually you get a million dollars anyhow." Looking back, he proudly stated, "I ain't had trouble with gangsters since I signed up with Joe Glaser."[34]

But to get to that point, Glaser had a lot of work to do. The first thing he did, he claimed, was insure his life and Armstrong's life for $100,000 each. He then gave up his other business ventures, including the Sunset Cafe. "Yeah, I remember him hocking the Sunset to get the uniforms, to get the band equipped and everything, to get out," Randolph remembered.[35] Rapidly running out of money, Glaser still felt confident about the opportunity. He ran into Armstrong's saxophonist Scoville Brown and his former trombonist Keg Johnson at a bar, telling them, "I'm going to buy you fellas a drink. It's my last five dollars, but I'm going to tell you this. I'm going to control everything in black show business before I'm through."[36]

Though Glaser had put on a few revues in recent years, he was not an official booking agent. To help, he approached Al A. Travers, a Chicago-based agent with the Associated Orchestra Corporation, known for handling the popular Don Albert and His Orchestra. Glaser and Travers put together some dates for a dance tour beginning in early July. When the *Pittsburgh Courier* announced on June 29, "Louis Armstrong O. K. Again," the story referred to "Al Travers, his manager"[37] and left Glaser out of it entirely, perhaps because he was trying to keep a low profile after the stolen liquor indictment; the *Des Moines Register* referred to Glaser as "a fugitive from justice" in a story later that summer.[38]

Next, Glaser settled with Lil Hardin Armstrong, who, once satisfied, withdrew her lawsuit and quietly went back to leading her band (and most likely went back to collecting her checks from Louis). But the biggest obstacle was still Johnny Collins. Glaser wasn't afraid of the man who pretended to be a gangster; he was the real deal. Still, it would require money, which he did not have, but with Armstrong going back to work soon, Glaser hoped he could accumulate it quickly. On June 29, Collins sold Armstrong's contract to Glaser for $5,000. Their agreement stated that Glaser would pay Collins $500 by July 4, another $500 by July 9, and then $100 a week for the remaining $4,000.[39] It was a deal. Armstrong was a free man; Glaser was officially his manager and they were set to go out on the road.

Before setting off on their tour, Armstrong and Glaser sat down with Ishmael Northcross of the Associated Negro Press for a long interview that appeared in multiple black newspapers. Armstrong was quick to mention his new manager. "There isn't a colored star on the boards or behind a stand who hasn't at one time or another been with or connected in some way with Joe," he said. "He's smart in the game. He knows where the money is and the two of us get together'll hit the top and hit it so hard that the top'll bust and we'll go swinging right on to the sky. Yeah man." Northcross gave Glaser's background, only hinting at his past troubles, writing, "Joe hasn't fared so well in recent years." But Glaser was enthusiastic about his new client, telling Northcross, "He originated the 'scat' song. Nobody will play a trumpet like he has. And then there's the fact that he hasn't let popularity, good fortune or anything else change him from the lovable Louie, the big man of fun."[40]

Armstrong also gave an interview to *Down Beat*, landing on the front page of the new music magazine.[41] Talking to a publication like *Down Beat* was a new sensation for Armstrong, as *Down Beat* didn't begin publication until July 1934. Now there was such a thing as a "jazz critic" and a "jazz journalist," and Armstrong would become the object of their scrutiny.

Down Beat also came into existence as big band jazz—now being called "Swing"—was becoming king. The turning point came in December 1934, when clarinetist Benny Goodman began featuring the arrangements of Armstrong's old boss, Fletcher Henderson, on NBC's *Let's Dance* radio program. Echoes of Armstrong could be heard on such Henderson arrangements as an updated version of Armstrong and King Oliver's composition, "Sugar Foot Stomp," or in the trumpet playing of Goodman's star soloist, Bunny Berigan. Berigan wasn't alone; Roy Eldridge finally made his first records with Teddy Hill's band on February 26, 1935, and immediately made an impression with his explosive, fast-fingered style. Louis Prima of New Orleans came to New York in 1934 and became a sensation at the Famous Door on the burgeoning 52nd Street scene in 1935 with his Armstrong-inspired playing and singing. And Henry "Red" Allen had steadily been continuing to make a name for himself, featured not only with the Mills Blue Rhythm Band, but also on his own series of recordings. "The Armstrong fanatics do not like [Allen] because he is the most serious rival to their idol," R. Edwin S. Hinchcliffe wrote in a new British periodical simply called *Swing Music* in May 1935. "In Henry Allen we have a player who can follow in the footsteps of Louis, without any accusation of copying; a player who may in time even surpass the true artistic Louis we all knew and admired so much."[42]

It was clear that much of the jazz world had finally caught on and caught up to Armstrong's influence and innovations in the 18 months he was overseas and the six months he spent resting. Later that summer, Goodman's phenomenal success at the Palomar Ballroom in Los Angeles would herald the official start of "The Swing Era" to many historians. Armstrong praised Goodman and the Casa Loma Orchestra as "mighty fine bands," but it was now time for him to prove he wasn't finished just yet. As he told *Down Beat,* addressing rumors that he "lost his lip," Armstrong said, "My chops is fine, now, and I'm dying to swing out again."[43]

With Joe Glaser in a Cadillac, Armstrong in a Packard (driven by Bob Smiley), and Zilner Randolph's band piled into a decrepit old bus nicknamed "Sophronia," Armstrong set out on his comeback on July 1, 1935. "We were all starting from scratch," he summed it up. "I'd been away so long and we hadn't made any records, and people had forgotten us. Then, too, I hadn't played for six months and had to take lessons all over to learn my weavin' and my bobbin'. We made any jumps just to get jobs. We thought nothing of going 500 miles a day for a one-nighter. We was Supermen."[44]

"Sophronia" started its journey in Chicago, went to Indianapolis, played Bluefield, West Virginia, on July 3 and headed straight for the Deep South. Glaser went along on the tour and ended up playing a critical role in protecting the band's well-being. Armstrong told *Ebony* about it in 1961:

> Years ago in the 1930's, we used to tour the South in a big Packard. Lots of times we wouldn't get a place to sleep. So we'd cross the tracks, pull over to the side of the road, and spend the night there. We couldn't get into hotels. Our money wasn't even good. We'd play nightclub and spots which didn't have a little boy's room for Negroes. We'd have to go outside, often in the freezing cold, and in the dark. When we'd get hungry, my manager Joe Glaser (who's also my friend, Jewish, and white) would buy food along the way in paper bags and bring it to us boys in the bus who wouldn't be served. Sometimes even this didn't work.[45]

In addition to demeaning treatment on the road, they hit a major snag in Baltimore on July 9, when Johnny Collins reappeared to cause trouble. Glaser had only paid Collins $240 of the first $500 he owed him, which was enough for Collins to show up at the New Albert Casino with a deputy sheriff to attach the box office and other movable possessions, including Glaser's car. The band earned $1,000 for the performance and gave Collins $260. It was a close call. "In the event that there is a default in payments, Collins's contract states Armstrong is to revert back to the management of Collins for a period of twenty months from the date of default," Levi Jolley wrote.[46]

Collins even managed to outline "previous difficulties the cornetist has run into during the past five years," telling Jolley about Armstrong's arrest for marijuana, his trouble with gangsters, his difficulties with Lil, and his problems with the Chicago musicians union. Jolley caught up with Armstrong at the Penn Hotel and wrote that "Armstrong readily admitted the indebtedness to his former manager, and explained that no attempt had been made to escape payment. In his southern drawl, Armstrong claimed that the attachment was an attempt of his former manager to embarrass him." Armstrong praised Glaser, stating that he "was easier to get along with and not insulting," and added that one of his goals was to "offset rumors that his lips can not stand the tremendous pressure of blowing 200 consecutive high C's, one of his feats."[47]

The truth is those days were over. By ending each show with over 100 high C's for so many years, Armstrong very nearly had to retire because of the damage he did to himself. Now that his lip was healed, he wasn't going to pull those stunts anymore. He actually saw the light and agreed with many of his toughest critics, later admitting that his pyrotechnics were done to impress one segment of the audience. "Just trying to please the musicians," he told Richard Meryman in 1965, adding, "And the audience, the ordinary public, thought I was a maniac or something, running amuck. I was only standing on my head, blowing my brains out, to please the musicians. I forgot about the audience—and it didn't do me no good."[48] Armstrong learned his lesson, but was not about to abandon high notes anytime soon. "Time and time again, he stood flatfooted and with as little effort as one would exert to smoke a cigarette, or say scat, he made notes utterly impossible," Rollo S. Vest wrote of a performance in Columbus, Ohio. "High C and notes ranging upward, fell in Louis' path, as conquered, each time he attempted to make them."[49]

Armstrong was breaking box-office records almost everywhere he played, and Glaser was now furiously working his connection with the black press; the July 13 issue of the *Pittsburgh Courier* featured four separate euphoric stories about Armstrong, along with a large photo, all on a single page. It didn't take long before someone else from Armstrong's past noticed: Tommy Rockwell. Though Collins had to continue paying Rockwell $150 a week after the court settlement in January 1932, Rockwell was never satisfied. He had written the blueprint for Armstrong's stardom but just as he started to skyrocket, Collins swooped in. Now running an agency with Cork O'Keefe and booking top artists such as the Mills Brothers, the Casa Loma Orchestra, and the Dorsey Brothers, Rockwell wanted Armstrong back, but Armstrong would only work with Glaser. Rockwell decided to take them both. On July 17, *Variety* reported, "Tommy Rockwell, who first discovered Louis Armstrong when he was recording manager for Okeh records, has taken on the colored bandsman for exclusive management via Rockwell-O'Keefe." Only at the end did the article squeeze in one line, "Joe Glaser, Chi rep, will be Armstrong's personal contact with the R-O'K agency."[50]

Glaser was now calling the shots and Armstrong was happy to just be playing anywhere, but he did have one request early on in the tour: he needed to go back to New Orleans and play for a black audience to make up for the debacle of his last night in his hometown in 1931. Armstrong had even told Ishmael Northcross before the tour began, "One thing I'm going to play my home town in New Orleans, and I'm really going to play it. They haven't heard me in person down that way and I'm going to put on the works for them when I get down there."[51] Armstrong made good on his word with a two-day engagement at the Golden Dragon on July 21 and 22. The *Pittsburgh Courier* reported that Armstrong "has set the town agog" and noted that Captain Joseph Jones welcomed him back home, once again brandishing Armstrong's first cornet.[52]

As the tour continued, Randolph increasingly found himself on the outs. Armstrong observed a lack of discipline and punctuality in the band and finally called Randolph over to say, "Randy, I'm going to have to take it and put it right in Mr. Glaser's hands and I'm going to have to give him the reins." Glaser would now control the hiring and firing of musicians, their salaries, getting them where they needed to be on time, and so on. Randolph, though, still tried exerting some power when he attempted to prevent an exhausted Armstrong from broadcasting in Washington, DC, after a run of record-breaking one-nighters through July and August. "That made Joe mad and made [Alpha] mad," Randolph said. "Alpha got mad because I was telling Louie what to do. But, see, I was looking out for the man's health."[53] Randolph's days were numbered.

Armstrong finally made his debut at the Apollo Theater the week of August 30. He was part of an all-black vaudeville bill, sharing the stage with the likes of blackface comedian Pigmeat Markham, straight actor and singer Jimmie Baskette (the future Uncle Remus in Disney's *Song of the South*), ballroom dancers Norton and Margo, rope dancers Danny and Edith, tap dancers the 4 Step Brothers, 16 chorus girls with choreography by Clarence Robinson, and more. Armstrong dominated, creating an uproar in the theater, breaking the box-office record and getting the media attention of Walter Winchell and *Variety*. In the black press, Allan McMillan of the *Chicago Defender* called Armstrong "a much improved salesman," illustrating that Armstrong's polished showmanship and lack of wild trumpet exhibitionism was well received by the Apollo audience.[54]

McMillan was soon hired to be Armstrong's press agent, specifically working to get all of Armstrong's moves mentioned in the black press; the *Pittsburgh Courier* began referring to him as the man who "came from nowhere" after a record-breaking week at the Howard Theatre.[55] Glaser also got the attention of the mainstream press and landed major spreads on Armstrong in the October issues of *Vanity Fair, Fortune,* and *Esquire.*[56] The *Courier* reported on the coverage and used the occasion to compare Armstrong to one of the fastest rising African American stars at the time. "One's first name is Louis and the other's last name is Louis, but both have 'crashed' the big-time magazines to loom as the most important men of their race in their particular division," they wrote. "You've heard the names . . . JOE LOUIS and LOUIS ARMSTRONG!"[57] The comparison between Armstrong and Louis was an apt one, according to trumpeter Harry "Sweets" Edison, at least when it came to trumpet players in this period. "He used to walk down Seventh Avenue in New York and all the young trumpet players would just follow him like you would follow Joe Louis," Edison said of Armstrong. "He was an idol."[58]

Glaser now needed to get Armstrong a new record contract. Many Rockwell-O'Keefe artists were now on Jack Kapp's new label, Decca Records, thanks to the relationship between Kapp and Rockwell forged at Brunswick. In addition to selling new recordings for the Depression-welcome rate of 35 cents per disc—or three for a dollar—Decca also had Bing Crosby, who regularly named Kapp as one of the people most responsible for his success.[59] Only RCA Victor stood in the way, but Glaser took care of them when they attempted to exercise their option with Armstrong once again that fall. He wrote back with a copy of his signed contract with Collins illustrating that he was now Armstrong's personal representative, insisting, "You are further notified that all payments due under and by virtue of the agreement herein referred to are to be made payable to the order of Joseph Glaser and sent to him care of Rockwell-O'Keefe Inc." Armstrong was now a Decca artist.

Armstrong's first Decca session was on October 3, but it was not made with Zilner Randolph's band. While Glaser was making all of these major deals, he once again had to settle an old score in Armstrong's life and booked his client to headline a revue at a new iteration of Connie's Inn, still run by Connie and George Immerman but now located on Broadway and West 48th Street in Manhattan. This would be an extended engagement beginning at the end of October and the New York Local 802 union insisted it use New York–based musicians. If Armstrong wanted to use the Randolph band, there would be a six-month waiting period for them to switch from the Chicago union to the New York union. Randolph claimed that Glaser could have pulled some strings, but Glaser refused and let Randolph's band go. As a parting gift, Glaser offered him $50 for a composition he had introduced to Armstrong, "Old Man Mose." "I had an idea it was good, but I sold it to save my home," Randolph said a few years later.[60] Randolph never had any hard feelings toward Armstrong, saying, "I idolized the man. . . . It was Jesus first, and I guess it was a tossup between Louis and my wife. Because I know Louis was right in there."[61]

Instead of assembling a band from scratch, Glaser rightly assumed it would be easier to hire an intact orchestra outright and have Armstrong front them. In late September, the *New York Age* reported that Glaser had signed Teddy Hill and His Orchestra, but days later, Hill had a change of heart. "Teddy has worked years to bring his organization to the heights it commands today and if he allowed his name to be submerged to another individual, no satisfaction for Teddy could be reached, so he says, and refused to sign a contract," read one report.[62] Glaser reached into Armstrong's past and instead secured the services of Luis Russell and His Orchestra to back Armstrong up on his maiden voyage on his new label.

This would also be Armstrong's first time in a studio with Jack Kapp overseeing a session since a rogue Hot Five date under Lil's name for Brunswick in 1926. Nearly ten years later, both Kapp and Armstrong were looking to achieve something different on Decca. Kapp was not a musician but he had a knack for knowing what the public wanted to hear, once remarking, "I know how to keep my pulse on the multitude."[63] He liked to have his artists record in diverse settings, not just in one genre of music. Crosby became the poster child of Kapp's methods, recording popular ballads, light classics, Irish lullabies, cowboy songs, and an occasional hot number. "And that kind of diversified record program, I believe, was the most important thing in the advancement of my career," Crosby said. "I thought he was crazy, but I did what he told me."[64]

This would now be Armstrong's recording life for the next several years: he'd record swing instrumentals, novelties, Mexican songs, Hawaiian songs, New Orleans throwbacks, early folk music, 19th-century material, spirituals, and more than anything else, love songs. This suited Armstrong just fine, as it allowed him to tap into his romantic side. And if the material was sometimes of subpar quality, that didn't stop him either. "He was a transformer," Dan Morgenstern said in 2019. "I mean, you could have given him a piece of shit and he would have done something with it."[65]

The only element that tied the different songs and settings Kapp sprung on his artists was a simple one: an adherence to the melody. If the melody was up front on his recordings, Kapp was content. "His brother, Dave, during a vacation in Virginia, photographed a statue of Pocahontas with her arms raised in prayer and added Jack's mantra as a caption, 'Where's the melody?,'" Gary Giddins wrote. "Dave mailed the picture to Jack, who enlarged it, printed several copies, and posted them in Studio A and other strategic places in the Decca offices."[66]

Armstrong did not need to be convinced of the wisdom of Kapp's beliefs as he had matured since that 1926 Brunswick date. He loved his vaunted 1920s recordings but even looking back on those, he saw room for improvement. In 1951, he made a private tape with some friends in Chicago, listening to the Hot Five's "Irish Black Bottom." During the shouted vocal from 1926, the Armstrong of 1951 grew frustrated and emphatically started scatting the written melody over the recording. After scatting, Armstrong moaned, "That's the lead!" before imparting some self-critical analysis: "In those days, we sang just what you call 'obbligato,' you know? And we commenced hollering, 'Where's the melody?' See? First thing you see when you walk in the Decca studio, chick with her hair down to her asshole, hollering 'Where's the melody?' holding both of her hands out."[67] It's a fascinating little insight hearing him made uncomfortable by his younger self, calling that vocal style nothing but an "obbligato" and recalling Kapp's advice, a true sign that he felt quite at home at Decca.

Kapp had four songs waiting for him on October 3, three of them new pop tunes. Up first was "I'm in the Mood for Love," with some Lombardo-esque reed work that surely pleased Armstrong (and Kapp). The vocal is nearly gravel-free, Armstrong trying to take his singing more seriously. A dramatic minor-to-major closing cadenza with a high note ending set up the template for many to follow. Armstrong also sings beautifully on "Got a Bran' New Suit," while he scats like a demon on the Mexican hit "La Cucaracha," a Kapp curveball choice. On "You Are My Lucky Star," he eschews the question posed by Kapp's Pocahontas image and offers a startling full chorus of improvisation in full command of his horn, offering some smooth, doubled-time lines and trying out some daring new harmonic choices. This was how Armstrong was now approaching the concept of "playing for musicians." And they were listening; trumpet rival Henry "Red" Allen told Dan Morgenstern that on "You Are My Lucky Star," Armstrong was "showing that he had something new for us."[68]

Two days after the session, Armstrong set about showing the world that he had something new for them with a high-profile radio appearance on Walter Winchell's *Shell Chateau Radio Show*, featuring excellent performances of "On the Sunny Side of the Street" and "Ain't Misbehavin.'" He still didn't have a band of his own, but after the Decca session, Glaser negotiated with Luis Russell's manager Sam Flashnick to hire the entire Russell organization to become Armstrong's full-time backing band. After their scintillating 1929–1930 recordings for OKeh, the Depression hit the Russell band hard. "They was trying days back in the '30s," Charlie Holmes, the band's alto saxophonist, remembered. "There was a Depression on here. And it was *terrible*."

Figure 12.2 Armstrong with his longtime friend Luis Russell, who became his music director in 1935, in Chicago in the mid-1930s.
The Jack Bradley Collection, Louis Armstrong House Museum

Glaser offered Russell six months at Connie's Inn to back Armstrong, which impressed the band. "That sounded *very* good," Holmes said.[69]

Percival Outram in the *New York Age* took Russell to task for giving up his band, saying Russell "has submerged his identity to the Orchestra he has fostered and built up for years to first class caliber."[70] Paul Kahn, Russell's son-in-law and biographer, provides an eloquent explanation for why Russell would have gladly made the deal to join forces with Armstrong:

> While there were pragmatic considerations in play, there is ample evidence to support a more holistic, artistic, and perhaps even spiritual explanation. Luis Russell and Louis Armstrong were musical yin and yang, Russell a reserved, supportive anchor, who created an unobtrusive backdrop, and Armstrong, a flamboyant dandy and charismatic front man who dazzled with brilliant trumpet playing, singing, and showmanship. Together, they were unstoppable, a complimentary [*sic*] team. Luis Russell loved and admired Louis Armstrong and realized

the transcendent nature of his talent. . . . Luis Russell knew deeply, from first-hand experience, that Louis Armstrong was a cut above everyone else. This realization made his decision easy.[71]

Armstrong went into rehearsal for his new revue, *Connie's Hot Chocolates of 1936*, featuring music by Sammy Cahn and Saul Chaplin and performances from an all-black cast of 97 members including young Billie Holiday, Ada Ward, Snakehips Tucker, Chuck and Chuckles, Kaloha, Ted Hale, and the Three Dukes. It was Cahn and Chaplin's first show of this kind and they were thrilled to work with Armstrong, whom Cahn called "just a marvelous, marvelous man." Armstrong's big showcase in the revue would be "Shoe Shine Boy," sung to a young boy during the finale. "If you listen to the recording of 'Shoe Shine Boy,' the song is based on a lick of Louie's," Cahn said before humming the melody. "You hear that in all of Louie's riffs." It was another example of Armstrong's language making its presence felt in various compositions of the era.[72]

When the revue opened on October 29, the show business trades and black newspapers deemed it a smash. "Overnight the supposedly smart attitude of lamenting Armstrong's decline, fashionable for five years, vanished," *Variety* reported. "'Satchelmouth' is still head man on that horn."[73] "Proof of Louis Armstrong's popularity was the overflow present at the premiere," the *New York Amsterdam News* wrote. "Some two thousand persons were turned away and a squadron of police patrolled the Times Square district for many blocks within the area of the nitery."[74] Six years after *Connie's Hot Chocolates*, Armstrong was once again a Broadway star. This would be his life for the next several months: three shows a night at Connie's Inn, plus five live radio broadcasts a week, two of them heard nationwide on CBS on Tuesday and Friday nights at 11. Radio was king and Armstrong was reaching bigger audiences nightly than he had in years.[75]

In November, Armstrong's initial batch of Decca records were released, immediately hitting *Radio Today's* "Best Sellers" charts. *Variety* approved, with Abel Green writing, "It's the same ole flannel-mouthed (or satch-mou,' as he's affectionately labeled) with his torrid trumpeting and his undistinguishable lyricizing whenever he essays a pseudo-vocal chorus. Hardly a word's distinguishable but who cares? He's in a class by himself."[76] The jazz writers told a different tale, as the material was knocked by former supporters John Hammond, Edgar Jackson, and Leonard Feather, the last of these writing, "Louis Armstrong has reached a stage where his showmanship overpowers his musicianship, his new Decca recordings showing that his greatest days are, alas!, over."[77]

Kapp didn't pay any attention to such reviews and continued recording Armstrong at multiple sessions in November and December, adding 10 more tunes to his oeuvre. Before Armstrong's November 21 session, E. F. Stevens of Decca assembled the Russell band in the studio and played them recordings Russell had made with Armstrong for OKeh back in 1929 and 1930 to try to regain some of the old, stomping rhythmic feel that was absent on the first session.[78] On "I've Got My Fingers Crossed," the band responded by recapturing their old verve, bassist Pops Foster really booting things along as Armstrong stretched out with two choruses of loose but intricate trumpet playing, closing with a surprising whole-tone passage. The same kind of rhythmic surprises infused "Shoe Shine Boy," which had become a big hit in the show and a favorite with African American audiences. Armstrong only plays one chorus, but what he plays is almost indescribable, building up to a dramatic closing cadenza, quickly becoming a hallmark of Armstrong's Decca work.

Armstrong's upper register work is cleaner than ever before on these recordings, which is almost unfathomable considering the state of his chops earlier in the year. He reaches a sky-high concert F at the end of both "I Hope Gabriel Likes My Music" and "Solitude," the latter making Walter Winchell's column: "Decca has just made a record (Louie Armstrong made it, I mean) of 'Solitude,' in which he hits an 'F' note at the end of the 2nd chorus. This is supposed to be wonderful among musicians."[79]

But of all the songs recorded at the end of 1935, none had the impact as the one Zilner Randolph sold for $50: "Old Man Mose." It wasn't "Star Dust" and there were no trumpet pyrotechnics, but the way Armstrong performed the singalong number, the results were magic. Reviewing it in *Esquire*, Frank Black wrote that "Old Man Mose" was "exciting and chasey and racial."[80] That might have been a clunky way of praising it, but "Old Man Mose" became one of Armstrong's biggest hits with black audiences. According to Jack Schiffman, son of Apollo Theater founder Frank Schiffman, "One song, 'Ol' Man Mose Is Dead,' stopped traffic every time, and in my recollections that song and 'Pops' Armstrong are indelibly etched."[81]

African Americans also might have seen another type of symbolism in the lyrics to "Old Man Mose," as "Mose" was slang for an older, more submissive type of black man. In February 1936, the National Negro Congress was held in Chicago, with almost 2,000 delegates—including Langston Hughes and the NAACP's Roy Wilkins—gathering to discuss important issues in the black community. The *New York Amsterdam News* sent its newest columnist, future Congressman and Civil Rights activist, Adam Clayton Powell Jr., to cover it. "OLD MAN MOSE is dead!" is how Powell opened his column. "So has puffed Louis Armstrong nightly over the radio waves for the past few weeks. The formal burial service, however, was held in Chicago this past week at the National Negro Congress." In his fiery conclusion, Powell quoted part of the lyrics and wrote, "But 'Mose has kicked the bucket and Old Man Mose is dead.' 'Old White Folk's Mose,' 'Old Sell-'Em-Down-the-River Mose,' 'Old Handkerchief-Head Mose,' 'Old Uncle Tom,' old self-styled race leader, buried in Chicago on February 14, the anniversary of Frederick Douglass' birthday.... In other words, friends, not 'I believe,' but I know, 'Old Man Mose is dead!'"[82]

The power of Armstrong's "Old Man Mose" and the success of his engagement at Connie's Inn were just part of a tremendously exciting and important period in African American show business. Yes, the "Swing Era" was taking off and providing more visibility for black jazz instrumentalists and singers, but Armstrong was also part of an equally important movement on Broadway. In addition to Connie's Inn, there was the opening of *Porgy and Bess*; the comedy *At Home Abroad*, starring Ethel Waters; the Langston Hughes–penned drama *Mulatto*; and the hit show *Three Men on a Horse* with black actor Richard Huey. To African American writer Floyd J. Calvin, "[A]t last the old 'Blackface' stereotype has been broken. White people now pay to see Negroes be themselves, and rate them on the faithful interpretation of character rather than on the faithful portrayal of preconceived prejudice notices."[83]

In a separate article, Calvin keyed in a reason why so many black entertainers such as Armstrong were finding newfound acceptance and fame. "There is but one answer—the new vogue of 'selling personality,' which began about six years ago and is now at its height of public favor." Bandleaders used to stay in the background, but starting with Armstrong and Cab Calloway, they were becoming stars of their own through the sheer force of their personalities. "So immediately a whole host of youngsters (few oldsters had the nerve to try it) began practicing before mirrors—conjuring up new facial workings and torso movements, all of which helped a nervous and depression worried public to forget the 'economic wolf' that was chasing them," Calvin added.[84]

Armstrong's personality and songs like "Old Man Mose" brought the trumpeter to new levels of fame in the African American community. Though Leonard Feather bemoaned that Armstrong's "showmanship overpowers his musicianship," that was just fine with Armstrong's black audience, as Feather experienced himself on one of his first trips to the United States when he attended a "Christmas Breakfast Dance" at the Savoy Ballroom in Harlem at the end of 1935. "All Harlem had been waiting for the night," Feather wrote, "And now Louis, the idol of his people, the Columbus, the Lindbergh, the George Washington of his race, had consented to come and play at the breakfast dance in the Savoy Ballroom, Harlem. O, what a ball was there, my countrymen!"[85]

Feather had been tough on Armstrong in print lately, but he had never quite seen anything like Armstrong in this setting, playing for a predominantly black audience, who sang along with every word of "Old Man Mose." "Say what you like about his Decca records, and I will probably agree; say what you will concerning his broadcasts, and perhaps again I will be of your mind," Feather said. "But nothing can erase my impression that on that night at the Savoy Louis Armstrong gave a show the like of which we seldom, if ever, saw during the entirety of his stay in Europe." He continued:

> We all know and appreciate that in his old days with Hines and Redman there was a more sincere or a purer and more musical Armstrong to be heard. But out of that purely musical Armstrong there has evolved another being, still a magnificent musician with good musical taste, but a musician who combines showmanship with his music in a subtle and spontaneous manner that makes it completely acceptable. There were no strings of a hundred and fifty high C's here; no wild gesticulations to the band or exhibitionism of the kind which brought him catcalls and pennies on that fatal Christmas night at the Holborn Empire just two years before. There were no wrong or cracked or offensive notes. When Louis worked up to a high note in the coda of "Ain't Misbehavin'" or "Confessin'," he made them wait for it and want it almost to desperation. His sense of dramatic values, of suspense and control of his audience, is fantastic.

Armstrong's long climb back to the top was nearly complete, ending a year of staggering highs and lows. For the rest of his life, he continued to give all credit to Joe Glaser for making it happen. N. J. Canetti, seeing all the attention paid to Armstrong, popped up at the end of 1935 to say that he still had Armstrong's music trunk and that Armstrong could have it for 12,000 Francs.[86] Canetti also added that Armstrong would never again be allowed to perform overseas. Armstrong told him through the press, "If I do sail, I'll not work under your direction."[87] Armstrong didn't need Canetti or anyone else; he had Joe Glaser—and peace of mind.

13

"Swing Is My Bread and Butter"

January–December 1936

One evening, trumpeter Red Hodgson asked Louis Armstrong how he played his high notes. "I don't know," Armstrong reportedly responded. "I just blow in here, and the music goes 'round and 'round and comes out here."[1] Hodgson turned that answer into a song, "The Music Goes 'Round and Around," and it quickly became the property of the team of trombonist Mike Farely and trumpeter Ed Riley at the Onyx Club on 52nd Street. Jack Kapp recorded it for Decca in September 1935; by December, it had sold over 100,000 copies and was the song most associated with the new "swing" craze.

It was only a matter of time before Kapp asked Armstrong to record his own version of "The Music Goes 'Round and Around." On January 18, 1936, Armstrong showed how to really swing it, adding some scat singing considerably more advanced than "whoa-ho-ho-ho." However, the arrangement was a little flat and the Russell band didn't play with much verve. Part of the reason could be exhaustion. *Connie's Hot Chocolates of 1936* went through some changes in January, meaning Russell's outfit had to now rehearse every afternoon from 2 to 5 P.M., play three shows between 7 P.M. and 3 A.M. and record at 9 A.M. Asked how this affected the band, Charlie Holmes said, "Well, it didn't help the band's performance, you know what I mean? . . . You be dead tired, you don't take no interest in what you do."[2] That tiredness is evident on the January 18 session. Kapp took notice.

Joe Glaser, meanwhile, was cashing in on the new craze in a big way. In early January, he negotiated a book deal with Longman, Greens and Company to have Armstrong write about swing music. "Book is in preparation now and due out as soon as it can be rushed thru," *Billboard* reported.[3] Writing was one of Armstrong's favorite offstage hobbies, but with his hectic schedule at Connie's Inn and the fact he had to have it "rushed thru," Armstrong would need some help. He got it in the form of Horace Gerlach, a 25-year-old white pianist, arranger, and bandleader from Philadelphia. Known to friends as "Dutch," Gerlach, in addition to being Armstrong's ghostwriter, soon began contributing arrangements for the band, though trombonist Jimmy Archey said, "he was nothing much as an arranger."[4] Still, he became a lifelong friend, saying of Armstrong, "He loved life. He was a real human being with a great sense of humor. And he was an exemplary representative of his race."[5]

It's possible that Gerlach was hired to give the Russell band a "whiter," more commercial sound. For Armstrong's next Decca session on February 4, Kapp decided to go all the way, replacing Russell with a band made up entirely of white musicians, including the sensational trumpeter Bunny Berigan. Berigan was a big part of Benny Goodman's success in 1935; Helen Oakley heard him then and wrote, "Bunny is, I believe, the only trumpeter today comparable to Louis."[6] Berigan modeled his style after Armstrong, saying, "All I can say is that Louis alone has been my inspiration, and whatever 'style' I play you can give Armstrong the credit."[7] Berigan soon became a favorite of Armstrong, who said of him "Now there's a boy whom I've always admired for his tone, soul, technique, his sense of 'phrasing' and all. To me Bunny can't do no wrong in music."[8]

Berigan doesn't solo on Armstrong's two Decca cuts, but his big tone can be heard happily leading the band through instrumental interludes on "I'm Putting All My Eggs in One Basket" and "Yes-Yes! My-My! (She's Mine)." The arrangements themselves are not great, but the band does play with more spirit than Russell's band did in January. The resulting record cracked Decca's top 10 best-sellers list and impressed Edgar Jackson in England, who concluded "there are times when white bands provide a much better support than Negro groups to colored soloists."[9]

The record was not as warmly received by at least one writer in the black press: Porter Roberts. Roberts was a songwriter in his spare time—and an elevator operator by day—but on April 11, 1936, he became a columnist for the *Pittsburgh Courier* with his first "Praise and Criticism" outing. For the rest of the decade, Roberts took aim at many of the top African American entertainers, dispensing much more "criticism" than "praise." In his very first column, Roberts went after Armstrong, up to this point, a sacred figure in the pages of the *Courier*. "Louis Armstrong's manager (white) is seeking some white boys to back up the king of trumpet high G's," Roberts wrote. "If Louis Armstrong accepts the proposition of leading a band of white boys, that will keep that many colored musicians out of work. No, no, Louis, that's all out of place. But if you, or your manager persists, the Negro Press should boycott you in every way."[10] Glaser "energetically and vehemently" called the *Courier* to say Roberts's story was "absolutely untrue." Glaser said he spent $3,000 to hire the Russell band and asked, "Would I want to turn over that set-up for a white band? I brought Louis back out of retirement and now he's the biggest name in the game."[11] It would be far from the last time Glaser would rush to Armstrong's defense and far from the last time Roberts would go after Armstrong.

On February 10, Armstrong closed at Connie's Inn after three and a half months in one place, something that would rarely happen again for the rest of his career. About to go on the road, Armstrong enlisted the excellent African American arranger Chappie Willet to finalize a library of new arrangements for the tour. Willet had worked on Armstrong's Connie's Inn arrangements with his partner Russell Wooding and according to Allan McMillan, "ol' Satchelmouth liked them so well that he contracted Chappie for exclusive services."[12] Some of the best arrangements of Armstrong's big band years would come from the pen of Willet.

Armstrong, now billed as "The King of Swing," was a sensation on the road.[13] Crowds wrapped around the Lincoln Theater in Philadelphia and he followed that by breaking his own record at the Apollo, where the *New York Age* reported that "Old Man Mose" and "Shoe Shine Boy" were the most popular numbers with the predominantly black audience.[14] From the Apollo, it was off to Boston where Glaser booked Armstrong and the Mills Brothers for $8,000 for the week, a record-breaking salary for African American entertainers. The *Pittsburgh Courier* reported that Armstrong "will become the highest priced colored star ever to appear at the spot," and added, "Armstrong's popularity seems to be increasing" because Glaser had "made the country 'Armstrong conscious.'"[15] In the jazz press, it was a different story. *Down Beat* covered the Metropolitan engagement with a front-page headline "ARMSTRONG IS PLAYING COMMERCIAL 'JUNK.'" "From the swing angle, it's really a bringdown show, giving Louis no opportunity to do anything but mug and play pure commercial junk," George Frazier wrote. "He sings 'Shoe Shine Boy,' 'Old Man Mose,' and 'I Hope Gabriel Likes My Music,' which should give you a faint idea of the Rockwell-O'Keefe influence."[16] Clearly, white jazz critics were not getting the same enjoyment of Armstrong as his legion of African American fans.

Armstrong was in great pain at the Metropolitan and took some more time off at the end of March to undergo a tonsillectomy, but was back in the studio on April 28, backed by a rested, rejuvenated Russell band on "Somebody Stole My Break" and "I Come from a Musical Family." "I wonder how many of those who listen to Louis' new records have realized that they are hearing something that is going to make a lot of difference to the jazz of the future," British writer Eric A. C. Ballard wrote of these sides.[17]

Armstrong topped himself on a May 18, 1936, session that resulted in six excellent recordings. The session got off to a terrific start with two new Hoagy Carmichael songs, "Lyin' to Myself" and "Ev'ntide," each featuring irresistible, walking, medium tempos, charming, gravel-free vocals, and extended closing trumpet cadenzas. On "Lyin' to Myself," the cadenza is 40 seconds long, while the one on "Ev'ntide" lasts 25 seconds, each quite majestic. "Pops has started playing codas again," Ballard wrote. "You all know what that means. The coda starts about two-thirds of the way through and carries on for the rest of the record. It goes up . . . and stays up for a couple of notes or so . . . then it comes down and rolls around below, below, below for a bit. Then it goes up again and you think, 'One more high note and that's all.' But you're wrong. It comes down again and you decide that Louis is going to finish on a low one. But you're wrong again. You always are when you try to figure out what he is going to do next."[18]

It was time for the main event: Armstrong and Gerlach's new composition, "Swing That Music," to be tied in with their soon-to-be-released book of the same name. There's no other way to view this recording other than Armstrong throwing down the gauntlet at his fellow trumpeters to let them know that he was still the king. Armstrong's Deccas up to this point featured some wondrous trumpet work, but of a more sober variety. He had matured and had given up the days of ending his shows with strings of high C's—but he decided to unleash those powers one last time on this recording, taking four demanding choruses and ending with 40 high C's, before ending on high E♭ (trumpet F). He's in the upper register for 1:41 and not only does his stamina never waver, he makes it sound easy—perhaps too easy. Roy Eldridge was already playing faster runs as jazz continued trending more toward speed, while other trumpeters—again, starting with Eldridge—started playing higher than Armstrong around this time. "Roy Eldridge almost plays sax on a trumpet," *Down Beat* stated in March 1936. "He hits em higher and faster than Louis."[19] That might have been true, but no other trumpeter topped Armstrong when it came to telling a story, endurance, and tone. Because he made it sound so easy, many 21st-century trumpeters don't study this period of Armstrong's playing, as they're more drawn to the intricate lines of later musicians such as Dizzy Gillespie and Clifford Brown. But few mortals could get through all four choruses of Armstrong's "Swing That Music" solo and live to tell about it.

Somehow, Armstrong still had three songs—"Thankful," "Red Nose," and another remake of "Mahogany Hall Stomp"—to get through and his chops never showed any signs of tiredness. This version of "Mahogany Hall Stomp" became a favorite of 17-year-old George Avakian, a student at the Horace Mann School in the Bronx. Avakian was to become one of a new breed of music fan: the hot record collector. With the publication of Hugues Panassie's *Le Jazz Hot*—due to be published later in the year in English as *Hot Jazz: A Guide to Swing Music*—there was now an interest in older jazz recordings from the 1920s. Panassie's influence as the president of the Hot Club Du France inspired Hot Clubs in the United States, resulting in a record label that started in April 1936, United Hot Clubs of America. Spearheaded by Milt Gabler, owner of the Commodore Record Shop in New York, UHCA went to the major record companies, made deals for jazz records from the 1920s that had fallen out of print, and re-pressed them on new 78s, complete with discographical information on the label.[20] When Avakian mentioned his appreciation for Armstrong's 1936 "Mahogany Hall Stomp" to classmate Julian Koenig, Koenig invited him home to meet his brother Lester, a hot record collector. Lester played the 1929 version for Avakian and then went backwards to the Hot Fives and Hot Sevens. "Well, I was floored," Avakian said. "I was 16, 17 at the time and the fact that I couldn't buy these records inspired me to start writing letters to Columbia Records which owned the rights. I suggested that they begin a program of reissues, a concept that was unknown."[21] Columbia ignored Avakian for the time being, but he would remain persistent over the next few years, as both he and Gabler would play major roles in shaping Armstrong's past and future discography.

On May 24, Armstrong took part at New York's first all-star "Swing Concert" at the Imperial Theatre, one of 17 bands on the bill. Armstrong was saved for the closing spot and had time for two numbers, "Shoe Shine Boy" and "Tiger Rag." In the eyes of many in the press, including columnist Louis Sobol, he walked away with top honors; *Variety* called him the "most penetrating" performer on the bill.[22] It was big news in the black press as well, with the *Pittsburgh Courier* reporting that Armstrong's "wild playing . . . had the conservative George Gershwin stamping his foot" and claiming that he had to close the program "because after he had demonstrated his idea of 'swing,' none of the other orchestras cared to go on."[23]

Once again, it was the jazz press that proved to be the sour voice of dissent. John Hammond took to the pages of *Down Beat* to write, "Louis Armstrong's band could not conceivably have been less suited to its leader's genius."[24] George Frazier agreed, headlining his negative review, "SATCHELMO'S BAND IS WORLDS WORST."[25] During this period, *Down Beat* was running a reader's poll to name an "All-Time Swing Band." Given *Down Beat's* coverage of white artists—and its patronizing, sometimes downright racist cartoons about black musicians—it wasn't a surprise that the leading vote getters were all white, with Tommy Dorsey and Gene Krupa amassing the most votes and Armstrong losing to his long-deceased friend Bix Beiderbecke in the trumpet category. In the overall "Swing Band" category, Benny Goodman led with 3,534 votes, followed by the Casa Loma Orchestra with 2,102. Armstrong received 38.[26]

The *Down Beat* audience might have believed that Armstrong was slipping, but they didn't represent public opinion. In June, Glaser booked Armstrong and his revue of singers and dancers into the prestigious Paramount Theatre in New York, the first time the Paramount booked an African American headliner. *Billboard* caught him there and reviewed his 45-minute show, reporting that there was dancing in the aisles and that Armstrong "left the house limp and begging for more." "Leader is a good showman," the review concluded. "He peddles his work and gets laughs with some of his antics."[27] The big surprise came when the Paramount had attendees fill out a popularity poll featuring all the artists who had been playing the venue throughout the year, which they would use to gauge who should receive repeat bookings. As of June 6, Armstrong, the only African American on the list, led the poll with 13,242 votes, topping Fred Waring's 13,002, Phil Spitalny's 11,803, and Paul Whiteman's 10,905. Benny Goodman came in ninth with 8,930; the Paramount patrons obviously were not readers of *Down Beat*.[28] Armstrong's ways with a love song still had an effect on his female fans, Walter Winchell reporting, "The chocolate-colored star was bombarded by white femme autograph seekers—almost caused a panic."[29]

All of a sudden, Armstrong was everywhere. The *New York Times* featured a big cartoon of him in promoting the Paramount engagement. He was caricatured in a new MGM cartoon, *The Old Mill Pond*. He appeared on the first episode of a new CBS radio show that debuted on June 13, *Saturday Night Swing Club*. And when syndicated columnist Jack Stinnett asked multiple musicians to answer, "What is swing music?" Armstrong replied, "Swing music is music as it should be played, with the whole heart and soul and not as a mechanical thing as so much is played today. I might also add, swing is my bread and butter."[30]

Armstrong continued touring theaters and playing occasional dances throughout the summer, breaking so many box-office records that the *Pittsburgh Courier* ran a headline "Louis Armstrong Beats Jesse Owens at Record-Breaking."[31] Armstrong welcomed a special guest for a stretch of his tour: Leonard Feather, back again on another trip from England. Feather had taken to anonymously reviewing records for *Melody Maker*, using the pseudonym "Rophone" to differentiate from Spike Hughes's pen name, "Mike." Hiding behind anonymity, Feather continued bashing Armstrong's recent Decca records, complaining that they presented "the worst features of Armstrong and his band" and calling "Swing That Music" the "weakest" of the May 18 recordings.[32] But when he showed up at Armstrong's last night at the Oriental Theatre on July 23, Louis and Alpha were surprised and happy to see him. Feather caught Armstrong's show and found himself fighting an internal battle between actually enjoying himself and remembering the negative views entrenched in his mind and in his writing. Noting that Armstrong played material like "Shoe Shine Boy," "Old Man Mose," and "I Hope Gabriel Likes My Music," Feather wrote that Armstrong "does them so perfectly that it's only after everything is over that you begin worrying about his complete surrender to commercialism."[33]

Armstrong invited Feather to join them on one-nighters in St. Louis and Kansas City and Feather was glad to accept. In St. Louis, the band played an all-black dance in front of 10,000 patrons at the Coliseum. Feather noted that "The whole city seemed aware of Louis's advent," as it was his first time there since the Johnny Collins era.[34] After dinner, Armstrong took Feather to hear his old boss, Fate Marable, still playing on the *Saint Paul* "colossal excursion queen" on the Mississippi River. Armstrong—"hailed as a prodigal son returned in triumph," according to Feather—and Marable reminisced while the band—which included a young saxophonist named Earl Bostic— "ploughed through popular song after popular song," disappointing Feather. Back at the Coliseum, Feather noted, "The entire colored population of Saint Louis seemed to have turned out to greet Louis. Marable, Carter Smith and I were soon knitted into a solid barrage of people, who, from the most beautiful of brown-skinned girls to the humblest rug-cutter, could imagine no greater thrill than to see this idol of their race to beseech him for autographs, to shriek for 'Shoeshine Boy,' and roar the whole auditorium's structure into vibrations as they applauded Sonny Woods' rendering of 'Ol Man River.'"[35]

Afterwards, Feather, Marable, and others joined Armstrong at a nearby tavern for beer, sandwiches, and musical discussion. What they discussed made a deep impression on Feather, who talked about this evening for the next several decades. Marable asked Armstrong to return sometime to play on the riverboat with him. "And Louis," Feather wrote, "whom his critics and best friends alike have been denouncing as completely in the thrall of commercialism, confessed that the whole distorted set-up is 'strictly for the glory of the cash,' and that he has to comply with what he is told is best for him commercially; and that in his heart of hearts he would still, to this day, prefer to be just one of the trumpeters in a swing band, enjoying his music and 'having a ball' just as he did years ago when he not so conscious that anyone believed it to be great music." Feather added, "At last I felt I knew the real Louis; the Louis that we all feared was dead; who, in fact, is nearly buried alive; the Louis who is one of the lads, who talks and plays and acts the way his nature dictates."[36]

The next night in Kansas City, Feather went with Joe Glaser to see Andy Kirk's band with pianist Mary Lou Williams, as Glaser was interested in signing Kirk. Armstrong then joined them to see Count Basie's group at the

Rhythm Club with Lester Young and trumpeter Oran "Hot Lips" Page, the latter particularly impressing Glaser who "murmured that he would like to form a band around that boy."[37] After another reception for Armstrong at another black venue, the Sunset Gardens, Feather and Armstrong went their separate ways, Feather calling him "one of the kindest and most generous hosts I have known."[38] But his time with Armstrong hadn't changed his views on the trumpeter's current music. In September, using yet another pseudonym, Geoffrey Marne, Feather published a poem in *Rhythm* titled "Satch'Mo," which included this stanza:

> The story of his triumph spreads abroad,
> "Who is this Louis Armstrong? Is he 'hot'?"
> Of course, if he plays 'West End Blues' they're bored,
> But to hear 'Old Man Mose' they'll pay a lot.[39]

Armstrong also parted with his entire band as he soon got on a train bound for Hollywood. Bing Crosby had started filming his latest picture, *Pennies from Heaven*, on July 6, but he insisted that Armstrong appear in the film with him. Columbia Pictures president Harry Cohn had no interest in paying for Armstrong but Crosby "refused to discuss the matter," according to Gary Giddins. "What's more, though his part was small (one musical number, two comic exchanges), Louis would be top-billed as part of a quartet of stars. No black performer had ever been billed as a lead in a white picture."[40]

It was another milestone for Armstrong, though of course it came at the expense of some typical Hollywood input regarding how it valued its black actors. Armstrong wouldn't be allowed to sing a duet with Crosby; his one big music number, "The Skeleton in the Closet," played up a stereotype of African Americans scared by ghosts; Armstrong was also shown stealing chickens and couldn't comprehend basic math in conversation with Crosby. But even with the deck stacked against him, Armstrong made the most of his time on screen, finally getting to unleash his acting ability at the start of "The Skeleton in the Closet" and displaying his natural flair for comedy in his scenes with Crosby.

African American columnist Bernice Patton was invited to the set and did not find anything objectionable with Armstrong's comedic scenes with Crosby, writing, "It may interest *The Courier* readers to know that there isn't anything in the entire cinema that you'll be ashamed of. There will be no chief cooks and bottle washers or Uncle Toms. Bing saw to that himself. He particularly informed the studio that his sepia troupe was the best in the business and he expected good dialogue in modern use, fine music and grandeur. He got it."[41]

Armstrong had to wake up every morning at 6 A.M. to get ready for his scenes, but didn't mind it as he was happy to be surrounded by so many friends in California, including Lionel Hampton, who appeared in "The Skeleton in the Closet" number, and Slim Thompson, there to film a supporting part in *The Petrified Forest* with Humphrey Bogart.[42] Armstrong's stand-in in the film was trumpeter Teddy Buckner, who became a friend. Over lunch, Armstrong imparted wisdom to Buckner, including the key to how he approached the songs he played on his trumpet. "When you're playing that horn, always play that melody," Armstrong told Buckner. "It's just like driving an automobile. You pass on the left side but you come back to the right side. Well, playing the horn is the same way: you improvise, then you come right back to that melody."[43]

With that philosophy, it was no wonder Armstrong remained a favorite of Jack Kapp, who set up three sessions for him while he was on the west coast. The first teamed him with another Decca star, Jimmy Dorsey and His Orchestra. They recorded a powerhouse version of "The Skeleton in the Closet," an exciting remake of "Swing That Music" that was shelved until 1941, and a rocking, two-beat tribute to King Oliver on "Dipper Mouth." Armstrong, Crosby, Dorsey, and Frances Langford met in the studio on August 17 to capitalize on the impending film, recording an extended version of "Pennies from Heaven" on one side of a 12-inch 78 and a medley of tunes from the score on the flip side. On his last day in California, Kapp threw Armstrong one of his curveballs and teamed him with a Hawaiian group, the Polynesians, adding Lionel Hampton on drums for good measure. The resulting sides, "To You, Sweetheart Aloha" and "On a Cocoanut Island," are among the most charming recordings Armstrong ever waxed, a stroke of genius from the mind of Kapp. As sweet and swinging as the results were, they were anathema to Feather, who simply wrote in his review, "Just play these two and then play 'Muggles' or 'West End Blues' or 'Save It Pretty Mama.' Then you'll know just how tragic it is that Louis has descended to making records with a Hawaiian orchestra."[44] It's an ironic choice of words since Armstrong's sunny records with the Polynesians are the least "tragic" records of his discography.

Armstrong rejoined Luis Russell's band in New Orleans and together, they set about breaking box-office records in each city they played in, including another outstanding engagement at the Apollo and a performance in front of 7,000 at the old Savoy Ballroom in Chicago. A *Pittsburgh Courier* headline from October 3 put it best: "Armstrong Is Called Answer to Theater Owner's Prayer."

By this point, Glaser was managing Kansas City–based Andy Kirk and his big band with pianist Mary Lou Williams, who would later write "Little Joe

from Chicago" in honor of Glaser. But the band's big break came when vocalist Pha Terrell recorded the ballad "Until the Real Thing Comes Along"
for Decca earlier in 1936. The result was a smash, though the diehard jazz
fans were upset that it was Terrell's crooning that put the band over the top,
and not the arrangements of Williams. But that kind of success was appealing
to Glaser, as it was proof that Armstrong could hit new levels of popularity
by peppering in more love songs and ballads in his repertoire. In September
1939, Glaser wrote that "in presenting the position of race artists in American
popular music I have drawn no line of distinction between sweet or swing
music. There is none."[45] Just like the popularity of Guy Lombardo in Harlem,
Glaser (and Kapp) had figured out that African American audiences also
wanted to hear pretty melodies and Crosby-esque love songs.

This romantic side to artists such as Armstrong and Kirk didn't endear
them, however, to the more vocal jazz critics such as Hughes Panassie, whose
Hot Jazz was released in the fall. It was an important work, but one with too
serious a tone for critic Robert Paul Smith, who had trouble with Panassie's
sometimes brutal opinions on who could and couldn't swing. "Swing is important, but importance of subject is never an excuse for a humorless attack,"
he wrote. He added presciently:

> Our only fear is that this will present opportunities for making swing even more
> esoteric than it is. I have seen fist-fights on their way because two parties couldn't
> agree who was playing a certain chorus on a certain phonograph record. Certainly
> it is a healthy sign but I am afraid that the outsider may fear to tread, and I have
> a deep personal conviction about swing critics who graciously let artists into the
> charmed circle or ban them to eternal darkness with absolute and final judgments
> as to their past, present and future value. Cults grow a little absurd from too much
> inbreeding.[46]

Armstrong himself entered the debate when *Swing That Music* was
published on November 4, complete with an introduction by Rudy Vallee.[47]
Armstrong only had 129 pages to tell his story, with Gerlach's fingerprints
evident in sections on Mark Twain and the Original Dixieland Jazz Band,
subjects Armstrong did not tackle before or after the publication of the book.
Still, reviews of *Swing That Music* were generally positive, especially in the
black press. Writing for the International Negro Press, Robert L. Nelson said,
"In the telling of his story, Armstrong has stuck to a natural style; the narrative is easy to read yet well enough done to satisfy the erudite. The story is
inspiring, for all the world likes to hear of those who have overcome great
odds."[48] John Hammond did not agree, writing that "in this brief pamphlet,

we see a self-satisfied, boastful artist, entirely uncritical of himself or his sur-roundings, with only kind words for everybody, including Canetti, Johnny Collins, Rockwell, and Joe Glaser, his various managers. About the real Louis, who is one of the most fascinating characters alive today, we do not get even a glimpse."[49]

Nevertheless, Armstrong made history with *Swing That Music*, becoming the first African American jazz musician to publish his own autobiography. He broke down another barrier when *Pennies from Heaven* opened on November 25, complete with Armstrong's historic top billing alongside Crosby and the other stars. The film became an instant hit, receiving many favorable reviews from film critics, who had almost unanimous praise for Armstrong's musical and comedic performance. "Dusky Louis Armstrong, the trumpetist, almost steals the picture with his novelty number, 'Skeleton in the Closet,'" wrote the *Film Daily*,[50] while the *Tampa Tribune*'s Henry Sutherland added, "his alter-nate trumpeting, husky singing and mugging are worth the price of admission alone."[51] The reception was similar at first in the black press, the *Pittsburgh Courier* running a huge headline, "Armstrong 'Steals' Bing Crosby's Picture." "The selective audience burst into spontaneous applause as Armstrong hit those high notes," Bernice Patton wrote of the private screening for the press.[52]

But as 1937 began, some dissenting views began to appear, starting with Porter Roberts, who was reveling in his role as the black press's hell-raiser.[53] "HEY, JOE GLASER, you are the manager of the world's greatest trumpet player (Louis Armstrong)," he wrote. "Well, why didn't you tell those Hollywood guys to go take a jump off of the Empire State Building when they started to make a CHICKEN THIEF out of the world's greatest trumpet player in his recent motion picture titled 'Pennies from Heaven?' Dear Joe Glaser, colored people did not like the way the great Louis Armstrong was 'typed' any more than your race would like to see you shining a colored bootblack's shoes (if you were the greatest trumpet player in the world), in pictures or other-wise."[54] Roberts was still hammering his point home in April, writing, "This column can't understand why any colored man who is as famous, and talented as Louis Armstrong, let Hollywood make an outright clown out of him!"[55]

An interesting debate on the subject took place in the black press between Calvin News Service columnist Marion Marshall and Alfred A. Duckett of the *New York Age*. "True, Mr. Armstrong played his part well or he couldn't have been permitted to participate but why did he have to take the part he did, risking the possibility of instilling deeper into the hearts of present-day people that the colored man is ignorant, and notorious for stealing chickens," Marshall asked. She did not believe in taking the long view, writing, "Probably you'll think we're being narrow-minded and we should be glad a colored man

LOUIS ARMSTRONG and BING CROSBY
In a scene from the Paramount Picture " PENNIES FROM HEAVEN "

Direction
JOE GLASER, Inc.
R K O Building Rockefeller Center
New York, N.Y.

Figure 13.1 Publicity still from the hit 1936 film *Pennies from Heaven*, featuring Armstrong with his friend and disciple, Bing Crosby.
The Jack Bradley Collection, Louis Armstrong House Museum

has a chance to act on the screen but I, myself, prefer not seeing one of my group in pictures than to see him belittle himself before the people whom youth is endeavoring with all his power to impress that, if given a chance, he will show the world that he can do more than is expected of him."[56]

The 20-year-old Duckett, who later helped Dr. Martin Luther King Jr. write his "I Have a Dream" speech and *Why We Can't Wait* book, did not agree. "We don't see anything debasing in his characterization," Duckett wrote. "We think it a fine job, artistically and well done. We believe that Armstrong and others like him are paving a way for the Negro to higher things in the world of Cinema." Of Armstrong, Duckett called him "a stylist," noting, "Through a style of unique exaggeration he has brought to himself glory in the field which he chose to conquer. He exaggerates the hoarseness of his voice; he exaggerates the beat of rhythm; he even exaggerated gestures and facial expressions. That is his style and through it he has covered himself with glory." But as to his appearing as a chicken thief, Duckett argued, "There were and are chicken-stealing Negroes just as there were and are horse-thieving whites. There was and is ignorance and there will always be. And it takes a heap of talent for a man of intelligence and ability to portray the ignorant."[57]

Marshall responded to Duckett's reasoning by writing, "You, as a young man, should be ashamed to come to such a conclusion. . . . Can't you see that in emphasizing these objectionable characters that we, who are struggling for advancement, are put to a great disadvantage because only ONE type of Negro is placed before the eyes of the public? Don't you understand that we can't go on allowing people to think Negroes are ignorant?"[58] Duckett answered that Marshall should "start applauding Louis Armstrong for all he's worth and concentrate less on panning him" and "her idealism and up-in-the-clouds theories will leave nothing for the Negro entertainment field but hungry artists and empty glory."[59]

Both sides made valid points, but such arguing must have confused Armstrong. He had just received top billing in a smash-hit film, played and sang at the height of his abilities, and got big laughs and critical praise for his comedic timing. For the rest of his life, Armstrong looked back at *Pennies from Heaven* with nothing but fondness. "I shall never forget *Pennies from Heaven*," he wrote to a friend in the 1950s. "Those Scenes I had with Bing in that picture were classics." He then recounted every line of his comedic exchange with Crosby, summing it up with a two word seal of approval: "GASSUH personified."[60] As the years passed, he never grew tired of re-creating his comedic scene, even doing it alongside Crosby on the *David Frost Show* in February 1971. He knew the times were changing but he also found it legitimately funny. At a friend's home in 1964, he again brought up the film, saying, "And the scene with the chickens, you know? Big laughs. Big laughs. See, you can't do scenes like that now in movies because of the NAACP. Oh, lord. That was the biggest laugh in the picture! Shit, you can't do those scenes now."[61] To Armstrong, who got his first laugh in public by re-creating a Bert Williams routine in his mother's church while still a child, getting the "biggest laugh in the picture" was a badge of honor.

The year 1936 was one that saw numerous record-breaking live performances, hit records for Decca, the first published autobiography by an African American musician, and a buzzworthy performance in a major motion film. Glaser's game plan for Armstrong was coming along better than even he could have imagined, but there was still one medium left to conquer: radio.

14

"A Boom to the Colored Race"

January–June 1937

Armstrong's tonsillectomy in March 1936 seemed to have caused more problems than it cured. K. K. Hansen saw him in Boston soon after and reported, "He mugged because he had his tonsils out two weeks before, his throat was hemorrhaging, and every note he sang was agony."[1] As 1936 came to an end, doctors deemed the first tonsillectomy unsuccessful and recommended another surgery to be performed on January 14 by Dr. H. T. Nash of the Provident Hospital in Chicago. This proved to be a nerve-wracking experience for friends and fans. "When word went out that 'ol' Satchmo' was under the knife, the entire Southside was thrown into consternation, and the *Chicago Defender*'s telephones started buzzing with inquiries," according to one report. "Crowds began to cluster on street corners and in barbershops, discussing the great musician."[2] The surgery was a success and Armstrong spent the next two weeks recuperating, welcoming visitors, and answering fan mail and get-well letters he received from around the world. Armstrong didn't have to worry about his hospital bills either, as Glaser paid them. "Now was'nt that a swell Xmas Present?" he wrote to a friend. "You bet your life it was."[3]

While Armstrong was convalescing, Glaser turned his attention to Luis Russell's band as he was tiring of reading so many critics call it the "worst in the world," bemoaning the glory days of 1929–1930, when Russell featured stars such as trumpeter Red Allen, trombonist J. C. Higginbotham, and clarinetist Albert Nicholas. If that's what it would take to restore the band to its former glory, Glaser would recruit them one at a time. Nicholas was first. A New Orleans native, Nicholas never had a bad word to say about Armstrong or about the Russell band. "We had a hell of a fine band," Nicholas said. "There were nothing but good sounds in the '30s. . . . Artie Shaw, Benny Goodman, Casa Loma, Duke, Basie, Fletcher Henderson, Chick Webb, Mills Blue Rhythm. They were tough bands, and they all had their own distinctive sound. But Louis really put the Russell band way out front."[4]

Glaser's next hire surprised many as he signed Allen, Armstrong's rival, to be a sideman. Allen had been recording as a leader for years but was now consciously making the decision to remain in Armstrong's literal shadow. "Glaser's strategy was very canny," John Chilton wrote. "Firstly he had someone on hand who could play magnificently should Louis ever be temporarily incapacitated; secondly, Red's talents allowed him to play trumpet features that kept up the crowd's interest before Louis came on stage; thirdly, Glaser was able to control the destiny of someone who was increasingly being described as Armstrong's nearest rival."[5]

Allen would not be featured on any of Armstrong's Decca recordings, nor would he engage in any public "trumpet battles." He took the job because he was assured of being featured in live settings and Glaser made good on his promise. When the band played four-hour dances, Allen got one hour to himself before intermission to feature himself and play and sing whatever he felt. "I mean, you don't work with many leaders like that!" Charlie Holmes said. "Especially when both are playing the same instrument. So Red would get up there and play, play, play, he'd play everything he knew. And Red could blow too. And Louis would come back, and just play one note—Toot—and bring down the house. . . . No, Louis was not the type to hold anybody back."[6]

The addition of Allen and Nicholas shifted the balance of power to the New Orleans musicians in the band, including Pops Foster, Paul Barbarin, and of course, Armstrong and (by way of Panama) Russell. "They had a worse clique in Louie's band than they had in Claude's [Hopkins]," trombonist Snub Mosley said. "Those New Orleans guys got on me, including Red Allen." Mosley left in May but the final push for him to leave was when the great J. C. Higginbotham was hired in April. Even with the New Orleans clique, the addition of Allen, Nicholas, and Higginbotham helped Russell regain some of his old glory and, along with the addition of new arrangements by black arrangers Chappie Willet and Jack Oglesby, immensely improved the band's sound.

Armstrong made his comeback after the tonsillectomy at the Metropolitan Theatre in Boston, playing in front of 17,000 fans on his opening night on February 25. His revue featured an African American blackface comedian and clarinetist in George McClennon, but also two up-to-date comedy acts, "The Two Zephyrs" and "Timmie and Freddie." "Timmie and Freddie" were Timmie Rogers and Freddie Gordon and they combined comedy with dancing, all while wearing loud zoot suits. Armstrong took young Rogers under his wing and kept him on tour with him for several years, teaching him about the stage, about comedy, and about timing. Rogers eventually felt confident enough to go on his own, exchanging his green zoot suit for a tuxedo and becoming a pioneering black stand-up comedian with a catch-phrase also associated with his mentor: "Oh yeah!" In a 1947 profile of the budding comedian, the *Pittsburgh Courier* simply stated, "Louis taught him," further proof that Armstrong inspired more than just jazz musicians in this period.[7]

As Armstrong's popularity continued hitting new heights, the *Pittsburgh Courier* ran a headline, "Satchmo's Ever-Working Magic Constant Puzzle to Music Critics.[8] Music critics be damned, Armstrong's Hawaiian recordings of 1936 proved popular enough to warrant a sequel on March 24, teaming Armstrong up with Andy Iona and His Islanders for two more winners, "On a Little Bamboo Bridge" and "Hawaiian Hospitality." On the former, Armstrong took a trumpet break and played a nifty little sing-song phrase, before scatting the exact phrase twice more before the end of the record. Just like that, Armstrong solidified what would go down as perhaps his most recognizable "lick," one he would use both with trumpet and voice countless times for the rest of his career. Longtime supporters such as Edgar Jackson were still not pleased; he gave both the new Hawaiian numbers one star each, and wrote, "The world's greatest swing man hob-nobbing with a bunch of grass skirts. Thus, do the mighty fall, and thus does the tragedy wend its pathetic way."[9]

Armstrong's next Decca collaboration, though, received a much warmer response as he was teamed with the Mills Brothers for the first time on April 7. The group had always been inspired by Armstrong, seeing him live in Cincinnati in 1931. "[H]is style, his delivery, the way of delivering a song, is what everybody tried to capture and it was pretty hard for any of them to do because everything Louie Armstrong did came from his heart and not just the fact that he wanted to do it; he did it because it was inside of him," Harry Mills said, adding that it was more than just Armstrong's music that was influential. "A lot of his slang, the musicians especially and the people in show business today are using these things purely because Louie Armstrong started them."[10]

Harry Mills described everyone's mood during the first session as "Just as happy as we could be. We never wanted to get out of the studio." The combination of the Mills's hornlike voices and the mellowness of Armstrong's singing and playing proved to be quite engaging. What's odd about their first pairing was the choice of material: "Carry Me Back to Old Virginny" and "Darling Nelly Gray." The latter was written in 1856 and was sung from the perspective a slave whose love was taken away by other slave owners. "Virginny" was written in 1878 by James A. Bland, a black man, and contained lines such as "There's where this old darkie's heart does long to go" and "There's where I labored so hard for dear ol' massa." It was risky for Kapp to choose these particular songs to be covered by two of the most popular black acts in America, but the combination produced two surprisingly wistful performances, transforming the Virginny of 1878 into the Harlem of 1937 with smooth vocal harmonies, hip slang, delicious scatting, and warm trumpet playing. Harry

Mills said of Armstrong, "And he was just tireless, this man, he could go from morning to night." Armstrong had to be tireless; in addition to squeezing in this Decca session, he was appearing at the Nixon Grand in Philadelphia, surpassing Tommy Dorsey's previously held attendance record, and preparing to make history again by hosting his first radio show just two days later.[11]

The radio rumors began in late March, with *Radio Daily* reporting, "Various angles are holding up the pens on the Louis Armstrong commercial contract, which will be a boom to the colored race!"[12] One week later, the rumor became reality: Armstrong signed a contract to take over hosting Rudy Vallee's *Fleischmann's Yeast Show* on the NBC Blue Network on April 9. Vallee was heading to England to attend the coronation of King George VI and heartily recommended Armstrong as his replacement. Executives at Fleischmann's Yeast (part of Standard Brands Inc.) and the J. Walter Thompson advertising agency didn't object, allowing Armstrong to make history again as the first African American to host a nationally sponsored, commercial radio show. The contract was for 13 Friday night broadcasts and if those proved successful, NBC had an option to pick up Armstrong's contract for five years, eventually switching him over to Sunday nights in the summer.

At the time of Armstrong's signing, African American representation on radio was most conspicuous on the hugely popular *Amos 'n' Andy*, where the titular characters were played by white actors Freeman Gosden and Charles Correll using black dialect. There was some rancor in the African American community, including a months-long protest by *Pittsburgh Courier* editor Robert Vann in 1931, but never enough to derail the show's momentum. Entertainers like Duke Ellington and Bill Robinson considered Gosden and Correll friends, while Armstrong himself, remained a loyal listener, writing to a friend in 1933, "Ol Amos 'N' Andy's just comin in on the radio. They are still funny. . . . Like Em? I do too."[13]

After the success of *Amos 'n' Andy*, African Americans still didn't get much of an opportunity to act on radio, as most black characters continued to be voiced by white actors using dialect. But this was all beginning to change in 1937, as Eddie Green started making regular appearances on Rudy Vallee's show and Eddie "Rochester" Anderson made his first appearance on Jack Benny's program on March 28. But having an African American such as Armstrong host a sponsored show was groundbreaking. Armstrong's deal was especially promoted in the black press, with Billy Rowe optimistically writing, "The success of the coming radio innovation depends largely upon the support of its listeners, therefore every ebony son and daughter from Maine to California, is urged to rally behind Armstrong and Fleischmann Yeast and

Figure 14.1 Armstrong signs the historic contract to host the *Fleischmann's Yeast Show* on radio, flanked by two of the most important managers of his career, Joe Glaser on the left and Tommy Rockwell on the right.
Courtesy of the Louis Armstrong House Museum

swing with them until March 31, 1942 at which time the first all-colored radio coast to coast commercial will come to an end."[14]

In addition to Armstrong and the Russell band, there would be various guest stars throughout the run, plus comedy by Eddie Green and Gee Gee James. The show would be retitled *Harlem* and every performer on the half-hour program would be African American. The same, however, could not be said behind the scenes. Without any explanation, the show hired a white man,

Octavus Roy Cohen, to write Green and James's comedy routines. Though he regularly wrote mysteries, the *Oakland Tribune* reported, "Cohen is at his best in portraying the life and character of the American Negro in its more humorous phases."[15] NBC might have acquiesced in having a pair of black comedians on the air, but not without the words of a white writer.

At 9 P.M. on Friday, April 9, Louis Armstrong made history yet again. He opened with a short version of his theme song, "When It's Sleepy Time Down South," glissing his way up to a sky-high E♭ at the conclusion.

"The makers of Fleischmann's Yeast bring you a new program featuring the best in Harlem entertainment with words by Octavus Roy Cohen, music by Louis Armstrong and His Orchestra, fun by Gee Gee James and Eddie Green," intoned announcer Graham McNamee, billing the one white writer first. "First, Louie Armstrong!"

The Russell band kicked off "Swing That Music" at a fast clip. "Look out! Look out!" Armstrong yelled. "Good evening, ladies and gentlemen! We are now swinging out on one of them good ol' good ones I wrote myself, 'Swing That Music.' Here we go!" With that, Armstrong took off on his showpiece, sounding stronger than ever as he sailed through the upper register of his horn, spurred on by cheers and hand-clapping by those present, cranking out 25 high C's before the final high E♭. The response was bedlam in the studio. Armstrong then served as emcee, introducing singer Amanda Randolph (later known as Sapphire's mother on the television version of *Amos 'n' Andy*), who performed "The Only Half of Me," followed by a fun version of "The Sheik of Araby" by the Four Nuts of Rhythm and a tap dance by Bill Bailey to the strains of "Honeysuckle Rose." Armstrong took center-stage to perform a laid-back version of "Pennies from Heaven" and romped on "Them There Eyes," both featuring excellent arrangements that Armstrong never recorded in the studio.

It was a very entertaining and exciting show—and then Eddie Green and Gee Gee James came on. Both fell back to familiar and degrading stereotypes of the angry dominating African American wife and the lazy, slow-witted husband.

"Of all the worthless, shiftless, slew-footed," James began to bark.

"Gee Gee, that sweet-talking is music to my ears!" gushed Green.

The result was near silence in the audience, with only a smattering of quiet giggles. It wasn't a good sign and it didn't get better. Green and James's routine lasted six and a half minutes, grinding the momentum of the show to a halt. Armstrong swooped in to close the show with his wild version of "Tiger Rag," now featuring five choruses at the end, complete with quotes and an astounding number of high notes, all with loud cheering from the band, audience members, and others in the studio. Graham McNamee returned to plug Fleischmann's Yeast and Arthur Murray's "new sensational dance book." The band struck up "When It's Sleepy Time Down South," the applause and cheering started all over again, and with the familiar sound of the NBC chimes, the first commercial radio broadcast hosted by an African American was over.

The reviews soon poured in from a variety of outlets. "Tempting the youth with swing music and comedy in all-colored show," is how *Radio Daily* summed it up, adding that in the comedy sketch, Octavus Roy Cohen's "familiar gag lines were missing."[16] *Variety* wasn't impressed with the comedy either, feeling "the chuckle score may not be sufficiently high," but their biggest complaint was about "the shrill jungle gutturalisms," calling it "the noisiest show on the air," and predicting, "It will be a guaranteed tune-off with thousands."[17]

For all the build-up, the reviews in the black press were decidedly mixed. Armstrong himself was singled out for praise. "Louie and his orchestra played their music faultlessly, Louie himself forcing his charm and personality across the audience and across the country," Billy Rowe wrote. "He is the most satisfying individual musician we have ever chanced upon. His efforts Friday night must have greatly enhanced his already established reputation."[18]

But it was Octavus Roy Cohen who became public enemy number one to many in the black press. The *Pittsburgh Courier* even ran a rare editorial on the broadcast, titled "Whose Commercial Was It? Armstrong's or Cohen's!" "[W]hat we heard Friday night was enough to disgust any Negro who had any pride of race," it read. "Instead of the famous trumpet player being 'Louis Armstrong,' fate, via the Fleischman's Yeast Company, decreed that he had to be Octavus Roy Cohen's version of a typical 'Uncle Tom' Negro."[19] The *New York Amsterdam News* agreed, writing that Green and James, "both known to be outstanding in their field, were considerably hampered by a very poor script."[20]

It was enough for Will Marion Cook to demand a boycott of the entire program. The 78-year-old Cook was a pioneering African American composer who studied with Dvořák, formed one of the first black orchestras, wrote multiple Broadway musicals, and served as a mentor of sorts to young Duke Ellington. But more than just calling for a boycott, Cook's telegram to African American newspapers and leading public figures took an ugly turn in the end, reflecting what was happening in Germany at the time. "Negroes should enmasse boycott the Fleischmann's Yeast and National Broadcasting Company for disgraceful Louis Armstrong program Friday night WJZ," Cook wrote. "The Jews of Hollywood, the stage and NBC only exploit the worst and basest of my race. Let's stop it now. Heil Hitler."[21]

Not all African American columnists agreed. Frank Marshall Davis was a journalist, poet, and political activist (he would later mentor young Barack Obama in Hawaii) who recently was named managing editor for the Associated Negro Press. Davis called Cook "a sorehead," writing "He falls into that officious grouping to which nothing is right unless they do it. It's a question as to which does most to retard our racial progress—they or the White Oppressor." Davis argued that this was one reason it took so long for an African American to get a commercial radio show, writing, "whenever any do receive broadcast work, the race either sends in virtually no congratulatory letters or else lays down a barrage of criticism similar to that of Brother Cook."[22]

Davis praised Armstrong, writing, "Louis Armstrong did nothing on the radio different from what he does ordinary. So far as I know he created his method of 'muggin'. You might as well condemn his individual and sensational trumpet style as flay his way of talking and singing. They go hand in hand." Davis even found James and Green's comedy sketch "inoffensive," saying it could have been done "with little variation" by any of the plentiful Greek, German, Russian, and Yiddish dialect comedians on the air.

Davis concluded that Armstrong's show was a "milestone" and implored readers write to NBC and Fleischmann's Yeast with "letters of thanks for the opportunity," before warning that if those entities "listen to the brayings of Brother Cook and his mentally constipated followers, they will soon throw this one out and pass the word around to other white companies. Then what we have gained will be utterly lost."[23] Davis was not alone in feeling that Armstrong's opportunity was too important to squander and required support from the African American community. "I know you were proud of Louis Armstrong on the yeast hour," Earl J. Morris wrote. "Get busy and write a letter to him. And to you cats, old Satchmo was a killer, a solid sender. . . . Get high on six cakes of yeast every day. We want the king to sell more yeast than Paul Whiteman and Rudy Vallee."[24] Both the *Baltimore Afro-American* and the *Pittsburgh Courier* published photos of Armstrong, Luis Russell, Eddie Green, and Gee Gee James in the NBC studio holding "a few of the hundreds of telegrams received attesting the success of the broadcast."[25]

Through all the controversy, Armstrong was receiving a tremendous amount of publicity—the April 17 issue of the *Pittsburgh Courier* featured no fewer than six different stories mentioning him, along with two photographs. In addition to the *Fleischmann's Yeast Show*, Armstrong also returned to the Paramount Theatre. Billy Rowe walked down Broadway and thought to himself, "Gee, the race lads and lassies are surely breaking down barrier by barrier, that which kept their talent in a restricted zone, in a type of atmosphere in downtown theatres."[26] Benny Goodman and His Orchestra returned to the Paramount on March 3, a storied occasion in jazz documentaries and history books as patrons began to dance in the aisles, further proof that the "Swing Era" had arrived. But it's rarely mentioned that Goodman's record was topped weeks later by pianist Eddy Duchin's commercial dance band. And on April 14, both white bandleaders were topped by Armstrong, who brought in $56,000 in his first week. E. Robertson reviewed a Paramount show for the *New York Amsterdam News* and noted, "[B]elieve you and me our Harlem people turned out in force. . . . The King of Swing had come!"[27]

As the weeks passed, some listeners noticed a change in the *Fleischmann's Yeast Show*. Billy Rowe called the second episode "a great improvement over the one before. The sponsors in an endeavor to check the wave of protest which flooded their offices, removed much of the uncivilized noises heard during the first program. As a result, it was more acceptable by race listeners."[28] The guests improved each week and included Ethel Waters, the Mills Brothers, and the Charioteers, while Armstrong continued his high level of musicianship

Figure 14.2 A joyous Armstrong takes a bow during his record-setting engagement at the Paramount Theatre in April 1937.
Photo by Charles Peterson, Courtesy of Don Peterson

on old standbys like "On the Sunny Side of the Street" and "Chinatown, My Chinatown." Chappie Willet even contributed sparkling new arrangements of many songs that were never recorded for Decca. Armstrong was sent acetate discs of five complete episodes and listening today, the results dispel the usual invective hurled at his band.

In the entertainment press, *Variety* gave it a second listen after the third episode and admitted that there had been a "slight moderation" to what it originally described as sounding like "a boiler factory in swingtime," but added, "hardly enough to win back many of those who were quick to tune out the opening barrage when it hit the air." *Variety* didn't have many kind words for Armstrong, arguing that "he should refrain from singing" and his "special type of rhythm, pushing melody in the background, seems of doubtful worth as a regular mid-evening show for general appeal."[29] In early May, a rumor surfaced in *Radio Daily* that "Edward Everett Horton and Ozzie Nelson are slated to replace Louis Armstrong's orchestra for the yeast people this fall."[30] The rumor caused panic in the black press. "With whites kicking to high heaven and the black wolves howling, it may be more than Fleischmann's Yeast can stand," Frank Marshall Davis wrote. "What marked a golden opportunity for our entertainers and might develop into a long time air contract may be taken off the air at the end of the trial period."[31]

Armstrong didn't have time to bother with the rumors or the criticism of the show. The Paramount engagement was a record-breaking smash and he followed that with a trip to Chicago for a week at the Chicago Theatre followed by a week at the Regal Theater, broadcasting his live *Fleischmann's Yeast* shows from Chicago's Merchandise Mart building. *Chicago Daily News* columnist J. C. Bulliet caught Armstrong at the downtown Chicago Theatre and reported, "While there was a sprinkling of Negroes in the audience, it was their white brethren and sisters who were responding most noticeably to the magic of the Armstrong orchestra."[32] Armstrong demonstrated his popularity with black audiences when he broke the box-office record at the Regal on the South Side of Chicago the following week, but Armstrong's white audience was starting to grow larger and more loyal.

After his week at the Regal and another excellent *Fleischmann's* broadcast on May 21, Armstrong, Joe Glaser, and Bob Smiley were immediately whisked away by a coast-to-coast TWA plane to Hollywood where Armstrong was set to film an appearance in the Paramount feature *Artists and Models*. To ensure that he wouldn't miss his May 28 broadcast, Paramount Pictures insured Armstrong's return, taking out a $5,000 policy from Lloyd's of London to indemnify Standard Brands in case he didn't make it back to New York by noon on May 27, as he had to open at the Apollo *and* broadcast the following day.[33]

Artists and Models had already been in production since April. The film was directed by Raoul Walsh and starred Jack Benny and Ida Lupino, but the threadbare plot was just an excuse for a series of musical numbers. For his sequence, Armstrong was paired with the brash singer and comedian Martha Raye, whose idea it was to include Armstrong in the film. "So when producer Lewis E. Gensler said he had *Artists and Models* on the fire," Raye said, "I told him I'd take the part if he would give Louis the part opposite me." Raye gushed to Bernice Patton that she had "every record Louis ever made, and I've been his fan, following him around from theatre to theatre, and all the hot spots for a long time."[34]

Like Bing Crosby, Raye had used her star power to get Armstrong in the film but unlike Crosby, she demanded she perform with him, which made the studio uncomfortable. If Hollywood wouldn't film an interracial duet featuring two men, having Armstrong interact with a gyrating white woman on screen would be even more problematic. It was decided the only way to make it palatable for white—specifically southern—audiences would be for Raye to wear a light coat of blackface to cover up any notions of interracial intermingling between the sexes. Armstrong and Raye performed a Harold Arlen–Ted Koehler composition, "Public Melody Number One," sending up gangster and "G Men" films in a sequence staged by young Vincente Minnelli, best known at the time for directing musicals on Broadway. It was Minnelli's first film work and he wasn't happy with the finished edit, saying, "As filmed, I found the involved production number a full scale mess."[35] Nevertheless, Armstrong and Raye brought undeniable energy to the sequence, with the trumpeter perfectly at home in the middle of such a big production number.

After the whirlwind week, Armstrong and his entourage boarded another TWA flight on May 26, making it back to New York on time on May 27 to open at the Apollo that evening before going back on the air live the next night. This is one of the broadcasts that survives and it captures Armstrong showing no signs of weariness, turning in a "Shoe Shine Boy" that topped the Decca record, taking a series of dazzling breaks on "Bugle Blues," and closing the show by soaring over the last four choruses of "Prelude to a Stomp," spurred on by Barbarin's percolating Latin rhythms and powerful backbeat. Even Eddie Green and Gee Gee James's routine on this episode induced heavy laughter in the studio audience.

But it was too late. On June 7, *Radio Daily* reported that Armstrong's show would be pulled off the air after its June 25 broadcast and NBC would not pick up his five-year option.[36] It didn't take long for the post-mortems to begin. "It is known now that the program fell short of expectations, and that the interference of several white script writers is being blamed in part," Billy Rowe wrote.[37] "I still want to know how much money Louis Armstrong GOT on that sponsored Radio program, don't you?" a gloating Porter Roberts asked. "I wonder just how many colored musicians would vote to pull out from white control from coast to coast?"[38] As time passed, Rowe remained unable to get the "bad taste" of Armstrong's cancellation out of his mouth, writing, "Race-conscious listeners all over the country have several answers as to the direct reasons for the untimely death of this program, and no doubt, as this is being written, many of them are crying race prejudice to high heavens." He did not agree with such reactions. "To that we say no, because Louie Armstrong, Duke Ellington, Chick Webb, Ethel Waters, Bill Robinson and those of like ability are daily smacking jim-crowism right on the button like Joe Louis hit Braddock," a reference to newly crowned heavyweight champion Joe Louis, who knocked out James J. Braddock on June 22, 1937, three days before Armstrong's final broadcast.[39] Rowe insisted black listeners bombard radio stations and sponsors to insist another African American get an opportunity to host a commercial show as soon as possible. It didn't work; it would be several years into the next decade before it happened again.

On July 14, Rudy Vallee returned to the air and hosted Armstrong as his guest. Radio critics were listening and this time, praised him. *Variety* wrote, "Armstrong had just got through laying an egg on a 13-week series of his own. Yet here as routined and built up he was a socko novelty."[40] One wonders how Armstrong felt about his show "laying an egg." He rightfully remained proud of his work on the *Fleischmann's Yeast Show*. In 1941, Leonard Feather asked Armstrong to name the most important events of his career. "As far as the most important events in Jazz during my 25 years" Armstrong responded, "well the first one was when Pops booked me for my first comercial program over the-N.B.C- for Flieshmans Yeast-(i guess that's the way you spell his name ha.. ha.)"[41] Even with the ultimate failure of the *Fleischmann's Yeast Show*, African Americans had a lot to feel proud about in the summer of 1937, as expressed in a column by Earl J. Morris devoted to "men who certainly excel in their particular line." Morris wrote about Joe Louis, Dr. George Washington Carver, Jesse Owens, Eulace Peacock, Duke Ellington, Cab Calloway, and Armstrong as "Just natural geniuses." He concluded, "The gifts of genius of our super race refutes all Nordic supremacy or Aryan line of chatter. The stuff has got to be there that's all. Give our group an opportunity to assert itself."[42]

15

"Just Glad to See Us"

July 1937–May 1938

Just days after the final *Fleischmann's Yeast Show* aired, it was business as usual at Decca as Armstrong squeezed in three more sessions in nine days. First up was an almost immediate reunion with the Mills Brothers, once again with a prime piece of antebellum material waiting for them: Stephen Foster's "The Old Folks at Home," better known as "Swanee River." Though acknowledged as a popular folk song, the content of the lyrics, with its references to "darkies," was no longer appropriate. Armstrong and the Mills Brothers didn't shy away from it, though, instead meeting the material head on and even burlesquing it, the Mills's singing the audible equivalent of an eye roll when they get to the epithet. Armstrong breaks into mock sermon mode in a thick black dialect, doing it in a way that black audiences would have understood as satire. Armstrong really lays it on, lamenting, "Oh, Darkies!" before a southern-fried ending finds him stating, "Well, lookie heah, we are far away from home"—until a hip, closing, "Yeah, man," punctures the message and punctuates the sermon. A daring, swinging, and hilarious way of bringing Foster's song up to date.

Next, the reconstituted Russell band hit the studio for the first time since May 1936. The difference in their playing is significant, thanks to new "old" hires Red Allen, J. C. Higginbotham, and Albert Nicholas, and powerful new lead trumpeter Shelton "Scad" Hemphill. Drummer Barbarin makes his presence felt more than usual, underpinning every song with slashing hi-hat work, street parade rhythms, rocking press rolls, cymbal backbeats, cowbell accents, and other tricks from his New Orleans arsenal. Only Armstrong's voice sounds extra gruff throughout (most likely affected by the throat operation), but his trumpet hits all the peaks on "Public Melody Number One" and the surprisingly glorious Cuban-themed novelty "She's the Daughter of a Planter from Havana." Armstrong also demonstrated his endurance on his latest collaboration with Horace Gerlach, "I've Got a Heart Full of Rhythm," taking two storytelling choruses that take up the final 90 seconds of the record.

The highlight of the July sessions, though, was an updated Chappie Willet arrangement of Irving Berlin's "Alexander's Ragtime Band" that pulls out all the stops. Armstrong again is confronted with out-of-date lyrics ("Dat 'am") and infuses his modern-day personality over them to make them more palatable ("Listen, Gate!"). After singing about hearing " 'Swanee River' played in ragtime," Willet actually writes an entire chorus of "Swanee River"—in swingtime—before Armstrong points the way out over a marching trombone section. The ending finds the dynamic trumpet section coming together to perform Willet's coda with panache, though it's Armstrong who breaks free for the final high note. Truly a performance that shows what Armstrong and the Russell band were now capable of in 1937.

Armstrong wasn't the only band Decca recorded on July 7; earlier that same day, Count Basie and His Orchestra recorded four selections. John Hammond brought Basie to New York in 1936 and though they received a rocky reception at first, they created enough of a buzz to be signed to Decca in January 1937. Featuring influential soloists such as tenor saxophonists Lester Young and Herschel Evans and a gliding, lighter-than-air rhythm section, the Basie band was changing the sound of "Swing."[1] Basie gained in popularity the longer he spent in New York, but it was Benny Goodman who exploded in 1937, with help from dynamic sidemen such as drummer Gene Krupa, trumpeter Harry James, and African American musicians with Armstrong experience, Teddy Wilson and Lionel Hampton. Goodman now led the Paramount Theatre's popularity polls, topping dance bands such as Guy Lombardo and Horace Heidt, proving that swing was not a fad. Armstrong was further down the list but still the top voted African American band, beating out Jimmie Lunceford, Chick Webb, and Cab Calloway.[2]

Armstrong did get a burst of publicity in early August when *Artists and Models* was released, featuring his "Public Melody Number One" with a blacked-up Martha Raye. The number was bound to get attention, as Walter Winchell pointed out that Raye had recently been named "the biggest individual draw in show business."[3] To the surprise of almost no one, their scene proved to be quite controversial. "There are a couple of misguided sequences, one of which may react negatively to the future of Martha Raye whom the studio has developed into sizeable b.o.," Abel Green wrote in *Variety*, adding, "While Miss Raye is under cork, this intermingling of the races isn't wise, especially as she lets herself go into the extremist manifestations of Harlemania torso-twisting and gyrations. It may hurt her personally."[4] "There's one jarring note," Dudley Glass wrote in his syndicated Hearst newspaper column from Atlanta. "It is the number in which Martha Raye, thinly burnt-corked does a Harlem specialty with a fat Negro trumpeter and a hundred other Negroes. It is coarse to the point of vulgarity. I have no objection to Negroes on the screen. I like them from Bill Robinson down the line. Their stuff is usually good. But I don't like mixing white folk—and especially a white girl—in their acts."[5]

The Theatre Owners of North Carolina and South Carolina, Inc. objected to what they described as "the appearance of Negroes in movie scenes with white persons on equal social basis," specifically mentioning *Artists and Models*.[6] W. A. Rush, manager of the Houston Theatre in Houston, Mississippi, took the extra step of writing a letter to the editor of the *Independent*, the official publication of the Independent Theatre Owners Association, to complain, "For some time, the producers have tempted fate by mixing whites and blacks on the screen, but they went too far in 'Artists and Models.'" In an ugly ending, Rush dared, "If the editor of *The Independent* wants to be a real champion of the Negro, he can convince the world in the next issue of his paper that he is really honest in his profession by announcing the name of the darky he is

Figure 15.1 Armstrong warns about the dangers of "Public Melody Number One" while a lightly blacked up Martha Raye poses in the background in this controversial scene from *Artists and Models*.
The Jack Bradley Collection, Louis Armstrong House Museum

willing to accept as a son-in-law, brother-in-law or even as a companion and social mentor of his women folks."[7]

All the controversy did nothing to dissuade Hollywood's interest in Armstrong, as Paramount soon announced that they had signed him for two more films. One would reteam him with Bing Crosby, obviously capitalizing on the success of *Pennies from Heaven*, but the other idea was much more enticing: *Chocolate Parade*. "Yes, indeedy, the current technicolor film is tentatively in the bag, paging such outstanding international Negro celebrities as Louis Armstrong, king of Swing; the Olympic star, Jesse Owens; Diva Marian Anderson, Paul Robeson, sensational baritone, and just about all the Who's Who in the sepia theatrical whirl," Bernice Patton reported in the black press. "The versatile filmmusical will carry a thread story of modern Negro life. Now, Hollywood sounds like it's got something!!!!"[8] Paramount went so far as devoting a two-page spread to the project in their 1937–1938 Exhibitors book, complete with a large color drawing of Armstrong playing trumpet and multiple mentions of him as the film's star. However, for reasons never published, *Chocolate Parade* was soon shelved; Hollywood was not ready for a major all-black musical at the time.

The movie work did boost Armstrong's wealth in this period. Joe Glaser, perhaps in an effort to answer questions about his star client's finances after the *Fleischmann's* cancellation, planted a story in late July that Armstrong had a $75,000 annuity and had already paid $5,000 into it, "preparing to live comfortably in his old age."[9] Though the financial arrangement between Armstrong and Glaser remained a secret, Armstrong did eventually pay off the annuity. "Cats come up to me, 'Well, what the hell, what you do with your money?'" Armstrong said in 1951. "I say, 'What you mean whatcha do with your money?' I said, 'Well, Goddamn, anytime a sonofabitch could put a horn down tomorrow and get $200 a week the rest of his life, he's got to be doing something with it. He's got to have at least a hundred-thousand-dollar trust fund, at least. And show me one colored man living that can bolster that. Not your biggest. Isn't that all right, Pops?"[10] Realizing the poverty Armstrong overcame during his upbringing in New Orleans makes one understand his excitement over the prospect of $200 a week for life ($200 in 1951 equaling $2,013 in 2020).

Up to this point, Glaser had good luck booking Armstrong on strings of week-long theater engagements for much of their time together, but he now realized that there was more quick money to be made with one-nighters. Armstrong and the Russell band went on the road in August and toured straight through October, playing predominantly one-nighters starting in New England before heading through the Deep South and the Midwest. Glaser learned to never turn down an offer during the Great Depression, even if it meant the band had to make some outlandish jumps between engagements such as traveling from New York to Miami for one night and then back up to Boston. This kind of traveling wore down many of the musicians, such as Charlie Holmes, who called it "bad booking," but of Armstrong, he said, "Louis didn't complain, he didn't say nothing. He didn't care."[11]

Holmes expounded on Armstrong's ability to play when tired, in a 1982 interview with Dr. Albert Vollmer:

> Now we had traveled eight hundred miles, you know, you'd get out, you can't hardly stand up, and you'd think he would take it easy the first few sets or something like that. Nooo. No. He'd get in there on that first number, boy, and pound-pound-pound. Well, the house was full of people. And there was no let-up. He was there to entertain the people, and believe me, that's what he believed in. People paid their money, they don't care what you go through. They paid their admission. They want to be entertained. He was absolutely right. Your feelings meant nothin'.[12]

In late August, the band hit Savannah, Georgia, where they encountered Joe "King" Oliver, down on his luck. Armstrong recalled Oliver was "so bad off and broke, he's got himself a little vegetable stand selling tomatoes and

Figure 15.2 Finding humor in the indignities suffered on the road, Armstrong titled this snapshot of himself and members of Luis Russell's band urinating on the side of their bus "Tire Inspection."
Courtesy of the Louis Armstrong House Museum

potatoes. He was standing there in his shirtsleeves. No tears. Just glad to see us. Just another day. He had that spirit."[13] In 1950, Armstrong reflected, "He didn't get his break like he should. See, in the first place, Pops, a whole lot of those musicians like Joe Oliver and Bunk [Johnson] and a whole lot of those boys, they didn't trust nobody, with agents or managers. . . . Well, that sort of thing was Joe Oliver's downfall." Asked why Oliver didn't trust managers or any outside help, Armstrong exclaimed, "Inferiority complex!"[14] Armstrong didn't mince words when it came to his mentor's sad fall from grace. "It was his fault, too," he said. "It was his fault because he had Chicago sewed up. The agents and everybody coming from New York had wanted to bring him in some place, *any* night club, with his band. But Joe wouldn't leave. 'I'm doing all right here, man,' he'd tell them. You know he had a good job, he was making good tips. So time ran out on him. He looked around, and when he came to New York—too late."[15]

After Oliver left New York, he began touring the south with lukewarm results. "From then on, he commenced to, what you call, getting a broken heart," Armstrong said. "You know what I mean, you wind up playing with little old musicians down in some place like Tampa, Florida, some cats that don't even know him. Lay off for two days, the band breaks up. And the landlady commenced to hold his trunks."[16]

In Savannah, Oliver was happy to see so many hometown men, especially since he had fronted Russell's band for a time in the late 1920s. "I gave him about $150 I had in my pocket, and Luis Russell and Red Allen, Pops Foster, Albert Nicholas, Paul Barbarin—all used to be his boys—they gave him what they had," Armstrong said. "And that night we played a dance, and we look over and there's Joe standing in the wings. He was sharp like the old Joe Oliver of 1915. He'd been to the pawn shop and gotten his fronts all back, you know, his suits and all—Stetson hat turned down, high-button shoes, his box-back coat. He looked beautiful and he had a wonderful night, just listening to us—talking."[17] It was the last time he would ever see Oliver alive.

Armstrong's grueling tour ended in October with another trip out to Hollywood to film his part in Bing Crosby's new film, an adaptation on O. Henry's story "The Life of Policeman O'Roon." To illustrate the impact the rise of swing music was having on the culture, Henry's story was retitled *Doctor Rhythm*. Armstrong had a production number written especially for him by James Monaco and Johnny Burke, "The Trumpet Player's Lament." Wearing a lavish satin suit and topped with a derby hat, Armstrong would dramatically—and ironically—lament about being forced to play "hot music, that's really not music," begging for Debussy and "Vesti la Giubba" instead of jazz.

Mae West was also on the Paramount lot and after she stopped in and heard him do "The Trumpet Player's Lament," she insisted he be hired to do a song in *Every Day's a Holiday*, her movie that was being filmed at the same time. He would appear in only one sequence of the film, dressed, in a white "sanitation department" uniform, performing a rousing version of Hoagy Carmichael's "Jubilee." It wasn't a grand showcase, but his appearance definitely livened up the middling comedy. (And without being directly related to the plot, his sequences could be edited out in southern theaters.)

With swing music hitting new heights of popularity at the end of 1937, it was only natural for the music periodicals to close the year by conducting readers polls to name their favorite artists. In the *Melody Maker*, Armstrong won first place in the trumpet category, over Bunny Berigan in second place and Bix Beiderbecke—who had been dead for six years, but who had some reissued records on the market—in third. The Associated Negro Press selected an "All-American Swing Band" based on the votes of a committee of seven black correspondents, musicians, and editors; Armstrong received unanimous first-place votes in the trumpet category, Frank Marshall Davis writing it was "proof both of his unquestioned domination of the field."[18]

Over at *Down Beat*, matters were much different. Except for tenor saxophonist Chu Berry and pianist Teddy Wilson, the winner of every category was white. *Down Beat* had been fixated on white musicians (and continuing to blast Armstrong), so it wasn't a surprise to see how their results were skewed, but it still sent off shockwaves in the black press, seeing Armstrong rated behind Harry James. Porter Roberts, calling *Down Beat* a "white magazine," called the poll a "joke" and this time, defended Armstrong. "Can you IMAGINE merely good white trumpet players like Bunny Burigan [*sic*] and Harry James rating above LOUIS ARMSTRONG?" he asked. "Naw, and neither can I. I am really getting a kick out of writing in defense of the superiority of colored musicians, mainly because they don't need defending! Their playing is their real defender."[19]

The *Down Beat* poll is sometimes used to paint a picture of Armstrong's diminishing popularity, but it's actually a representation of the racially biased readership of *Down Beat* and the general shunning of Armstrong by many jazz journalists. He was at the peak of his popularity to this point in his career, breaking records in California both at the Vogue, where he drew more people in a week than the nightclub had seen in a month, and the old Cotton Club (the *Pittsburgh Courier* referred to him as "Hollywood's Miracle Man"), broadcasting on NBC five nights a week, getting good reviews for *Every Day's a Holiday*, which opened in December, and appearing on Bing Crosby's *Kraft Music Hall* in early January.[20]

On top of all of this, Armstrong's own trumpet playing was stronger than ever, hitting new peaks on a pair of Decca sessions on January 12 and 13 that found him in especially Herculean form on "Jubilee" and "Struttin' with Some Barbecue."

"Jubilee," featuring an arrangement by Chappie Willet, is really pushed along by Barbarin's drums. Listening to it on one of his tapes in the 1950s, Armstrong erupted at the conclusion of the record, "Wow! How about that!? That's that old Barbarin', you know, with that street parade jive. . . . You have to be from the old country to put that out."[21] Inspired by Barbarin's "street parade jive," Armstrong pulls off one of his most staggering feats of endurance, staying in the upper register for the final one minute and 37 seconds of the record, not just hitting high notes, but holding them. "See, the thing that Louis had on everybody else," Charlie Holmes said, "Most trumpet players, the higher they go, the thinner the tone got, and they would end up just squeaking, like a flute. But with Louis, the higher he went, the *broader* his tone got—and it was beautiful!"[22]

Perhaps not surprisingly, "Jubilee" was not well received by Armstrong's detractors at the time, Leonard Feather giving it two stars in *Melody Maker* and writing, "Armstrong's band makes some horrible noises in 'Jubilee,' "[23] while Edgar Jackson gave it one star and mentioned "a stumbling climb up to one of those ghastly high note finishes."[24] But in recent years, "Jubilee" has become a special favorite with modern-day trumpeters. Young Wynton Marsalis grew up in New Orleans and admitted, "I didn't necessarily like [Armstrong's] music because I grew up in the Civil Rights era and the post–Civil Rights era and we felt like he was an Uncle Tom, always smiling with his handkerchief." He finally gave in and listened to one performance after much prodding from his father, Ellis. " 'Jubilee' was the name of the song," Marsalis recalled. "I tried to learn that song one night when I was 18 and I couldn't make it through the song. . . . But when I tried to learn one of his solos, just the endurance it took, let alone the type of soul and feeling he was playing with, it was revelatory for me. And then I began to study his music."[25]

Trumpeter Nicholas Payton spotlighted "Jubilee" on his Instagram page in 2019, writing, "He makes the most of so little information. He never allows for one note to escape him. He finesses each one as if they are all his lovers. His phrasing defies metronomic explanation. He's mastered the ability to place each beat exactly where he wants to for maximum effect. He single-handedly turned a hokey (Hoagy Carmichael) show tune into a magnum opus. This is real trumpet playing here, folks. He says more in under 3 minutes than most people say their whole lives."[26]

It was seemingly impossible for Armstrong to top "Jubilee," but he did just that on the next song he recorded that day, "Struttin' with Some Barbecue." Originally recorded by the Hot Five in 1927 and credited to Lil Hardin,[27] the tune was brought into the modern age by Willet with a sparkling new arrangement, complete with an ultra-hip unison break in the first chorus. Once again, Armstrong's up in the stratosphere for two full choruses, sticking to the melody the first time around and then unleashing the variations, making it sound easy when it was anything but. Like "Jubilee," it was a favorite of a wide range of trumpet players. In a 1959 *Down Beat* cover story on a "New View" of Armstrong, trumpeters Bobby Hackett and Maynard Ferguson—who had about as different styles as imaginable—both named the 1938 Decca "Barbecue" as their favorite Armstrong recording.[28]

Armstrong's high level of playing can also be gleaned on radio broadcasts in this period at the Grand Terrace in Chicago. Acetate discs of some of the performances, discovered in 2016 by Luis Russell's daughter, singer Catherine Russell, and her husband Paul Kahn, showcase Armstrong in even better form than on the *Fleischmann's Yeast Show*, taking a seemingly unplanned, wild extra chorus on "Them There Eyes," using the coda of "Pennies from Heaven" as a canvas for some surprisingly playful work, and shooting out the lights on a hot "I've Got a Heart Full of Rhythm." But the broadcasts also find Armstrong featuring the band on Chappie Willet's modernistic "Blue Rhythm Fantasy" arrangement, as well as Mary Lou Williams's "Riffs" (soon to be recorded by Andy Kirk as "Dunkin' a Doughnut"). With high-caliber soloists such as Armstrong, Allen, and Higginbotham and a top-notch rhythm section, the acetates show they could hold their own against any big band of the period.

Joe Glaser was happy to be back in Chicago and back at the Grand Terrace—home of the old Sunset Cafe—attending most of Armstrong's shows and working out a deal to follow Armstrong with his other major client, Andy Kirk. Glaser had been very successful with Rockwell-O'Keefe but was now looking to expand, incorporating "Joe Glaser, Inc." in October 1937 and moving out of the Rockwell-O'Keefe office into a separate suite shortly after.[29] He remained the agency's "key man" with black bands, but by March 1938, rumors were swirling that Glaser wanted to go out on his own.[30] Armstrong continued being Glaser's prime client, becoming the highest paid African American to perform at Loew's State Theatre in Times Square at the end of March, earning $6,500 a week for a revue featuring new female vocalist Midge Williams and acts such as Nicodemus, Alma Turner, the Two Zephyrs, and Mayes and Morrison.[31]

Soon after, though, Armstrong received the news that King Oliver died in Savannah on April 10. He was only 53. The official cause of death was a hemorrhage, but Armstrong, aware of Oliver's final months, knew the real cause. "A little time after we left Savannah, the owner of a bar, an old fan, give Joe a job as a flunky cleaning up—emptying those cuspidors like the ones he used to tap his foot on," he said. "And pretty soon he died—most people said it was a heart attack. I think it was a broken heart. Couldn't go no further with grief."[32]

The Negro Actors Guild of America paid to bring the body up to New York, though Armstrong later said that he should have been buried in New Orleans. Armstrong met the body when it arrived at Grand Central Station and attended the funeral, which took place at a chapel across from the Lafayette Theatre in Harlem. "Everyone was there," he said. "Most of the musicians turned out. . . . Very sad inside. Very sad." The Reverend Adam Clayton Powell gave the eulogy, which left a bad taste in Armstrong's mouth for years to come. "I didn't like the sermon this preacher gave," Armstrong said in 1950. "The preacher was laying it on him. They said he made money, and he had money [but didn't keep it]. Well, the Guild isn't supposed to say that; that's what we donate our services for when they give benefits and them things where they make a *lot* of money. A lot of the cats didn't like that sermon. . . . I mean, they ain't got no business saying that! . . . It was a drag, a real drag."[33]

The *Baltimore Afro-American* reported that Armstrong played a "dirge" for Oliver and was the only soloist to perform at the funeral. He was quoted at the time as saying, "He started all of us youngsters off, and there isn't a riff played today that he didn't play more than fifteen years ago."[34] Oliver was buried the next afternoon at Woodlawn Cemetery with Armstrong in attendance. For the rest of his life, Armstrong continued to tell the story of Oliver's importance not only in his life, but in jazz in general. "Ain't no trumpet player ever had the fire Joe Oliver had, I'm sorry," he said in 1950.[35] But he also used Oliver as a cautionary tale of what happens when a brilliant trumpeter doesn't take care of his lips, doesn't take of his business, and simply lets the times pass him by.

Perhaps with Oliver and the memories of his New Orleans days flooding his mind, Armstrong decided to finally record his jazz version of "When the Saints Go Marching In" the next time he entered Decca's studio on May 13. Made with another small contingent from the Russell band, the recording was joy personified from the opening notes as "Reverend Satchelmouth" announced the coming of "Brother Higginbotham down the aisle." Together, they swung the sacred melody as it had never been swung before on record, Barbarin's parade drumming adding the perfect touch of home. Like OKeh, Decca must have had trepidation and sat on the release of the record for almost a full year. In the meantime, the label recorded Armstrong frequently in the spring and early summer of 1938, mostly on a string of pop tunes, some better

("So Little Time (So Much to Do)," "It's Wonderful") than others ("Mexican Swing," "As Long as You Live, You'll Be Dead If You Die"). Decca did give him a choice George and Ira Gershwin composition to record in "Love Walked In," as well as two excellent Irving Berlin numbers, "The Song Is Ended" and "My Walking Stick," recorded in a June reunion with the Mills Brothers that captured all parties at the top of their game. But remakes of two of his 1929 hits, "I Can't Give You Anything but Love" and "Ain't Misbehavin'," with an all-white studio group resulted in somewhat lackluster performances that didn't make anyone forget the originals.

But the most publicized recordings Armstrong made in 1938 were something entirely different: four spirituals with choir backing by Lyn Murray and "The Decca Mixed Chorus." He didn't play a note of trumpet on the session, but Jack Kapp and Joe Glaser knew they had something different and quite terrific and rushed out a single of "Shadrack" and "Jonah and the Whale" to great publicity. The *Brooklyn Daily Eagle* said it was "highly recommended to hepsters," *Billboard* named it one of "The Week's Best Records" (in the "vocal" category), and Walter Winchell gave one of his "New Yorchids" to "Louis Armstrong's platter of 'Shadrack,' a weird and compelling jungle rhythm."[36] Even Leonard Feather begrudgingly gave it three stars, writing, "In fact, it's an odd disc altogether, but not unattractive," though he couldn't resist a closing dig: "And what a marvellous job he could have made of it ten years ago!"[37]

Armstrong's multimedia onslaught was to continue in June with the release of *Doctor Rhythm* but when it hit theaters, he was nowhere to be found. This seemed to catch everyone by surprise as he was performing "The Trumpet Player's Lament" in live performances and was prominently mentioned in all the promotional materials for the film right up to its release. Billy Rowe wrote, " 'Is there a Sherlock Holmes in the house?' That was the query of many theatregoers here last week when they got their first glimpse of Bing Crosby in 'Doctor Rhythm,' not because they needed someone of his fame to find the entertainment in the screen fare, but to find out just what had happened to Louis Armstrong the trumpeter."[38] The black press, led by Earl J. Morris of the *Pittsburgh Courier*, went into investigation mode to see exactly what happened. Morris implored his readers, "Write Bing Crosby at Paramount studios for his photo and demand to know what happened to Louis Armstrong in his picture, 'Dr. Rhythm.' "[39]

Crosby's brother Larry Crosby eventually spoke to Morris, saying Armstrong's scenes were removed not "due to racial or professional jealousy," but rather "to technical imperfections," adding that Bing and co-star Andy Devine also had several scenes cut to make room for more scenes involving British performer Beatrice Lillie. Morris reported that any theaters wanting to show Armstrong's sequence could write to the Paramount Film Exchange to obtain a copy.[40] Apparently some black theaters did just that, which Morris took as a victory. "We have won the first round," he wrote. "We raised plenty hell about Louis Armstrong in the pix, 'Dr. Rhythm.' Jules Wolf and James Thomas are showing the entire sequence at the Lincoln theatre here. Oh yes, we can get the Negro recognized if you do your part."[41]

But Morris was still disturbed by the overall trends in Hollywood, which he saw as "controlled by a few Jews. This small group by its un-American methods is causing a widespread increase of Nazism, Fascism and Communism. It is an American tragedy. . . . These few Jews are either consciously or subconsciously slowly, but surely destroying everything that America has stood for or is striving for."[42] The timing of Morris's comments was especially grisly considering Nazis had destroyed the Nuremberg Synagogue just 17 days earlier. Fascism was on the rise, but Adolf Hitler was dealt a moral defeat on June 22 when Joe Louis knocked out Max Schmeling in the first round of their heavyweight championship bout at Yankee Stadium. Armstrong was playing the Apollo Theater that night, pausing his show so the live radio broadcast of the fight could be played for the audience in Harlem.[43]

The result of a boxing match did nothing to slow down the eventual start of World War II. As Hitler's power grew, Armstrong's music and that of his contemporaries were prohibited in Nazi Germany. On May 24, 1938, the Nazis opened an exhibition titled "Entartete Musik" ("Degenerate Music"), which took aim at American popular music, specifically the Jewish influence on what was referred to as "nigger music."[44] But a group of Germans known as the "Swing Kids" defied orders and gathered secretly to listen and dance to the best American jazz. One "Swing Kid" was Heinz Praeger, who was born in 1911 and who attended one of Armstrong's Paris concerts in November 1934. As the Nazis took control, Praeger remembered listening to jazz music in Berlin in "Basements—with the windows blackened out or covered with curtains." Asked by writer Mick Carlon who their favorites artists were, Praeger responded, "Louis and Duke." Asked why Armstrong, Praeger said, "Back then, Louis' horn symbolized to us the freedom and open heart of America. There was something so majestic, so glorious, so free in the sound of that horn."[45]

16

"A Solid Man for Comedy"

May 1938–December 1939

Joe Glaser moved into his new office in the RKO building at 1270 Sixth Avenue in Manhattan in May 1938, still technically a part of Rockwell-O'Keefe, Inc., but now operating as Joe Glaser Inc. As soon as his contract expired on August 1, he went out on his own, having "had a peeve on with R-O'K office for some time now."[1] This got a small paragraph notice in *Variety*, but it garnered a huge headline in the *Pittsburgh Courier*, acknowledging Glaser's power in the world of black show business.

Glaser was serving as personal representative to Louis Armstrong, first and foremost, but also bandleaders Andy Kirk, Noble Sissle, Willie Bryant, and Claude Hopkins and two other top trumpeters, Oran "Hot Lips" Page and Roy Eldridge. Page was an engaging singer and a dynamic trumpeter with a true affinity for the blues, but he would never replace Armstrong in Glaser's eyes or those of the American public. Reviewing his first Decca single, the *Brooklyn Daily Eagle* wrote, "A miniature Louis Armstrong comes out of Harlem in the shape of 'Hot Lips' Page, whose trumpet playing and vocalizing show the influence, but not the excellence, of the original 'Satchelmouth.'"[2] Armstrong continued to support the fiery Roy Eldridge, sending him a congratulatory telegram after hearing his 1937 recording of "After You've Gone," but Eldridge, too, wouldn't overtake Armstrong in Glaser's plans, much to his frustration. Still, with Red Allen in Armstrong's trumpet section and Eldridge and Page under his representation, Glaser was now representing three of Armstrong's greatest black disciple/rivals. His influence could also still be felt on numerous white trumpeters, namely Bunny Berigan and Harry James, the latter performing a snippet of Armstrong's "Shine" solo at Benny Goodman's Carnegie Hall concert in January 1938. "I still think Louie is the father of them all," James wrote in August 1938.[3]

However, none of these trumpet men had quite the personality and pure natural comedic ability as Armstrong. Comedy had been an important part of Armstrong's life since he first heard Bert Williams's records when he was still a child in New Orleans. He continued collecting Williams's records and learning his routines, which paid off when Decca allowed him to record two of Williams's "Elder Eatmore" sermons in full, each one lasting nearly four and a half minutes. It's doubtful the recording sold many copies but it's still a fine example of Armstrong's acting and comedic ability, as well as his ultimate public tribute to one of the first great black stars of the 20th century. Armstrong's most graphic private tribute to Williams came in a 1953 conversation at home with George Avakian, when he said, "Like Bert Williams, if that son-of-a-bitch was here right now, I'd walk in that room and suck his dick, I guess. I'm just that thrilled to be with him. . . . But that's how much I think of Bert Williams, see what I mean?"[4]

One week later, Armstrong traveled to Hollywood to appear in a new Warner Brothers comedy, *Going Places*, starring Dick Powell and featuring other black stars Maxine Sullivan and the Dandridge Sisters. The score by Johnny Mercer and Harry Warren included "Jeepers Creepers," named for the horse in the film, who only responds positively to Armstrong's stable worker "Gabe." It was Armstrong's juiciest comedy role and he couldn't be any more excited to do it. On August 18, he wrote to his friend Elmer Lewis while "Enroute to Hollywood," "I don't know yet—just what part I'm to play in Mr. Powell's Flicker . . . I do hope it's a Comical'one . . . I love to do Comedy for those Picture Stars . . . Something like the part I had in Papa Bing's Picture . . . . . Remember Pennies?"[5]

Armstrong's excitement dimmed when he began shooting scenes with Jeepers Creepers, the horse. "He was a rough horse," Armstrong related in the 1960s. "He would stand way up in the air and the first time I looked up at him, there was nothing but hoofs! I said, 'Well, wait a minute man, let's start this thing over. Don't pull me in with this horse until you're going to shoot.'" Jeepers Creepers had a trainer who prepared the horse before each scene but even when Armstrong got in front of the camera, the trainer's presence wasn't a guarantee that everything would go smoothly. One day the horse hurt Armstrong's hand so badly, he remembered, "I was ready to quit the whole picture! It hurt so bad. They begged me to carry on."[6]

Armstrong also had to fight the painful dialect-heavy dialogue given to his character in the script. Reporters caught the scene on Warner Brothers' Stage 12 as Armstrong struggled to master the line, "If yo'll pahdon me sayin' so, Mistah Randall, of all the gen'lmen who ain't got no right to ride that Jeepers Creepers, you got the most right not to," taking three times to get it right.[7] Armstrong delivered his lines with the usual southern black dialect expected of most black comedians at the time, though he never spoke that way on the stage or on record; in fact, on his recent record of "Going to Shout All Over God's Heaven" with Lyn Murray's choir, every time the white choir sang the

Figure 16.1 Shortly before filming his role in *Going Places*, Armstrong wrote to a friend, "I love to do Comedy for those Picture Stars." He was widely praised for his comic work in the film, but many in the black community felt the role was too demeaning and offensive.

The Jack Bradley Collection, Louis Armstrong House Museum

titular word as "Hebben," Armstrong responded with a clearly enunciated, "Heaven." Even with the imposed dialect in the film, Armstrong's timing was impeccable and the conviction in his delivery was responsible for several laugh-out-loud lines.[8] Still, it's hard not to wince at white actor Allen Jenkins referring to Armstrong as "Uncle Tom," which would definitely have a different effect on black audiences than on most white ones.

Just days after filming ended, Armstrong received word that Lil had filed for divorce in Chicago, charging him with "desertion." Though they had been officially separated since the summer of 1931, neither Louis nor Lil seemed in a rush to officially divorce. "Louis didn't really want to marry Alpha, but she was threatening him with a breach of promise suit, and he was afraid of all the publicity, so he asked me *not* to give him a divorce, because that would be the only way he could really get out of it," Lil remembered. "I gave him the divorce just to spite him, I guess."[9] Louis and Alpha were now free to marry while traveling through Houston on October 11. Perhaps feeling spiteful himself, Louis diminished the effect Lil had on his career, telling reporter John R. Williams, "Alpha has stuck with me through thick and thin. She has been a wonderful inspiration; indeed my very back-bone. Whatever success I may have attained has come about largely because of her never-failing interest in my welfare along all lines."[10]

But truthfully, he was growing weary of her high maintenance—and high spending—ways. "Alpha was all right but her mind was on furs, diamonds and other flashy luxuries and not enough on me and my happiness," he wrote in 1954. "I gave her all the diamonds she thought she wanted but still she wanted other things. She went through most of my money and then walked out."[11] He alluded to some uglier moments in a conversation with William Russell in the 1950s. "Alpha was always getting drunk," he said. "She was swinging at my mouth too often, and it always scared me. What good is a trumpet player if his chops are no good? We were on the train one night with the band and she was trying to hit me in the mouth with the lock on her purse. I hit her, and my fist kept traveling through the double plate glass window." Armstrong said it was a "miracle" that he didn't cut the tendons in his hand. He also told Russell, "There were other times when I would have thrown her out of the hotel window if nobody had been around."[12] Armstrong was now married for the third time but it was clear to anyone who knew them that it was not built to last.

Louis and Alpha celebrated their marriage in Armstrong's hometown, performing a one-nighter in New Orleans in front of a record-breaking crowd that assuredly contained Armstrong's friends and family members from way back. But soon after, while touring through New Iberia, Louisiana, Armstrong ran into a real forgotten figure from his early days, trumpeter Bunk Johnson. Johnson had lost his teeth and hadn't played the trumpet in years, instead spending his time working in the sugarcane fields. At the 1938 reunion, Armstrong autographed a photo for him, "Best Wishes To My Boy 'Bunk.' He's my musical insparation [sic] all my life— 'yea man' from Louis Satchmo Armstrong."[13] He inflated Johnson's actual impact on his musical development, most likely an effort to make the old man feel good, but he did start letting people know that Johnson was alive. Coincidentally, three white historians, Frederic Ramsey Jr., Charles Edward Smith, and William Russell, were already working on a book on the history of jazz and multiple interview subjects had mentioned this mysterious "Bunk" figure. When Armstrong told the writers that he saw him in New Iberia, they immediately began corresponding with Johnson, initiating the birth of a new folk hero.

Interest in the early days of jazz in New Orleans was growing, as well as in pure, no-frills jamming, seen by some as an antidote to the heavily arranged work of the big bands. Small group swing was the hallmark of the nightclubs on 52nd Street, of the new Commodore record label (the brainchild of Milt Gabler of the United Hot Club of America), and of radio shows such as Martin Block's *Swing Show* on WNEW. On December 14, Armstrong appeared on Block's show to take part in a once-in-a-lifetime jam session with Fats Waller and white musicians Jack Teagarden, Bud Freeman, Bob Spergel, Pete Peterson, and George Wettling. Even though the broadcast featured numerous stars, all deferred to Armstrong, allowing him to lead exciting jams on standbys such as "On the Sunny Side of the Street," "I Got Rhythm," and "Tiger Rag." Block aptly summed up the summit meeting as "The jam session to end all jam sessions." Armstrong sounded right at home jamming with Waller and Teagarden, but no more at home than at the Apollo, where he broke it up with his versions of "Shadrack" and "Jeepers Creepers" at the end of December, or at his Carnegie Hall debut on Christmas night, leaving his trumpet behind to sing spirituals with Lyn Murray's choir at Paul Whiteman's eighth "Experiment in Modern American Music." "Receiving the greatest ovation meted out by the huge audience, Louis Armstrong captured the spotlight as soon as he stepped upon the stage," Billy Rowe wrote in the *Pittsburgh Courier,* calling him "still the most magnetic personality in the world of modern music."[14]

Going Places opened on New Year's Eve and gave Armstrong the best notices of his film work to date. "Here and elsewhere dusky, gusty Armstrong is the dominant entertainer," Roscoe Williams wrote in *Motion Picture Daily.*[15] "Incidentally, Armstrong registers agreeably as a comic possibility," said Philip K. Scheur in the *Los Angeles Times.*[16] And in the *New York Times,* which didn't often mention Armstrong, Frank S. Nugent wrote, "Satchel-Mo' blows a mean horn; better still, he's a solid man for comedy."[17] This was music to Joe Glaser's ears, who took out a full-page ad in *Variety* quoting multiple reviews, topped by the giant headline, "A SOLID MAN FOR COMEDY."[18]

Over in the black press, though, matters were more varied. Porter Roberts wrote, "I think Louis Armstrong was perfectly terrible in Dick Powell's picture 'Going Places.' Haw! Imagine the so-called king of the Trumpet serenading a horse with his trumpet, while dressed like a weather-beaten hobo. You laugh this time!"[19] But Earl J. Morris, who crusaded against "Uncle Tom" parts in Hollywood, was pleased, urging his readers to "Write and thank Hal Wallis out at Warner Brothers' Studios in Burbank, Cal., for giving Louis Armstrong and Maxine Sullivan such long parts. Then thank them for the way they are going after the Negro trade. Write to Mr. Wallis and thank him. It may mean more big roles for Louis Armstrong and Maxine Sullivan."[20]

Going Places opened at Strand Theatre in New York, which simultaneously presented its "first all-colored stage show" featuring Armstrong, Sullivan, and the Dandridge Sisters, all from the film. The headliner, though, would be Bill "Bojangles" Robinson, the first time he and Armstrong would share a bill for an extended period. The result was a smash hit for the Strand, as the pair brought $35,000 in their first week. But more important, it gave Armstrong the opportunity to study Robinson every night, learning even more than he already knew about timing and how to tell a joke. "To me he was the greatest Comedian + dancer in my race," Armstrong wrote about Robinson toward the end of his life. "He didn't need black face to be funny."[21]

"Jeepers Creepers" was nominated for an Academy Award and became a fixture of the Strand performances and an eventual hit on Decca, recorded on January 16, 1939. It's a triumphant record, with a sunny vocal and a trumpet solo that must have pleased Jack Kapp's "Where's the melody?" mentality. But the drumming also captures the attention of the listener and for once it's not

Figure 16.2 The finale at the Strand Theatre in 1939, featuring from left to right: Putney Dandridge, Midge Williams, Luis Russell, the Dandridge Sisters, Louis Armstrong, Freddie Gordon, Bill "Bojangles" Robinson, Timmie Rogers, and Sonny Woods.

Paul Barbarin, but rather Big Sid Catlett, a man Armstrong later called "the finest drummer to ever pick up a pair of sticks" and "a born genius."[22] Catlett had recorded with Armstrong once for RCA in 1933, but now he became the Russell band's regular drummer. He also possessed a sense of humor that matched his leader's, Armstrong calling him a "funny summitch" as the two spent much of their time on the road swapping dirty jokes.[23] Armstrong and Catlett would forge one of the great partnerships in the music's history.

Catlett immediately made his presence felt on the flip side of "Jeepers Creepers," another Armstrong original co-composed with Horace Gerlach titled "What Is This Thing Called Swing" and featuring a full chorus drum solo with Catlett working out on the snare drum like a New Orleans master. Armstrong and Gerlach's lyrics, delivered in a proto-rap, half-spoken/half-sung fashion, displayed Armstrong's lack of tolerance for musical categories, lumping "swing" in with "jazz," "drag time," and "futuristic ragtime." Armstrong was getting a little tired of now being asked to analyze the music he had spent his life performing. Asked about an unnamed critic who said that "swing was too commercialized," Armstrong responded, "Don't say I said he can go to hell or anything like that; just say Armstrong disagrees with him."[24]

The growing interest in jazz history perhaps led him to look backward more than usual in 1939, leading to remakes of past triumphs such as "Rockin' Chair" (made with the white Casa Loma Orchestra), "Hear Me Talkin' to Ya," "Save It Pretty Mama," "West End Blues," "Savoy Blues," "Confessin' That I Love You," and "Monday Date." More than being re-creations, each one was updated for the modern era with new arrangements, dynamic, dancing drumming by Catlett, invigorating outings by soloists such as J. C. Higginbotham and Charlie Holmes, and stirring new contributions from Armstrong. Perhaps none of the remakes made anyone forget the originals— except in 1939, many listeners had indeed forgotten the originals, as they had been out of print for much of the decade. While Leonard Feather frequently brought up Armstrong's 1920s masterworks as evidence of what he determined to be Armstrong's decline, not every critic felt that way. Edgar Jackson, who could run hot and cold on Armstrong's Decca recordings, wasn't the least bit nostalgic over Armstrong's past triumphs, giving a reissue of 1927's "Weary Blues" and "Willie the Weeper" in 1937 only one star, saying "they just sound hopelessly crude and corny. I don't see how any record made ten years ago could be anything else, no matter who played it."[25] When the remakes started appearing, Jackson gave them his approval; of the 1939 "West End Blues," Jackson wrote, "Louis himself plays even more brilliantly on the new record."[26]

Still, Decca couldn't fully embrace the nostalgic trend. The pop songs continued in this period as even the remake of "West End Blues" was backed by a trifle, "If It's Good (Then I Want It)," while "Savoy Blues" was paired with a new comedic Armstrong novelty, "Me and Brother Bill." The 1939 pop sides have their moments, but the songs aren't as durable as the ones from the mid-1930s and even the arrangements lost a little of the craftsmanship of the Chappie Willet heyday.

The one record Armstrong released in this period that made the most headlines was another one that looked backward, his 1938 take on "When the Saints Go Marching In." Many were not pleased, especially in the African American community. The Reverend George W. Harvey, associate religious editor of the *Pittsburgh Courier*, wrote, "The sacrilegious desecration of Spirituals, the only real American music as it is swung in gin shops dance halls, over the radio and on records in various non-descript amusement places is a disgrace to the whole race."[27] Harvey called for a protest and in the ensuing weeks, 60 churches representing a total of 8,000 members protested Armstrong's recording. Harvey followed up with harsher criticism of Armstrong, the *Courier* reporting, "Our age needs a new demonstration that there are some militant and courageous Negroes. [Harvey] says all the 'Uncle Tom's' are not dead yet, but there are members of the race old and young, whom he believes will gladly support and take a stand on his side, on curbing and stopping all irreligious use of the songs of our foreparents."[28]

Armstrong was perplexed by the controversy. "I don't think there's any harm in my record, 'When the Saints Go Marching [In],'" he told reporter Isabel M. Thompson. "That's the same way I played it years ago in brass bands down in New Orleans, my old home-town. We played it in parades and at church affairs, and no one took offense. In fact, various ministers and other church persons have praised me for the recording of this piece."[29] Fifteen years before Ray Charles inspired similar controversy by mixing gospel chord progressions with rhythm and blues on "I Got a Woman," Armstrong upset the religious community by mixing gospel with jazz. But Armstrong did not back down and it's his version of "When the Saints Go Marching In" that turned it into the anthem of New Orleans jazz. And instead of discouraging him, Armstrong had the support of Jack Kapp and Joe Glaser when he jazzed up another traditional spiritual, "Bye and Bye," later that year.

The year 1939 was a time of transition for Glaser as he expanded Joe Glaser Inc. He had now been on his own for almost a year and was starting to struggle, which meant that for the first time in the partnership, Armstrong also started to struggle. A hot night in Nebraska netted a box-office take of only $600, not even breaking even, and even *Down Beat* mentioned "that profitable dates for Satchmo and his cohorts had been few."[30] Glaser needed some help and ended up merging with Consolidated Radio Artists to form Glaser-Consolidated, set up strictly to book black dance bands. Glaser brought his acts to CRA, but also would now be responsible for booking many of CRA's over 100 black acts.[31]

Glaser was finally able to get Armstrong off the road in the fall with an extended engagement at the Cotton Club. This was no longer the famed Harlem nightspot, but rather a midtown club that opened on Broadway and 48th street, the previous location of Connie's Inn when he played it in 1935–1936. That ended up being something of a last hurrah for the Immerman brothers. Hounded by gangsters—George had already been kidnapped once in 1933— they sold the short-lived midtown Connie's Inn to the Cotton Club owners. George Immerman went on in show business for a few more years, booking shows at small venues before dying in poverty in 1944. Connie Immerman stayed during the regime change but as a waiter. He lived until 1967 spending his final years as a maître d' at Kenny's Steak Pub in Manhattan. Armstrong lost touch with both but was still venting about them on a private tape he made in 1951. "This sonofabitch died like a dog, peckerwood did," Armstrong said of George Immerman. "Broke. In fact, both of them went broke. And they were riding on the crest of the wave there. I say the Lord don't like ugly. And they died like a dog—poor. You just can't do them things. Johnny Collins, same way. He thought, 'You're just a nigger' but the Lord, he don't worry about that color; you're wrong, you're wrong and in some kind of way, you're going to pay for it."[32]

Armstrong once again teamed up with Bill Robinson at the Cotton Club in early October, doing a straight vaudeville bill with a variety of acts. The *New York Times* praised Robinson as "the complete entertainer" but of Armstrong, added, "Though we could get along without Mr. Armstrong's apeman antics, his trumpet tooting is phenomenal."[33] A more spectacular revue was being written and rehearsed for November but for a full month, Armstrong got to enjoy being in the company of his idol.[34] He also spent his free time reading *Jazzmen*, the recently published history of jazz compiled by William Russell, Frederic Ramsey Jr., and Charles Edward Smith. Armstrong wrote Russell to congratulate him on his "absolutely Wonderful" book and thanked him for helping to get Bunk Johnson, the book's star, to the dentist to get his teeth fixed so he could play again. "That was very nice of you boys," he wrote. "Honest-Gate—that's something that we will be talking about the rest of our lives."[35] Armstrong also wrote to another friend to say that *Jazzmen* was "really taking Harlem by storm."[36] That opinion was corroborated in the black press, with the *Pittsburgh Courier* writing, "Well, well, well! Here it is at last!

A book that gives full credit to Negroes for what they have done in an impor-tant branch of the arts."[37]

While Armstrong was at the Cotton Club, Joe Glaser was entertaining offers for a more serious Broadway role for his star client, including the part of Bottom in a proposed musical version of Shakespeare's *Midsummer Night's Dream*.[38] This was the brainchild of Erik Charell, a successful German the-ater director and actor who had staged the popular production of *White Horse Inn* on Broadway in 1936. Charell had a history of mixing classic operettas with the sounds of jazz, something he had done in his German adaptations of works such as *The Mikado* and *Madame Pompadour*. Perhaps inspired by the success of *The Hot Mikado* with Bill Robinson on Broadway, Charell and cultural critic Gilbert Seldes set off to combine Shakespeare and jazz in *Swingin' the Dream*, to be staged at the expansive 3,500-seat Centre Theatre in Rockefeller Center. By early October, Benny Goodman and Maxine Sullivan had been signed and rehearsals began.

Armstrong agreed to attend rehearsals but would not commit to per-forming the role because of interest from producer Vinton Freedley, who wanted Armstrong to provide the live trumpet playing in a Broadway ad-aptation of Dorothy Baker's 1938 novel, *Young Man with a Horn*, based on the tragic life of Bix Beiderbecke. Soon, both Freedley and Charell began claiming they had Armstrong under contract.[39] Columnist Louis Sobol was present one night at the Cotton Club when Glaser let Armstrong make the final decision. "Pops—Good news for you," Glaser opened. "Vinton Freedley wants you to co-star with Margaret Sullivan and Burgess Meredith in Young Man with a Horn. Howzzat?" According to Sobol, Armstrong responded, "Not for me. I'd do anything for you boss—you're my poppa—but dat's voodoo to me. Dat's a play about Bix—Bix is daid—I don't want no ghosts fingerin' my horn, Pops." "Okay, Pops," Glaser responded. "I'll sign you for Swingin' the Dream—but don't forget—Shakespeare is dead, too—very dead." Armstrong replied, "That's solid, boss, but Shakespeare ain't no Bix, no suh."[40]

Armstrong was now officially part of *Swingin' the Dream*, but in many ways, his headaches were just beginning. His first opponent, as it was, was Benny Goodman. On October 14, Armstrong appeared on Goodman's *Camel Caravan* radio show, something he looked forward to, telling Bill Russell about it and referring to "my pal Benny Goodman" in his letter of October 3. But the relationship between the two "Kings of Swing" soured just before the broad-cast while discussing the rehearsal for *Swingin' the Dream*. "Reminds me of the time I wanted to strangle him," Armstrong recalled of the incident on one of his private tapes in 1953. Condescendingly, Goodman asked Armstrong,

"Well, how are you on lines, there? You know it ain't like moving pictures." Armstrong responded, "What difference does it make? I study both of them and memorize them. I didn't come here to talk about no damn lines. I'm supposed to do a broadcast with you. Now do I or shall I cut out?"[41] Once Armstrong officially signed to be in the production, the war continued, this time over billing. On November 15, two weeks before the official opening, *Variety* reported on a "Billing Battle," writing, "Armstrong threatens to pull out if he doesn't get top name and Goodman ditto."[42] The matter was settled a day later with each man agreeing to equal billing, their portraits appearing at the same height on the program, as drawn by famed artist Al Hirschfeld, with Hirschfeld's sketch of William Shakespeare "truckin'" in the middle.[43]

Hirschfeld wasn't the only big name brought in by Charell for *Swingin' the Dream*. The sets would be designed by no less than Walt Disney. Original songs were composed by the team of Jimmy Van Heusen and Eddie de Lange, and included future standard, "Darn That Dream." Lyn Murray provided the "swing choir" of singers and Agnes de Mille choreographed the dancing, while Herbert White enlisted his famed troop of "jitterbugs," "Whitey's Lindy Hoppers," including future lindy hop ambassadors Norma Miller and Frankie Manning. And in addition to Goodman's famed integrated Sextet with Lionel Hampton, Fletcher Henderson, Charlie Christian, Artie Bernstein, and Nick Fatool, music would also be provided by tenor saxophonist Bud Freeman's similarly integrated Summa Cum Laude band with Max Kaminsky, Brad Gowans, Pee Wee Russell, Eddie Condon, Dave Bowman, and Zutty Singleton.[44]

There'd be a *Going Places* reunion as, in addition to Armstrong, Maxine Sullivan was cast as Titania, Queen of the Pixies, while the Dandridge Sisters served as pixies. The sheer amount of African American talent was staggering, including Jackie "Moms" Mabley, Nicodemus, Butterfly McQueen, Bill Bailey, and many more. "It appears that the theatre season holds great prospects for the Negro, if the preparations now in the making mean anything," Floyd G. Snelson wrote. "Broadway will be darker, and that means that many Negro performers, who are badly in need of employment will come into their own, and rightful place in the theatre."[45]

Armstrong had his work cut out for him in preparing for *Swingin' the Dream*. He might have battled Benny Goodman to a draw over equal billing, but Goodman and his band got to sit in a box all night and play music. As Bottom, Armstrong had one of the biggest speaking roles in the play, appearing as a fireman in the first act and later, as a donkey in the "Pyramus and Thisbe" operatic sequence. Reminiscing about it with his friend Stuff Crouch on tape in early 1951, Armstrong said:

You know, I had a real heavy part in it. I played the part of Bottom . . . the part in Shakespeare's play where he comes out there and this princess, which is Maxine Sullivan, her sweetheart or something that they wanted her to do—I don't know what he asked her, evidently she refused terribly. So, he told her the next person that comes out of those woods is going to turn into a jackass, see? That was the torture he was going to lay on her. And sure enough, I was the first one to come out. And here I come with a head of an ass. [laughs] So I think they're all glad to see me and things like that and come to find out, they all run away! You know, they tipped away the first chance they got. And I'm standing out there on this great big stage by myself. Stuff, you're talking about a speech? My speech was 10 minutes long.[46]

Crouch responded, "My goodness. How'd you memorize that?" "Oh man, I used to memorize all my lines, you know, when I'm sitting on the toilet before I go to bed," Armstrong replied, summing it up by saying, "It was a helluva show."[47]

Figure 16.3 Armstrong in full costume as Bottom during the "Pyramus and Thisbe" sequence of the short-lived Broadway production *Swingin' the Dream* in 1939.
Courtesy of the Louis Armstrong House Museum

Previews for *Swingin' the Dream* began on November 25 and Armstrong immediately created a buzz, with George Ross writing, "The reports on Louis Armstrong as Bottom in *Swingin' the Dream* are raves."[48] Dorothy Kilgallen agreed, giving a "Gold Star" to "Louis Armstrong's historic trumpeting as the black 'Bottom' in *Swingin' the Dream*—just caught a preview."[49] It was an encouraging sign but on November 29, *Swingin' the Dream* officially opened and the good buzz disappeared almost immediately. "If Shakespeare turned over in his grave, that was his affair," Arthur Pollock wrote in the *Brooklyn Daily Eagle*. "The audience at the Center would have liked to turn over a good deal more."[50] *Billboard* summed up the show as "an orgy of wasted talent."[51] In the black press, Philip Carter of the *New York Amsterdam News* called it a "nightmare of Lindy Hoppers and buck dancing" and "pure and simply a vaudeville show and not a play."[52]

Armstrong's role in the production received decidedly mixed reviews, not because of his acting but because of his lack of trumpet playing. "Although Louis Armstrong carries his golden horn whenever he appears, he hardly has a chance to warm it up until the show is well over," Brooks Atkinson wrote. "He is put in irons in a stupid version of 'Pyramus and Thisbe.'"[53] But in the *Pittsburgh Courier*, National Editor William G. Nunn wrote, "Armstrong comes into his own as a legitimate actor. His naturalness adds to his greatness. And Armstrong, the actor, refuses to be miscast. He moves into his part and gives a commanding performance, holding the audience with his matchless wizardry on the trumpet."[54]

The very next night, Armstrong and Sullivan had yet another premiere on Broadway with the debut of the new Cotton Club revue.[55] The show opened with film footage of Armstrong and Sullivan in *Going Places*, partially to kill time and provide more glimpses of Armstrong, who had to miss much of the dinner show because of his commitments to the second act of *Swingin' the Dream*. Once there, Armstrong was singled out for praise in all the trade reviews, *Billboard* writing, "Armstrong's foghorn singing and his outstanding trumpeting combined with his winning personality to put him over."[56] Seeing Armstrong shine at both *Swingin' the Dream* and the Cotton Club led Nunn to write, "[N]ow you can feel that the musical genius of the trumpeter is approaching the apex of a new career."[57]

While the Cotton Club revue was thriving, *Swingin' the Dream* was sinking fast. Charell listened to the critics and did his best to tinker with the show. "*Swingin' the Dream*, insofar as the Shakespearean text is concerned, has been submitted to an alum bath and the customers are getting more Benny Goodman and Louis Armstrong," the *Los Angeles Times* reported on December 7.[58] Pointing out that Armstrong went from having no solos to "several" and that the show now ended with "six or seven" numbers by the Goodman Sextet, Joseph Dorfman, writing in *Science and Society* ("A Marxian Quarterly"), said, "If the show runs a month maybe Louis and Benny will have chased the troop of bungling *regisseurs* out of the thing altogether."[59]

But on December 9, Goodman, sensing the inevitable, announced that he would be leaving the show after six weeks.[60] The show would barely last six more hours; *Swingin' the Dream* gave its 13th and final performance that same evening.[61] Billy Rowe, writing in the *Pittsburgh Courier*, blamed it on "lack of patronage and a thorough-going-over by the critics," adding, "the show sadly closed Saturday after the last performance, putting more than 200 performers again on the help wanted list, most of them colored."[62]

Armstrong emerged unscathed from the debacle; columnist George Ross called it "the peak of his trumpet-playing career."[63] He probably felt relieved to have one less thing to do, allowing him more time to focus on the Cotton Club engagement, which now also included regular radio broadcasts. Decca brought him in on December 18 to record two new Sammy Cahn–Saul Chaplin numbers from the Cotton Club show, "You're a Lucky Guy" and "You're Just a No Account." The result was one of his best singles for the label. "His last chorus on the latter tune is amazingly clear and beautiful," George R. Dempsey wrote of "No Account." "You begin to think Louis is slipping, then he surges back with a record like this one to reassert his immortality."[64]

Far from slipping, Armstrong had just finished the most successful decade of his career and he could not have accomplished half of it without Glaser's strategy of having his star client conquer records, film radio, live performances, and even Broadway, as well as publishing an autobiography. *Motion Picture Herald* named Armstrong one of "The Biggest Money Making Stars of 1939," a list with only four African Americans: Armstrong, Maxine Sullivan, Louise Beavers, and Bill Robinson.[65]

Yet, the success did not come without disappointment: the failure of *Swingin' the Dream*, the failure of the *Fleischmann's Yeast Show*, and the criticism of some in the African American community toward his film appearances. Armstrong remained proud of his accomplishments in film, on the radio, and on the Broadway stage, but he wasn't as able to have the same impact as he did when simply playing and singing on recordings or in live performances. And even that impact was lessening as the "swing" scene continued turning out so many white stars. *Down Beat's* 1939 poll only placed three African Americans in first-place positions—Ella Fitzgerald, Coleman Hawkins, and Charlie Christian. Armstrong finished fourth in the trumpet category, behind three white trumpeters, Harry James, Ziggy Elman, and Bunny Berigan, all of whom were quick to call him their idol. Academy Award–nominated songs,

Broadway spectacles, and Cotton Club revues were not enough to get the plaudits from the jazz press or votes from the jazz fans.

And not everything in Armstrong's off-stage world was stress-free as the 1930s came to an end. In November, he was sued by California-based night-club entertainer Polly Jones, who claimed Armstrong promised to marry her after he divorced Lil. When he married Alpha instead, Jones sued for $35,000, making headlines. Armstrong and Glaser released a joint statement claiming, "We don't know anything about this breach of promise suit. We don't know the girl even. . . . It's all a mystery to us."[66] Jones soon disappeared from the press, but it's no surprise that Armstrong was unfaithful and it's quite possible the publicity of Armstrong's affair with Jones drove him even farther apart with Alpha. Alpha needed an operation at the end of December, the *Pittsburgh Courier* reporting that she had to have three tumors removed, and Louis was there to tell reporters that she was doing well and would be home in a few weeks.[67] But he couldn't tell anyone what only he himself knew:

He was in love with a Cotton Club dancer.

17

"He Is Like the Armstrong of the Old Days"

January 1940–July 1941

Lucille Buchanan Wilson was born on January 13, 1914, in New York City, spending part of her childhood in Corona, Queens, but the majority in the Bronx. As her father does not seem to have been a reliable presence, Lucille dropped out of school and went to work at the age of 15.[1] "The Depression was on when I went into show business," she later said. "I was the oldest of four children, so I had to pitch in." Lucille's mother, Maude, objected at first, but Lucille confidently told her, "You raised me and if you've done a good job, you shouldn't be afraid."[2]

Lucille spent three years dancing at the Alhambra in Harlem, before making the transition to the Cotton Club, an unusual occurrence because of her dark skin. "Lucille was the first girl to crack the high yellow color standard used to pick girls for the famous Cotton Club chorus line," Louis later wrote. "I think she was a distinguished pioneer."[3] In July 1935, Lucille appeared in the 26th edition of the *Cotton Club Parade*. Though it starred Nina Mae McKinney and featured 18-year-old Lena Horne, Babe Wallace, Butterbeans and Susie, and more, according to one critic, "the most important contribution to the city's ha-cha-cha is in the person of an obscure youngster in the chorus by the name of Lucille Wilson.... With practically nothing to do outside of the chorus routine, the Wilson girl frequently diverted the attention of the audience from the principals."[4]

"I graduated into specialty turns at the club," Lucille said, "and into roles in such shows as the original *Showboat, Flying Colors* and *Blackbirds*. In 1936, I went on tour to London with *Blackbirds* . . . which just kept running on and on."[5] Lucille became something of a sensation in the British run of Lew Leslie's *Blackbirds of 1936*, Leslie calling her "the most perfect ebony beauty I have ever encountered in the theatre."[6] Lucille spent a year in Europe but admitted she "got lonesome for New York," adding, "Well, Hitler was acting up in Europe, so I decided not to return. I went back to the Cotton Club, which had moved downtown by then, into their 'Tall, Tan and Terrific' revue."[7] Lucille also became a fixture in the black press, often referred to by Billy Rowe as "the 'Brown Sugar' of the Cotton Club."[8]

Louis and Lucille first made contact at the Cotton Club when Louis shared the bill with Bill Robinson in October 1939. To him, it was love at first sight, relating in *Ebony*, "When I first saw her the glow of her deep brown skin got me deep down."[9] He had the best seat in the house to admire her dancing. "All those Beautiful notes along with Lucille's perfect dancing," he wrote. "Me-diggin those Cute Lil Buns of Hers." Louis instantly saw how hard she was working to support her mother and three siblings and thought, "In fact our lives were practically the same." Lucille even sold homemade cookies to the other entertainers to make extra money. One night, Louis asked her, "Honey, how many boxes do you bring down here every night?" When she answered, Louis responded, "I'll take all of them." Lucille brought him the cookies and after a long night of performing, Bob Smiley drove them uptown in Armstrong's rust-colored Packard, where they handed the cookies out to the kids of Harlem.[10]

This continued for a few nights, as Louis's feelings grew deeper and deeper. Both parties acted like teenagers, using Luis Russell as a go-between until Louis finally said, "See here, little girl. I think you're very cute, you know? And I know all the cats are sharkin' after you. And I want you to know I'm in the running, too!"[11] Louis knew it was time for her to pass his most important test. "Then I stopped her from talking slowly reaching for her Cute little Beautifully manicured hand, and said to her, can you cook, Red Beans and Rice? which Amused her very much," Louis wrote. "Then it dawned ON her that I WAS very serious." Lucille asked for some time, consulted her mother for advice and then invited Armstrong over to meet her family and to taste her cooking. "The Red Beans + Rice that Lucille cooked for me as Just what the Doctor ordered," Louis recalled. "Very much delicious and I ate just like a dog."[12]

Louis and Lucille became inseparable, seeing movies in between shows and spending their nights in Harlem, going to the bar at the Braddock Hotel "where all of the show Folks (colored) would congregate after we all Had finished our last show. And go there to Sort of Signify, etc." At dawn, they would devour spaghetti and meatballs and sleep all day, sometimes at Lucille's apartment, where her mother relinquished her master bedroom to the new couple. Yet, through it all, Louis was still very much married to Alpha. In July 1940, after the Cotton Club engagement ended, he wrote to Elmer Lewis, "I want you to meet the Mrs . . . Yea Man—you must meet my Alpha (my little hatchetmouth wife) . . . All the musicians—Actors—Record Fans—and everybody has met the Madam Armstrong."[13] But Alpha would not be "Madam Armstrong" much longer.

The Cotton Club engagement represented one of the most peaceful and fulfilling periods of Armstrong's life. Except for the short-lived doubling in "Swingin' the Dream," he remained in one place from October 1, 1939, through April 25, 1940, as the venue kept extending his contract four weeks at a time, with Midge Williams returning to replace Maxine Sullivan in the final month. The band seemed rejuvenated by not having to travel, sounding in excellent form on a series of surviving broadcasts and especially a Decca session on March 14 that ranked with Armstrong's finest for the label. Armstrong sounds like the grandfather of rap and hip-hop on "Hep Cat's Ball" and "You've Got Me Voodoo'd," both featuring proto-rap spoken vocals with heavy slang on the former and incessant rhyming on the latter. The highlight of the day was an instrumental romp on Jelly Roll Morton's "Wolverine Blues" where Armstrong doesn't play a note for the first minute and 50 seconds and for maybe the first time, isn't missed. It's a top-notch swing band and then Armstrong enters and pushes them over the top with a two-chorus solo plus coda, undeniably inspired by Catlett's drumming.

"Wolverine Blues" showed that Armstrong's band could stand alongside the best swing records of Ellington, Basie, and Goodman. However, to many, swing was already on the way out. The year 1940 began with a series of nationwide columns by Paul Ross of the Associated Press on the subject, writing that "Swing is 'dead'—as a national craze" and that "sweet" music and novelties from leaders such as Kay Kyser were now more popular than the "swing" of leaders like Goodman.[14] The Swing Era might have represented the closest jazz ever got to being America's popular music, but Ross pointed that it was always "music of-by-and-for a minority," adding that the majority of American people "want a catchy or a sentimental tune to sing, a funny song to smile over, a steady tempo to dance to." Harry Moss of Music Corporation of America listed the most popular bands of 1939: Kay Kyser, Horace Heidt, Orrin Tucker, and Guy Lombardo.

Of course, jazz periodicals such as *Down Beat* and *Metronome* disagreed, as they regularly mocked the sweet bands for being hopelessly corny. Hardened jazz fans scored a victory when Coleman Hawkins returned to the United States in 1939 and had a hit record with an instrumental version of "Body and Soul" that featured stirring improvisation and very little melody. To supporters of jazz as a harmonically daring, constantly evolving, improvising music, the big swing bands, black and white, suddenly seemed a little too stagnant and commercial compared to what Hawkins was playing.

One such writer was Barry Ulanov, a 21-year-old recent graduate of Columbia University who wrote a savage review of Armstrong's big band at the Cotton Club for *Metronome* in March 1940. "If the band has a style, it is chiefly one of playing without discipline or musical organization," was his opener before systematically criticizing each section of the band. Eventually, he came to Armstrong: "Even Louis is limited to spectacular blasting and monotonous one-note repetitions which suggest nothing so much as a circus entertainer." Ulanov summed up his feelings by reiterating how he was "disappointed," writing, "For it is a disgrace to the art, and even to the commerce, of jazz, that so many fine people should be buried in such musical desolation, so that, as one of them said to me, 'Man, we don't get a chance to really play no more!'"[15]

Ulanov sounded like he was reviewing a completely different band from the one on the March 14 session but when they reassembled on May 1 to wax four more songs for Decca, they did sound defeated by inferior material such as "You Run Your Mouth, I'll Run My Business," "Cut Off My Legs and Call Me Shorty," and another swing sermon on "Cain and Abel." The arrangements are lacking, the novelty vocals are too repetitive, and Armstrong, perhaps suffering from tired chops after the seven months in the Cotton Club, strangely stays out of the upper register for much of the time, most conspicuously on a remake of "Sweethearts on Parade" that features a relaxed, lyrical improvisation but none of the bravura of the 1930 version. Occasionally, Catlett lights a fire under Armstrong and inspires him to really blow, but overall, it's a mostly forgettable session that lends some credence to Ulanov's critique.

Perhaps Glaser heard the uninspired recordings, perhaps he read the scathing *Metronome* review, perhaps the various cliques in the band had gotten out of hand, perhaps Luis Russell was burned out, perhaps Glaser was angered by an unnamed member of the band criticizing the organization to Ulanov—whatever the reason, Glaser fired six musicians, Lee Blair, Bingie Madison, Charlie Holmes, Bernard Flood, Pops Foster, and Russell himself, all but Flood having been with Armstrong since he took over the band in 1935. "Armstrong's front office states that the men in the band do not work in harmony, that many have been in the outfit too long; that some of the men actually refuse to speak to each other," the *Pittsburgh Courier* reported.[16]

Forty-eight-year-old Pops Foster was told he was "too old" for the band and remained bitter about the firing, writing in his autobiography that "Glaser fired the whole band to get a cheaper band. . . . Some of the new guys he hired couldn't play the music and that was the end of the band. They went downhill fast after that." Foster even took out his resentment on Armstrong, writing, "Louis is real jealous of other players who put out. If you play bad you won't be in the band, and if you play too good you won't be there. When I'd get to romping along on the bass, he'd yell at me, 'Hey, man, if you want to play trumpet come down here and play.' I'd say, 'Go on man and play your horn.' He's lucky he's lived so long. He works too hard because he don't want nobody to do nothing but him. Louis shouldn't be so jealous because he's an outstanding man."[17]

Charlie Holmes and Luis Russell chose to combat being fired by agreeing to stay for less money. Russell stayed as only a pianist, officially turning over the music director role to saxophonist Joe Garland, who immediately instilled more discipline than Russell ever did, insisting on constant rehearsals. "Damn," Holmes thought to himself, "this is worse than going to work in a damn factory. We come off the stage and we've got to go to rehearsal right away." But he did admit, "It really did improve the band."[18] Holmes didn't last much longer, though, officially leaving in September. "I was tired, that traveling was too much for me," he said. Unlike Foster, Holmes retained warm feelings toward Armstrong and even praised him for his confidence. "Everybody looked up to him cause he looked up to himself," he said. "He knew he was the king. Something funny about them geniuses, they know they are that great. I mean he wasn't biggity or anything, he was a fine person. But he did not lose any self-confidence when anyone else come around blowing the trumpet."[19]

Red Allen and J. C. Higginbotham departed in October, the last major ties to the glory years of the Russell band. There was no animosity, as Glaser immediately signed them both up to co-lead their own band, but Armstrong was cautious about Allen. "We're still in good terms," he told *Swing* magazine. "I'm always glad to see a man better himself. Of course he doesn't know all the worries of having a band these days, but it won't hurt him none to try. He won't be bettering himself financially. My boys are the best paid of all the colored bands, that goes for Duke or anybody."[20]

Garland now had an opportunity to construct the band he wanted and immediately set about "raiding" Coleman Hawkins's orchestra to sign guitarist Lawrence Lucie, bassist Johnny Williams, and trumpeter Bill Dillard, in addition to veteran reedman Prince Robinson.[21] *Down Beat* immediately noticed a difference, Onah Spencer writing that his "revamped outfit . . . is a great improvement over the one he had here a year ago."[22] Armstrong agreed. "In America, when I had my big band with Joe Garland as musical director, I was very pleased," he said in 1970. "Joe Garland, to me, is one of the finest musicians that I have ever met. With him on the mound, I didn't have to ever worry about the band playing good or sounding right. He rehearsed them very strictly. He disliked bad notes the same as me."[23] Unfortunately, he would

Figure 17.1 A 1943 reunion with two New Orleans homeboys with whom Armstrong had somewhat complex relationships: Henry "Red" Allen (left) and Zutty Singleton (right).
Courtesy of the Louis Armstrong House Museum

not be able to showcase Garland's improvements for quite some time as Decca would not make any recordings with the big band between the May 1, 1940, session and November 16, 1941.

Instead, Armstrong's Decca sessions in that period would be small group affairs, mostly looking to the past for inspiration. The success of *Jazzmen* in late 1939 put a new spotlight on the sounds of early jazz. RCA Victor's Bluebird label was the first to capitalize on the new trend, bringing back Jelly Roll Morton to record two sessions in September 1939, in addition to recording 16 well-regarded small group numbers with King Oliver disciple Muggsy Spanier's "Ragtime Band." That same year, Decca hired 20-year-old Yale student George Avakian to oversee new recordings for what would be the first jazz concept album, *Chicago Jazz*. Avakian's idea was to record three different small groups who played the free-wheeling small-group "Chicago" style and package the resulting six 78s in an "album," complete with liner notes. Decca followed up with an album of *New Orleans Jazz* to be supervised by Steve Smith of the Hot Record Society. The album would feature different combinations led by Red Allen, Zutty Singleton, Johnny Dodds, and Jimmie Noone, but the main attraction would be four songs reuniting Armstrong and Sidney Bechet.

In 1924 and 1925, Armstrong and Bechet had teamed up for a series of incendiary recordings that bubbled over with competitive spirit. But their lives went in very different directions after those sessions. The hot-headed Bechet was arrested in Paris and spent 11 months in jail while Armstrong's star ascended. Back in America, Bechet was a sideman in Noble Sissle's orchestra, but without Armstrong's brand of showmanship his career stalled, and he turned to running a tailor's shop in Harlem for a spell in the 1930s. Writing in his autobiography, Bechet seemed to be discussing Armstrong without mentioning him by name. "If a man can really play where the music is, he's entitled to all the personality they'll give him: but if the personality gets to come first, that's bad for the music," he wrote.[24]

Bechet scored a hit with his recording of "Summertime" on the new Blue Note label in 1939, lending him to approach the reunion with Armstrong with a bit of a chip on his shoulder. He also had a distrust of trumpet players, working best with those who knew how to stay out of his way, such as Spanier. Adding to the potential tension, Lil Hardin was the project's "Musical Advisor" and the drum chair would be filled by Zutty Singleton, with whom Armstrong hadn't played since their 1929 falling out. Trombonist Claude Jones was affected by the tension, mostly because he wasn't a New Orleans musician. A veteran of the swing bands of Fletcher Henderson, Cab Calloway, and Don Redman, Jones had already been called into service on Jelly Roll Morton's 1939 Bluebird sessions and was once again in the "tailgate" role here. Jones remembered, "Louis and Bechet were in peak form that day, but the recording manager just wore me down. He kept coming out of his sound-proof box and shouting, 'Give that horn more tailgate, Jones, more tailgate,' and he got me so mad in the end that I messed up my solo in 'Down in Honky Tonk Town.'"[25] The thought of a white producer telling a black trombonist from Oklahoma to play authentic New Orleans style is indicative of one of the main problems with what became known as the "New Orleans Revival."

But even in a room filled with potentially combative personalities, Armstrong remained calm. Charles Edward Smith was there and noted that Armstrong deferred to Bechet when it came to make decisions about the music because Bechet was four years older. Guitarist Bernard Addison described the date as "distinctly harmonious, particularly between Louis and Sidney" and Singleton was proud that the reunion produced, in his words, "some of the greatest recordings ever made in jazz."[26] Singleton's assessment might be a little hyperbolic as the four Armstrong-Bechet selections don't quite reach the heights of their 1920s work, but they're still very satisfying recordings on their own. "Perdido Street Blues" rocks from the start, allowing both Bechet and Armstrong to show their affinity for the blues. Armstrong sings beautifully on "2:19 Blues" and the two principals harmonize nicely on the charming "Coal Cart Blues." The only real fireworks occur in the last chorus of "Down in Honky Tonk Town," when Armstrong ascends to the upper register and more or less steamrolls Bechet, who fights for space and loses. In his autobiography, Bechet painted a sour portrait of the session, claiming Armstrong was "a little hungrier" and "seemed like he was wanting to make it a kind of thing where we were supposed to be bucking each other, competing instead of working together for that real feeling that would let the music come new and strong." Bechet even remembered producer Steve Smith telling Armstrong, "Louis, take it easy. Just *play* Louis. Play natural. Don't worry about what Sidney's doing."[27] But British drummer Barry Martyn got the story from trombonist Jones that it was Bechet who needed calming down in the studio, and it was Armstrong who pulled him aside to give the older man a little pep talk.

Nevertheless, the *New Orleans Jazz* album was warmly received when it was released that fall. "This is the righteous stuff, spirited, easy flowing and yet intense," Frank Marshall Davis wrote for the Associated Negro Press. "If you have any liking at all for real jazz played by its masters, get this album."[28] Edgar Jackson gave the package four stars in *Melody Maker*, writing that "in all four of his sides we are taken back once again to the real Louis of the good old days."[29] But in the mainstream music press, *Billboard* put the album in its place, calling it "A field day for record collectors and jazz lovers, but meaningless to anyone else."[30]

Armstrong didn't know it at the time of the May session with Bechet, but he was about to come into a lot more contact with "the real Louis of the good old days" thanks to young George Avakian. After years of writing Columbia Records to get them to release their out-of-print jazz recordings of the 1920s and getting nowhere, he was hired by Columbia president Ted Wallerstein in 1940 to come to the label's headquarters in Bridgeport, Connecticut, to research their collection and offer input on what he thought should be released.[31] Avakian got to work, cutting classes at Yale occasionally to conduct research, including going through artist files in Columbia's legal department. He picked out Armstrong's folder and found two pages of recordings he made in 1927 and 1928—many of them titles unfamiliar to Avakian. He submitted the master numbers to the plant and received test pressings of a slew of previously unissued—and unknown—performances, including "Chicago Breakdown," "S. O. L. Blues," "Twelfth Street Rag," "Ory's Creole Trombone," "Symphonic Raps," "Savoyager's Stomp," and more.

In July 1940, Avakian played test pressings of the unissued recordings for Armstrong in his dressing room at the Apollo Theater. Armstrong was thrilled to hear the recordings, identifying the musicians, the song titles, even the composers. Avakian floated back to Connecticut to continue working on what would become the first volume in Columbia's "Hot Jazz Classics" series, *King Louis*, released in October. Similar albums were issued with material by Bix Beiderbecke, Fletcher Henderson, and Bessie Smith, in addition to a series of singles. Thanks to the Columbia juggernaut, the albums received an overwhelming amount of publicity. "Big news of the month in record circles is the barrage of re-issues unleashed by Columbia," *Radio Varieties* reported. "Jazz collectors are in for the time of their lives with the large store of classics in tempo now available at bargain-basement rates."[32] The *Cincinnati Enquirer* noted that record sales were booming, with 60,000,000 records sold in the previous year, up from 40,000,000 in 1938. "Reissues of original recordings that made musical history years ago, early masters that somehow got shelved in the files without ever being issued to the public, and 'second masters,' which have had heretofore very little circulation, are being brought out along with new and modern recordings to supply the booming market," Mark Baron wrote.[33]

All of a sudden, Armstrong's 1920s recordings were being reviewed as the latest "New Releases" in newspapers and magazines across the country. Some weren't impressed, such as a critic from the *Tampa Tribune*, who wrote of the single of 1927's "The Last Time" and "Ory's Creole Trombone," "Hot disc collectors will count this a valuable addition to jazz mania, but it comes out as rather corny stuff compared to contemporary recordings."[34] On the contrary, Robert White of the *Arizona Daily Star* gushed, "All eight sides were recorded before Armstrong adopted the exhibitionistic upper register finales that are his trade mark today, and they are all the better for that."[35]

In the jazz press, however, the same self-discovery of these recordings led many to conclude that Armstrong reached his peak in the 1920s and never did anything of merit after 1928. A majority of jazz writers viewed Armstrong this way over the last 30 years of his life and it is still how many view him today. While some like Leonard Feather had been peddling this theory for years, the release of *King Louis* and other similar Columbia albums that followed turned it into a widely accepted ideology in jazz circles. In January 1941, Paul Eduard Miller wrote a column titled "Musical Blasphemies" in which he laid out the feelings and theories that would follow Armstrong for decades to come:

> Creatively and artistically, Armstrong is dead. . . . Armstrong's showmanship improved, but sadly enough, it improved so much that it became an outright commercial attitude. His forehead was dotted with beads of sweat as he reached for high C. Gradually he substituted these meaningless pyrotechnics for the more sober, more sincere performances of the days of the Armstrong Hot Five. Armstrong

had chosen to play exclusively for the box-office. . . . Therein lies Armstrong's failure.[36]

Part of this reaction was a result of the tracks Avakian selected, focusing on soon-to-be legendary performances like "Potato Head Blues" and "Heebie Jeebies." Avakian chose all winners, but also purposely omitted "King of the Zulus" with its "chitlin' rag" comedy interlude, "Who'Sit" with its slide whistle solo, "Sunset Cafe Stomp" with its booming vocal by Mae Alix, "Big Fat Ma and Skinny Pa" with its square dance parody, and "Irish Black Bottom" with its silly vocal ("If I were born in Ireland—HA!"). Meanwhile, Decca had recently issued inferior sides such as "You Run Your Mouth and I'll Run My Business" and "Cut Off My Legs and Call Me Shorty." And anyone who saw Armstrong live would have to sit through the comedy of Timmie and Freddie, the dancing of one-legged "Big-Time Crip," the love songs crooned by Sonny Woods, and finally, Armstrong's latest hits like "Old Man Mose" and "Jeepers Creepers." Never mind that the majority of the country actually preferred such a varied bill; *Variety* caught him live at the Oriental Theatre in Chicago in February 1941 and reported that "Armstrong proves once more that he belongs among the top band presentations" and that "he presents a well-balanced, all-colored surrounding bill. . . . [He] had the audience rocking in rhythm and hanging onto every high note."[37] To a certain type of jazz fan and especially a certain type of jazz critic, the release of *King Louis* made it appear that Armstrong had once been a serious artist in the 1920s but had long since sold out.

Decca was paying close attention to everything that was going on, especially after Armstrong's single with Sidney Bechet of "2:19 Blues" and "Coal Cart Blues" proved to be a surprising jukebox hit. With all the uproar surrounding the release of *King Louis*, the label capitalized on the appeal of Armstrong in a small group setting and recorded eight numbers in March and April 1941 with Armstrong's "Hot Seven," even borrowing the name of his vaunted 1927 studio group. However, instead of going back to the aesthetic of the *New Orleans Jazz* album, Decca couldn't quite figure out what it wanted the new Hot Seven to be. In the end, they decided to showcase Armstrong doing a little bit of everything—except the type of music he recorded in the 1920s. From a repertoire standpoint, they reached way into the past for the March session, even beyond the New Orleans days, selecting "In the Gloaming" from 1877 and "Long, Long Ago" from 1833. From the 1930s, Armstrong finally got to record a lovely "I Cover the Waterfront," and, as something of a comment on the whole trend of looking backward, 1935's "Ev'rything's Been Done Before." In April, the Hot Seven tackled "Hey Lawdy Mama," a Piedmont blues song popularized by Buddy Moss, and "Now Do You Call That a Buddy," an ominous minor-keyed tale of revenge that had recently been the first Decca hit for Armstrong disciple Louis Jordan. Finally, Armstrong went country with a cover of Buddy Jones's "I'll Get Mine Bye and Bye" (originally recorded for Decca and also recorded by Bob Wills) and combined everything with "Yes Suh," an almost vaudeville-esque number by Edgar Dowell and Andy Razaf that was covered by the integrated "Rhythmmakers" jazz group in 1932 and the western swing outfit Milton Brown and the Brownies in 1936.

The source material was varied, but the new Hot Seven presented it all with sleek, up-to-date arrangements that swung gracefully thanks to the simpatico rhythm section. These smart records show off Armstrong's versatility and natural ability to shine in the context of a smaller ensemble. They also received a large amount of publicity and a string of good reviews. "Ole Satchmo sings a brace of blues in a way that will make the jook nickels roll in," said the *Tampa Tribune* of "Now Do You Call That a Buddy" and "Hey Lawdy Mama."[38] Frank Marshall Davis wrote in the black press, "Truly King Louis has hit his stride again with these."[39] But with the Columbia album still fresh on everybody's mind, mainstream newspaper critics now began lacing compliments with references to Armstrong's past, such as "He is like the Armstrong of the old days"[40] and praising the "honest attempt to recapture his lost sincerity."[41] In the jazz press, the recordings were dead on arrival. "They've turned our Louie into nothing more than a comedy singer," *Down Beat* complained.[42] *Metronome* agreed, saying the material he was given to record "are insults to the great one."[43] Because of such reviews, the 1941 Hot Seven recordings remain among Armstrong's least known.

Armstrong had been on the road without a break since the summer of 1940 (often traveling with Lucille Wilson), finally returning to New York in March 1941. He had a successful week at Loew's State on Broadway in April and then went back to headline the Apollo in May, now featuring Ann Baker, his latest female vocalist. Avakian caught up with him again at the Apollo, Armstrong greeting him warmly and telling him, "George, let's get some ice cream. I'm going to take some ice cream to my darling." Avakian assumed it was Alpha, whom he had met before, but was surprised when they headed to the Bronx and visited Lucille at her mother's apartment. "We'd bought a quart of vanilla ice cream," Avakian remembered. "Louis was acting like a little boy. His eyes were sparkling. He was practically dancing, toe dancing. I could see he was in love with this girl." Avakian found both Lucille and her mother "charming" and watched as Armstrong finished three-quarters of the ice cream. Avakian also brought a gift: a copy of *King Louis*. He signed it, "Lucille—This Louis guy really is something—hope you'll go for him and these records a long time—George." Armstrong added, "Yas ma'am—From, Louis Armstrong."[44]

"We had a great time," Avakian remembered, but they had to leave quickly because Armstrong had another show to play. "When he left, I went to the car and turned around," Avakian said. "Louis was on the stoop of the building, and he was pirouetting with his arms out, and he was saying, 'Oh, my darling, my darling.' He was talking about Lucille. I thought, oh gosh, isn't this beautiful. This man is in love." Avakian also felt that in that moment, he had become something more to Armstrong than just a fan or a record collector or a reissue producer. Armstrong, Avakian recalled, was "expressing himself to me, a relative stranger, just somebody who had discovered these records and turned out to be a fan of his, neither of us ever dreaming that I would ever be his record producer and that we would become fast, beautiful friends, see each other abroad, be with our wives and all that, having dinner, etc. That was a marvelous relationship."[45]

It was probably the last thing Avakian expected to accomplish, but with his Columbia reissues, he put the Armstrong of the early 1940s in direct competition with the Armstrong of the 1920s. In June 1941, Columbia once again overshadowed the latest Decca singles with another Hot Jazz Classics album, *Louis Armstrong and His Hot 5*, featuring eight more selections from 1925–1926. Martin Mack reviewed the set for the Marxist *New Masses* magazine and predicted "some day the records he made ten and fifteen years ago will be placed among the highly important contributions to American music."[46] Decca, not wanting to be left behind, issued an album of their own the same week as Columbia, *Louis Armstrong Classics*, including many of Armstrong's remakes for the label, such as "Confessin'," "West End Blues," "Mahogany Hall Stomp," "Dipper Mouth," and "On the Sunny Side of the Street." The *New York Times* gave Armstrong a rare rave, saying the Decca compilation "deserves unreserved recommendation," but Don Woodrum spoke for many in the jazz world, writing, "Not the greatest of his recordings, perhaps, but still fine examples."[47]

Armstrong was alive and well and still in demand, but now most of his press was either about past triumphs or painted him a "grand old man" of sorts, resting on his laurels. Writer Peter Dana captured an interesting scene after one of Armstrong's Apollo performances in May, dining at the Hotel Theresa with two professional musicians and three experts on jazz, all of whom remained anonymous. Armstrong was the subject and the conversation was one of praise, but mostly for his showmanship and humor. Dana described Armstrong as "the world's great minstrel man," adding, "It was as if these men were intent on celebrating the minstrelsy of Louis for the sheer pleasure of it, for the truly remarkable phenomenon of folk art it is. Again, it was as if they were saying that Louis had created out of the solid tradition of modern folk music a musical language of his own, as indeed every great artist does." It was clear that those present were celebrating a folk artist, not a cutting-edge musician. After two hours, one of the men said, "Well, I hope Louis will be around a long time yet 'beating' up them chops."[48]

Armstrong indeed still had 30 more years of "beating up them chops" and no one could have predicted that his greatest success still lie ahead, but his 1920s triumphs would now be shadowing him for the rest of his life—and beyond.

18

"I Never Tried to Be God"

July 1941–July 1942

In the summer of 1941, Leonard Feather moved to the United States and immediately began working as a writer, radio host, and press agent. Joe Glaser used him frequently to drum up publicity for his clients, including Armstrong. Feather's first idea was to have Armstrong name his favorite trumpet players for a *Down Beat* column, perhaps expecting him to go way back and name New Orleans greats like King Oliver and Bunk Johnson. Instead, Armstrong named Bunny Berigan first, followed by Harry James, Roy Eldridge, Erskine Hawkins, and the other trumpet players in his own orchestra, Shelton "Scad" Hemphill, Frank Galbreath, and Gene Prince.[1] Zilner Randolph remembered Armstrong getting criticized for naming Berigan instead of a black trumpeter such as Red Allen, who didn't even make the list. "You know, Randy, I picked somebody that played Louis Armstrong," Armstrong said. "If I picked any of the other trumpet players, that mean that I don't like Louis Armstrong style."[2]

Feather's next idea was to celebrate Armstrong's 25th year in show business, arbitrarily choosing the year 1916 for Armstrong's debut. He asked Armstrong to name "the most important events" of his life in those years, again, possibly assuming that "West End Blues" or the music of the Hot Fives and Sevens would be listed. Instead, Armstrong first choice was the *Fleischmann's Yeast Show* in 1937, his second was a listing of his films (naming *Pennies from Heaven, Artists and Models, Every Day's a Holiday,* and "that fine" *Going Places*), and he finished by detailing his Broadway run in *Connie's Hot Chocolates* in 1929. In each instance, Armstrong valued the result of higher visibility or breaking down a racial barrier rather than something he played on the trumpet.[3]

Armstrong's visibility was about to soar when it was announced that he had signed on to star in a big-screen film about his own life that would be directed by Orson Welles, fresh off *Citizen Kane*.[4] The black press immediately noted the importance of this news. "I believe this is the first time a Negro has ever been honored in this particular manner by Hollywood, unless we consider the two biographical films on the career of Dr. George Washington

Carver, the Tuskegee scientist," Edgar T. Rouzeau wrote.[5] A lot was riding on this role; writing in the *Daily Worker*, Bill Newton called Armstrong "a clever comedian" but added, "He's been in movies before, playing Jim Crow 'comedy' parts. One that stands out in memory saw this great artist portray a menial and slow-thinking stable groom in a film that starred the feeble crooner Dick Powell. But we can probably expect far different treatment of Louis from the talented and progressive Welles. It should be a film to look forward to."[6]

Welles named Elliot Paul as screenwriter—Armstrong wrote to Paul and immediately recommended the services of Feather, telling him, "if there's anyone that know's about my life is Leonard Feather"[7]—but soon raised eyebrows when he announced that "he can't see" Lillian Hardin Armstrong playing herself; *Down Beat* called it a "tragic irony."[8] Instead, rumors floated that either Una Mae Carlisle or Hazel Scott—both talented pianists who also sang—would be signed in the role of Miss Lil, while Billie Holiday was signed to play Bessie Smith.[9] Duke Ellington also was brought in at $1,000 a week to supervise the music of Welles's film, which was now to be titled *It's All True*.[10]

But Ellington ran into a problem when he met Technical Director Dave Stuart, described as a "well-known west coast swing radical" by *Metronome*. Stuart was one of a growing number of disciples of *Jazzmen* who strictly adhered to the principles of early New Orleans jazz and nothing else that followed (Stuart owned a record store and refused to sell Glenn Miller's big band recordings). Stuart insisted he was hired to "set writer Eliot Paul right on the intricacies of jazz" and was also not impressed with Ellington. "I spoke with him for a long time," Stuart said, "and I'm convinced he knows nothing about jazz. Why he never even heard of Buddy Bolden!!!"[11] There was obviously a lot of work to be done and in October, it was announced that filming would be delayed until March 1942 to allow time for the script to be prepared properly.[12]

Stuart revealed himself when he announced, "There's only one band in the world that is playing real jazz today, and that's Lu Watters's band in San Francisco. They copy all the old Louis records, note for note." Watters was at the forefront of what was becoming known in some circles as the Dixieland or New Orleans "Revival," as he looked past swing and began painstakingly re-creating the jazz records of the 1920s. When the *Jazzmen* authors discovered Bunk Johnson, it was Watters who took up a collection to help buy Johnson a new trumpet. It was now 1941 and Johnson still hadn't recorded, but with a new set of teeth and the new instrument, he felt confident enough to sit in with Armstrong's big band during an engagement in New Iberia. "Hope I can still play like that cat when I'm his age," Armstrong wrote in *Down Beat*. "His lip work is tops and he still has original ideas aplenty."[13]

The New Orleans nostalgia, the resurgence of Johnson, the novelty of Watters, the publicity of Columbia reissues, and the release of Decca Hot Seven singles led to new rumors that Armstrong was planning on ditching his big band to return to a "Hot Five"–type setting. But truthfully, Armstrong had no desire to go back to roots; on the contrary he was keeping up with the times. "Lots of new ideas circulating and I try to keep hep to the jive, because if I live to be as old as 'Old Man Mose' I'd like to be up to the minute," Armstrong wrote in the same *Down Beat* column in which he praised Johnson.[14] For proof, all one had to do was look at the drummer on the stand when Johnson sat in: Kenny Clarke.

The 27-year-old Clarke had already begun making a name for himself with his somewhat unorthodox style of drumming, interacting creatively with the soloists and "dropping bombs" with his bass drum instead of keeping straight time. Clarke had associations with Armstrong-related figures such as Joe Garland and Sidney Bechet before settling in as the house drummer at Minton's Playhouse, the destination for those who tired of playing the same charts in big bands night after night. Soon, musicians like Dizzy Gillespie, Charlie Christian, Mary Lou Williams, Joe Guy, Thelonious Monk, and others began descending on Minton's for jam sessions in which stretching out was encouraged and daring explorations of harmonies became the norm. Minton's became the incubator for the next new trend in jazz, a place for young musicians looking to experiment.

Sid Catlett put in his notice to join Benny Goodman and strongly recommended Clarke as his replacement. Armstrong agreed, over protests from Joe Glaser, who never heard of him. Catlett rehearsed with Clarke for a week, showing him just how Armstrong liked his drums played. It paid off; on his first night, Clarke's playing so impressed Armstrong, the trumpeter repeatedly exclaimed, "Doggone, Gizzard!"[15] Armstrong and Clarke became fast friends and regularly indulged in marijuana together, though Armstrong's days of getting the band high before a gig were long gone. One night, Clarke got too high before playing, causing his drumming to suffer. He knew it and waited to be scolded afterwards. Instead, Armstrong went to Clarke's hotel room—and immediately rolled two joints. After spending the night smoking and talking, Armstrong prepared to leave, but not before sticking his head back in to impart a lesson: "Klook," he said, "*after* the gig; not before."[16]

Clarke was there for a tour of the south, featuring Armstrong's first military base performance, playing for over 5,000 soldiers at Fort Barrancas in late August. Armstrong donated his appearance "in the interest of national defense," received gold crossed cannons from Col. Lloyd B. Magruder, and opened and closed his show with "The Star Spangled Banner."[17] He wrote about the experience to Feather, "And was it thrilling when—we started the Star Spangled Banner and every one of those Soldiers stood up and every one of them gave the same right hand Salute as they stood attention . . . Good Gracious was I thrilled."[18] After the concert for the soldiers, Armstrong visited the base's hospital. "And Feathers you've never seen anything like it the way those soldiers—colored and white all brightened up just at the sight [of] me," Armstrong wrote. "Gee—whata wonderful feeling that was to know that I cheer'd them all so." Armstrong even led the sick soldiers in a chorus of "When the Saints Go Marching In" and joined them for lunch.[19]

The next stop was Georgia, where Clarke's short stay in the band came to an end. Glaser had been against Clarke's hiring from the start and wanted to fire him almost immediately, but Armstrong always stuck up for him. "You've got to get that Kenny Clarke out of there," Glaser would huff. "Leave Little Gizzard there," Armstrong would respond. "He's modern." That always impressed Clarke, who said years later, "Oh, Louis was the first modern musician. So

Figure 18.1 Entertaining the troops at a military base in Pensacola, Florida, in September 1941. Vocalist Ann Baker is on the left. Such venues kept Armstrong's big band working steadily through World War II.
Courtesy of the Louis Armstrong House Museum

therefore he could understand, you know, when he heard something that was akin to what he had been doing all his life, he recognized it immediately." But when drummer O'Neal Spencer quit the popular John Kirby Sextet, Glaser made his move and hired him. Armstrong took the news hard. "So when I left the band, he gave me a picture and cried and his tears were on the picture," Clarke recalled. Clarke never forgave Joe Glaser, hanging up on him years later when he called to inquire about booking the Modern Jazz Quartet. "So I kind of got my revenge, you know," Clarke said.[20]

Armstrong admired having a "modern" musician like Clarke in his band, but jazz critics weren't paying attention to such a hiring (or firing). In September, George Avakian released his third Armstrong "Hot Jazz Classics" album in less than a year, *Louis and Earl*, containing Armstrong's ground-breaking recordings with Earl "Fatha" Hines. Leonard Feather, writing under the pseudonym "Geoffrey Marne," reminisced about "West End Blues" being the record that introduced him to jazz. "The Album of the Month is, for my money, also the album of the year," he concluded. "If any of the younger jazz fans wonder about the adulation which every trumpet player expresses for Louis, this album will help them to understand."[21]

But *Louis and Earl* also inspired hostility toward Armstrong, especially in a column in *Music and Rhythm* by D. Leon Wolff, who argued, "Louis Armstrong has ceased to be God. He remains technically and creatively under today's niveau. Even in 'West End Blues,' which was recorded when Armstrong was at the peak of his powers, one senses his struggle with the instrument. This is perfectly evident in the frayed solo introduction and in the ending." Wolff hammered Armstrong's technical ability, saying he was "forced" to "ride slowly or even half-time" because he eschewed playing fast runs and concluded that Armstrong "stopped being God back in 1932."[22]

This time, Feather leapt to Armstrong's defense. "Louis is not *forced* to 'ride slowly or even half-time' on fast numbers," he wrote. "He has learned the value of simplicity. Anyone who has heard him warming up in the dressing room can confirm that he can play scales, exercises and technical runs with great proficiency, but he has sense enough to know that technique in jazz is only a means to an end. In fact it is undeniable that Louis leaned more on superficial virtuosity in 1932 than he does today. No more does he play 250 high C's in succession. The high-note endings still remain, and they are as near infallible technically as any jazz trumpet man has ever come."[23]

Feather showed Wolff's article to Armstrong himself and reported the trumpeter's "explosive" reaction. "I never tried to be God," Armstrong said. "If some of the fans made an idol out of me I couldn't help it, but I'm just a trumpet player like thousands of others; maybe I play better than some and maybe a lot of 'em try to copy me—but I never wanted to be put in a class by myself!"[24] Armstrong was growing frustrated by the constant analysis of his style and the newfound admiration for the way he played 15 years earlier. He remained proud of the improvement of his big band under Joe Garland and wanted to record those sounds instead of anything that sounded like 1928.

Armstrong got the opportunity on November 16, in the middle of a four-week engagement at the Grand Terrace in Chicago with Sid Catlett back on drums. Armstrong turned back the clock, remaking one of his biggest selling singles of 1931, coupling "I'll Be Glad When You're Dead You Rascal You" with "When It's Sleepy Time Down South." The new versions were improvements on the originals, the latter a glorious, rare instrumental rendering of a song Armstrong performed thousands of times. Armstrong also threw Joe Garland a bone by recording his "Leap Frog," a catchy riff-based instrumental in the mold of Garland's "In the Mood." Armstrong only played on the last 18 seconds, sacrificing his solo work on a number guaranteed to be more popular on jukeboxes and with black audiences than anything in the style of the Hot Five. Armstrong was front and center on the fourth song recorded that date, but it was still an unusual selection: a completely instrumental, slow, deadly serious rendering of "I Used to Love You (But It's All Over Now)," clearly aimed at third wife Alpha as their marriage was indeed, for all intents and purposes, all over now.

Armstrong broke all existing records during his luxurious month at the Grand Terrace before setting out to conquer some different territory: Minnesota, North Dakota, and Canada. During his week in Minot, North Dakota, Japan attacked Pearl Harbor, kicking off American involvement in World War II.[25] Arriving in Winnipeg, Armstrong was immediately asked about how Americans were taking the news about the United States going to war. "The way those people were jitterbugging last night, I would say they were taking it kind of calm," Armstrong said. He also said that people were singing "The Star-Spangled Banner" with more enthusiasm than ever, adding, "And I love to play it." Regarding how he might be used by the military Armstrong said, "I'm ready willing and able. Whatever they want me to do is fine with me."[26]

Meanwhile, Joe Glaser was preoccupied with two of his other clients. In 1940, Glaser split with Consolidated Radio Artists to go back on his own as Joe Glaser Inc. His first major hire was Armstrong's old friend, Lionel Hampton. Hampton's big band made its debut at the Apollo on December 11, 1941, and "did something to this town that hasn't been done in a long time," according to Billy Rowe.[27] But ironically, the client that was making the most waves for Glaser was one of the few white artists on his roster: Les Brown.

The 29-year-old Brown had been a struggling bandleader until, according to a *Radio and Television Mirror* report, "like the hero with the mortgage money, came veteran manager Joe Glaser." With Glaser running the show, Brown said, "We started working for a change."[28]

In 1941, Brown's "Band of Renown" suddenly became the hottest band in the country and all eyes turned to Glaser in the booking world. At the end of the year, he made a major deal to move his stable of artists to Music Corporation of America, *Variety* admitting "the band around which the entire deal revolves is Les Brown's."[29] Overnight, Glaser became the subject of multiple profiles in the mainstream press based on his association with Brown. Bob Musel of the *Times Herald* spent a day with Glaser at his Radio City office and mentioned Glaser's championship Boston bulldogs, his six-room penthouse, complete with a kennel, his four automobiles, sixty suits, and twenty pairs of shoes. He did not mention the multiple rape charges. And he did not mention Louis Armstrong.[30]

Not that Armstrong needed help getting publicity. After traveling for much of 1940 with Lucille Wilson, he seemed to temporarily reconcile with Alpha, praising her in letters to Feather from his tour of the south in August and September 1941. But as they drifted apart and their fighting grew more violent, it was clear that there would be no saving the marriage. "I Used to Love You (But It's All Over Now)" was released by Decca at the end of December, while Armstrong was playing the Paradise in Detroit. The message was received loud and clear by Alpha, who drunkenly responded with a message of her own: she was cheating on him with Cliff Leeman, a white drummer in Charlie Barnet's orchestra.

Armstrong poured out any sorrow or anger he felt into a letter to Walter Winchell, still quite an influential columnist. He said he wasn't surprised— "I always become Surprised when a Woman does 'Right' and not when she does 'Wrong'"—and claimed Alpha bragged about Leeman paying her gas bill. "Brother Winch," he wrote, "Can . . . you imagine my wife 'Bragging about this Lad paying a few lousy gas bills—when I've been giving her THOUSANDS and 'THOUSANDS of Dollars for 'Furs—Diamonds, Jewelry, etc . . . It really 'Kills, One Doesn't It?" Regarding Leeman, Armstrong wrote, "If I only could see him and tell him how much I appreciate what he's done for me by taking that 'Chick away from me. . . . So if you should run across him 'Please thank him for me 'Wilya Mr Winch? . . . And with all of that—I still think he is one of the greatest drummers that we have here in our-U.S.A."[31]

Winchell removed Leeman's name, but he printed just about everything else Armstrong wrote in a column titled "The Love Letters of a New Yorker."[32] The result was widespread shock. "The whole town is talking about Louis

Armstrong who shouldn't have written Winchell that letter about a wife he once loved and vice versa," Billy Rowe wrote in the *Pittsburgh Courier*.[33] Alpha immediately hit back, filing a suit for separation, charging "inhuman treatment, refusal to provide and abandonment," and asking for alimony of $250 a week, plus $5,000 for counsel fees. Alpha told the press that since they were married, Armstrong's "repeated instances of infidelity have made life (with him) unbearable."[34] Rowe reported about this and couldn't resist a dig at Alpha's materialistic tendencies, writing, "Alpha Armstrong peeped out from one of her six fur coats in domestic court here last week to ask Louis Armstrong, her estranged hubby, for a two hundred and fifty dollar allowance per week for life as a parting gift. What would you say? Well, so did Louie!"[35] The mess would not be straightened out any time soon, but Louis was now free to spend as much time as he wanted with Lucille Wilson.

The year 1942 began like all other recent years with the release of various readers' polls; Armstrong wasn't even mentioned in *Down Beat* and *Metronome*, losing to Ziggy Elman, Cootie Williams, and Roy Eldridge.[36] But again, showing that the jazz press reflected only one viewpoint, he still won the top trumpet spot in the *Pittsburgh Courier* annual poll.[37] And he certainly wasn't struggling; he became the only African American entertainer to perform at President Franklin Roosevelt's Birthday Ball on January 30. Glaser kept the one-nighters to a minimum for the first half of the year, allowing him to reign at favorite old venues such as the Royal Theatre in Baltimore, and the Apollo in Harlem and Frank Sebastian's old Cotton Club, now renamed the Casa Manana. His band was now being hailed by some "As Finest He's Had In Years"[38] and featured an upgrade in the female vocalist department when Velma Middleton replaced Ann Baker in April. Middleton was Armstrong's fourth female vocalist since Glaser signed him in 1935, but where the others were content to sing pop tunes of the day, Middleton was an all-around entertainer, singing, dancing, and doing comedy.

Frank Sebastian still had his radio hook-up in place and Armstrong broadcast regularly from the Casa Manana through April. Surviving broadcasts find him in peak form, playing new arrangements of old favorites "Shine," "Basin Street Blues," and "I Surrender Dear," as well as another striking ballad inspired by Alpha, "You Don't Know What Love Is."[39] He also broadcast performances of four songs he was due to record for Decca on April 17, "Get Your Cash for Some Trash," "Among My Souvenirs," "Coquette," and "I Never Knew." This was usual practice for Glaser, who wrote in *Billboard* in September 1941, "Another important issue is that we don't want our bands to go into the recording studios cold—we want them to have the feel of the song to be recorded way in advance. We have our bands play instrumental numbers at least a month at various jobs before they are recorded."[40] As a result, the April 17 session continued the high level of the November session from Chicago, especially on "I Never Knew," which swings effortlessly thanks to the fruitful partnership of Armstrong and Catlett.

Armstrong didn't know it at the time, but it would be the last single Decca would release until 1945. James C. Petrillo, president of the American Federation of Musicians, was threatening to strike. More and more "disc jockeys" had taken over the radio airwaves by playing commercially recorded music, which Petrillo argued was taking away jobs from the many studio musicians who made careers in playing live music on the radio. Armstrong was off on tour and was not able to record before the recording ban officially went into effect on August 1. Just as this particular edition of Armstrong's Garland-led band hit its stride with two successful Decca sessions, they would never record again.[41]

Armstrong's recording career was not the only work that disappeared. In early April, he received the news that the planned Orson Welles film about his life had been shelved; a spokesperson for Welles said "it was just another project that never got beyond the talk stage."[42] Armstrong received $15,000 for not doing anything, but many in the black press were disappointed. "Let it be known that by filming the life of an important Negro musician like Louis, [Welles] could weave into the story the more important theme of the race and its contributions to music," Peter Suskind wrote in Norfolk, Virginia's *New Journal and Guide*, adding "There is always the possibility that Hollywood just wasn't 'ready' for an all colored show."[43]

The disappointment reflected Armstrong's high standing in the black press, but that momentarily changed in 1942, sometimes because of self-inflicted decisions. After the letter about Alpha, Armstrong continued writing letters to Winchell, who continued publishing them. Armstrong always peppered his letters with slang and jokes and even misspellings, but Winchell went one step further and "edited" Armstrong's letters by rendering them in a type of painful dialect that Armstrong never used. "Dear Pappy Winch," began a letter in Winchell's column in March, "Open up dem Madison Square Garden gates, but wide, yo hear? I mean on March 10th, pappy. Because I'se comin'! Ah'm playing a date in Akron, Ohio dat night and can hop a plane and get to N'yawk about 3 ayem. Is dat time enuf? . . . Betcha mistah FDR plenty satisfied wif wot yo Is doin' for de USA."[44] Two weeks later, Winchell published another, quoting Armstrong, "Ah'm headed for Hollywood and will be at de Casa Manana and to make a pitcher for RKO, beginning April 1, no foolin.'"[45].

The "letters" aren't remotely close to how Armstrong typed, but they didn't seem to bother him. "You'd be surprised at the people telling me about they have been reading about you and me in your column constantly," Armstrong wrote in a private letter from May 31—without a trace of the dialect. "Pops I won't take up too much of your time this time," he concluded. "I just wanted to tell you how all the folks everywhere seem to be so glad when they see something in your column concerning me. . . . And of course you know how grateful I am for it."[46]

But Armstrong was wrong because many of his own people were disgusted by Winchell's fabricated letters. In the black press, Edgar T. Rouzeau felt that "his recent attempts at inveigling publicity out of the white press have been on the cheap side and seem to indicate that the man is frantically grasping at a waning popularity." Rouzeau had a problem with Armstrong's first letter concerning Alpha, saying it was "written in a Jeeter Lester–Uncle Tom dialect that neither man would own," but the later letters with the over-the-top dialect were too much for him to handle. "It made you feel ashamed of your own folks and it made you wish with all your heart that no white people would read the column, as impossible as that is," he wrote. Rouzeau concluded, "I wish someone would tell Louis that the white folks are laughing at him and that we aren't laughing at all."

Rouzeau and like-minded black fans would not be laughing at Armstrong's latest film work either. To make up for the loss of the Welles film, Glaser signed Armstrong up with Sam Coslow for some quick work shooting four Soundies in April for R. C. M. studios. Soundies were the first music videos, a series of low-budget three-minute shorts featuring a visual of a band performing one of their signature songs, miming to a pre-recorded track. The films would then be shown in a coin-operated booth known as a "Panoram," which sprung up in nightclubs, bars, restaurants, and most places that already had a jukebox. Hollywood put its fingerprints on two of the numbers, "Shine" and "When It's Sleepy Time Down South." An improvement on *A Rhapsody in Black and Blue*, Armstrong sang "Shine" as himself, wearing a sharp pinstriped suit and looking "youthful" in the words of a *Billboard* reviewer, thanks to a diet he picked up in *Harper's Bazaar*. But the set featured a prop of a gigantic shoe being shined in the background, while comedian Nicodemus was brought out "for a few mugging bits."[47] And on "When It's Sleepy Time Down South," Armstrong not only sang the "darkies" lyrics he hadn't uttered in public in many years (he normally played it as an instrumental theme), but also performed it on a set that was one step removed from a plantation. Black fans already having trouble with Armstrong's letters in Winchell's column and his previous film appearances could not have been pleased.

Nevertheless, Armstrong remained a major draw, especially with black audiences, breaking records at both the Orpheum in Los Angeles (where trumpeter Frank Galbreath had to take over for a few days because Armstrong had weakened himself, reducing to 135 pounds for the aborted Welles film[48]) and at the Grand Terrace in July, his July 4 date "attracting more patrons on a single day than any band or show ever to hit the Southside house," according to the *Chicago Defender*.[49] A string of one-nighters followed, this time through the south, but the band now had to travel via train instead of bus because the Office of Defense Transportation put a ban on charter buses owing to rubber and gasoline shortages. "Since the Office of Defense Transportation banned the use of buses by musicians," Glaser said, "colored bands have been up against an unprecedented problem. It cost almost $1800 last week to move Louis Armstrong and his band by train for seven one-nighters. A trip which can be made for $75 by bus may cost anything from $250 to $350 by train, including the extra charges for trucks to move the instruments and other expenses." Glaser predicted "eventually half of the bands will have to get off the road."[50]

Traveling by train was not necessarily an improvement for the musicians, either. Trains were overcrowded to begin with and though Glaser tried to book his bands in a private car, it didn't always turn out that way—especially in the south. "We'd have reserved cars on trains, going through the South," Armstrong's new bassist John Simmons said, adding, "And they would even stop and take that away from us. You know some woman would come back there and she'd say, 'Oh, here's some seats back here,' Big Sid says, 'Ma'am, this car's reserved.' She said, 'Don't any [niggers] have any reservations.'" While Catlett argued with her, Simmons remembered Armstrong "standing there, guarding his lips. . . . Everything that happened, he was guarding his lips all the time."[51]

The traveling was brutal, and the actual gigs in the south weren't much easier. "Boy, but that Louis Armstrong tour was something else, baby," Simmons recalled. "We got to Atlanta, Georgia and they had chicken wire down through the middle of this auditorium. It was a dance. Whites on one side, blacks on the other. If the dance gets too good, the blacks got to leave, you know. If the music got too good, and some more whites wanted to get in there, the blacks had to go." Armstrong remained in his dressing room after shows but had an open-door policy for visitors. Simmons was with him when a white fan—"he's real hip, clean"—approached and said, "Man, some of my best friends are colored." Simmons said, "That didn't rub me right. I'm waiting for him to say that magic word so I can jump down his throat." The fan continued, "We had a colored mammy. We nursed her breast." Simmons couldn't resist. "Well, man, you're a lucky S.O.B.," he said. "I was 21 years old before I sucked a Caucasian breast." Armstrong exclaimed, "Oh!" and immediately held his mouth as though he had been struck, telling Simmons, "You're going to get us killed down here." Simmons replied, "Well, he asked for it." A new generation of African Americans weren't going to put up with comments like that anymore. When the tour ended, Simmons "kissed the Pennsylvania Station's ground, time I got there. Never no more. One trip through the South was enough for me."[52]

It had been quite an up-and-down year so far, with record-breaking engagements balanced with tiring one-nighters, a series of excellent Decca recordings brought to a halt because of a recording ban, the disappointing cancellation of the Welles film, and copious praise and criticism from the black press and the jazz press. But as the calendar hit August, things were looking up: Louis officially filed for divorce from Alpha and was prepared to walk down the aisle for the fourth—and final—time.

19

"A Little Higher on the Horse"

August 1942–December 1943

"Hollywood Goes Glaser!"

So stated an ad in *Variety* in August 1942, mentioning that Les Brown just completed filming *Seven Days' Leave* for RKO, Lionel Hampton was appearing at the Casa Manana, Stuff Smith was at the Trouville, and Louis Armstrong had just been signed for a major role in the all-black film *Cabin in the Sky*, beating out Cab Calloway for the part.[1] Glaser, feeling confident in California, bought a large home in Beverly Hills, promising to start spending six months a year on the west coast.[2] After the expenses of train travel, Glaser was relieved to bring in the big film money with *Cabin in the Sky*, laying off the band during the filming; some members, such as Sid Catlett and John Simmons, did not return.

While in California, Armstrong reunited with another one of his elders, trombonist Kid Ory. Ory had retired to a chicken farm in Los Angeles for many years but was now playing again as part of a band led by clarinetist Barney Bigard. Armstrong went to see Bigard and Ory at the Trouville in Los Angeles, and quickly became impressed with their 20-year-old bassist, Charles Mingus. Mingus joined Armstrong's outfit as they went back on the road, heading north to Washington and into Canada. Mingus would go on to become a legendary figure but at the time was one of several younger, unheralded musicians who joined Armstrong's big band because of the draft; never again would it feature the veteran name musicians it did in the 1930s and early 1940s.[3]

On September 25, Armstrong wrote a letter to William Russell while passing through Evansville, Indiana. "By the time you get this letter—I'll have my Divorce from my third wife and I'll be on my way to the Altar with my fourth wife . . . Which is the sharpest one of all of them," Armstrong wrote. "Yessir—Madam Lucille Wilson is gonna make all of the rest of the Mrs. Satchmo's look sick when she walks down the Aisle with Brother Satchmo Armstrong looking just too-pretty for words with her little Brown Cute Self . . . Lawd today." Armstrong's first three marriages didn't produce a child but he was now hoping that Lucille would change that. "And if Lucille and I have more than one Satchmo—I'll name one of them Russell," he wrote, adding, "And believe me Pal—we're really going to get down to real—*Biz'nez* this time... Catch on? ... Oh Boy."[4]

Armstrong's lawyers had filed a petition for divorce on September 15, but Armstrong was unable to get to court until he passed through Chicago in early October. "When I divorced Alpha I had two witnesses who weren't very bright," he recalled. "Those cats talked so slow they not only almost kept me from getting the divorce, they almost got me some time. The judge asked me a few questions and when he heard my voice, said, 'Hey, boy, you got a cold?' I said, 'No, sir, that's just that saw-mill voice of mine.' We both laughed and the judge said, 'Divorce granted.' "[5] The 16-year relationship with Alpha Smith was over but his hurt over her cheating on him never quite went away, once literally haunting his dreams in North Dakota. When he awoke, he wrote down music and lyrics that came to him in his sleep: "Some Day, you'll be sorry/ the way you treated me was wrong." Asked about the origin of the song a year before he died, Armstrong said, "It could have come back to the days of my third wife, you know. One of the finest women I ever met—until she got two or three drinks in her."[6]

However, he never forgot his indebtedness to Alpha's mother, who watched his developmentally disabled adopted son Clarence Hatfield Armstrong for so many years. "My divorce from Alpha didn't end my friendship with her family," Armstrong wrote years later. "After she died I took care of her mother for a number of years. It was a pleasure to help her because she was such a wonderful old lady. I did it too out of respect for Alpha's memory and the years we were together."[7] There was one problem with Armstrong's statement: he wrote it in 1954—Alpha Smith didn't pass away until 1960.[8] Armstrong always maintained that he had positive relationships with all of his ex-wives but Alpha disappeared from his life the day of their divorce; there are no letters, no photographed reunions, she doesn't appear on his tapes, etc. And except for a blurb about her funeral, there was no obituary for Alpha and no stories of her post-Louis life in Beverly Hills. It says something that Armstrong told *Ebony* readers that she was dead—evidently, she was dead to him.

With the divorce out of the way, Louis and Lucille planned to wed immediately. On October 12, while passing through St. Louis on tour, they had their ceremony at the home of Blanche Smith, Velma Middleton's mother. Lucille's mother, Maude Wilson, made the trip and Bob Smiley served as Louis's best man; Luis Russell and Sonny Woods were the only members of Armstrong's band in the wedding party. The celebration lasted the afternoon, but then it was time to perform and go on the road. "My honeymoon was eight months of one-nighters," Lucille recalled. "I hadn't traveled like that before and I was really weary and tired. Louie had, you know, Louie was bubbly all the time. I got to thinking, 'My God, do I have to live like this the rest of my life? I can't stand it!' And I almost decided, 'Well, this marriage is not for me,' but you know, love will prevail. We came home and I rested and finally, I just made up my mind, 'If this is the way it's got to be,' and I learned to cope with it."[9]

At the end of October, Armstrong headlined for another week at the Apollo, sharing the bill with two old friends from his Chicago days in the 1920s, Butterbeans and Susie. *Variety* called it "One of the better Apollo stage shows," but criticized Butterbeans and Susie and their "alleged funny talk. The material is mostly old and much of it is borrowed, but the audience here seemed to go for them."[10] There was a gap widening between what *Variety* found funny and what the Apollo audience found funny. But it wasn't just *Variety*; the NAACP had always had a problem with some of the comedy exhibited at the Apollo—most notably blackface, which was still hanging on—but increasingly, more socially conscious, liberal white fans also began voicing their

Figure 19.1 Louis plants a kiss on his newlywed bride Lucille Armstrong shortly after their wedding in 1942.
Courtesy of the Louis Armstrong House Museum

uncomfortableness with the jokes told on the Apollo stage. Brooklyn resident H. P. Goldstein noted a Butterbeans and Susie routine where Butterbeans strutted around the stage in a loud zoot suit. "Who do you think you are?" Susie asked. "Frank Sinatra," replied Butterbeans. "Who?" asked Susie incredulously. Butterbeans responded, "I'm Frank Sinatra—'cept that I'm in technicolor."

"The audience, which was predominantly Negro, reacted very favorably, but somehow I, a white person, found the line objectionable," Goldstein wrote, in a letter to the editors of *PM* and the *Pittsburgh Courier*. "Perhaps I'm being very picayune, but I've heard similar material on the Apollo stage before (I visit the theatre because I'm addicted to jazz and like to hear some of the bands featured there) and I can't help but wonder how Negroes can object to 'Uncle Tom' caricatures and material with an objectionable connotation, when they burlesque themselves so crudely."[11]

Armstrong avoided such criticism for the time being, but his love of comedy was not an act he just turned on for Hollywood or for the public. He had long included jokes in letters to friends, such as this one he shared with Leonard Feather, which he attributed to blackface comedian George Williams:

He (George Williams) said—when he was a little boy living way out in the country—one day his mother sent him down to the Pound [ed. Pond] to get a Pail of Water . . . She said—Boy run down to the Pound an fetch me a pail of water right away . . . So he went runnin down to this pound to get this water and the minute he went to dip his pail into this water he looked overthere and spied an Alligator lying in this water . . . George said he'd gotten so terribly frightened until he clear forget to get the water and immediately started to runnin to home . . . And no sooner then he'd gotten to the porch of his home his mother said to him—Boy—Wheres that water that I told you to get? . . . And George said—Mother—theres, an Alligator in that water-and his mother said—Aw—Boy—go an get me that pail of water—don't you know that that Alligator was As Afraid of you as you were of him—and I said (sez George) well mother—if that Alligator was as Afraid of me as I was of him—that Water Isn't Fit To Drink. . . I guess he told her something . . eh?[12]

In late 1942, Armstrong began working on his third "joke book," which survives at the Louis Armstrong House Museum and is a priceless anthology of underground black humor of the early 1940s.[13] Armstrong had a public audience in mind for this 87-page document, opening with a four-page "Forward" [*sic*] in which he gave credit for the jokes to Bill "Bojangles" Robinson, Stepin Fetchit, Big Sid Catlett ("a funny 'Sommitch 'Too"), Earl Hines, and Zutty Singleton, spending much of the introduction writing about playing in the 1920s with the latter two.[14] He then explained the background of the jokes and why he felt them to be so important to collect: "So you see—the main reason for this book is to 'Kill the 'Cats . . . That means, to—'Knock 'Em out in the Isle . . . To 'Floor Em . . . To 'Bust their Vest—to Gas Em—to 'bust their Konk'—Aw Hell—To 'Send Them and make them feel—and put them in a rather 'Jovial Mood . . . Or should I say Jovial'Moods? . . . Or should I say—make them 'Laugh their 'ASS OFF . . . . haw haw haw."[15]

Armstrong might have loved to laugh offstage and on, but one youngster quickly grew tired of what he perceived as "Tomming and Mugging": Charles Mingus, who put in his notice when he learned that the band was due to tour the south.[16] A complex figure, Mingus spent the rest of life bad-mouthing Armstrong. "As for Armstrong—he was only an Uncle Tom," Mingus said in 1977. "He was doing, in the music he played, just what the boss man told him to do. 'Hello, Dolly,' and 'Mack the Knife'—he was helping separate the races. Duke Ellington wanted to integrate the races."[17] But for all of his harsh criticism, Mingus held on to one artifact from his stint: a battered publicity photo of Armstrong signed, "Best Wishes To My Boy, To Mingus, A Real Fine Youngster. From Louis Armstrong."[18]

As Armstrong headed south, he was faced with an itinerary filled with military camps, which now became his main type of performance venue. Over the next several months Armstrong performed at locations such as Fort Benning in Columbus, Georgia; Duncan Field in San Antonio, Texas; and the Tuskegee Army Flying School in Tuskegee, Alabama. The black press covered Armstrong's visit to Tuskegee, where he was photographed frequently, broadcasted on the radio, and was generally treated as a hero. But the military was still painfully segregated, leading to an altercation at Fort Benning when the camp decided to exclude black soldiers from Armstrong's show on Christmas Day. "Every colored soldier was turned away," the *Baltimore Afro-American* reported. "Two were beaten by MP's when they insisted the announcement said 'all soldiers were invited.'" Armstrong, who was used to playing in front of segregated audiences, didn't know what was happening behind the scenes. "One group, refused admission, waited until the program was over and when Armstrong came out, gave him a piece of their mind for consenting to play at a U.S. Army Camp from which his own race was excluded," the story continued. "When one of the orchestra members said that Armstrong did not know about the camp's lily-white policy, soldiers replied he should have made it his business to find out ahead of time."[19] Just like Mingus's refusal to play the south, younger African Americans were rightfully getting angry at segregationist policies that excluded them altogether. Armstrong didn't set the policy, but he paid for it that Christmas.

Armstrong might have been disturbed by the altercation, but he was soon focused on something much more personal and heart-warming: his first Christmas with Lucille as his wife. She recalled:

> I had this Christmas tree. He hadn't mentioned it, but I had always had a tree at home. I put this tree up and then Louie told me, he just looked at it and looked at it and told me, "This is the first tree I've ever had. I've *never* had it." We were on one-nighters and the next day . . . I was going to leave the tree, Christmas is over, you know, this is the 26th. And Louie said, "No, we'll pack the tree!" Wherever we'd go, I'd have to protect the tree. The first thing, instead of unpacking bags, he made me put the tree up first.[20]

Louis's and Lucille's traveling wasn't about to stop anytime soon. "On his way to Hollywood to make another picture, Louis Armstrong will play at 54 Army camps," Harrison Carroll wrote in January 1943.[21] "This is a funny kind of a honeymoon, playing both day and night with little time to rest, but I don't mind it because those boys fighting out there aren't resting," Louis said at the time. "Just as long as they are willing to carry a gun, I will be willing to blow my trumpet, day and night, for them."[22] Lucille put up with it but in early 1943, she returned to New York to get some rest—and to strategize.

At the start of 1943, *Billboard* published an article by Paul Denis, "The Negro Makes Advances," listing Armstrong as one of the top African American figures of the year. Denis noted, "Negro performers are being presented with more dignity, their employment opportunities have increased, their race is being portrayed more sympathetically in films, radio and stage, and they are getting publicity in publications hitherto closed to them."[23] A lot was riding on the success of *Cabin in the Sky*, due to open in February. While performing at a week at Fay's Theater in Philadelphia, Armstrong and Glaser went to see a preview of the film, anxious to see Armstrong's big "Ain't It the Truth" production number on the screen. Instead, they were in for a shock; the number had been edited out entirely. Armstrong considered it a learning experience in a 1960 interview, bringing up the rest of the film's stars and saying, "See, they all had their managers when they cut that picture and Joe Glaser was in New York." Glaser told Armstrong, "I'll be there next time!"[24]

Armstrong displayed his talent for comedy in his single scene, more than holding his own with black actors and comedians Rex Ingram, Mantan Moreland, Willie Best, Fletcher Rivers, and Leon James. Armstrong played a few seconds of hot trumpet, and in private, bragged that his lines "saved that scene." Though he had done comedy in many of his previous films, the concept of him not even getting a song of his own was hard to reconcile, especially as Duke Ellington got to portray himself, leading his band through an exciting version of "Going Up" in a nightclub scene.[25]

Nevertheless, *Cabin in the Sky* received above-average reviews and was a box-office smash. "Don't be afraid of the all-colored cast," said *Showmen's Trade Review*. "This is darn swell entertainment that will more than please the average theatre-goer."[26] The black press put a lot of stock into it, Leo Roa writing in the *New York Age*, "If it is greeted with public approval, it will start a trend in the making of both all-colored and mixed cast pictures that will give the Negro a strong entertainment and talent outlet in Hollywood."[27] But the jazz press was rightly upset with the scant amount of Armstrong on screen,

Figure 19.2 Armstrong's "Ain't It the Truth" production number was cut from *Cabin in the Sky*, but he still bragged about how his comedic lines "saved the scene" with Lucifer (Rex Ingram) and his Idea Men (Fletcher Rivers, Leon James, Willie Best, and Mantan Moreland).
The Jack Bradley Collection, Louis Armstrong House Museum

despite being billed fourth in the all-star cast. Fats Baker (possibly a pseudonym) saw it and wrote about his feelings in *The Jazz Record*, saying, "It's the deal Louis got that hurts."

So Hollywood gets Satchmo, and has him play ten—or was it eleven?—notes, and speak about two-bits worth of lines, as one of Lucifer's idea men. Giving him a role as a comic, instead of musician, would have been grand in its way, Louis being Louis; if he had had Rochester's part, MGM would have had itself a picture. But as it is all he really got was a slap in the face. Incidentally, he goes to town with it as with all he does, but hell! This guy is one of the real greats in the history of America. You just can't forget it. We hope it haunts MGM.[28]

Glaser promised Armstrong it wouldn't happen again. In March, he signed Armstrong to appear in an upcoming Columbia film, *Jam Session*, in which he would only have to film a new version of his old standby "I Can't Give You Anything but Love." There would be no comedy, no acting, just one dynamite little performance of a song Armstrong had been performing since 1929. Armstrong would not have another big acting or comedic role for several years.

Glaser was spending more time in California in order to make more lucrative film deals. Around this time, Leonard Feather wrote about visiting "the nearby home of Mr. and Mrs. Joe Glaser, a palatial residence surrounded by a mouth-watering orchard of oranges, grape fruit and everything else growable."[29] Armstrong did not have a "palatial residence"; he had an apartment in Harlem's Olga Hotel, which he hadn't seen in some time. But that was about to change.

When Lucille went back to New York, she had a mission: find a home for her and Louis. Since getting married, Lucille repeatedly said, "Let's get a house," but Louis wouldn't hear of it. "What do you want a house for?" he'd respond. "We'll be traveling, we can get a hotel room." "I wasn't about to be cooped up in a hotel room," Lucille recalled, "and after being married to Louie for a few months I found that it wasn't very easy to argue with Louie if he made his mind up about something; he was very, very positive and you couldn't change his mind. So he kept not wanting this house and I'm a very stubborn person myself and so I said, 'This guy doesn't know what a house is all about.'"[30]

In early 1943, Lucille was contacted by Adele Heraldo, an old friend from her early days in Corona, Queens. Heraldo alerted Lucille that the two-family house next door at 34-56 107th Street in Corona was for sale. Lucille immediately envisioned her and Louis living on the first floor and her mother on the second. She worked out terms with attorney John P. Gering and on March

3, 1943, closed on her new home with a purchase price of $8,000, putting down $300 from her own bank account as a down payment.[31] There was only one issue.

"I bought the house myself and didn't tell him," Lucille said. "My mother was ill when I married Louie . . . [and] I wasn't about to leave my mother, I couldn't do that, so I bought a place large enough . . . [so] we wouldn't be in each other's way." Lucille helped move her mother in and paid her sister Janet to stay and watch over her. She rejoined Louis in Los Angeles in April and since he wasn't due back in New York for several months, chose to not tell him about their new home in Queens until the time was right.

Armstrong dominated Los Angeles as usual, this time at the Trianon Ballroom in Southgate, and immediately broke the records of Ellington and Basie during a triumphant three-week engagement. "Louis' thinness has added years to his appearance but hasn't done anything to his playing," the difficult-to-please Leonard Feather wrote. "I'd still like to hear him some time jamming with a great small group."[32] While in California, Armstrong's big band was regularly featured on a new radio program aimed at African American servicemen, *Jubilee*. The *Jubilee* recordings and other broadcasts of the period allow listeners to hear what Armstrong was doing during the recording ban, performing new arrangements of old favorites like "The Peanut Vendor" and "Dear Old Southland," and putting his own spin on current pop hits like "I've Got a Girl in Kalamazoo" and "As Time Goes By." Interestingly, demanding trumpet features such as "Struttin' with Some Barbecue" and "Swing That Music" seemed to disappear entirely after 1941, following the fate of longtime specialties such as "Tiger Rag," "Dinah," and "Chinatown," which didn't survive the 1930s. He still pushed himself to the limit every time he put his trumpet to his lips, but with age came experience on how to feature his horn work with a little more strategy.

Armstrong left California and headed back on the road in the summer, but this time minus a few of his best-known musicians. While in Los Angeles, Velma Middleton was offered a spot in Bill Robinson's variety revue, *Born Happy*, at the Alcazar Theatre. Middleton welcomed the chance to stay in once place and left Armstrong, with Ann Baker resuming her old role.[33] Sonny Woods, who had been there since 1935, left to join the service, becoming a private first class and singing with military bands during the war.[34]

But the biggest loss occurred when Luis Russell finally decided to call it quits. Relegated to the role of a band pianist for the last several years, Russell left to form a new big band of his own, signing with Glaser's rival Moe Gale (though he would return to Glaser in 1946). Russell left Armstrong with one last present: the two men collaborated on a new song, "Back O'Town Blues," set in New Orleans but potentially referring to Armstrong's marital woes with lines like "Never mistreat your woman, cause it's gonna bounce right back on you." Armstrong began performing it on broadcasts in 1943 but wouldn't officially record it until 1946. It also proved to be a parting gift from Armstrong to Russell; as the flip side of Armstrong's 1955 smash hit, "Mack the Knife," it earned Russell enough royalties to buy his family a brand-new car.

While touring through Portland in July, Glaser put out a blurb in the *Pittsburgh Courier* announcing that " 'King Looic' is available for one-nighters on his way back from the Northwest."[35] It might seem unusual that Glaser was seemingly booking Armstrong on the fly instead of having him booked well in advance, but Armstrong was now just one in an ever-expanding stable of clients and Glaser had his work cut out for him in keeping everyone working. In fact, Glaser was featured in more major news stories than Armstrong between May and October 1943, including a profile in *Billboard* about how Glaser was "riding high on a rising market with plenty of bands to feed hungry spots."[36] In October, he received a life-changing offer: Jules C. Stein, president of Music Corp. of America, wanted to partner up with him. Glaser sold MCA a 50 percent interest in Joe Glaser, Inc. for $100,000 with a two-year option that would allow MCA to buy out the remaining 50 percent. According to *Variety*, MCA wanted a piece of Glaser because he "does an annual gross comparable with some of the better known agencies and surpasses most of the smaller outfits."[37] Glaser would continue managing his acts, including Armstrong, but increasingly, it looked like his goal was to dispose his booking business and move full time to California. Also, as a condition of the deal, he would no longer be operating as "Joe Glaser, Inc."; in December he began conducting business as the Associated Booking Corporation.[38]

A few weeks after Glaser's blockbuster merger with MCA, Armstrong returned to New York to play Loew's State on October 29, his first time in New York since playing the Apollo in November 1942. As the grueling tour wound down, Louis began talking to Lucille about how he was looking forward to spending time together in his Harlem apartment. Lucille knew she could no longer keep the new home a secret. Two weeks before the tour ended, Lucille broke the news.

"Pops, I've got something to tell you."

"Well, now what have you done?"

"Well, I haven't done anything I don't think you're going to be unhappy about what I've done but, uh, I have to tell you that we've moved."

"We've what!?" Louis erupted incredulously. "We've moved? Well, that's all right, you got a larger apartment?"

"No, I bought a house in a little town called Corona."

In telling the story, Lucille remembered that Louis "looked at me like I was . . . a cow with seven horns." She showed him some photos and he admitted it was beautiful but now had another question he wanted answered.

"Well, how did you pay for it? You didn't ask me for any money."

"Well, you have to remember that I had been working for 13 years," Lucille responded. "I have money saved up and so when I had approached you about a house and you were so down on it, I didn't ask you, I just took my money and put the down payment on the house and I've been keeping the payments up."

"You have?"

"Yes—but now that you know about the house you can take the payments over!"

They decided it would be best for Lucille to return home a little early so she could make sure everything was okay before Louis arrived. Finally, the day came, and Louis called from Penn Station in Manhattan at 6 A.M, saying he was about to get in a taxicab and asking her to have breakfast waiting for him. Lucille set out to start cooking hominy grits, sausage, eggs, and biscuits, figuring it would take Louis about 30 minutes to arrive. But after 1 hour and 45 minutes passed, he was nowhere to be seen. "Of all the cab drivers, he gets one that doesn't know how to get to Corona, he says he's never heard of it, and they're riding around for hours," Lucille said.[39]

"So the cab driver finally found the house," Louis wrote. "And when he looked around to the back of the cab and said to me, O.K. this is the place. One look at that big fine house, and right away I said to the driver 'Aw man' quit kidding, and take me to the address that I'm looking for." In Louis's version, he got "up enough courage to get out of the Cab, and Ring the Bell. And sure enough the door opened and who stood in the doorway with a real thin silk night gown—hair and curlers."[40]

But according to Lucille, she looked out the window and saw Louis and the cab driver outside, Louis standing there, swaying from side to side with his arms on his hips. Lucille opened the window and said, "Why don't you come in this house? How long have you been standing out there?" Nervous, Louis turned to the cab driver and said, "Man, you better come into this pad. This is the first time I'm seeing it so we might as well inspect it together."[41] Lucille gave them a tour and Louis finally sat down for breakfast—inviting the cab driver to eat with them. "The more Lucille showed me around the house the more thrill'd I got," Armstrong wrote, adding, "I felt very grand over it all. A little higher on the horse (as we express it)."[42] Years later, Lucille summed it up by saying, "I've never been able to move Louie from that place. Once he got in that place, he loved it."[43]

In addition to falling in love with the home and neighborhood where he would live for the rest of his life, Armstrong was thrilled to be performing in New York again—and New York was thrilled to see him. At Loew's State, he brought in an astronomical $40,000 in his first week at a time when the average was $23,000, obliterating the house record—but it still wasn't enough to get him back in the recording studio.[44] Decca had broken away from the other record companies and made their own separate deal with the AFM to start paying royalties, allowing them to begin recording again in October.

Figure 19.3 Armstrong joined by three young neighbors, Patricia, Gracie, and Annie Maguire, on the front steps of his Corona, Queens, home in the 1940s.
Courtesy of the Louis Armstrong House Museum

Armstrong and Glaser might have expected to be called back to the studio, but that call didn't come as the label set about recording the likes of Bing Crosby, Louis Jordan, Roy Eldridge, Jimmy Dorsey, Sister Rosetta Tharpe, and Lawrence Welk first. Perhaps it was best, as Armstrong's band was consistently receiving negative reviews in the press and losing more veteran musicians such as Frank Galbreath, Henderson Chambers, Bernard Flood, George Washington, and Lawrence Lucie, the last of whom having been drafted. Younger musicians, such as alto saxophonist Joe Evans, were brought in and they weren't necessarily thrilled to be there. Evans came from Jay McShann's band, where he picked up some of the stylistic mannerisms of that group's breakout soloist, Charlie Parker. Armstrong paid more but Evans felt "it was not as exciting as playing with the McShann band."[45]

Billboard praised Armstrong personally at a concert at Philadelphia's Town Hall in November, but added, "However, the orchestra that tags along with the master is a story in an entirely different tempo. And it ain't so good. As background for Armstrong's individual instrumental and vocal talents, a small rhythm-bound combo could easily mean as much as the large aggregation of 14 men rounded up in this instance."[46] Those begging Armstrong to perform again with "a small rhythm-bound combo" were about to have their wish granted.

20

"A Great Deal Less Than Grown Up"

January–December 1944

In 1943, *Esquire*—"The Magazine for Men"—asked Belgian jazz authority Robert Goffin to select his personal "All-American Jazz Band." "To begin with, it's very simple," Goffin wrote. "Opposite the place where it says 'Trumpet,' you merely set down the name of Louis Armstrong. After that, you go gently mad."[1] When it came time to select another "All-American Jazz Band," Goffin didn't want to do it alone. This time, he would consult a panel of 16 experts and the winners they chose would perform at the Metropolitan Opera House on January 18, 1944. It wasn't quite as simple as Goffin made it sound— Leonard Feather, Barry Ulanov, and George Avakian voted Armstrong in second place and John Hammond didn't vote for him at all—but Armstrong amassed enough votes to win first place in both the Trumpet and Male Vocalist categories.

Armstrong would be joined by first place winners Jack Teagarden on trombone, Coleman Hawkins on tenor saxophone, Art Tatum on piano, Al Casey on guitar, Oscar Pettiford on bass, Sid Catlett on drums, and Red Norvo and Lionel Hampton on xylophone and vibraphone respectively. Due to previous commitments, first place winner Benny Goodman and second place trumpeter Cootie Williams could not make it to the concert and were replaced by Barney Bigard and Roy Eldridge respectively. It would be—and remains—one of the greatest assemblages of jazz giants ever to play together. The *Pittsburgh Courier* rejoiced at the selections of the experts, Izzy Rowe writing, "For the first time in the history of swing music contests, Negroes have swept most of the choice spots on a jazz poll not conducted by a colored publication."[2]

For those critics wishing to see Armstrong perform in an all-star small group, the occasion seemed like cause for celebration. But even surrounded by old friends Bigard, Teagarden, Hampton, and Catlett, there would still be some tension brought on by the presence of Hawkins and Eldridge. Hawkins and Armstrong still weren't especially close and now the saxophonist was taking more of an interest in the newer, "modern" sounds coming out of the jam sessions at Minton's.[3] Eldridge made headlines by integrating the big bands of both Gene Krupa and Artie Shaw, won "Top Small Combo" honors in *Down Beat*'s readers' poll, and was now recording for Decca, but still felt like he was in Armstrong's shadow. A gladiator at heart, the chance to finally "battle" Armstrong in public was something he could not pass up.

Unfortunately, Armstrong would not be in shape for such a battle: he was suffering from kidney stones. At rehearsal, Glaser called Eldridge aside, told him about the kidney stones, and according to John Chilton, "pointed out, with no room for negotiation, that it would be appreciated if Roy did not attempt to outblow an ailing Louis."[4] Eldridge decided to tone it down a little bit—but not much. Armstrong wasn't in peak form, but still played and sang very well on his multiple features, swatting away the challenge of Eldridge on a potent "Back O' Town Blues," though in his haste to push the younger man out of the way, he cracked a note or two.

But on songs where they shared solo duties, Eldridge did not hold back. After Armstrong's two melodic choruses on "I Got Rhythm," Eldridge followed with three, building higher and higher and finally unleashing torrents of notes in a way Armstrong never did, not even as a young man. Eldridge and Hawkins flawlessly tackled Pettiford's intricate, modern feature, "For Bass Faces Only," while Eldridge took center stage on "Flying Home" and "Jivin' the Vibes," the audience screaming in bedlam as Armstrong seemed to disappear. But at the conclusion of "Jivin' the Vibes," Armstrong suddenly emerged in the lead— on a concert-ending "Star Spangled Banner." Eldridge later talked about this with a smile, saying that Armstrong went into the national anthem without warning just as Eldridge "was getting up steam."[5] Numerous photos survive from the concert and in nearly every single one, Armstrong looks miserable, most likely a combination of pain caused from the kidney stones and the mental strain of sitting next to a younger disciple out for blood.

Press on the concert was plentiful, but most of the mainstream outlets focused on the novelty of jazz music—and jazz fans—taking over the hallowed Metropolitan Opera House. The Associated Press quoted "one conservative looking, middle-aged usher" who said, "If I said what I think of this, I'd be jailed."[6] But to those paying close attention, the real story of the evening was Armstrong and Eldridge. "A different Louis Armstrong didn't hit a high note all night while Roy Eldridge raised the roof with his horn," Dan Burley wrote in the black press. "Armstrong was cut to ribbons by Roy Eldridge, who blew some high and fancy horn," said Elliott Grennard in *Billboard*.[7] Barry Ulanov, champion of "modern" jazz, wrote, "Next year, if this concert is given again, let's hope we'll be spared the pathetic spectacle of a giant of the past, like Louis, hopelessly trying to play with his younger betters."[8]

Figure 20.1 A solemn Armstrong, playing in pain, wearily looks over at Roy Eldridge, Coleman Hawkins, and Barney Bigard during *Esquire*'s "All-American Jazz Concert" at the Metropolitan Opera House in January 1944.
Courtesy of the Louis Armstrong House Museum

But the most vitriol was dispensed by Leonard Feather. In March 1943, Feather was still bemoaning the lack of opportunities to see Armstrong with a small band, but after watching the ailing Armstrong next to the Herculean Eldridge, Feather couldn't hide his disgust. Leaving the *Esquire* concert, Feather was asked if he enjoyed it. "It was not too good," he reportedly replied, "but then how could it be, with Louis Armstrong playing?"[9] Feather was just getting warmed up for his official *Melody Maker* review of the concert, in which he claimed there were only "three wrong things" with the concert: Jack Teagarden, who "seemed ill at ease and out of place in this combination; "a stupid, undiscerning audience, which reacted to showmanship instead of musicianship"; and Armstrong's "pathetic" performance. "Louis is simply getting old and hasn't got the power, the imagination or the lip to keep up with the younger stars who have built on the foundations he set so many years ago and have since gone far ahead of him," Feather said, adding, "Louis was hopelessly outclassed by Roy Eldridge, whose playing inspired the whole band."[10]

Feather's review wasn't published until March. On February 9, Armstrong wrote to "pal Leonard," praised the staff at *Esquire* as "wonderful," and thanked him for the "Esky" award he was presented with at the concert. He certainly didn't seem like he was licking his wounds, saying the awards left him with "nothing but beautiful memories."[11] But then Feather published his review—and simultaneously stopped his regular correspondence with Armstrong, which seemed to ruffle him. "I still haven't heard from Ol Leonard Feather," Armstrong wrote to Goffin on July 19. "I'll never forgive him for that . . . [He] could have eased my mind a little—by no more than sending a short Wire, etc. . . . I've done ever'so much for him and didn't even charge him one nickle . . . He know I'll tell him so too. . . . Oh Well—that's not so important anyway . . . So lets forget about him."[12]

Perhaps the most balanced reaction came from *Esquire* itself, which devoted its April 1944 "Editorial" to "a tale of two trumpets." Summing up the various reviews stating that Eldridge embarrassed Armstrong or that Armstrong outclassed Eldridge (such opinions came from passionate defenders of New Orleans jazz such as Charles Edward Smith), *Esquire* warned about such "odious" comparisons that seemed "to be mistaken for the thing that makes the music go round in jazz circles," turning the Metropolitan concert into "a spectacle." Of Armstrong and Eldridge, *Esquire* stated:

> As for us, from where we sat, listening and watching Louis and Roy, we couldn't help thinking in terms of fiddlers. It was like seeing Kreisler and Heifetz side by side, and trying to take in at one and the same the great Kreisler heart and warm golden tone and the terrific Heifetz technique and smooth oiled-steel precision. Like trying to multiply peaches by pears, it just can't be done. The error, it seems to us, is in confounding different qualities and trying to reduce aesthetic abstractions to a basis for argument. People don't go to an art exhibition to see whether Gauguin "cut" Van Gogh, or study drama to try to determine whether Ben Jonson "made a bum out of" Shakespeare. To that extent, it seems to us, the attitude toward jazz, on the part of its amateurs and experts alike, is still a great deal less than grown up.[13]

Armstrong at least enjoyed his time in New York for the *Esquire* concert, spending it in his new Corona, Queens, home, telling Harry Faulkener that his future plans were to "settle down and enjoy life rearing about six babies."[14] But soon, it was time to go back on the road with his big band, still weakened because of the draft. Joe Glaser was in Hollywood, setting up a new Associated Booking Corporation office on the west coast, but he knew something needed to be changed.[15] Glaser reached out to Teddy McRae, a tenor saxophonist, composer, bandleader, and arranger who was currently helping Glaser with

Lionel Hampton's organization. McRae saw Armstrong's band live and thought to himself, "Jesus, the band do need changing." He said, "Louie was going like mad, and nobody was getting any hands."[16]

At the end of January, Glaser fired Joe Garland and replaced him with McRae. McRae recommended Glaser cancel the next couple of scheduled radio broadcasts to allow him time to get the band reorganized. McRae then hired Benny Carter's brass section and began working on the book of arrangements, scaling down Armstrong's role so he was utilized in smaller doses, but with more impact. "I think Joe disagreed with me for a while," McRae said. "But then he finally came up and he found out when we was on the air that it was better, you know. Louie was showing off better, the spots were better for him to play, and the band was backing him better, and everything like that."[17]

Many broadcasts survive from McRae's year and a half and though the band still sounds haphazard some of the time, one can hear the difference in arrangements. For one thing, many favorites from the Garland era, including "Shine," "You Rascal You," "Basin Street Blues," and others were retired or at least not broadcast in this 1944–1945 period. On "Confessin'" and "Lazy River," Armstrong now had a choice at the end, whether to end with a high trumpet note or, if his chops were feeling down, a vocal. On "Ain't Misbehavin'," an elongated climb up to the last high note was eliminated. There were new instrumentals, such as "Keep on Jumpin'," "Groovin'," and an updated version of "Swanee River," but now Armstrong shared the solo spotlight with his younger trumpeters, who weren't afraid to explore some more modern harmonies and phrasing in their solos.[18]

Armstrong still wasn't recording for Decca, but he was all over radio, breaking the record for most appearances on Coca-Cola's *Victory Parade of Spotlight Bands* series, appearing 19 times, according to McRae, causing someone to say to him, "Oh, you got more air time than God."[19] Velma Middleton also returned in 1944, often given pop hits of the day to perform solo. But it was McRae's idea to team Armstrong and Middleton up for a vocal duet on "Don't Fence Me In," the first time Armstrong had performed with any of his female singers. The result went over so well, they immediately added Louis Jordan's "Is You Is or Is You Ain't My Baby" to their repertoire and one of jazz's funniest partnerships was officially off and running.

As "straw boss" of the band, McRae helped Armstrong pick different sets and stick to them night after night, something that bothered Pierre "Frenchy" Tallerie, Armstrong's former bus driver and current road manager who took over when Bob Smiley was felled by tuberculosis (Tallerie also took over as company spy). Tallerie asked McRae, "Why do y'all open with the same set every night?" "We're in a different town," McRae said. "That's our show. Don't you see the circus open up—what does a circus do when it comes to town? This is our show!" McRae noted that the band had three different sets they could call at a given time, saying, "Even that gets the band in the mood. If they're feeling low, they know these numbers. . . . We got a number two set, number three set—well, one of those sets is gonna get you."[20]

But the music business was changing rapidly, and it was becoming much harder to keep a big band working night after night. Songs of love and loss were more popular than ever with World War II raging on, so the Swing Era gave way to the era of the vocalist, led by Frank Sinatra. Small bands like those of Louis Jordan and the Nat King Cole trio were also succeeding without orchestral backing, leading Glaser to begin booking similar combos led by John Kirby, Stuff Smith, Eddie South, Red Norvo, and the team of Red Allen and J. C. Higginbotham.[21] Yet Glaser kept Armstrong in his big band format because of a saving grace. "The only thing that kept us going during the war years was Joe Glaser had worked out a deal for us to play these Army and Navy hospitals and benefits and things," McRae said, adding, "Why we had to do that was because the Army and Navy flew us around. We couldn't get transportation."

In between the endless military bases, Glaser continued booking Armstrong at theaters such as the Apollo, the Royal, and the Panther Room of Chicago's Hotel Sherman; on radio shows such as *Command Performance* with Jimmy Durante; and in movies such as *Atlantic City*, which began filming in April in California. While there, someone from Armstrong's organization—possibly Glaser—went to a jam session in Los Angeles and was immediately impressed by a young tenor saxophonist. Armstrong showed up the next night and told the tenor player, "Son, say son, I really liked that sound you get." "Thank you, thank you very much," replied the saxophonist, 21-year-old Dexter Gordon. Armstrong didn't usually get involved in such affairs, but he made it known that he wanted Gordon for his band and the next night, Glaser signed him up. As with Kenny Clarke and Charles Mingus, Armstrong heard the more modern aspects of Gordon's playing and instead of dismissing him, insisted that he become a part of his big band.

"Oh, that was a thrill," Gordon wrote of his time with Armstrong. "Every night. He had such a big, beautiful, fat, blaring sound, just ran right through you. And that was really the reason I joined the band, to play with him. To play with him every night. The band was a mediocre type band. He was playing the swing type arrangements from the '30's . . . especially 'Ain't Misbehavin'' and 'I'm Confessin.' The arrangements were just a showcase for him. But, he liked me and he always gave me a chance to blow. He featured me a lot."[22] Indeed, multiple broadcasts survive of the band with Gordon, often performing "Ain't Misbehavin'," with Armstrong gleefully turning proceedings over to "Brother Dexter!" On three separate versions of the song, Gordon takes three completely different solos, each one showcasing his heavy Lester Young influence, but he's quickly followed by Armstrong playing the solo set he perfected back in 1929. The two different approaches to jazz—improvising every night or sticking with something tried and true—were on display on each broadcast, but they co-existed peacefully. Gordon played like Gordon and Armstrong played like Armstrong and they kept their individual voices without feeling the pressure to play more "modern" or more "old-fashioned."

Gordon was with the band for two film appearances as Armstrong performed "Ain't Misbehavin'" in Republic's *Atlantic City* and "Whatcha Say" in Warner Brothers' *Pillow to Post*, both with Dorothy Dandridge. But his one studio record date with the group was a failure. Armstrong was finally invited back to record for Decca on August 9, his first session for the label in over two years. But this time, instead of Jack Kapp, there was a new producer waiting for him: Milt Gabler. In 1938, Gabler started Commodore Records to record the small group brand of jazz he loved best, but when he joined Decca in the early 1940s, he immediately displayed a Kapp-like affinity of knowing what the public wanted to hear. He oversaw Louis Jordan's continued meteoric rise and was about to record Billie Holiday with strings, resulting in the hit "Lover Man."

Gabler had high hopes for the session and was pleased just to be in the same room as Armstrong, calling him "the most lovable man you ever met in your life." But when the band—exhausted from coming straight from a string of playing army camps—started to play, Gabler grew dismayed. "And the band was so tired, guys were falling asleep in their chair," Gabler said. "So how are you going to get a thing like that to swing? How are you even going to like the tunes? I could have cried, I was so broken hearted. And here's a guy, traveling with a tired band, doing his bit, playing for servicemen and probably a USO tour and we only got three sides in, we didn't get four. And they weren't good."[23] None of the three sides would be released until the LP era.

Gabler also ran a series of popular Sunday jam sessions at Jimmy Ryan's but noted that Armstrong never showed up to those either because he was rarely in New York or when he was, he spent so much energy in his own performances, he didn't have anything left in him to blow anywhere else. But the jam session scenes at Minton's in Harlem and 52nd Street in midtown Manhattan were where the latest sounds in jazz were being worked out. Younger musicians such as Dexter Gordon wanted to be a part of this movement, and when offered an opportunity to join Billy Eckstine's groundbreaking big band (featuring Dizzy Gillespie, Gene Ammons, Art Blakey, and more), he quit Armstrong. "Pops asked me if I wanted more money," Gordon wrote. "I told him that wasn't the problem. It was that we young guys wanted to play some new music. He wished me the best and said I always had a place in his band if I wanted to come back." Though he only spent six months with Armstrong, it was enough for Gordon to continue admiring Armstrong—and defending him against criticisms—for the rest of his life; in fact, if Gordon won the Academy Award he was nominated for the film *Round Midnight*, his plan was to dedicate it to his former boss. "He was a born ambassador, and he really was a beautiful, warm human being, just the way you hear him and see him on stage and on film," Gordon wrote at the end of his life. "That was Louis. He was always the same, always a beautiful man."[24]

Throughout the year, Glaser was still featuring Armstrong in Associated Booking advertisements, billing him as "KING OF THEM ALL."[25] But he was no longer Glaser's top money-maker. "Joe Glaser, a veteran Broadway smarty who is not bound by the territory around Times Square, has just bought a Hollywood home, complete with swimming pool and all the traditional movieland adornments such as private movie theater, for $87,000," the *Salt Lake Tribune* reported on July 16, 1944. "It is the profit from only 1 account— Bandleader Les Brown!"[26] Brown single-handedly earned $350,000 in the previous 12 months, allowing Glaser to purchase his Hollywood mansion, as well as a new office for Associated Booking, leaving 30 Rockefeller Plaza after nine years to head to 745 Fifth Avenue. In March of the following year, Glaser returned the favor. "Joe Glaser, the band tycoon, gifted Les Brown, his protege, with an eight-room house in Beverly Hills," Dorothy Kilgallen wrote. "It was a combination wedding anniversary and birthday gift."[27]

Meanwhile, the Armstrongs were paying their mortgage in Corona and Louis was on the road and away from home for nearly the entire year just to stay ahead. Early on in their marriage Lucille wasn't afraid to say she had a problem with the setup, once telling Louis, "You gotta let the white man do everything!?" Armstrong was offended and responded, "No, it ain't that! It ain't one of them old fogey, phony things like that. Here's a man I know is in my corner and he's just like a father to me and we come up together. We've both had our ups and downs. See? He's been broke three times. He's been a millionaire three times. So you know he knows life and he knows his friends, you understand? So it ain't like that, see?" Lucille eventually came around to Louis's way of thinking and though she personally never got especially close to Glaser, she did learn to trust him and even defended him after both Louis and Glaser were dead. "[E]verybody will tell you Joe Glaser was stealing from Louie, but outsiders always speculate," she said in her widowhood. "You know, this has been said, I know you've read it, that Joe Glaser was stealing from Louie and all that sort of thing—well, if he stole, he still left a couple of million! How could he steal? The man was making money himself! It just doesn't make sense for anyone to even say that. That was a very, very close relationship. Fortunately, Joe, after getting to know me, had a great respect for me. We became great friends, you see. But Louie didn't have—I think that was the tightest friend he had, really."[28]

Glaser finally got Armstrong an extended engagement in New York in December at the Cafe Zanzibar with fellow headliners Bill "Bojangles" Robinson, Maurice Rocco, the Nicholas Brothers, the Delta Rhythm Boys, and the Peters Sisters.[29] This was a true variety revue of professional entertainers, not jazz musicians, performing specialties they had worked out over the years and Armstrong felt right at home with his old standby "Ain't Misbehavin.'"

There were plenty of options when it came to African American entertainment in New York in December 1944. Also on Broadway, Count Basie was at the Hotel Lincoln while Lionel Hampton was playing the Strand. Uptown, Billy Eckstine was featuring Dizzy Gillespie and other like-minded "modern jazz" musicians at the Apollo. Fifty-second Street was still buzzing as New York's "Swing Street," with various small configurations performing nightly, while in Greenwich Village, Nick's became the destination of choice for those who liked the "Nicksieland" music served up by Eddie Condon's groups. Bebop was still being worked out up at Minton's, a scene Armstrong never discussed, quite possibly because he might not have been welcome there. His former bassist John Simmons told Patricia Willard about how the bop musicians began playing different sets of chord changes to standbys like "Dinah" and "Sweet Sue" to dissuade inferior musicians from sitting in. Simmons recalled that Red Allen turned up with his trumpet and called "What Is This Thing Called Love." The band started playing, "But they had some different changes," Simmons said. "And Red Allen couldn't press a valve whereas he wasn't playing the right note. So he quickly put his horn back in the case and got off the bandstand. Now, this should have been done years before this, you know." Even though Allen was African American, it didn't matter. Allen frequently played with Coleman Hawkins in the early 1930s, but Hawkins had adapted to the new music, so he was accepted; Allen didn't and was shunned. Willard asked Simmons, "But are you saying that the bop—so-called bop revolution was strictly conceived to eliminate people from jam sessions?" "Yeah," Simmons replied. "That was the only reason . . . the sole reason for the new music?" Willard asked. "Yes," Simmons insisted.[30]

That was not the spirit in which Armstrong approached music. On December 7, 1944, he illustrated how inspired he could still be in a small group setting when surrounded by the right combination of musicians and friends, an integrated group who all spoke the same cooperative—not competitive—musical language. The occasion was a midnight V-Disc jam session, made strictly for US military personnel and featuring cornetist Bobby Hackett, drummer Cozy Cole, guitarist Herb Ellis, pianist Johnny Guarnieri, and trombonists Jack Teagarden and Lou McGarity. The last two were in the middle of singing the blues when Armstrong walked into the studio, stopping the proceedings cold. Armstrong was given a hero's welcome before all present stopped to watch him simply unpack his horn and warm up. Finally, they struck up their blues again, now named "Jack Armstrong Blues" after the radio serial, *Jack Armstrong, the All American Boy*. Two takes survive, each highlighted by chorus after chorus of ferocious trumpet playing, most of it spent in the highest parts of his upper register, a destination Armstrong was unable to reach at the Met earlier in the year.

Metronome writer George T. Simon was present and was in awe. Simon had heard Armstrong's big band at the Zanzibar and wrote that "the band behind him [is] positively abominable. Nothing could possibly do more harm to such a great artist. It's absolutely murderous."[31] Now, of the V-Disc session, he said that it was "the first time in my life that I'd ever heard the Real Armstrong in person. I've never heard anything like that in all of my days. The way he blew! The feeling, the tone, the phrasing, the heart! It was something that just doesn't come out of anybody's else's horn." Armstrong had to get back to the Zanzibar, but he left the other musicians in a state of shock. Trumpeter Billy Butterfield was asked to record a feature but refused. "How can I?" he asked. "How do you expect me to play after that?" Bobby Hackett, meanwhile, was walking around muttering, "They're all fakes, all of 'em. He's the only *real* thing."[32] Everyone else agreed.

Simon noted that trumpeters like Cootie Williams, Harry James, and Muggsy Spanier still followed Armstrong's every move, but he noticed an "Armstrong Apathy" forming in "younger listeners [who] don't know and don't feel what Louis is doing."[33] Simon put the blame for this on close-minded critics. "If only these critics would take time off from themselves and their own preconceived opinions long enough, before making judgement, to perceive what the musician is doing and to judge him upon standards covering his efforts, I think we'd have much faster progress in jazz and/or swing and, I might add, probably lots less broken hearts, spirits and even heads," he concluded.[34]

As a V-Disc, "Jack Armstrong Blues" was aimed at servicemen in World War II not the world of jazz critics, though it still had its desired effect on those who heard it, especially African American sailor William Green. Green was already a fan of the recording when he came down with a 104.6 degree fever while stationed in the Pacific. Nothing made him feel better—until he heard "Jack Armstrong Blues" being played on a Navy LCT boat. He continued:

> It seemed to give me a big shot in the arm, a big boost up. It made me feel like I was alive again. I said, "I could do it" because it was my kin that was blowing and I had to honor that beautiful tone. And all the fellows on the ship said, "Hey Green! Hey Green! I know you feel better now—there's your boy playing. Don't that sound pretty? Look at that big tone he got, man! Sounds good, doesn't it?" I said, "Yes." I felt better. I felt like I could lick the world then. And all the fellows on the ship, their morale boosted 100%, too, because we felt although we was many miles from home, we was still surrounded by friends as well as foe and it gave us courage to go on. I want all you jazz cats to know what these tunes *really* mean. They're not just something that is played for a moment of zest. It's something you have to feel and *live*.[35]

Green eventually became friends with Armstrong and in the 1950s, Armstrong had Green record his story on one of his private reel-to-reel tapes. It meant so much to him to hear the effect his music had on not only a sailor but also a real jazz fan and an African American, too, coming at a time when his confidence still might have been shaken by the reviews of the *Esquire* concert. He closed 1944 in a much better place as the Zanzibar revue was a big success on Broadway; the V-Disc session illustrated that he still had a lot of fire left in him; he appeared along with Robinson and most of the Zanzibar cast at a Police Athletic League benefit at Madison Square Garden, performing in front of 20,000 people; he was broadcasting nightly on the radio; and Decca wanted him back in the studio in January. Things were looking up but with another *Esquire* concert around the corner, they would not stay that way for long.

21

"Why Should I Go Back?"

January 1945–December 1945

Joe Glaser began 1945 by placing a full-page advertisement in *Variety* to tout his various clients. The ad that ran on January 3 was the same one he had used at the start of 1944, except for one difference: in 1944, the top spot was filled by Louis Armstrong; in 1945, it was now occupied by Lionel Hampton.[1] *Billboard* reported that Armstrong grossed over $250,000 for Glaser the previous year, but Hampton grossed $350,000. Both numbers were impressive, but Duke Ellington grossed $600,000 in 1944, while Cab Calloway topped all with close to $750,000. *Billboard* noted that 1944 was "the best in history" for African American entertainers; clearly, the big bands were not dead just yet.[2]

Neither was Armstrong's recording career as he returned to Decca on January 14. Milt Gabler learned his lesson from the rejected session of the previous August, and, taking a page from Jack Kapp's playbook, left Armstrong's regular band behind and instead put together a large ensemble of top white studio musicians, arranged by bassist Bob Haggart. He also put a bigger premium on selecting better material to record, making an inspired choice of Pvt. Cecil Gant's tender blues ballad hit, "I Wonder." Armstrong rose to the occasion, singing with real pathos before uncorking a trumpet solo with some surprising harmonic choices. It was a completely contemporary-sounding recording with a good chance of becoming a hit. Armstrong left the studio and headed to the Zanzibar for another evening as part of one of the most popular revues on Broadway. The year 1945 was off to a great start.

This feeling would be short-lived, thanks to the amplified voices of the supporters for the various factions of jazz springing up. The end of the recording ban in 1944 led to a flood of new recordings of all styles. Bunk Johnson spent the summer of that year recording for William Russell's American Music label. "The music of Bunk's 1944 band, both their fast stomps and the slow blues they play after midnight, is the most thrilling I have experienced during the 37 years of my interest in music," Russell wrote in September 1944.[3] The records became something of a Bible for fanatics of New Orleans jazz as Johnson became their king and an example of folk art untainted by commercial aspirations. "Bunk now considers himself as the savior of jazz," Leslie Smith wrote in traditional jazz bible the *Record Changer*. "He may well be."[4]

But the more modern sounds of jazz being spearheaded by Dizzy Gillespie and Charlie Parker were also starting to appear on the market, complete with a new name, as christened in a recording Gillespie made on January 9, 1945: "Bebop." That same day, Gillespie also recorded "Salt Peanuts," based partially on a line Armstrong played on "I'm a Ding Dong Daddy," and further threw down the gauntlet by recording "I Can't Get Started," a song most associated with Armstrong's favorite trumpeter, Bunny Berigan, who passed away in 1941. Armstrong respected Berigan so much, he never dared to record his theme song, but that didn't stop Gillespie from making a statement on it in his own fashion.

Leonard Feather prided himself on being up on the latest progressive trends in jazz and spent much of 1944 beating up those who played in older styles,

Figure 21.1 Armstrong looks admiringly at Bunk Johnson, hero of the New Orleans jazz revival, during an appearance on KSAN's *Jive at Eleven Five* radio show in San Francisco, c. 1943.
Courtesy of the Louis Armstrong House Museum

such as Johnson ("hopelessly incapable of producing anything that could be called real music, or real jazz or real anything except real crap"), Armstrong ("All I hope is that next year we won't hear Louis's pathetic efforts to get the release of 'Stomping at the Savoy'"), and pianist Art Hodes ("an amateur band entertaining in an air-raid shelter"). Feather's criticism of Hodes was so over the top, Hodes sued for $100,000 and settled out of court. But Feather also wasn't a fan of Gillespie at first, mostly because he had issues with Billy Eckstine and Eckstine's manager Billy Shaw and did everything he could to knock Eckstine's big band.[5] Bassist Oscar Pettiford was the one who asked him one night at the Onyx club in 1944, "Hey, why don't you write something about Dizzy sometimes, man?"[6] Feather started paying attention and on December 31, 1944, produced a session with Gillespie and Sarah Vaughan—with Feather himself on piano and Vaughan singing two of Feather's compositions. Feather claimed his participation was because of a low budget but it was known among musicians that if an artist used Feather on piano or recorded one of his compositions, he or she would receive good reviews.[7] Having been ac-cepted a bit into the inner circle of the new music, Feather began devoting his considerable power in the media to spreading the word about bebop. "We favor progressive music and advanced ideas," he wrote in *Metronome* (he also continued to write statements such as "Baby Dodds's drumming is absolutely anathema to us," "Bechet is a dwarf," and "Django Reinhardt is not a real jazz musician").[8]

The different factions were preparing for what were to become known as "The Jazz Wars." Armstrong, with his popular Broadway revue and hip new Decca recording, wasn't taking sides, but the jazz critics did that for him when the second annual *Esquire* Jazz Concert took place on January 17, 1945. Using a larger pool of voters, Armstrong won first place in the male vocal category, ensuring his participation in the concert, but his ego was dealt a blow when he went from winning the trumpet category the previous year to not even placing in 1945. But the sniping of the critics led to another format change: figuring it was unfair to pit older musicians championed by Russell against the more modern musicians supported by Feather, *Esquire* decided to split the concert across three locations. In New York City, Benny Goodman's Sextet would per-form, along with Mildred Bailey. In Los Angeles, Duke Ellington, winner of the "Outstanding Band" Gold award, performed many numbers and shared the stage with features for Art Tatum, Billie Holiday, Al Casey, and Sid Catlett. Neither venue featured any bebop, just pure contemporary swing.

That left New Orleans, the birthplace of jazz and the home for *Esquire's* de-cidedly "old-fashioned" segment with Sidney Bechet, James P. Johnson, Bunk Johnson, J. C. Higginbotham, Paul Barbarin—and Armstrong. What could go wrong? The answer was everything. Armstrong most likely did not appreciate being relegated to the old-timer's portion of the concert and needing to take his frustration out somewhere, took it out on Bechet. At rehearsal, when Bechet got characteristically boisterous in the ensembles, Armstrong stopped playing and yelled at him, "I ain't gonna have no two leads in my band!"[9] Things got worse at the actual concert, which was broadcast coast-to-coast on radio. Armstrong did everything in his power to not let Bechet solo, which, coupled with the loud, erratic playing of Higginbotham, led to some overcrowded, unpleasant ensembles; during the entire New Orleans segment, Bechet didn't get a single solo. He never performed with Armstrong again and wrote bitterly about him in his posthumously published autobiography.

Variety wasn't impressed with the three-concert layout and though they praised "the incomparable Armstrong," they also referred to the music of the New Orleans set as "some primitive jive."[10] Over at the *Record Changer*, matters seemingly weren't primitive enough for Nesuhi Ertegun, who complained of the "utter mediocrity" presented at the concert. "Bunk's playing was heard over the air for less than half a minute," Ertegun wrote. "It was enough to convince musically sensitive listeners that he was a great artist and that he played the best jazz on the entire broadcast."[11]

Armstrong was doubtlessly pleased to get back to New York, where the Zanzibar revue proved so popular, it began doubling as a vaudeville bill at the Roxy Theatre in late January. The entertainers presented a shorter version of the revue at a cheaper ticket price (and with fewer "Zanzibeauties"), but the workload for those weeks was almost unbearable. "That was enough for anybody," Teddy McRae said. "That was some hard work. Imagine playing three long shows in the Zanzibar. In the meanwhile you're doing from 12 o'clock to 12 o'clock at the Roxy—you're doing five shows over there. And packed everyday with Bill Robinson, Louie Armstrong, Delta Rhythm Boys, the Peter Sisters, Nicholas Kids. Some show."[12]

Billboard praised the show at the Roxy and noted of Robinson, "For the Roxy date, he has dropped many of his Uncle Tom, racist jokes and act benefits accordingly."[13] Black comedy was becoming more common in Broadway theaters and nightclubs and that was making some in the African American community nervous. Harold Timberlake wrote about this in a March 3 column in the *New York Age* called "Keep It Uptown." Of the Roxy show, Timberlake described it as "tops—almost." "Bill Robinson came out, did some 'mugging' and told some of his ancient jokes," he wrote, adding, "All William had to do was dance, not make faces or be funny."[14]

Timberlake also took aim at the Apollo Theater, reprimanding black comedians who still used blackface and calling out Butterbeans and Susie for their "I'm Frank Sinatra in technicolor" joke. "Until we Negroes learn to re-spect ourselves, we can't demand or command respect from anyone else," he said. Timberlake might have been dismayed to know that Armstrong found the humor of Bill Robinson and Butterbeans and Susie legitimately hilarious. Less than a week before Timberlake published his column, Armstrong wrote a letter to his old friend Joe Lindsey and couldn't resist slipping in a joke. "Dig this—this is a cute one about the Church," he started.

> A colored boy had a sweetheart . . .The boy was a Church Goer and the girl was not . . . However, one evening he prevailed upon her to attend Church Services with him . . . They entered, sat down, when she observed an Eurdite appearing person moving about and speaking to Members of the Congregation . . . "Mose," asked the girl, "Who Am Dat Distingushied Pusson 'Urinating up and down the Aisle?" . . . "Shh! not so loud—'dat am the 'Rectum of 'Dis Yare' Constipation!" responded the lad.[15]

One can judge Armstrong for finding such a dripping-with-minstrelsy joke funny, but the fact that he wrote it in a private letter to a black child-hood friend—in addition to compiling multiple volumes of jokes in his spare time—is proof that he did find the humor in it, and wasn't just doing it for white audiences. And the laughter of the black audiences at the Apollo told him he was not alone.

Armstrong returned to the Apollo at the end of April, with Joe Garland back as his musical director as McRae stayed behind to oversee the musical offerings at the Zanzibar. Armstrong shared the bill with the controversial Stepin Fetchit, who remained a popular stage attraction though his film career had stalled. *Variety* reported the standing-room-only section was five deep and the combination of Armstrong and Fetchit provided "some of the heft-iest applause fodder heard at this house in some time." Fetchit "did his usual lazy act for powerful appreciation," while Armstrong was praised for his "solo and vocal work, as well as showmanship."[16] Showmanship was still the name of the game for Apollo attendees and for reviewers in trades such as *Variety*. A few months earlier, Billy Eckstine's famed big band played the Apollo with Dizzy Gillespie, Charlie Parker, Dexter Gordon, Art Blakey, and more. *Variety* admitted Parker's and Gillespie's solo work was "good" but otherwise, was not impressed. "As a stage attraction, band is weak in its present shape, there being no showmanship in evidence, and a complete lack of sight novelties," *Variety* wrote of Eckstine's band. "Coupled with the overworked blare emphasis, it places severe limitations on the band's theatre values."[17]

At the Apollo, Armstrong featured his big new hit, "I Wonder." Released in February, Walter Winchell immediately recommended it, reviews were good, and sales were strong, with the *Pittsburgh Courier* reporting that "I Wonder" "had no longer hit the music stalls before the first pressing of 75,000 of the tune were gobbled up."[18] Charles Menees summed it up by writing, "Louis Armstrong proves he is far from through on his first record (Decca) since 1942."[19] One of the men most responsible for the thinking that Armstrong *was* through was Leonard Feather, who also attended Armstrong's April stand at the Apollo and reviewed it for *Metronome*. Feather had a few criticisms that were probably warranted, namely that the arrangements were so loud it "often made it impossible to hear what [Armstrong] was doing." But he praised Armstrong's "superb" singing and concluded, "As a stage showman, Louis is as personable as ever. The audience liked Louis and Louis liked the audience; and they made each other know it."[20]

After savaging Armstrong's performance at the 1944 Met concert and ceasing to correspond with him for several months afterward, Feather now did an astounding about-face, resulting in him and Barry Ulanov dedicating the entire April 1945 issue of *Metronome* to Armstrong's achievements. In an opening editorial, they stated, "The purpose of this issue of METRONOME, devoted to his life and work, is to call attention to two things: (1) the size and shape and substance of Louis Armstrong's accomplishment; (2) to point with pride to the present-day beauty and taste and style of his playing, to the fact that Louis is a genuine contemporary in his musical thinking."[21] Both men now defended Armstrong's 1944 Metropolitan Opera House showing, blaming his performance on his "poor physical condition," with Ulanov noting, "But even at that concert, as records will attest, there were great Armstrong moments. There will always be, as long as that inspired Satchel- or Dipper- or Gatemouth wraps itself around a horn."[22] What could have caused this change of heart?

The answer seemed to lie elsewhere in the issue. Ulanov mentioned that he and Feather visited Armstrong at his Corona, Queens, home during a three-week break in March. They asked him questions about music and to their surprise, many of Armstrong's answers fell right in line with their way of thinking. "What about the other musicians of that time, Louis?" Ulanov asked about the past. "How would they stand up today? "Most of 'em couldn't stand the gaff— the pace is too fast for them today," Armstrong answered. "They wouldn't hold your interest the way they did. You can't go back thirty years, man. It's all right for a novelty. But missing notes and not caring nothin', not a damn, about 'em, you can't play music like that nowadays. Take me back thirty years—I could play that stuff with one finger! Why, I'd live forever!"[23] Ulanov couldn't contain his glee, writing, "That's Louis Armstrong's answer to the fanatics of the old school who want to take jazz back twenty, thirty, forty years." Armstrong continued with his thoughts about the importance of moving forward:

Why should I go back? I want to stay up with the times. That's why I surround myself with youngsters. Every once in a while I lay an old-fashioned phrase on 'em, but
music's better now than it used to be, it's played better now. Whether it's arranged
or improvised, the music of today is way ahead of what it used to be. We've advanced a lot since the early day. Music should be played all kinds of ways, anyway.
Symphonic stuff, beautiful things, everything goes. If there are people who want to
omit arrangements, omit scored backgrounds, omit any kind of music, you tell 'em
I said, "Omit those people!"[24]

That was all Feather and Ulanov needed to hear. They repeated that passage in their editorial, writing, "His acceptance of his own time and his rejec-
tion of a retrogressive jazz aesthetic are not so well known."[25] Never mind that
Armstrong also, for the first time, hinted at his feelings toward modern jazz,
saying, "Some of that fantastic stuff, when they tear out from the first note and
you ask yourself 'What the hell's he playing?'—that's not for me. Personally,
I wouldn't play that kinda horn if I played 100 years; you don't have to worry
about my stealing those riffs."[26] Feather and Ulanov ignored such words
and continued leaning on his other comments for months to come, even in
other publications. Feather mentioned the visit to Corona a few months later
in *Modern Screen*, writing, "Louis also spoke very forcefully about the need
for progress—he just can't understand some of the jazz fans who worship
the musicians he played with in the 1920's in preference to the great young
musicians of today."[27]

A new term for such fans was coined in *Esquire* in March 1945 when
the magazine published a letter from a reader in France insisting that New
Orleans "was—and is—the birthplace of the true 'stuff'" and "The only true
Jazz I ever heard off the record was that of Lu Watters in San Francisco, and
Brad Gowans & Co. in New York." Closing with a list of records the reader considered "the finest"—works of Oliver, Morton, Armstrong, Johnson, Watters,
and Spanier—the reader signed off, "Sincerely, France, MOLDY FIG."[28]

The reader never revealed his or her true identity, but the phrase "Moldy
Fig" was too perfect to ignore. Feather and Ulanov didn't pick up on it immediately but other *Esquire* readers did. First was Paul Wachtel in the May issue,
who addressed the figure as "Mr. Fig," writing, "Mr. Fig seems to belong to that
group of people who live in a pre-historic era of jazz glory, for whom nothing
is good unless it's old."[29] But it was another reader, a sailor in the Navy named
Sam Platt, who really transformed the phrase into what it came to be, writing
in the June issue that he wished "to protest against the 'Moldy Fig' genre of
music lovers." Platt observed, "There seems to be some perverse streak in
critics such as [George] Avakian or 'Moldy Fig' which prevents them from

liking anything but the very oldest available."[30] Platt's letter sealed the deal; even Feather himself only referred to Platt as coining the term "Moldy Fig" to refer to anyone who only listens to early jazz.[31]

But the moldy figs, as they were now known, had a field day in March when, just three days after Armstrong closed at the Zanzibar, Bunk Johnson made his New York debut at a Sunday afternoon jam session at Jimmy Ryan's on 52nd Street. His first words to the crowd were, "Don't expect me to sound like my boy Louis. When Louis does up, I does down." "Bunk didn't let anybody down," Jean Gleason wrote in the *Record Changer*. "In his own way he is as great a showman as his boy Louis Armstrong, and despite the fact that his lip was weak from lack of recent practice, and his hands shockingly calloused from working in the rice fields, Bunk showed New York how a trumpet is really supposed to be played!" Gleason breathlessly wrote of Johnson's rendition of "Confessin'," "Louis could have learned a lot more from his teacher than he did!"[32] Armstrong was getting a little tired of reading about how Johnson was his teacher. "And where'N' the devil did they get that stuff—that Someone else showd'me the real rudiments on a trumpet-I really don't know," Armstrong wrote to Robert Nutt on May 9. "King Oliver was always kind and willing to help the under dog and the younger fellow . . . God Bless him." Armstrong proved that he also still had a good deal of moldy fig in him, praising one of Leonard Feather's enemies, Muggsy Spanier. In February, Spanier, angry over one of Feather's negative reviews, knocked Feather out with one punch outside of a Chicago nightclub and soon after, recorded "Feather Brain Blues" in his dishonor. "He still sounds as good as ever," Armstrong said of Spanier. "Muggsy and I—both are King Oliver's Deciples [*sic*]."[33]

By the time Armstrong wrote to Nutt—an amateur trumpet player who interviewed Armstrong for his high school newspaper and ended up corresponding with him—he was back on the road, traveling by train and still dealing with humiliating situations in the south. "And coming from Lexington into Cincinnati to change trains to come here (in Chicago) we ran into one those 'James Crow Cars—(Jim Crow to you) tee hee . . . But we are so used to that mess until it really isn't funny," he wrote. "But what amuses me about the whole affair is—There wasn't but one car for us 'Spades (the colored folk) and when the train hit Lexington where we gotten on-that colored car was already crowded-and me and my whole 'Tribe had to stand up all the way to Cincinnati . . . Tee Hee—we get a great big boot out of those situations."[34] A textbook example of laughing to keep from crying.

Earlier in the year, Armstrong's sister Beatrice, better known as "Mama Lucy," traveled to New York to spend some time with him and Lucille. She didn't leave the south often and was "worried to death." Armstrong, too, was nervous about her traveling by train, writing to Joe Lindsey to ask him to tip a porter extra to make sure Mama Lucy got her meals delivered to her room. "Then by that," he explained, "I know she want [sic] have to come in touch with that awful 'James Crow . . . (Jim Crow) to be exact."[35] He also referred to the south in a letter he wrote to his ex-wife Lil on June 1, mentioning he was "traveling down in Germany (down south)." "V-E Day" had just taken place a few weeks earlier, but that didn't stop Armstrong from equating the south with Nazi Germany.[36]

In the same letter to Lil, Louis mentioned that Lucille had been touring with him, writing, "This road beats her down to her socks 'Sho-Nuff."[37] One day later, the *Chicago Defender* ran a profile of Lucille, making note of how much time she spent traveling with Louis. "So you see, he's my career these days," she said.[38] A few months later, Lucille's "career" almost came to an end. "All is not well, in fact all is far, far from being well in the Louis Armstrong ménage here," Lawrence F. Lamar wrote in September. "A rift that can be well authenticated here as true, has broken out with great suddenness and threatens to see the matrimonial ship piloted by the famed King of the Trumpet and his ex-chorine glamour girl wife, Lucille Wilson, crash on the shores of marital difficulties." Lamar reported that while Louis was playing the Trianon in Los Angeles, he and Lucille split up as she "found it hard to remain home of late at night alone." After his evening performances at the Trianon, Louis continued going out until dawn "with some of his own alleged male friends." Lucille didn't buy it and they separated. "In the meantime, Armstrong declares he is through with trips to the altar for happiness," Lamar wrote. "He asserts he will, henceforth, might love all, but marry nary."[39]

It's no stretch of the imagination to assume that Lucille caught Louis cheating on her. Louis loved her but would never turn down the opportunity to get intimate with a member of the opposite sex. Louis himself relished the advice he received from Black Benny while still a teenager in New Orleans: "Dipper, you're going out in this wide wide world. Always remember, no matter how many times you get married—always have another woman for a sweetheart on the outside. Because, mad day might come, or she could be the type of woman who's ego, after realizing that you care deeply may—for no reason at all, try giving you a hard time. And with no other chick whom you're just as [fond] of on the outside—two chances to one you might do something 'rash' which is a mild word." Armstrong took the advice to heart, writing to Joe Glaser in 1955, "That's why I have several chicks that I enjoy whaling with the same as I do with Lucille. And she's always had the [choicest] ass of them all."[40] That was in 1955; ten years earlier, Lucille made the decision that she'd rather be "Mrs. Louis Armstrong" than go through a divorce, even if that meant she had to deal with his cheating on the road. "Let's say the eye sees what it wants to see," she told a reporter in 1964. "There are all sorts of women in the entertainment field. They throw their arms around Louis. I have partial vision on purpose. I don't see these things. I know Louis loves me. I am his fourth wife, but we've had a wonderful marriage." She also alluded to a lesson she must have learned the hard way in 1945. "I don't believe in surprises in our marriage," she said. "I call Louis when I am going to join him while he is on tour."[41] By October 24, Walter Winchell was reporting, "The Louis Armstrongs have patched up their silly estrangement."[42]

By the time the Armstrongs made up, the sounds of bebop had begun spreading outside of the scenes at Minton's and on 52nd Street—with disappointing results. The Nicholas Brothers hired Dizzy Gillespie's big band—featuring Charlie Parker, Miles Davis, Fats Navarro, Max Roach, and more—to join them as part of a revue, "Hepsations of 1945," for a tour that would feature nothing but dances in front of what Gillespie later termed "the unreconstructed blues lovers down South."[43] Gillespie wouldn't bend an inch toward what the audiences wanted and continued serving up nothing but the most complex arrangements played at demanding, fast tempos. Fayard Nicholas approached Gillespie and told him to "Kinda compromise. . . . Play a little 'Stormy Weather,' or something that they're familiar with. And then maybe give them a little bit of jazz that they know. Then come on out with your bebop, your modern jazz, maybe they'll appreciate it better, a little bit more. But you don't give it all to them, something that they don't know. They'll walk out on you ever time."[44] Gillespie didn't bend, and the southern tour remained a struggle to the end.

Though the south was not ready for bebop, the sounds of the music had crept onto the pop charts in a roundabout way. In January 1945, Louis Jordan continued his string of hits for Milt Gabler and Decca with his boogie-woogie blues, "Caldonia," reaching number one on the "Race Records" chart and number six on the pop charts. Sensing a hit, Woody Herman recorded a turbocharged version of it in February. Neal Hefti scored a special chorus featuring the band's five trumpets ripping through some Gillespie-influenced bop lines. Used as a seasoning in the middle of the otherwise roaring performance, the public approved and Herman's version rose to number two on the charts.

"Caldonia" also allowed Armstrong to dip his toe in bop waters. As had been his practice for over 15 years, Armstrong tackled the popular music of the day and began featuring the Herman band's arrangement of "Caldonia" in live performances and on radio. However, Armstrong only sang the vocal on it, leaving his young trumpet section to handle the Gillespie passages by themselves. It was proof that while Armstrong was showing no interest in playing bop, he was not averse to featuring modern sounds with his big band.[45]

But Armstrong never got the opportunity to record "Caldonia" in a studio; instead, the only new Armstrong records that hit the market in the summer of 1945 were old ones, such as Brunswick's *Louis Armstrong Jazz Classics*, an album of sides Armstrong recorded as a sideman between 1924 and 1927. *Chicago Tribune* critic Will Davidson said of it, "There is solo work in these dates that makes some modern 'jazz' musicians look like the egotistic technique fiends they are."[46] Leonard Feather did not agree, taking to the pages of *Esquire* to write that with the exception of two sides with Earl Hines, "the records sound just like what they are—records made two decades ago."[47]

Feather spent September 1945 profiling Gillespie—"The 21st Century Gabriel"—in *Esquire* and ramping up his attacks on fans of early jazz in *Metronome*, writing, "Thus the Moldy Figs are frustrated by their musical illiteracy, just as they are frustrated by their inability to foist their idiotic views on the public, and frustrated by the ever-increasing public acceptance of the critics and musicians they hate."[48] But that same month, Bunk Johnson's band opened at the Stuyvesant Casino in New York City, an engagement that did sensational business and brought out reporters from *Time, Life, Vogue, Glamour, Harper's Bazaar, View, Down Beat, Jazzways, PM*, the *New York Times,* and the *New Yorker.* The moldy figs did a victory lap, with Frederic Ramsey Jr. (of *Jazzmen*) writing, "There has never been such ensemble playing, such brilliant solo work, all going at once, in New York jam sessions."[49]

Modern jazz fans would have disagreed. While Johnson was at the Stuyvesant Casino, Gillespie was achieving what he referred to as "the height of the perfection of our music" at the Three Deuces on 52nd Street with Charlie Parker, Bud Powell, Curley Russell, and Max Roach.[50] It was no surprise when *Metronome* named Gillespie "Influence of the Year" and that he placed second only to Roy Eldridge in the magazine's trumpet poll. But a December trip to spread the sounds of bebop to the west coast at Billy Berg's in Los Angeles proved nearly as much of a disaster as the "Hepsations" tour of the south. "They didn't know what we were playing, and in some ways they were more dumbfounded than the people were down South," Gillespie recalled.[51]

Where was Louis Armstrong through all of this? On the road, busy as ever but also experiencing one of the quietest periods of his life from a publicity standpoint. There were no films, no recording sessions, only occasional radio broadcasts and very few high-profile gigs. He still traveled with a full revue, now featuring trombonist Russell "Big Chief" Moore and vocalists Leslie Scott and Velma Middleton. Otto Eason tap-danced on roller skates, the husband-and-wife team of "Slim & Sweets" (including Lucille "Sweets" Preston, Armstrong's future mistress and the mother of his alleged love child) danced and did a comic sketch based on *Romeo and Juliet*, and the Two Zephyrs (with comedian Slappy White) were brought back for their slow-motion crap game, still a hit after so many years. "The Satchmo's emphasis on jive rhythm and a strong group of supporting acts makes this top grade entertainment for the younger fans," *Variety* wrote of a September engagement at the Orpheum in Los Angeles. "At show caught, every act earned honest encores and went off to plenty of palm-smacking."[52] The applause was nice and Armstrong remained busy, but without the controversy of a Gillespie or Johnson, he had disappeared from the headlines. Before a dance at the Radio Rondevoo in Twin Falls, Idaho, reporter Ian Sanderson asked Armstrong about his plans to retire. "I'll just keep on playing till I fade out," the 44-year-old trumpeter said. "I like to play. Why should I quit?"[53]

22

"We Really Did Romp"

January 1946–February 1947

After not setting foot in a recording studio for a full year, Armstrong had two sessions over a span of eight days in January, resulting in his first recorded pairings with Duke Ellington and Ella Fitzgerald. The session with Ellington was as part of an "Esquire All-American 1946 Award Winners" date supervised by Leonard Feather. *Esquire* skipped its annual concert in favor of the session and Armstrong's Gold award for best male vocalist was enough to get him on the date, even though he remained absent in the trumpet category. Feather couldn't resist giving the band two of his own compositions to record, a blues titled "Long, Long Journey" and "Snafu," a boppish instrumental on "I Got Rhythm" changes that caused some difficulties. "Louis read his part accurately, but it was too evident that he was reading; the notes came out staccato and self-conscious," Feather wrote. Without insulting Armstrong, Feather had an idea to let trumpeter Neal Hefti play the melody, allowing Armstrong to improvise around it. It worked, inspiring Armstrong to take one of his most "modern" solos, though mostly in terms of some surprising harmonic choices; rhythmically, it was a long way from bebop. Feather approved of Armstrong's "masterfully improvised thirty-two-bar solo" and wrote, "The myth that he was set in his ways and had forgotten how to play spontaneously was immediately dispelled."[1]

Eight days later, Milt Gabler paired Armstrong and Fitzgerald for the first time, the start of what would become an immortal partnership. Gabler selected the new composition "You Won't Be Satisfied" and a recent Nat King Cole hit, "The Frim Fram Sauce" and hired Bob Haggart to once again write arrangements and conduct a top-notch studio band. The results are terrific—both Armstrong and Fitzgerald had a deep affinity for "You Won't Be Satisfied"—but oddly, the two great voices and personalities only interacted briefly at the very end of "Satisfied." The record still became a jukebox hit and the jazz press took notice of the notable partnership, with *Metronome* writing, "The material is not great, but the singers are, and the result is delightful listening."

Armstrong went back on the road, playing three weeks at the Plantation Club in St. Louis in February when his regular bassist Al Moore notified him that he had to suddenly go back home to Philadelphia because his wife was expecting. Twenty-two-year-old Arvell Shaw got the call and was hired for three weeks. Shaw was petrified at first, until Armstrong eventually signaled his approval, asking Shaw, "Are you sure you're not from New Orleans, cause you have a New Orleans beat."[2] He ended up being associated with Armstrong for much of the trumpeter's remaining life, including playing his final public engagement at the Waldorf-Astoria in 1971.

With Shaw on board, Armstrong headed home for New Orleans, performing on March 2 and 3 at the Coliseum. It was perfect timing, as he was able to catch his first Mardi Gras in years, ending up as part the Zulu King's float. Armstrong had long been a proud member of the Zulu Social Aid and Pleasure Club and understood the long tradition of the black King of the Zulus—with blackface makeup, grass skirt, and lard can crown—mocking the traditions of the white king, Rex. "You should have seen me—bowing—ana waving to the folks—and Cats as they cheered at the sight of me (their home boy)," Armstrong wrote to Joe Glaser's secretary, Frances Church. "Oh its only great."[3]

In another letter to Church, Armstrong recounted his annoyance with a personal appearance at a record store in Texas where he expected to sign his own records—only to find that the place was overrun with collectors who wanted to talk about the old days. "There I have to sit-signing a lot of old crap they've bought that's recorded by someone else," Armstrong wrote, adding, "Now you can imagine me sitting around some 'E-flat-record shop waiting for some—Pimply Face boy—come in—ask me a lot of silly questions just to impress me that he's so Hep—til it hurts . . . Ump . . . And then too—the way I see it Mrs. Church—thats old time stuff. . . . If they were my own recordings I wouldn't mind so much . . . But just the same—keep me away from all that mess in the future if you can."[4]

Armstrong, like many, was growing exhausted by being accosted by collectors and critics wanting to talk—and argue—about the various schools of thought in the jazz world. "Last night two kids were punching each other in front of a 52nd St. swing club and, when separated, divulged that the fisticuffs started over an argument as to who is the greatest living saxophonist. Recently, a jazz pianist sued a critic, and collected, over a particularly vicious magazine attack on his art," Robert Sylvester wrote in the *New York Daily News* in April. "Another jazz critic has been flattened three times in the Village for saying what he meant a little too firmly. You'd think that jazz music was meant to be enjoyed. Instead, it's apparently something to fight about."[5]

Sylvester didn't name the critic—Leonard Feather—who was now exerting a greater influence on the jazz recordings made for RCA Victor. In December 1945, RCA recorded an album by Bunk Johnson, but Feather soon took over and put an end to any Moldy Fig leanings. After having Armstrong and the "Esquire All-Stars" record his own compositions in January, Feather convinced the label to record Dizzy Gillespie in February, including another Feather original, "Ol Man Rebop," using the pseudonym "Floyd Wilson." Five days later, Feather supervised a Coleman Hawkins date and once more included one of his compositions "Low Flame." The resulting eight sides by Gillespie and Hawkins were eventually packaged together as the album *New 52nd Street Jazz*, the label avoiding the word "bebop."

In March, perhaps because of the influence of Feather, Joe Glaser ended Armstrong's long association with Decca and signed a new contract with RCA. Milt Gabler might have been two-for-two with jukebox hits "I Wonder" in 1945 and the first pairing with Fitzgerald in 1946, but RCA promised to release 12 sides a year, an improvement over the four sides Decca had issued in the previous four years.[6] Still, without Gabler's intuitive knack for selecting the right material for his artists, Armstrong's first session for RCA in April produced only average results, including two so-so pop tunes, "Linger in My Arms a Little Closer" and "Whatta Ya Gonna Do," Armstrong and Middleton's first recorded duet on "No Variety Blues" (which didn't include a note of trumpet) and a fun "Joseph 'N' His Brudders" that's marred by some atypically stiff trumpet playing in the middle. A rare fifth song was also recorded, perhaps at Armstrong's insistence, "Back O' Town Blues," which he had been performing since 1943. It's no surprise that the familiarity led to the best performance by the band and by Armstrong of his inaugural RCA date.

Armstrong's big band was by no means bad on the session, but it was loud to an unpleasant degree. A holdover from the Teddy McRae era, it now had four trumpets (five, including himself) and four trombones, leading to an overly brassy sound that was in keeping with the trend of the day.[7] The arrangements also included some modern harmonies and dissonant touches (the opening of "Linger in My Arms a Little Longer" contains the seeds for Thelonious Monk's later composition "Blue Monk").[8] It was enough for the *Negro Soul* to report, "Louis is still going ahead, he is keeping right up with the current trends in popular music, that's why he keeps young men in his band."[9] Armstrong also praised this younger edition of his big band, telling the *Baltimore Afro-American* "those boys are the best bunch of musicians I ever had under my wing."[10] Most critics did not agree. "Satchmo arrived with one of the biggest (19 pieces), brassiest, and worst bands he ever had—a kind of unintentional satire on everything wrong with big bands: saxophonists who stood up and writhed as they played; a brass section with a nose for noise rather than an ear or melody," *Time* reported on an April engagement at the Aquarium in Manhattan.[11]

The first two RCA Victor singles were released in June to a flurry of publicity Decca hadn't given Armstrong in years. Reviews were generally good, but *Billboard* predicted, "Sides won't excite the hot jazz fans much and the phono fans even less."[12] What did excite "phono fans"? In July, *Billboard* published a "Most-Played Juke Box Race Records" chart, topped by Lionel Hampton's "Hey! Ba-Ba-Re-Bop" and featuring multiple entries by Louis Jordan and the Ink Spots, as well as the rhythm and blues of Lucky Millinder and Roy Milton and ballads from Buddy Johnson and Andy Kirk. Of the 11 selections listed, nine were Milt Gabler productions at Decca.[13] Singers were now leading the way. The best-selling popular recording in early July was "The Gypsy" by the Ink Spots, another Milt Gabler–produced opus on Decca.[14] Armstrong and Garland were paying attention. Armstrong's male vocalist Leslie Scott began performing "The Gypsy," while Velma Middleton did her own version of "Hey! Ba-Ba-Re-Bop," climaxing each performance with a split. In the early 1930s, Armstrong was the one leading the way on the pop charts; now he was handing the covers of the hottest pop songs over to his vocalists while he continued featuring himself on older numbers like "I Can't Give You Anything but Love," "Stompin' at the Savoy," and "Back O'Town Blues."

Meanwhile, the band business was nosediving, especially where one-nighters were concerned. *Billboard* spelled this out with an article in its July 13, 1946, issue, "Did Atomic Bomb Double on Bikini (Pacific) and the Road (U. S. A.)? 1-Niters Die." "The road is shot," the article stated. "Many big city locations are not making money. The nation's economy is so unstable that there is no prospect of an improvement on the situation without positive action on the part of leaders, agencies and promoters."[15]

A glimpse into the state of the music business and into the state of Glaser's work can be found in a letter he sent to Joe Garland at the Band Box in Chicago on July 25. "I am heart sick at what is happening to the band business," Glaser wrote. He continued:

> Promoters all over are going broke—bookings are being cancelled at the last minute—I can name at least half a dozen Colored bands that will disband in the next 30 days and at least 20 White bands that will disband so if our men are complaining then all I can say is God Bless them all and my only hope is that they change before it is too late as I assure you they will be very unhappy unless the situation changes in the immediate future.[16]

But almost immediately, the situation did change as Glaser came through with one of the biggest deals he made in years: he finally signed Armstrong up to star in "the movie of his own life," to be titled *New Orleans*.[17] The *Pittsburgh Courier* called it "the most important news to come out of Hollywood in a decade." Billy Rowe wrote that if done right, "it will be the greatest break the race has had in film in the history of America. All and sundry agree that it couldn't happen to a better artist than Louis Armstrong, the evergreen trumpet king of swing."[18]

Perhaps a troubling sign was the next star announced, Arturo de Cordova, who would portray Nick Duquesne, ostensibly the white star of the film. Why did the film need a white star? But more greats from the jazz world were signed up, including Billie Holiday, Kid Ory, Zutty Singleton, Barney Bigard, Charlie Beal, Bud Scott, Mutt Carey, Red Callender, and Lucky Thompson. With the cast in place, Producer Jules Levey, Director Arthur Lubin, and an entire crew headed for New Orleans to begin filming locations and recording examples of live traditional jazz, receiving advice from the National Jazz Foundation on "technical aspects."[19]

Back in California at the end of August, Glaser was suddenly feeling powerful and called for a meeting with Jules C. Stein, MCA president, to discuss the future of Associated Booking Corporation. "In the two and a half years or so since Glaser set up ABC, the agency has become one of the four largest in the field," *Variety* reported. Stein's original two-year option to buy out the other 50% of ABC had lapsed but he still could have offered to buy Glaser out at any time. Instead, Glaser surprised many by buying out Stein's 50% interest for $100,000, making Glaser the sole 100% owner of Associated Booking Corporation. *Variety* reported that Glaser had always been "anxious to shift his own activities to Hollywood" but those plans were now off. Glaser would continue to have ABC offices in Chicago and Beverly Hills but, recently separated from his wife, he would settle down and become a celebrated New York character (whose Chicago skeletons in his closet would never again be publicized during his lifetime).[20]

Armstrong arrived in Los Angeles at the beginning of September and immediately checked into his old headquarters, the Dunbar Hotel. Leonard Feather was in town and spent his time shadowing Armstrong on his first day on the set of *New Orleans*, a reunion with hometown friends Ory, Bigard, Beal, Scott, and Singleton, the last of whom smiling constantly at the chance to once again play with his still somewhat estranged best friend. The producers then sat the musicians down to play the music they had recorded in New Orleans, resulting in one of the most vindicating moments of Feather's life. "As Louis, Barney and the others gathered around the machine, they broke into roars of laughter at the welter of wrong notes, the horrible out-of-tune horns and the generally unbelievable wrongness of the music," he wrote. Ory "almost doubled up with laughter," Armstrong said, "[Shit], man, I could put down my horn for six months and pick it up and blow better than that!" and Bigard added, "How in the hell do they expect us to play that bad?" Feather called it "sheer bad music by any standards" and was relieved that Armstrong and the New Orleans men didn't listen to it "in terms of nostalgia and cultism."[21]

The next day, Armstrong was to record for Charles Delaunay's French label, Swing. Delaunay was the founder of the Hot Club du France, the author of the landmark *Hot Discography* and, along with Hugues Panassie, started Swing in 1937. News of *New Orleans* had spread around the world and Delaunay wanted to record Armstrong with the ensemble from the film. Delaunay

Figure 22.1 A reunion on the set of *New Orleans* with (top row) Louis Armstrong, Kid Ory, Barney Bigard, (bottom row) Bud Scott, Zutty Singleton, Charlie Beal, and Red Callender.

The Jack Bradley Collection, Louis Armstrong House Museum

couldn't get to the United States but he trusted Feather to oversee the proceedings and wired $2,000 to his friend Walter Schaap to see that Armstrong got paid.

Feather couldn't help himself and, without Delaunay present, took over the planning of the date. Instead of old-timers Ory and Scott, he replaced them with two excellent swing musicians, trombonist Vic Dickenson and guitarist Allan Reuss. Two standards were agreed upon, "I Want a Little Girl" and "Sugar," but then Feather had them record two of his own compositions, "Blues for Yesterday" and "Blues in the South"—with Feather on piano. He protected himself a few months later, by saying it wasn't his idea, writing, "When we got to the blues, Zutty completely knocked me out by insisting that I play on the date myself. I wondered what some of the Moldy Fig jazz fans would have said if they had heard Zutty talking that way, and Louis seconding him."[22] Whether or not it happened like that, it was not what Delaunay wanted. "Feather, who had some skills as a composer and pianist, put himself on the record on two of the titles and Delaunay knew that he had immortalized himself by recording with Louie," Phil Schaap, Walter Schaap's son, recalled in 2017. "And Delaunay would take 38 years to forgive Feather."[23] Drama aside, the date was a gem, with Armstrong sounding much looser here than he did on the big band session in April, though he eschewed any high note endings, quite possibly at the suggestion of Feather, who usually complained about such "exhibitionistic" tendencies. Feather, after being given so much control, now concluded "that Louis still sounds best with a small band, and second, that the Armstrong of 1946 is greater than the Armstrong of a couple of years ago, and one of the very greatest figures in all jazz, just as he has been for a quarter of a century."[24]

Armstrong remained in terrific form for the soundtrack recordings for New Orleans, but any hopeful expectations for the finished film were killed almost immediately after the film began shooting. Though the original script was based on "Conspiracy in Jazz," a story written by Elliott Paul—the screenwriter of Orson Welles's aborted jazz film in 1941—and Herbert J. Biberman, Biberman recalled that producer "Levey was scared to death that too many Negroes will come to the theaters to see this picture because there will be too many Negro artists in it."[25] Thus, more emphasis was placed on the white leads in the film, De Cordova's Nick Duquesne, a club owner in New Orleans's Storyville, and Dorothy Patrick's Miralee, a wealthy opera singer who gets bitten by the jazz bug after being introduced to it by her maid Endie, played by Billie Holiday.

Holiday was deep in the throes of her heroin addiction, but Joe Glaser was attempting to help his client, booking her to appear with Armstrong back in July and then getting her signed up for New Orleans. She arrived 12 days late

Figure 22.2 Leonard Feather takes over the piano during a September 1946 recording session for the French Swing label, much to the consternation of the date's organizer, Charles Delaunay.

The Jack Bradley Collection, Louis Armstrong House Museum

and, once on set, met with a dialogue coach "trying to brief me on how to get the right kind of Tom feeling into this thing."[26] Holiday also tangled with Patrick, who was angry at Holiday for "stealing scenes." Holiday couldn't take it and began crying. "Better look out," Armstrong told everyone on the set. "I know Lady, and when she starts crying, the next thing she's going to do is start fighting."[27]

Armstrong, at least, was happy to have Holiday around, writing to a friend afterward, "Of course Billy and I are doing quite a bit of acting (ahem) she's also my Sweetheart in the picture. . . . Ump Ump Ump . . . Now isn't that Something? The great Billy Holiday-my sweetheart? . . . Likes, that very very much."[28] Holiday and Armstrong introduced new songs by Eddie De Lange and Louis Alter, "The Blues Are Brewin'," "Endie," and the one song to destined to become a standard, "Do You Know What It Means to Miss New Orleans." Holiday was under contract with Decca, but Armstrong recorded all three songs for RCA on October 17, the first two with his big band and the latter with the small "Dixieland Seven" group from the film, the only substitution being drummer Minor Hall in for Zutty Singleton. With Ory's growling trombone, Bigard's creole-flavored clarinet, and the stomping rhythm section prodded by drummer Hall's backbeats on "Where the Blues Was Born in New Orleans" and Armstrong's fourth studio recording of "Mahogany Hall Stomp," the free-wheeling "Dixieland" date seemed to be aimed squarely at the Moldy Figs.

Yet, it still wasn't enough to win unanimous praise in the various bibles of traditional jazz. "Let's face it; Louis is completely and irretrievably the star soloist and no longer the greatest of all lead men for a small ensemble," Armstrong's friend George Avakian wrote. "Every record date with a pick-up unit in the past decade has shown this, and these sides are no exception."[29] William C. Love, writing in the *Jazz Record*, said, "The band is called Louis Armstrong and His Dixieland Seven but the music resembles dixieland about as much as Kate Smith resembles Lena Horne."[30] And in the *Chicago Tribune*, Will Davidson said "Mahogany Hall" "isn't bad . . . altho you could wish for a little more authenticity."[31] Davidson did not further define the criteria what would be more "authentic" than a band made up of New Orleans pioneers such as Armstrong, Ory, Bigard, and Hall.

The "Dixieland Seven" records were issued at the same time as RCA's *New 52nd Street Jazz* album with the modern sounds of Dizzy Gillespie and Coleman Hawkins. It was impossible not to notice Armstrong recording in the "Dixieland" style at the same time his old Henderson-bandmate and rival Hawkins was recording with the vanguard of the bop scene. Davidson again demonstrated the problems with the convoluted definitions of the various styles of jazz in this period, writing of the Hawkins sides, "This isn't rebop at all—just good modern jazz."[32]

The RCA Victor album helped position Gillespie a bit more comfortably into the spotlight after another rough year of trying to get the mainstream public to accept bebop. In July, Gillespie "laid an egg in Detroit that a mama ostrich would have cherished," according to *Esquire*.[33] A tour with Ella Fitzgerald helped, as Fitzgerald had a built-in audience and proved receptive to Gillespie's sounds, soon incorporating bop into her own scat solos. Still, Gillespie was having the most difficulty with African American fans, especially in the south. "I remember one night we was packing up and five of 'our brothers' came up to the stand," Gillespie's drummer Joe Harris recalled. "They said 'Man, if you niggers ever come down here playing that Bebop shit with that Dizzy Jill-e-spy with that trumpet and that goddamned drummer!' We were a long way from [blues and shuffles]. I don't remember ever playing a backbeat with Dizzy's band, but the booking agent wanted to give the band some exposure and the do-gooders would say, 'It's good for the black people to hear this music.' It really didn't work out."[34]

The results were borne out in the *Pittsburgh Courier*'s annual readers' poll, published in early 1947. There was barely a trace of bop in the results, with Louis Jordan leading the Small Combo category, Johnny Hodges in front on Alto Sax, Lester Young winning Tenor Sax, and Cab Calloway named the most popular leader. But perhaps the biggest surprise was Armstrong once again winning the Trumpet category, edging out Cootie Williams.[35] An even bigger shocker occurred in *Esquire* when Armstrong, after not even placing in 1945 and 1946, won the Gold Award in the Trumpet category, with Silver going to Gillespie and the New Star award going to Miles Davis. "Perhaps the comeback of the year is that of Armstrong on trumpet," Louis Sidran wrote in *Esquire*. "Unplaced in the balloting last year and singled out for his singing alone, Louie snapped back off a so-so season to re-establish himself in the first horn seat. More people saw and heard him in '46 than in some time; seeing and hearing is believing, for what Satchmo' has lost in lip strength, he makes up for in that fabled drive he never seems to lose."[36]

Armstrong was proud of his "Esky" awards, writing to readers of *Melody Maker*, "Haven't done so bad during these Esquire Polls, etc. . . . My home in Corona Long Island is just full of oscars. [. . .] I only mentioned those trophys at my home sos you can see for yourself that I'm still not a lazy man musically and its still in my veins."[37] Thanks to his Gold Awards, Armstrong was heavily featured in *Esquire*'s *1947 Jazz Book*, a hardcover work that was published in January 1947. The book included Armstrong's first published statement directly on bebop (which some, including Armstrong, were still referring to as "rebop"). "Don't you know I'm crazy about that 'Re Bop' stuff? I love to listen to it," he was quoted as saying. "I think it's very, very amusing. One thing, to play 'Re Bop' one has to have mighty good, strong chops from what I've witnessed. I'm one cat that loves all kinds of music."[38]

Armstrong didn't want to air any negative feelings in the press, but when it came to New Orleans Jazz and Dixieland, many of his contemporaries weren't as kind, as evidenced in Leonard Feather's new *Metronome* series, "The Blindfold Test." Feather began the series in late 1946, playing 10 records at random for musicians and eliciting their comments without telling them what they were hearing. It was a perfect setup for Feather, who was able to play lesser recordings by the likes of Bunk Johnson and Eddie Condon in order to get musicians to knock the earlier styles. "These oldtime musicians and fans romanticize themselves into a false conception of how things were played years ago," drummer Dave Tough said in the December 1946 installment, blasting Kid Rena's Jazz Band of New Orleans with the caveat, "All the same, these musicians are less ridiculous than the fans who idolize them. How can they be sincere? It's just one of those esoteric cults." "I think it's a bad idea for kids or youngsters who are interested in music to pick up on Dixieland; everyone should try to progress," Mary Lou Williams said in the September 1946 installment after beating up Feather targets Johnson and Art Hodes. Feather played Coleman Hawkins his 1925 recording of "Money Blues" with Armstrong and Fletcher Henderson. Hawkins said, "I'm ashamed of it," gave it "No stars," and concluded, "It's an amazing thing, there are kids 22, 23 years old who get hold of these records and they don't think anything has ever been made that's better than that sort of thing and never will be. I don't understand it! To me, it's like a man thinking back to when he couldn't walk, he had to crawl."[39]

The January 1947 installment was devoted to Dizzy Gillespie, who was more than ready to attack the "moldy figs." Reacting to a recording with Sidney Bechet and Mezzrow, Gillespie gave it "No stars" and erupted, "That must have been made in 1900. . . . No harmonic structure here; two beats; bad rhythm, nothing happening; just utter simplicity, but how simple can you get? You can get a little boy eight years old to play that simple." Played a Wild Bill Davison record with Eddie Condon, Gillespie said, "No stars, no nothing." Finally, Gillespie reacted to two Armstrong performances, "Savoy Blues" from 1927 and "Linger in My Arms a Little Longer" from 1946. Of the Hot Five classic, Gillespie allowed, "Louis *always* sounds good to me—he might not have the chops he used to have, but his ideas are always fine." Admitting, "No, I wasn't influenced by him because I'd never heard his records," he gave it one star, saying, "I only like Louis on this." For "Linger in My Arms," Gillespie said, "Louis shouldn't play a solo with a straight mute—it only sounds good with a section . . . I prefer to hear him play legato . . . the tune holds him down here; it's a wasted effort. Vocal is wonderful. No voice, but lots of feeling." On the surface, there are plenty of complimentary phrases—"Louis *always* sounds good to me," "Vocal is wonderful"—but there's just as many backhanded comments: "He might not have the chops he used to have," "No, I wasn't influenced by him," "No voice," "It's a wasted effort," "One star." Critics had been taking shots at Armstrong for years, but musicians did not, especially in print. Armstrong would not forget Gillespie's words.

Besides, Gillespie *was* being influenced by Armstrong, if in an entirely non-musical way: he now realized the importance of showmanship. After the cold reactions of African American fans on the road, Gillespie played the Apollo in January 1947, sharing the bill with two of Armstrong's friends and favorite comedians—and two men who were becoming the bane of existence for younger, more progressive audiences—Mantan Moreland and Stepin

Fetchit. Gillespie indulged in more showmanship and dancing than before, but *Variety* still didn't buy it, scoffing at "Gillespie's hogging the spot with his unsharp clowning" and concluding that the "Great favorites in this house" remained Fetchit and Moreland.[40]

Gillespie was in attendance at Armstrong's next major performance on February 8, 1947, his first time headlining at Carnegie Hall. Feather produced the show to be a celebration of Armstrong's entire life and hoped to coax him into playing with a small group. Armstrong was apprehensive, though, and needed to speak up if he wanted to avoid the fiascos that were the *Esquire* concerts in 1944 and 1945. "I understand you and the Boss Mr Glaser's planning a concert for me and my gang," he wrote to Feather. "Well I'll tell ya planning a concerts alright—but if any an every old Tom Dick & Harry will be interfering I'd just sooner forget about the concert. . . . They have all been awfully messy anyway-from what I can gather . . . So if you boys intend on doing the thing—for God's sake—don't have a lot of guys whom think they know whats going down—and come to find out—the'yre no wheres." Armstrong suggested, "It really wouldn't be a bad idea to have the seven piece band (the one I used in the picture) in that concert," adding, "We really did romp."[41] The *New Orleans* band, though, was too old-fashioned for Feather's tastes. Feather instead suggested a suitable working sextet led by clarinetist Edmond Hall, a musician from New Orleans with an instantly identifiable dirty sound. Armstrong, for his part, insisted that his regular big band and vocalists perform the second half of the concert, augmented by guest stars Big Sid Catlett and Billie Holiday.

Though Hall's sextet had the makeup of a traditional New Orleans ensemble with a trumpet-trombone-clarinet front line and piano-bass-drums rhythm section, the musicians all came out of the big band era and sounded a little ill at ease on the earlier material at the start of the concert. Armstrong, too, sounded slightly less assured than usual, but everyone grew more confident as the concert wore on, Armstrong especially dazzling on ballads "Save It Pretty Mama," "Confessin'," and "Black and Blue." The band cooked on "Ain't Misbehavin'" and "St. Louis Blues," and the old routine on "Rockin' Chair," performed as a duet with somnolent bassist Johnny Williams, elicited gales of laughter from the Carnegie crowd. The audience was still buzzing as the big band launched into a storming version of "Stompin' at the Savoy" and played old favorites "I Can't Give You Anything but Love" and "Back O'Town Blues," before featuring regular vocalists Leslie Scott and Velma Middleton and special guests Holiday and Catlett.

Reviews were sensational, at least as far as Armstrong was concerned. *Variety* wrote, "From start to finish, this performance was strictly a one-man

concert. In the first three-quarters of the program, Armstrong had to over-
come the uninspired accompaniment of the Edmond Hall sextet while in the
last quarter he had to contend with the comparative mediocrity of his own
orchestra. But despite the obstacles, or perhaps, because of them, Armstrong's
genius as trumpeter and showman flashed brilliantly from the bandstand."[42]
Down Beat's Michael Levin agreed, saying the big band portion "was artistically unsatisfactory," though he added, "The producers said that the entire last
section was completely picked by Louis himself," noting that the inclusion of
Scott and Middleton was to not hurt the feelings of his two loyal vocalists.[43]

Interestingly, in the black press, Armstrong's big band was warmly received.
"The last section of the program found Louie framed by a large, well disci-
plined orchestra," the Reverend Ben Richardson wrote. "It formed a perfect
back drop for his offerings." Richardson also praised Armstrong's stage persona, writing, "His facial antics added zest and positive charm."[44] Billy Rowe,
who had been following Armstrong since he came to New York in 1929, wrote,
"Not since the early days of his career in New York when he caused a blasé
Lafayette Theatre audience to stand up and cheer his playing has the writer
seen the great master of the modern musical idiom in such rare form."[45] Even
Dizzy Gillespie exclaimed, "Didn't he play wonderfully!"[46]

The concert seemed to thrill everyone in attendance—except for the
members of Armstrong's big band, who now saw the writing on the wall. "That
spelled the death knell for the big band," Arvell Shaw said of the Carnegie
Hall concert.[47] He was right, though no one could quite predict what was still
to come.

23

"Ain't No Music Out of Date as Long as You Play It Perfect"

1947 and Beyond

Shortly after the applause at Carnegie Hall died down, Armstrong had to take a full month off to deal with pain caused by ulcers. While convalescing in Corona, he received a visit from concert producer and press agent Ernie Anderson. Anderson was most closely associated with Eddie Condon's crew, producing a series of popular concerts at Town Hall. *Esquire* asked Anderson to edit its annual *Jazz Book* earlier in the year, but he used the opportunity to publicize Condon and his circle of musicians, although they hadn't won any awards. Almost instantly, 18 of the 20 critics who voted in the poll—including Leonard Feather, John Hammond, and Barry Ulanov—severed their connections with *Esquire*, claiming Anderson turned the 1947 *Jazz Book* "into a press manual for Eddie Condon." (*Billboard* wrote, "One of the critics pointed out that this mass resignation is truly a historic event, since it was the first time in his recall that so many of his brood had concurred on a point involving mass opinion."[1]) Next came a letter from 34 angry musicians asking, "Why does the list of so-called 'best' records ignore good recordings made by younger jazz musicians in favor of records made by Dixielanders?"[2] The letter was signed by, among others, Miles Davis, Duke Ellington, Nat King Cole, Ella Fitzgerald, Dizzy Gillespie, Coleman Hawkins, Billie Holiday, and, topping the list, Louis Armstrong. It marked the end of the *Esquire* era in jazz journalism. Three years later, Armstrong was still grumpy about it, saying, "Music got to be politics in America; that's what ruined it—all them awards and things. I won the last *Esquire* award, and when you opened *Esquire,* every page you turned it was Ernie Anderson and Eddie Condon. How about that?"[3]

Armstrong might have been salty, but Anderson didn't want to talk about *Esquire,* he wanted to talk about Town Hall's "One Night Stand" series of concerts that he booked with disc jockey Fred Robbins. Anderson had what he thought was a sure-fire idea: he wanted Armstrong to fill in their open May 17 Town Hall date, playing with a small group. "Louis was wonderful," Anderson said. "He obviously loved the idea, he loved the musicians we had picked out to play with him, and he loved the selections we had listed." But there was a problem. Armstrong told Anderson, "I can't do this unless Joe Glaser wants me to."[4] Anderson knew what he had to do, and he knew the one way he could get Glaser's attention: money. One of Glaser's bookers told Anderson that Glaser was now charging $350 for a weekday one-nighter for Armstrong's big band, $600 on weekends. Anderson came to Associated Booking's Fifth Avenue office with a cashier's check made out to Glaser for $1,000. A skeptical Glaser barked, "What are you trying to do, you jerk?" "That's for Louis for one night without the band," Anderson replied. Glaser—"still snarling"—invited Anderson into his office. "If this works as I think it will, instead of $350 a night for Louis, you'll be getting $2500 a night," Anderson told him. Glaser continued to glare at him, but agreed to the May 17 date.[5]

Town Hall was booked, but that was over two months away and Armstrong had to go back to work. He began with an RCA Victor session with his big band on March 12, cutting five sides and sounding completely rejuvenated, the ulcer-related layoff probably doing him some good. RCA's choice of material was better here than in the April 1946 session, if not exactly a slew of future standards, with Armstrong recording lesser numbers associated with Frank Sinatra ("I Believe"), Nat King Cole ("You Don't Learn That in School"), and Doris Day ("It Takes Time"). The band was still a little too brassy and showcased more modern touches; in fact, the arrangement of "I Wonder, I Wonder, I Wonder" opens by directly quoting a line Dizzy Gillespie played at the end of "Groovin' High" in 1945, immortalized by Tadd Dameron in the ballad "If You Could See Me Now" in 1946. Armstrong plays well but is really on fire vocally throughout the date, as his vocals were now officially the main attraction. Thanks to the popularity of Sinatra's version, "I Believe" became a bit of a hit and immediately became a part of Armstrong's live act, but this mixed bag of material wasn't enough to please John Lucas at the *Record Changer*, who wrote of the sides, "Armstrong is downright disappointing. Louis has had frightful material like this for many, many years; it's certainly time for a change."[6]

Armstrong went back to work on March 14 at the Paradise Theatre in Detroit, while awaiting a wave of publicity the likes of which he hadn't experienced in a decade. Armstrong had supplied Belgian Robert Goffin with several notebooks of autobiographical material back in 1944 and Goffin finally turned it into the biography *Horn of Plenty*, published in March and re-familiarizing the public with Armstrong's improbable rags-to-riches story (though Goffin's work was plagued by too many fictitious quotes rendered in painful dialect).

On April 26, Jules Levey's *New Orleans* had its official world premiere in the titular city's Saenger Theatre, with both the governor of Louisiana and mayor of New Orleans present. The finished film was a disappointment as the melodrama featuring the white characters overshadowed the music, eventually erasing all the African Americans from the story; when jazz is finally accepted and showcased at Carnegie Hall at the end, it is Woody Herman's white band, not Armstrong's, that closes the film. This kind of kowtowing to southern audiences could be seen in a two-page spread for the film in *Motion Picture Daily* that featured only photographs of the white actors and musicians.[7]

Reviews were mostly disappointing. "*New Orleans* brought to the Orpheum screen yesterday one of the silliest plots, most stilted dialogue and acting deficiency, the combination of which makes the new film a bidder for the 10 worst films of the year—so far, that is," according to Theresa Loeb in the *Oakland Tribune*. "However, there is a redeeming feature in *New Orleans* reserved for jazz fans only. Said redeemer is Louis Armstrong and his horn. . . . Armstrong not only plays his style of music so that it must melt the most hardened-against-hot-notes member of the audience, but he displays a naturalness and ease in acting himself on the screen, which puts the veteran actors in the cast to shame."[8] Donald Kirkley agreed, more or less rolling his eyes at "the customary love story" before writing, "But it is Satchmo, with his oversize smile and educated cornet, who steals the picture every time he gets a chance. It is a pity they did not write the whole story around him, for he displays an unexpected gift for comedy."[9]

Perhaps surprisingly—or maybe not considering the history of poor representations of African Americans in film—the black press was very kind toward *New Orleans*. "The picture is unique in that Negro entertainers are on a parity with white entertainers," the *New York Age* wrote. " 'Praise be to Allah' the stereotype role for the Negro has definitely been removed from this film."[10] "Saw a preview of it last wk. and came away feeling that it was the best cinematic tribute to jazz and those who further its cause than any ever filmed," Billy Rowe wrote. "Using the life of Louie Armstrong as the dominant theme, it is by far the most democratic mixed film to ever come out of H'wood."[11] But Edwin Schallert of the *Los Angeles Times* spoke for many when he wrote, "It is regrettable that *New Orleans* couldn't have been more solid in a documentary way, because there is doubtless an interesting story to tell about the birth and growth of a popular music heritage in America."[12] Such a movie would not be made in Armstrong's lifetime.

On April 26, the same day *New Orleans* had its New Orleans premiere, Armstrong appeared on two high-profile radio shows, leaving his big band behind to instead perform with two very different small groups. Up first was

This Is Jazz on WOR, a kind of paradise for moldy figs that was the brain-child of Rudi Blesh, a man with a very strict definition of what constituted the "this" in the title of his show. In 1946, he expounded on the subject in his book *Shining Trumpets*, a problematic "History of Jazz" that sneered at any form of music that wasn't the original polyphonic sound of New Orleans jazz, which he felt peaked with Jelly Roll Morton. Armstrong was featured prominently in *Shining Trumpets* but to Blesh, Morton was a greater figure. "Events robbed Morton in his later years of the opportunity to serve the music of his race," he wrote. "Armstrong had the opportunity and threw it away. . . . Armstrong's path led him elsewhere and herein lies not merely a serious blow to art but the tragedy of Louis Armstrong, the artist."[13] This was the first time "the tragedy of Louis Armstrong" was written up in a major book. It would not be the last.

Now, Armstrong was face-to-face with Blesh, but also with musicians who were longtime associates and close friends, such as Pops Foster, Baby Dodds, Albert Nicholas, and Art Hodes. There was a feeling of excitement and apprehension at the rehearsal the day before the broadcast. "Everyone in the studio talked about one thing: how would Louis sound with a small group of really great jazzmen?" Bob Arthur wrote. "It had been a long time."[14] Armstrong answered any questions on the air, sounding highly inspired on selections that ran the gamut from "When the Saints Go Marchin' In" to "Do You Know What It Means to Miss New Orleans." When it was over, Wild Bill Davison said, "Anybody says Louis can't blow the best, I'll spit in his eye." Arthur concluded, "He did exactly what everyone was hoping he would do. He played like he hasn't played in about twenty years."[15] A few hours later, Armstrong appeared with another small group on Art Ford's *Saturday Night Swing Show* on WNEW, sounding even more stimulated by the presence of Jack Teagarden and Sid Catlett. It was undeniable that both ensembles on April 26 inspired some of Armstrong's best playing and singing of the period, topping even the Carnegie Hall show, but if one had to choose, it was Catlett and Teagarden who spurred him on to even greater heights than Blesh's crew.

Armstrong resumed performing with his big band, doing a week with Billie Holiday at the Earle Theatre in Philadelphia in May.[16] In addition to a short set by Holiday, Armstrong featured his entire revue, including vocalists Leslie Scott (described by the *Philadelphia Inquirer* as "a sepia Sinatra who had the ladies in the audience shrieking") and Velma Middleton, as well as the comedy-and-dancing teams of Slim and Sweets and Myers and Walker. Armstrong featured the band on "Let's Have a Session" and was in the spot-light for a total of four selections, "Stompin' at the Savoy" and three songs he had recorded for RCA in the past year, "Back O'Town Blues," "I Believe," and "Do You Know What It Means to Miss New Orleans."[17] Without a trace of "the tragedy of Louis Armstrong" present, *Variety*'s critic noted "enthusiastic audience response" and summed it up, "All in all, show stacks up as good entertainment"—which is all Armstrong cared to provide.[18]

The day after the Earle engagement ended, Armstrong headed back to New York for the Town Hall concert. Cornetist Bobby Hackett had put together an all-star band made up entirely of members from Eddie Condon's circle: Teagarden, clarinetist Peanuts Hucko, pianist Dick Cary, bassist Bob Haggart, and two rotating drummers, Sid Catlett and George Wettling.[19] Famed guitarist Andrés Segovia was booked to play Town Hall at 8:30 P.M. so Anderson booked two hours of rehearsal time between 6 and 8. Armstrong arrived and after greeting everyone warmly, told Anderson, "We don't have to rehearse. We'll just hit at eleven thirty and play the show!" With that, he left to spend his evening at home in Corona, putting the pressure on Hackett to formalize the tunes, tempos, and keys with the other musicians, and putting panic into Anderson. He surely calmed down at showtime when confronted by a completely sold-out house, with a gross of $4,000 at the box office (Segovia grossed $1,000 and Anderson's concert with Mildred Bailey on May 10 made less than that).[20]

After an emotional introduction by Robbins, Armstrong strode onstage at 11:40 P.M., with only the rhythm section of Cary, Haggart, and Wettling waiting for him. He threw down the gauntlet on the opening number, "Cornet Chop Suey," a vaunted Hot Five masterpiece, the kind of instrumental showcase that purists bemoaned the lack of in Armstrong's big band repertoire. Armstrong created something new, never trying to re-create the sound of the 1920s, instead approaching it as music of the present, not the past. He topped himself on selection after selection: a dramatic duet with Cary on "Dear Old Southland"; two new rhythmically advanced, surprising choruses on "Big Butter and Egg Man"; a gentle lullaby treatment of "Sweethearts on Parade"; and a gorgeous "Pennies from Heaven" with a note-perfect obbligato from Hackett. Even when on familiar ground like "I Can't Give You Anything but Love," "Back O' Town Blues," or "Ain't Misbehavin'," the "set" portions of his solo sounded fresher in the small band context, especially when spurred on by Catlett's backbeats.[21]

The evening climaxed in a version of "Rockin' Chair" that stands among the very highest peaks of Armstrong's career. Without any rehearsal, Armstrong and Teagarden teamed up to provide a performance for the ages, radiating an obvious love between the two that the audience in Town Hall felt that evening and that still translates to listeners today. After the vocal, Armstrong led the ensemble out, Hackett right in there with him, driven by more Catlett backbeats; the emotion of it all is enough to bring one to tears. In many ways, it's a quintessential Armstrong performance: laughter, warmth, and heavy drama, all in about five minutes, but it had the added statement of being performed by an integrated band, 18 years after Armstrong and Teagarden first made history on "Knockin' a Jug."

"It's ridiculous for anyone to be able to play that good," Hackett said when it was over.[22] "The concert was a smashing success," Anderson said. "The audience gave ovation after ovation. I had given Joe Glaser the best box in the place and I looked up from time to time to see how he was taking it. He seemed to be having the time of his life. When I spoke to him at the end of the show, there was a dynamic change in his attitude to me. No longer hostile, he was affable."[23] Glaser's first order of business was to invite Teagarden to his office, where he signed him to a seven-year contract. He had also seen the future: it was time to break up the big band.

Glaser convinced RCA Victor to do a session on June 10 to capitalize on the buzz of the Town Hall concert, reuniting Armstrong with Teagarden, Hackett, and Hucko, but adding Ernie Caceres on baritone saxophone, Johnny Guarnieri on piano and celeste, Al Casey on guitar, Al Hall on bass, and Cozy Cole on drums. Leonard Feather was also back in the studio to supervise and as usual, had Armstrong and Teagarden record one of his blues compositions, a fine if forgettable "Fifty-Fifty Blues."[24] But the rest of the session was a classic, including an excellent reprisal of "Rockin' Chair" and Armstrong's first recording of his original composition—and personal message to Alpha—"Some Day," an ode to heartbreak in the guise of a lullaby. The highlight of the date was a remake of "Jack-Armstrong Blues" that topped the V-Disc version, concluding with six masterful, storytelling trumpet choruses. Tellingly, Feather must not have fully supported Armstrong's embrace of the small group polyphonic sound; he rarely wrote about or took credit for any part of this landmark session.

An amazing snapshot of the different trends in the black American music scene could be glimpsed in June 1947, just days after the RCA session. Armstrong celebrated the New York City premiere of *New Orleans* at the Winter Garden on June 19, once again performing in a small integrated group with the likes of Hackett, Teagarden, and Catlett. While Armstrong was performing "Muskrat Ramble" and "Basin Street Blues" on Broadway, Dizzy Gillespie was uptown at the Apollo with his new big band and vocalist Sarah Vaughan, sharing the bill with dancers the Four Step Brothers, the comedy team of Garner and Wilson, and African American skaters Nick and Virgie Ball. *Variety* finally gave him a fully positive review, complimenting not only Gillespie's "torrid trumpet" on numbers like "Cool Breeze" and "Bebop," but also a humorous scat-singing duet with Kenneth Haygood and "a wacky dance" during a Milt Jackson solo.[25]

While Gillespie was at the Apollo and Armstrong was at the Winter Garden, Louis Jordan was at the Earle Theatre in Philadelphia, still wearing loud suits and performing hits such as "Texas and Pacific," "Jack You're Dead," and "Look Out." *Variety* was there, too, and noted, "Jordan and lads not only make music, but make merry in a manner calculated for plenty laughs. Their principal ingredients are fun and informality."[26] Gillespie was now trying to tap into some of that brand of showmanship, but he was alone, as other boppers such as Charlie Parker and Miles Davis preferred to play their music with an absence of histrionics. When Jordan hired young modern saxophonist Paul Quinichette, it was a disaster, Quinichette later referring to Jordan as "a dictator with Uncle Tom qualities."[27] Jordan's biographer John Chilton said that such accusations could result in "a backstage explosion of fury as Louis countered such allegations by pointing out that all of his showmanship had been learnt from black performers, all of his tricks of the trade mastered while he was playing to black audiences. If later, white audiences also found them funny this was not, in his eyes, a disgrace. Jordan was particularly proud that he was popular at the Apollo Theatre, which boasted the hippest audience in the world, and pointed out that the audiences there were 'too damn busy laughing at me, and at themselves, to make any complaints.'"[28]

Louis Armstrong felt the same exact way and he got to demonstrate just how popular he remained at the Apollo when he brought his big band—and special guest Jack Teagarden—there for one final week beginning on July 4. The Harlem faithful were still with him all the way, 12 years after he first broke the box-office record. Armstrong featured his big band and the other acts in his revue, but closed each night by spotlighting Teagarden, reprising "Rockin' Chair" "to sock returns" before closing with an explosive "Jack Armstrong Blues."[29] On July 11, Armstrong's big band years came to an end on the Apollo stage.

Three days later, Armstrong flew to California to begin shooting Howard Hawks's remake of *Ball of Fire* titled *A Song Is Born* and starring Danny Kaye. During the month-long filming, the market was flooded with Armstrong releases old and new, including Vox's *Paris 1934*, the first US release of the material N. J. Canetti recorded for French Brunswick in November 1934. Armstrong gave a copy to Kaye, who surprised him by playing it on the set. "And while they was reloading the cameras, he turned on that 'Sunny Side' and everybody on the set—quiet," Armstrong recalled. "It was beautiful."[30]

Glaser used the month Armstrong was filming his part to begin assembling a new small group. Teagarden, Dick Cary, and Sid Catlett were hired to reprise their roles from Town Hall, while clarinetist Barney Bigard was brought in after appearing in *New Orleans*. The band was rounded out by Los Angeles–based bassist Morty Corb. With three white musicians and three African Americans, Armstrong was the leader of an integrated band for the first time. His and Mezz Mezzrow's idea of "the millennium" had finally come true.

Glaser, trading in on Armstrong's *Esquire* awards (not to mention Teagarden's, Bigard's, and Catlett's), named the new group the "Esquire All Stars" and booked them for two weeks at Billy Berg's in Hollywood at $3,000 a

Figure 23.1 Armstrong and his musical soulmate Jack Teagarden share a laugh onstage during the inaugural engagement of the All Stars at Billy Berg's in August 1947.
Courtesy of the Louis Armstrong House Museum

week guaranteed against 50 percent of the gross, already more lucrative than the big band. The Esquire All Stars made their debut on August 13, sharing the bill with saxophonist Jack McVea and vocalist Nellie Lutcher. "Louis Armstrong's opening at Billy Berg's last night was more like a Hollywood premier than a night club session," Dorothy Kilgallen wrote.[31] Among those in the crowd were Danny Kaye, Frank Sinatra, Benny Goodman, Hoagy Carmichael, Abe Lyman, Freddie Slack, Woody Herman, Buck and Bubbles, Sarah Vaughan, Woody Herman, Stan Kenton, Red Norvo, and Johnny Mercer. Pianist Jess Stacy had tears in his eyes, saying, "I can't tell you how happy this makes me."[32]

Reviewers were unanimously ecstatic. "Armstrong is playing again as he played several years ago, with imagination, a sharp attack and great technique," *Variety* gushed.[33] Over in the jazz press, John Lucas of *Down Beat* exclaimed, "Right now, more than ever before, Louis Armstrong is the real, the only King of Jazz!"[34] The black press took notice, too, with Herman Hill writing in the *Pittsburgh Courier*, "Beaming in complete satisfaction was Joe Glaser, Armstrong's manager who set the deal and convinced club owner Berg that he had the cure for his box office doldrums."[35]

That was an understatement. "Satchmo Socko," declared *Billboard* on the band's first week, noting "Armstrong pulled in over $12,000 for the management, of which a nice hunk is his, since he went on a $3,000-plus-percentage deal."[36] Originally booked for two weeks, Glaser was able to extend the engagement two more weeks into mid-September and start booking a tour for the new group in the fall, mixing nightclubs such as the Rag Doll in Chicago with concert halls such as Carnegie Hall and Symphony Hall. The jazz fraternity prepared to write a happy ending to the saga of Satchmo. As *Time* magazine declared, "Louis Armstrong had forsaken the ways of Mammon and come back to jazz."[37]

But had he? How does one come back to something they never really left? Hughes Panassie remembered "a famous person" remarking, "Pops, you made a wonderful come back." "A come back?" Armstrong asked. "Where was I?"[38]

The goodwill generated by Armstrong's small group debut at Billy Berg's only lasted a couple of weeks. Many of those celebrating assumed that the formation of the All Stars meant a return to the good old days of the 1920s and the Hot Five. But even within the small group format, Armstrong had learned too much during his big band period to throw it all away. He dug out older songs like "Muskrat Ramble" and "Black and Blue" but soon developed routines and "arrangements" for those numbers, performing them the same way each time out. He regularly featured his sidemen and made sure to find time for love songs and comedy numbers, even rehiring Velma Middleton so they could reprise their crowd-pleasing duets. That alone was enough to harm Armstrong's reputation with the moldy figs. Albert S. Otto of the *Record Changer* reviewed the All Stars at the Dixieland Jubilee in Pasadena in 1948 and complained about "some Uncle Tom stuff by Louis." "If Satch had any desire to kick over the traces, here certainly, at a Dixieland Jubilee, was his golden opportunity to do so," Otto wrote. "Everyone expected it, hungered for it. But no; the Armstrong unit gave the evening's most incongruous performance. Theirs was a vaudeville act."[39]

"Vaudeville" now became one of the most commonly hurled epithets at Armstrong, but he should have worn it as a badge of pride. Vaudeville taught Armstrong everything there was to know about the stage. It especially helped him in the pacing of his shows, though now he had to work harder than ever without an entire troupe of performers to fall back on. He still opened with a series of demanding trumpet specialties but did not rest during the sideman features, always present to back them up with trumpet riffs worthy of a big band. He would assume the role of the crooner when he sang material like "La vie en rose" or "The Gypsy" before turning into a comedian, telling one of his off-color jokes, such as the "alligator story" he got from blackface comedian George Williams. He later referred to his pianist as "Liberace in technicolor"; somewhere, Butterbeans and Susie were smiling. By applying the lessons he learned during the big band years, Armstrong ensured that the All Stars would remain in demand with the general public for the rest of his career. But ironically, Armstrong's shift to a small, traditional jazz setting diminished his popularity with his black fan base, who greatly preferred his contemporary big band sound to the inherently old-fashioned setup of the All Stars.

Armstrong also lost whatever goodwill remained with younger musicians and proponents of modern jazz when he decided to unburden himself of his true feelings on bebop during the initial Billy Berg's engagement. Except for his compliment of "re-bop" in the 1947 *Esquire Jazz Book*, he remained quiet, quiet through the attacks after the 1944 Metropolitan Opera House concert, quiet through Dizzy Gillespie's veiled shots in his January 1947 "Blindfold Test," quiet through all the various criticisms from various musicians in Feather's columns about all of those outdated, Uncle Tomming New Orleans musicians. Now, he could no longer remain silent. "Take them re-bop boys," he told *Time* magazine.

> They're great technicians. Mistakes—that's all re-bop is. Man, you've gotta be a technician to know when you make 'em. . . . New York and 52nd Street—that's what messed up jazz. Them cats play too much music—a whole lot of notes, weird notes. . . . That don't mean nothing. . . . You've got to carry a melody. Some cats say

Old Satch is old-fashioned, not modern enough. Why, man, most of that modern stuff I first heard in 1918. Ain't no music out of date as long as you play it perfect.[40]

Armstrong's remarks were published just as Dizzy Gillespie was about to perform at Carnegie Hall on September 29 in a concert produced by Leonard Feather. The concert was a sellout, a critical and commercial hit. Soon after, *Esquire*'s Gilbert S. McKean profiled Gillespie in a long piece, "The Diz and the Bebop." "Dizzy is a very lovable guy—it is said that he hasn't an enemy in the world," McKean wrote. "The Savoy Ballroom clique copy his walk, clothes, glasses, mustache and goatee, his laugh, his bizarre voice which often sounds off-pitch. It is startling to go to Harlem of late because you see a reasonably accurate facsimile of Dizzy everywhere."[41] If one substitutes the name "Louis" for "Dizzy" in that passage, it could have accurately described Armstrong's impact on Harlem just 15 years earlier.

With the tide turning toward Gillespie, black columnist Roy W. Stephens addressed Armstrong's *Time* comments in a syndicated column picked up by many black newspapers:

Armstrong is 47 years old, possibly too old to jam dozens of notes into a couple of bars at a nerve-wrangling tempo, possibly too old to rip off [a] cascade of rich, full and resonant tones, and possibly too old to remember when his own wonderfully-phrased solos brought a few nods of discord from persons whose ears had become accustomed to "progressive" music. . . . Because of his position in music and be-cause he has been—perhaps he still is—the glistening idol of countless youngers, Armstrong should be wary of discouraging these creative young minds merely because he seems to think "them cats play too much music—a whole lot of notes, weird notes that don't mean nothing." The statement itself is absurd.[42]

Armstrong and Gillespie were now embroiled in a bona fide rivalry. Armstrong let the in-fighting and criticism get to him in France in 1948, as he gave an emotional interview to George T. Simon, complaining, "You know, one trouble with the beboppers is that they can give it, but they can't take it! They tear you down, but if you say somethin' against them, they yell you're old fashioned and you don't know nothin' about jazz any more."[43] Ironically, Armstrong omitted one musician from his criticism: Gillespie. "I'd never play this bebop because I don't like it," he told Simon. "Don't get me wrong; I think some of them cats who play it real good, like Dizzy, especially."

Gillespie did not return the favor. After a concert at the Civic Opera House in Chicago in January 1949, Gillespie sat down for an interview with the Associated Negro Press and decided to give his own history on how bebop

Figure 23.2 From left to right: Dizzy Gillespie, Charles Carpenter, Louis Armstrong, Arvell Shaw, and Big Sid Catlett share a laugh at a nightclub in the late 1940s.
Courtesy of the Louis Armstrong House Museum

was created. "A couple of us who hated straight jazz used to get together at Minton's playhouse in New York and blow our brains out," Gillespie said. "We couldn't take any more of that New Orleans music. That was Uncle Tom music. It was for kids and birds. We simply had to get away from that!" The reporter asked about Armstrong and Bunk Johnson, who were now being lumped together. "They're squares," Gillespie said. "Man, how can you listen to that old-fashioned beat?"[44] The following month, when *Time* magazine needed a voice of dissent in a cover story on Armstrong, they found Gillespie. "Nowadays, we try to work out different rhythms and things that they didn't think about when Louis Armstrong blew," Gillespie said, referring to Armstrong in the past tense. "In his day all he did was play strictly from the soul—just strictly from his heart. You got to go forward and progress. We study."[45] After Armstrong appeared as King of the Zulus in New Orleans in March 1949, Gillespie told *Down Beat*, "Louis is the plantation character that so many of us . . . younger men . . . resent."[46]

There is no doubt that Gillespie's words further hurt Armstrong's reputation in the jazz and African American communities. But just as Gillespie was getting more brazen in his public attacks, he had to come to terms with an undeniable fact: the sound of bebop was not catching on with the general public. "We'll never get bop across to a wide audience until they can dance to it," he admitted. "They're not particular about whether you're playing a flatted fifth or a ruptured 129th as long as they can dance."[47] Unhappy with RCA Victor, Gillespie left the label in October 1949 with eight months remaining on his contract to sign with Capitol Records to begin recording material like "You Stole My Wife, You Horse Thief." At the same time, Charlie Parker had success with his album, *Charlie Parker with Strings*, with *Billboard* writing, "Jazz collectors, boppers or non-boppers equally, will find a great deal to delight in with these sides."[48] All of this was happening at the end of 1949, proof that for all the revolutionary aspects of bebop, at the end of the day, all musicians want to connect with a large audience. It had taken a few years, but Parker and Gillespie now learned the same lesson Armstrong did back in the 1930s: "[T]he music ain't worth nothing if you can't lay it on the public."[49]

But at the end of 1949, Armstrong topped both Parker and Gillespie and surprised everyone in the jazz and pop world by recording the biggest hit of his career to that point: a trumpet-free single of "That Lucky Old Sun" and "Blueberry Hill" for Milt Gabler at Decca Records. Gabler just applied an updated version of Tommy Rockwell's old formula to Armstrong's new sessions. Rockwell took the hottest pop sound of the day—Guy Lombardo's— and selected the best-known songs and watched Armstrong work his magic. Gabler took the hottest pop sound of the current day—Gordon Jenkins's—and hired Jenkins himself to start writing arrangements on pop tunes. By intelligently choosing the songs for him to cover and placing him in contemporary settings, Gabler was able to get Armstrong back on the charts regularly in the early 1950s. As he had done before—and would continue to do—Armstrong proved that he was bigger than jazz.

With the boost in popularity came more pushback from many in the jazz world, ever distrustful of success. In 1950, *Record Changer* editors William Grauer Jr. and Orrin Keepnews traveled to Armstrong's home in Corona to interview him for his 50th birthday. Since taking over the magazine in 1948, they gradually began relaxing its "moldy fig" policy, profiling modernists Tadd Dameron and Thelonious Monk—and taking aim at Armstrong. "[Armstrong] brought nothing with him but his exuberance, and a pretty commercialized, Uncle Tom version of it at that," Keepnews wrote of an All Stars performance in 1948. He was most disgusted by any and all hints of showmanship in the All Stars' act. "[W]hy then can't they just play some straight, shallow but unphonied music and get the hell off the stage," he demanded, adding that Armstrong's "responsibilities are to his art, and to all of jazz."[50]

Two years later, Keepnews and Grauer were now face-to-face with Armstrong. They turned the tape recorder on, just in time to hear an angry Armstrong bark, "That's what ruined *all* music, that 52nd Street."[51] It was clear that he had been waiting for years to unburden himself of some strong feelings about the state of jazz and where he saw it heading. "The only reason for bop, it comes from the soloists keeping the lead in their head and playing variations on their instruments," he vented. "So you get the variations and they keep the lead. . . . What good is that to the untrained ear? . . . Sure, it was created for the musicians. There's no point in that if you can't let somebody else know what you're playing outside of yourself." Armstrong grew nostalgic. "There's too many young players that skate; the old timers knew their instruments and they knew how to take advantage of the instrument," he said. "They were musicians among musicians in the old days."

Not that Armstrong believed the old-timers were faultless. Grauer brought up past *Record Changer* heroes like Bunk Johnson and Kid Ory, remarking that they continued staying true to the New Orleans traditional style but Armstrong had made "tremendous changes" in his playing "That's what I'm trying to tell you!" Armstrong exclaimed, knocking the choices of his elders. "Why would a musician want to stay in one style? I call it a rut! Because when I was coming through, I got a little taste of all kinds of music."

Grauer, feeling Armstrong's 1920s recordings with his Hot Five to be the pinnacle of his career, asked him point blank, "Which group would you rather play with, the group you're with now or the old Hot Five?"

"This group."

Almost incredulously, Grauer asked again, "You prefer this group to the old Hot Five?"

"See, the old Hot Five was all right but a little crude. They was a little crude. . . . We play them same records and they sound better." Continuing, he talked about the "arrangements" the All Stars played and how they played songs the same way every night. "See, that's the best part of jamming: remembering! See? We remember every riff we have to make together and that we think should stay in, it stays in, and we never forget it. . . . We don't tire people out with one number to the extent. . . . A number goes over five minutes, it gets monotonous. You better watch that."

Asked to choose between musicians past and present, Armstrong selected Jack Teagarden over Kid Ory, Barney Bigard over Johnny Dodds, and Arvell Shaw over Pops Foster, praising their ability to play in different styles and to command the stage in their feature spots. Keepnews finally grasped the trumpeter's philosophy: "In other words, what you have to do in this band is put on a show without losing anything in the music at the same time." "If we're going to give concerts, that's the only kind of band I've got to have," Armstrong replied. "We got to stand out there two hours and a half, three hours and play. You've got to get somebody more than just play ordinary."

Armstrong was offering sharp insights into his way of thinking, but he was also representing an endangered species: a black traditional jazz musician. Grauer asked, "How do you account for the fact that there are no young Negro bands playing New Orleans style and Dixieland style?" Armstrong shot back, "Why, I can tell you: they're 'overhip.' They think we're old-timers. We're old grandpas. They go according to our age." He continued:

> I had some trumpet players in my big band, making all that *fly* stuff. They just only respect me because they had to cause I was the leader. But with them, they feel I was an old man. But still in all, everything I played showed them that it was played right. So much for that. And I got respect from them for that. But still in all, within themselves, they don't think Dixieland is modern music. And Dixieland is just as good as any classic. That's the way Europe put them together. When you play Dixieland with full value, notes and tone, they appreciate that. But I mean, your young colored musicians, they figure, 'Why should I play like that? . . . It's old-timey.' "

He then grew dead serious as he discussed a slight hurled at him by one of his disciples. "A certain trumpet now that's making a good living playing Dixieland made a crack that I play '1918 trumpet.' I don't go to him and say, 'Why you'—you know what I mean? I just kept on blowing my horn *right*. And every time he get any decent hand at all, he's playing the same horn that I play—if he can." Asked to name the trumpet player, Armstrong did: Hot Lips Page. "And that same little cat," he said, "*I* was the one that was instilling everything in him cause when I played the Albee, way back there when I was headlining the RKO show [in 1931], he hung around me all day long backstage and we talked over things like that." His pride wounded, Armstrong continued, "Every time I look around, I was on Winchell's program, Al Jolson, your biggest chain programs—but still in all, I'm playing '1918 trumpet'? And he's walking the streets? So why fight a man like that?" Unable to hide his hurt, Armstrong immediately recalled his success on the radio during the big band years. He must have sensed that the jazz world was coming dangerously close to forgetting what he accomplished during the previous 20 years.

A lot of this was a result of the "jazz wars" of the 1940s, which petered out by 1950. Leonard Feather toned down his rhetoric over the years, admitting in his 1986 autobiography, "Controversy played a significant and in some ways helpful part in establishing my credentials; however, I lean towards the

328 Heart Full of Rhythm

view that the intramural fights of the 1940s were foolish and avoidable."[52] Still, the effects of such tactics could still be felt as jazz musicians continued to be placed in strict categorical boxes, never to mix with those outside of their preferred style.[53] In the early 1950s, Armstrong and Gillespie's public "feud" played out in their recordings, with Gillespie mocking Armstrong on "Pops' Confessin'," and Armstrong responding with a parody of "The Whiffenpoof Song" retitled "The Boppenpoof Song." Neither backed down as the 1950s wore on, with Armstrong continuing to slam bop in public, while Gillespie referred to Armstrong's "Uncle Tom–like subservience" in *Esquire* as late as 1957.[54]

But in the late 1950s, Gillespie and his wife Lorraine moved to Corona, Queens, living literally around the corner from Louis and Lucille Armstrong. Lucille and Lorraine were both friends going back to their days as dancers so as they fraternized, so did their husbands. As Gillespie began hanging out with his new neighbor, he had his big revelation, which he wrote about in his autobiography:

> Later on, I began to recognize what I had considered Pops's grinning in the face of racism as his absolute refusal to let anything, even anger about racism, steal the joy from his life and erase his fantastic smile. Coming from a younger generation, I misjudged him.[55]

Armstrong and Gillespie grew to be close friends and finally buried the musical hatchet with their immortal televised duet on "Umbrella Man" in 1959, neither man giving an inch or changing anything about their individual, groundbreaking styles. But in the second half of the performance, both men also revel in their natural talents as singers, showmen, and comedians, inducing waves of laughter from the studio audience just seconds after dazzling them with their virtuosity.

Armstrong and Gillespie remained friends until Armstrong's passing in 1971. "Never before in the history of black music had one individual so completely dominated an art form as the Master, Daniel Louis Armstrong," Gillespie wrote in a tribute in the *New York Times*, adding, "His melodic concept was as near perfect as possible, his rhythm impeccable. And his humor brought joy into the lives of literally millions of people, both black and white, rich and poor."[56]

Gillespie had spent years telling reporters that Armstrong had no influence on his playing and that he never even listened to his records. But in 1982, Gillespie named Armstrong as his favorite trumpeter of all time. In the accompanying article, Gillespie imparted his personal philosophy of performing: "When I play, I try to find out quickly what kind of mood the audience is in, and I'll sacrifice my feelings that night for the mood of the audience."[57] It turns out that Gillespie was a dedicated disciple to Armstrong after all. As he famously said of Armstrong, "No him, no me."

Perhaps it's better to ask, "No him—what then?"

Epilogue

"I Can't Give You Anything but Love"

Unlike the tragic endings that felled earlier black superstars and influences Bill Robinson (who died broke in 1949) or Bert Williams (who suffered from alcoholism and depression and died before the age of 50), Louis Armstrong continued thriving until his death in 1971. He made it a priority to not end up as they did, which is one reason he maintained total faith and loyalty in Joe Glaser. Glaser had spent much of the mid-1940s blinded by the spectacular success of other clients such as Les Brown and Lionel Hampton and though he kept Armstrong working, he didn't seem especially plugged into the struggles of his supposed number one client. That all changed after the establishment—and box-office success—of the All Stars. By the time Armstrong became the first jazz musician to appear on the cover of *Time* in February 1949, Glaser was quoted as saying, "I'm Louis and Louis is me. There's nothing I wouldn't do for him."[1] That is how it remained until the end of Glaser's life, though Associated Booking Corporation continued growing, bringing in clients ranging from Noël Coward to Barbra Streisand to Duke Ellington. Ellington knew that Glaser was perhaps the only agent who could keep a big band working steadily in the rock 'n' roll era, but he had reservations. "Joe Glaser doesn't care as much about me as he does Louis," Patricia Willard remembered Ellington saying. "He gives Louis better dates." Upon hearing that, long-time All Stars trombonist Trummy Young remarked, "Well, I don't think Joe Glaser cared as much about his own mother as he did Louis, if you really want to know the truth."[2]

Armstrong remained devoted to Glaser but the same could not be said of some of the other earlier influences in his life. Tommy Rockwell sued Armstrong in 1947 after Armstrong named Rockwell in Robert Goffin's *Horn of Plenty* as being a part of the gunpoint incident with the Immermans and Frankie Foster in Chicago in 1931. According to Armstrong, Rockwell realized he bit off more than he could chew and eventually said, "Just ask him to remove my name out of the book and forget it." "Yeah, he's going to raise so much hell," Armstrong said privately. "Let him do whatever he wants, I'm still going to tell it!"[3] Rockwell continued as an agent after parting ways with Cork O'Keefe and Joe Glaser, first as General Amusement Co. and later, General

Artists Corp, doing much work in television. The man who really set Louis Armstrong on the path toward being a pop star died of peritonitis in May 1958, just shy of his 57th birthday.

Johnny Collins disappeared after Glaser bought him out in 1935. He turned up booking vaudeville at the Star Theater in Portland, Oregaon in the late 1930s and early 1940s, moving to that city's Gaiety Theatre, in 1945. In 1953, Armstrong received a curious package from Collins at his home: a scrapbook Collins helped him compile of clippings related to Armstrong's first tour of England in 1932. "I guess he got tired of looking at them or there's a method in his madness," Armstrong told George Avakian in a privately recorded conversation soon after receiving it. "He just would be the type. You know what I mean, he's got something else in mind. . . . He's about broke, on his ass now." Armstrong did not respond to Collins, but instead knew where to turn. "So I told Mr. Glaser about it right away," he said. "I said, 'Now, you watch this motherfucker. You know I had trouble with him once. I had to pay $5,000 to him just to get his contract. $100 a week til I was blue in the face. So I don't want no part of him.' So he brings all these old fucking clippings about London and things. . . . Well, I appreciate that, but I don't want to get in close quarters with Johnny Collins because he done forgot all that shit we had in the ocean."[4] Clearly, Armstrong was not the type to forgive and forget—except in two instances.

In 1929, Louis, his wife Lil, and drummer Zutty Singleton were inseparable. When Louis received copies of his latest publicity photo, he signed one for Lil and one for Zutty. To Lil, he wrote, "To my Dear wife whom I'll love until I die." To Zutty, he inscribed it, "May we never part." The good times did not last, as Armstrong viewed Singleton as betraying him by staying at Connie's Inn at the end of 1929, while Lil and Louis separated in 1931. Armstrong did remain on good terms with both for several years, though he did all he could to avoid playing with them again.

But by the 1950s, Armstrong was growing more sensitive around these two important figures from his past. Perhaps his guard was up, hurt from what he viewed as unfair attacks from younger musicians and jazz critics, as well as the gradual abandonment of his African American audience. Now, you were either with Armstrong or you could go to hell. The publication of Mezz Mezzrow's *Really the Blues* in 1946 seemed to rip open Armstrong's old wounds with Singleton. Singleton didn't seem to realize there was a problem and campaigned to be the drummer in the All Stars, even sitting in with the band in 1954. "Wasn't that terrible?" Armstrong vented afterwards. "And he's the one who kept telling me he should be in my band. You know that boy's not all right for this shit, man, time has marched on. He'll never get in that band."

Joe Glaser even sensed something was wrong and asked Singleton, "What's wrong with you and Louie Armstrong? You all have an argument or something?" "No, we're the best of friends!" Singleton responded. "He done forgot that shit," huffed Armstrong.[5]

Regarding Lil, matters were a little more complex. She moved to Paris in the 1950s and had a happy reunion with Louis and Lucille there in 1952. When Louis returned in 1955, Lil met up with him in Brussels but to hear her tell it, something was off from the start. "I went back into his dressing-room, and he took one look at me and out of a clear blue sky said: 'Hump! For someone who went to Fisk University you sure don't know much,'" Lil recalled. "Lucille, his present wife, was there, and we just looked at each other, not knowing what was bugging him. So finally I said, 'For someone who went to Fisk University, I at least know one thing, and that's not to trouble myself over someone who didn't go to Fisk University.'" Lil decided to unburden herself of something she had been holding in for over 30 years. "And then I did something I never intended to do," she said. "I told him for the first time what Joe Oliver had told me about Louis being better than him even then. He was stunned. All his life he'd worshipped Joe Oliver, and now he was finding out for the first time how Oliver had tried to keep him buried. I thought he was going to cry, and so did Lucille, so she and I went out and got drunk together." When Lil and Lucille rejoined Armstrong, the press wrote about Armstrong traveling "with six musicians, two valets and two wives." "I thought it was pretty funny," Lil said in 1965, "but Louis was furious, and we haven't had much to say to each other since."[6] Armstrong remained angry enough to have trouble even saying her name. "A woman I knowed once, she was pretty smart and she was always rubbin' it into my mind she was smarter than I am, and I used to rub in her mind that one of my thoughts would bust her goddam brains from my experience, though she was the valedictorian of her class in some university," Armstrong told Gilbert Millstein in 1960. "I say, 'I think you an educated fool, you see, your ego makin' an ass out of you, chick.'"[7]

Louis remained estranged from both Hardin and Singleton for the next several years, but as the 1960s wore on, he grew tired and depressed, with mortality staring him dead in the eye. And in the final, declining years of his life, he made up with both crucial figures in his story.

Lil was first and seemed to have initiated the reconciliation herself. She now split her time between the home she bought with Louis in Chicago and their old vacation property in Idlewild, Michigan, purchased by Louis and given to Lil after they divorced. She talked about selling the Chicago home, but couldn't do it, because, as her friend Chris Albertson pointed out, "She would never admit, but it was hard for her to part with any reminder of Louis."

In June 1967, Lil surprised Louis before a performance in Highland Park, Illinois, holding court in his dressing room, reminiscing about their "wild" times in Idlewild. "Hey, Pops," Lil asked, "remember when you'd ride the horse in your bathing suit?" "And Pops would crack up," clarinetist Joe Muranyi recalled. "He'd crack up and Pops started chortling again and they got a little hysterical actually. Pops said, 'Would you excuse us?'. . . They shut the door and I could hear them scream inside, laughing and breaking up. It sounded like quite a fun, jolly moment." By 1970, Armstrong was ready to give Lil the credit she deserved. While setting the record straight for a biography being prepared by Max Jones, he admitted "that the woman was in my corner at all times," adding that Lil "did engineer my life" and "she had a perfect right to." "I listened very careful when Lil told me to always play the lead," he said. " 'Play second trumpet to no one. They don't come great enough.' And, she proved it. Yes sir, she proved that she was right, didn't she? You're damn right she did."[8]

After Louis's death in July 1971, Lil traveled to New York to attend his funeral, shaking her heat and repeatedly muttering that she "couldn't imagine Louis being dead."[9] Lucille Armstrong made sure Lil rode with her to the funeral. "If I had not put Lil in that family car," Lucille said, "I am sure Louis would have found a way to come back and haunt me."[10] Soon after, Lil was asked to perform at a memorial concert for her late ex-husband in Chicago on August 27. Cameras captured a beaming "Miss Lil" at the piano, stomping her way through "St. Louis Blues." At the conclusion of the number, she collapsed and died onstage. The photograph Louis inscribed, "To my Dear wife whom I'll love until I die" still hung in their home. The feeling was mutual.

Shortly after returning home in 1969 from his second stint in intensive care, Louis received word that Zutty Singleton suffered a debilitating stroke and would not be able to play again. Both men had come dangerously close to dying within months of each other, leading Louis to finally bury the hatchet. "And God, Louis loved Zutty," Marge Singleton said. "Now when Zutty got sick, Louis came here, and everything and was carrying on something awful and told me, 'Marge, I believe if Zutty would die, I think I'd kill myself.' " When Zutty returned home, Louis visited him and spotted the 1929 photo he had signed, "May we never part." "Well," he said, "we picking up from where we left off!" "And the way he bathed Zutty and wheeled him out to the house like Zutty was a piece of gold," Marge Singleton recalled. "And tried to shave him, tried to do everything. Because he knew Zutty loved him and he loved Zutty."[11]

Louis and Zutty's friendship blossomed again in the final year of Armstrong's life. Louis invited Zutty to be his guest in the audience during tapings of the *Tonight Show* and the *Mike Douglas Show*, making sure to introduce him on-air each time. The *Tonight Show* sent a black limousine to pick up the Armstrongs and Singletons. When it arrived, Louis helped Zutty into the car and marveled, "Look at this, isn't this something, isn't this something?" The two old New Orleans friends had come a long way. "Now, I mean, you know that showed he was still—didn't realize how big he was, you know," Marge admitted. "He really didn't. He was just such a down to earth, down to earth man."

In February 1971, Louis visited Zutty at his apartment and brought along his tape recorder, capturing the two men reminiscing about the old days, laughing like teenagers. Louis sounded like the life of the party but was ailing inside, complaining of shortness of breath to his doctor in private. In March, he finished two weeks at the Waldorf-Astoria—one night with Zutty present— and then had a major heart attack, needing a tracheotomy to survive. He was in the hospital for eight weeks, during which time Zutty was one of the few people allowed in to see him. "He wanted Zutty to the bitter end," Marge said.[12] Back home, Louis soon went back to his hobby of making reel-to-reel tape recordings. He made an entire reel of his recordings with Singleton, handwrote all the details, and sent it off to him. He died a short time later. "That was the real Louis," Zutty said after Armstrong died, "going to all that trouble because he knew it would cheer me up—even though he also knew he was dying himself, and don't let anybody tell you he didn't. But that, more than anything else, was what made him the greatest. He was the warmest, kindest man who ever lived and it all came out in his music." Armstrong's body lay in state at the Park Avenue Armory but Singleton "couldn't stand" to see him that way. "I want to remember Louis the way he was the last time I saw him in the hospital—that great big warm smile, in spite of all the pain, and still making everybody who came to see him feel good all over," he said.[13]

At the end of the day, that is what Louis Armstrong's life was all about: he made everybody who came to see him feel good all over. As Stanley Crouch put it, "He was a one-man carnival of joy."[14] In the fractious Civil Rights era of the 1950s and 1960s, feeling good was not enough for certain segments of Armstrong's audience. But one must remember that Armstrong's sense of humor developed in the dangerous, segregated, poverty-ridden "Battlefield" section of his New Orleans upbringing and it blossomed on stages around the world as a way of bringing great joy and laughter in the Great Depression. Invoking Ralph Ellison, Robert O'Meally wrote of "Ellison's law" in discussing Armstrong: "If blacks could laugh (even if only laughing to keep from crying), who could dare to frown?"[15] Armstrong lived through hell, through racism, was arrested multiple times, held at gunpoint, belittled, scorned, and resented yet through it all, he retained his laughter and the power to bring joy to audiences all over the world. As Armstrong said in 1933, jazz was "a reaction, because now we dare to laugh and smile—we got human dignity."[16]

Perhaps the best way to close is with a song. "When You're Smiling" is a natural choice to sum up Armstrong's mission in life but perhaps a more appropriate autobiographical text can be found in one of his own compositions:

Let the great think I'm small
I can laugh at them all
Cause I've Got a Heart Full of Rhythm

Acknowledgments

It was never my intention to write about Louis Armstrong in "backward" fashion. After my first book, *What a Wonderful World: The Magic of Louis Armstrong's Later Years*, was published in 2011, I honestly didn't think about writing another book about the trumpeter, instead focusing on ways to change perceptions of the All Stars years, giving lectures around the world, and producing numerous reissues and boxed sets. But while giving such lectures and in speaking with numerous musicians, I learned that it was Armstrong's middle period, the big band years, that really constituted uncharted territory for so many listeners and fans who only knew the 1920s masterworks and the popular albums and singles from the 1950s and 1960s.

With the seed planted, my agent and chum Tony Outhwaite supported moving forward with the idea. We found enthusiastic support at Oxford University Press, where Lauralee Yeary proved to be an unwavering advocate for my work and an excellent editor whose advice and insight was invaluable. Multiple memorable evenings were spent at Birdland with Tony and Lauralee and I cannot thank them enough for their encouragement during the researching and writing of this book.

I'm extremely fortunate make a living as director of research collections for the Louis Armstrong House Museum, but I've been even luckier to work with so many great colleagues over the years, including Sarah Rose, Hyland Harris, Adriana Filstrup, Pedro Espinoza, Junior Armstead, Rafael Castillo-Halvorssen, Ben Flood, Brynn White, Peter Moffett, Jennifer Walden-Weprin, B. J. Adler, and the late Michael Cogswell, not to mention all the wonderful docents and fellows who are devoted to the cause of Armstrong. Thanks also to Jeff Rosenstock at Queens College and Wynton Marsalis, Stanley Crouch, Jackie Harris, Robin Bell-Stevens, Robert O'Meally, and the rest of the Louis Armstrong Educational Foundation for their support.

My alma mater is Rutgers Newark and I was honored to receive a Berger-Carter-Berger fellowship to conduct research at the Institute of Jazz Studies. Big thanks to Vincent Pelote, Tad Hershorn, Elizabeth Surles, Adriana Cuervo, Angela Lawrence, and the rest of the staff for their assistance—and for the laughs!

An early draft of this book weighed in at an obscene 296,494 words. Thanks are in order to David Ostwald, Michael Steinman, Loren Schoenberg, Dan

Morgenstern, Sharone Carmona, and Marc Caparone for taking the time and energy to work through the manuscript and offer indispensable advice that hopefully have made the finished product a much more interesting and readable work. Extra thanks to David Ostwald for his friendship and advice and for opening up the "Riccardi Room" whenever it is needed! And just knowing Dan Morgenstern, Jack Bradley, and the late George Avakian has provided priceless insight into Armstrong the man. I treasure my friendships with all three and miss George tremendously.

Catherine Russell is not only my favorite living singer today, but also one of my favorite humans and a loyal friend. She and her husband Paul provided not just support, but also access to recordings, letters, and photos I never would have known about otherwise. Paul is doing wonderful work on Luis Russell, Catherine's father, and he was gracious enough to share his research, too.

Researching and writing is fun but the best way to experience Armstrong's genius is still to listen. I have been fortunate enough to have worked on over a dozen Armstrong releases in the past decade and have loved every moment spent in the company of producers such as Scott Wenzel of Mosaic Records, Harry Weinger of Universal, and Jerry Roche of Dot Time. More projects are planned at the time of this writing so I thank them for their dedication to Armstrong and for including me on the ride.

Perhaps the most gratifying experiences I've had regarding Armstrong have been through teaching. Thanks to Antonio Hart at Queens College and to Seton Hawkins at Jazz at Lincoln Center for giving me the opportunity to "preach" about Pops.

I'd be nowhere without my European contingent of Armstrong scholars, namely Björn Bärnheim, Håkan Forsberg, Sven-Olof Lindman, Peter Winberg, Franz Hoffman, Fernando Ortiz de Urbina, and two dear, departed friends and mentors, Gösta Hägglöf and Jos Willems. Extra special thanks to Jonathan David Holmes for his help in providing access to numerous rare important audio and video artifacts that greatly enriched my research. In New England, my thanks go to Matt Glaser, Andrew Sammut, Mick Carlon, Mike Persico, Phil Person, and Dave Whitney, and in New Orleans my thanks go to seemingly everyone, but especially to Jon Pult and my friends at French Quarter Festivals, WWOZ, the Louisiana Music Factory, and the New Orleans Jazz Museum.

There's literally too many other people to list, but I must take the time to thank Rich and Vicki Noorigian, Maxine Gordon, Randy Fertel, Stephen Maitland-Lewis, Joni Berry, Gary Giddins, Nicholas Payton, Jon Faddis, Laurelyn Douglas, Terry Teachout, James Karst, Donna and Perry Golkin, Jean-Francois Pitet, Dave and Sue Dilzell, Don Peterson, Ryan Maloney,

Maristella Feustle, Matt Snyder, Allen Lowe, Sascha Feinstein, Brendan Castner, Tom McGovern, Tracy Morgan, Shaun Redick, Yvette Yates, Reno Wilson, Mike Wellen, Bria Skonberg, Alphonso Horne, Phil Schaap, Matt "Fat Cat" Rivera, Steve Jordan, Chris Pizzolo, Denny Illet, Phil Dunlap, Dennis Lichtman, Vince Giordano, Dr. Colleen Clark, Byron Stripling, John Crocken, Lewis Porter, Andreas Meyer, David Adler, Adrian Cox, David Sager, Evan Christopher, Ted Gioia, Ted Panken, Marcia Salter, and anyone else who has supported my work, whether on social media or in person, over the years.

I commute 2.5–3 hours—one way—every day to go work. When people ask why I stay in Toms River, NJ, the answer is simple: family. Big love to my brother Jeff Riccardi, sister Michele Riccardi-Mees, nephews Connor Mees, Tyler Mees, and Nicky Riccardi, niece Gianna Riccardi, brother-in-law Gary Chrzan, and in-laws Joe and Anne Adams.

I would be absolutely nothing without the support of my parents, Dan and Marilyn Riccardi. They encouraged all of my bizarre interests, which started from a young age, and when I discovered Armstrong at the age of 15, they became fans of his, too. From my first lectures to my first book to all the CD releases and accomplishments at work, they have been there cheering me on the entire time. They're my biggest fans and I hope to always make them proud.

Finally, biggest thanks go to the ladies in my life, my wife Margaret, and my three daughters, Ella, Melody, and Lily. My kids weren't around the first time I wrote a book, but they were with me every step of the way this time. It wasn't easy for them, two straight years of trying to find time to research and write, in between my day job, teaching, producing, and commuting. "Daddy needs to write" became a common refrain as they'd see me hunched over the computer at all hours of the day. But I think they're excited to see the finished product and I hope they know that everything I do is motivated by my love for them. That especially goes for Margaret, who often had to pick up the slack in and around her own full-time job during the writing of this book. On our third date in 2004, I vowed to one day write a book on Louis Armstrong and assured her I would not make a lot of money if I chose this path; I was right on both counts, yet she loyally remains by my side! She and all three of our kids are simply the greatest—and all of them would kill me if I did not close by thanking our dogs, Frida, Daisy, and Louie, for their love and support, too.

Notes

Epigraph

1. Mel Watkins, "That Vaudeville Style: A Conversation with Honi Coles," *Alicia Patterson Foundation Reporter* 2, no. 6 (1979), http://aliciapatterson.org/stories/vaudeville-style-conversation-honi-coles.
2. Leonard G. Feather, " 'I Never Tried to Be God,' Cries Louis," *Music and Rhythm*, September 1941, 9..

Prologue

1. Abel Green, "Variety House Revues: Apollo, N. Y.," *Variety*, September 11, 1935, 16.
2. Walter Winchell, "On Broadway," *Reading Times*, September 5, 1935, 6.
3. "Armstrong Triumphs at the Apollo Theatre," *New York Amsterdam News,* September 7, 1935, 7.
4. "Armstrong Coming for Mammoth Benefit," *Pittsburgh Courier*, April 18, 1936, 17.
5. Isadora Smith, "Apollo Is Packin 'Em In; Reason!—Louis Armstrong," *Pittsburgh Courier*, May 20, 1939, 20.
6. "Wood," "Apollo, N. Y.," *Variety*, July 10, 1940.
7. Peter Suskind, "Stardust: 'Old Satchmo' Is More Than an Artist," *New Journal and Guide*, November 14, 1942, B24.
8. "Jose," "House Reviews: Apollo, N. Y.," *Variety*, April 25, 1945, 46.
9. "Louis Armstrong and Jack Teagarden Come to the Apollo," *New York Age*, July 5, 1947.
10. "House Reviews, Apollo, N. Y.," *Variety*, July 9, 1947, 18.
11. "House Reviews, Apollo, N. Y.," *Variety*, July 16, 1947, 41.
12. "Jose," "House Reviews: Apollo, N. Y.," *Variety*, December 31, 1952, 45.
13. Jack Schiffman, *Uptown: The Story of Harlem's Apollo Theatre* (New York: Cowles Book Company, 1971), 31–32.
14. Nicholas Payton, "I Love MJ but Satchmo Was the Original King of Pop," April 3, 2012. Accessed at http://nicholaspayton.wordpress.com/2012/04/03/i-love-mj-but-satchmo-was-the-original-king-of-pop/, December 30, 2016.
15. Rudi Blesh, *Shining Trumpets: A History of Jazz* (New York: Knopf, 1946), 257–258.
16. Private tape made with George Avakian, October 24, 1953. Courtesy of David Ostwald and George Avakian.
17. Gunther Schuller, *Early Jazz: Its Roots and Musical Development* (New York: Oxford University Press, 1968), 90.
18. Ibid., 130, 133.
19. Bill Grauer Jr. and Orrin Keepnews, "Louis on the Spot," *The Record Changer*, July–August 1950, 23. The only non–big band side Armstrong listed was "West End Blues."

20. Gunther Schuller, *The Swing Era: The Development of Jazz, 1930–1945* (New York: Oxford University Press, 1991), 158.

21. James Lincoln Collier, *Louis Armstrong: An American Genius* (New York: Oxford University Press, 1983), 342.

22. Ibid., 344.

23. Tape 1987.3.70, Louis Armstrong House Museum.

24. It should be noted that other writers such as Gary Giddins, Terry Teachout, Brent Hayes Edwards, and Stanley Crouch have been much more sympathetic to Armstrong's post-1928 output. But as recently as 2014, Thomas Brothers treated Armstrong as a fallen hero in his *Master of Modernism*, a fallen hero who had to live the rest of his life tortured by choosing what Brothers calls "The White Turn."

25. Even his longtime manager Joe Glaser admitted in 1939, "When a tune . . . comes along to be recorded the band works its head off, rehearsing it dozens of times over again. Then, we make the recordings in private session to pick out the flaws. After the clinkers have been removed then it's ready for a regular recording session, and we know that the coin machine operator is going to get a perfect product. That is how we operate. So far it's been successful." Joe Glaser, "To Make Better Records," *Billboard*, October 28, 1939, 13.

26. "Roses for Satchmo," *Down Beat*, July 1970, 19.

27. "Miles Davis Interviewed by Bill Boggs," 1986, https://www.youtube.com/watch?v=6XnLblYNfIg&t=2266s. Davis does offer some oft-quoted apprehensions about Armstrong's and Dizzy Gillespie's stage persona in his autobiography, but that work was heavily ghostwritten by Quincy Troupe. It's almost impossible to find examples of Davis himself actually critiquing Armstrong before that. See Ethan Iverson's 2014 blog post for more: https://ethaniverson.com/2014/03/11/louis-armstrong-and-miles-davis/.

28. *Jazz: A Film by Ken Burns*, episode 9, "The Adventure."

29. Fitzgerald's recording situation was the closest to Armstrong's as she recorded a similar run of pop and jazz material for Decca at the same time as Armstrong. Yet the narrative in jazz circles is that Norman Granz had to "rescue" her from Gabler in order to concentrate on jazz-centric recordings and the songbook series instead of any more pop records. Like Armstrong, Fitzgerald seemed perfectly happy making pop recordings for Decca. Nat Hentoff once wrote, "Left to herself, I think you would find Ella would pick many more of the pop hits of the day than she would material better suited to jazz." He could have said the same about Armstrong. Nat Hentoff, "Ella Fitzgerald: The Criterion of Innocence for Popular Singers." Reprinted in Dom Cerulli et al., *The Jazz World* (New York: Da Capo, 1963).

30. Jake Feinberg, "The Bobby Womack Interview," March 11, 2014, http://www.jakefeinbergshow.com/2014/03/jfs-152-the-bobby-womack-interview/.

31. Giovanni Russonello, "Louis Armstrong's Life as He Saw It," *New York Times*, November 18, 2018, A1.

32. Max Jones and John Chilton, *Louis: The Louis Armstrong Story, 1900–1971* (St. Albans: Mayflower, 1975), 228. Note: This book was originally published by Little, Brown and Company in 1971. An expanded paperback edition came out in St. Albans, England, by Mayflower in 1975 and in the United States by Da Capo in 1988. All page numbers refer to the expanded paperback editions.

Chapter 1

1. Stanley Dance, *The World of Earl Hines* (New York: Charles Scribner's Sons, 1977), 146.
2. Charlie Holmes, interviewed by Albert Vollmer, Jazz Oral History Project, October 11, 1982.
3. Lawrence Lucie, interview with Phil Schaap, July 1980, 2005.1.2155, Louis Armstrong House Museum.
4. Holmes, interviewed by Albert Vollmer, Jazz Oral History Project, October 11, 1982.
5. Danny Barker, *A Life in Jazz*, ed. Alyn Shipton (New Orleans: The Historic New Orleans Collection, 2016), 122.
6. Louis Armstrong, acetate disc of April 1950 interview for *The Record Changer*, 2013.70.27, Louis Armstrong House Museum.
7. Holmes, interviewed by Albert Vollmer, Jazz Oral History Project, October 11, 1982.
8. Louis Armstrong, acetate disc of April 1950 interview for *The Record Changer*, 2013.70.27, Louis Armstrong House Museum.
9. Bill Coleman, Jazz Oral History Project Manuscript, JOHP 24.4.1, 120.
10. Holmes, interviewed by Albert Vollmer, Jazz Oral History Project, October 11, 1982.
11. Lucie, interview with Phil Schaap, July 1980, 2005.1.2155, Louis Armstrong House Museum.
12. Coleman, Jazz Oral History Project Manuscript, JOHP 24.4.1, 120.
13. Holmes, interviewed by Albert Vollmer, Jazz Oral History Project, October 11, 1982.
14. Charlie Holmes, interviewed by Albert Vollmer, Jazz Oral History Project, December 5, 1982.
15. Armstrong, acetate disc of April 1950 interview for *The Record Changer*, 2013.70.3, Louis Armstrong House Museum.
16. Lucie, interview with Phil Schaap, July 1980, 2005.1.2155, Louis Armstrong House Museum.
17. Garvin Bushell, interview with Phil Schaap, July 1980, 2005.1.2155, Louis Armstrong House Museum.
18. "Disk Reviews," *Variety*, January 16, 1929. The specific records *Variety* reviewed were "Skip the Gutter" and "Knee Drops," released on OKeh's general series as OKeh No. 41157, and "Two Deuces" and "Squeeze Me," released on the race series as OKeh No. 8641.
19. OKeh Records Advertisement, *Pittsburgh Courier*, January 26, 1929, 2. On February 20, though, an OKeh ad for two more December tracks, "St. James Infirmary" and "Save It Pretty Mama," on the race series used a blackface caricature with copy written in dialect, "Yeah! It's 'St. James Infirmary. See dis Strutter! He's Jess like that. Jess like that! And he don't give a doggone whut you say 'bout his clothes." *New York Amsterdam News*, February 20, 1929, 8.
20. "Louis Armstrong Takes New York by Storm," March 15, 1929, clipping found in scrapbook 1987.8.83, Louis Armstrong House Museum.
21. Eddie Condon and Thomas Sugrue, *We Called It Music: A Generation of Jazz* (New York: Da Capo Press, 1992 edition), 199–200.
22. Lucie, interview with Phil Schaap, July 1980, 2005.1.2155, Louis Armstrong House Museum.
23. Louis Armstrong, interview with Phil Elwood in 1962, 1995.28.1, Louis Armstrong House Museum.

24. Mezz Mezzrow and Bernard Wolfe, *Really the Blues* (New York: New York Review Book Classics, 2010 edition), 256.

25. Larry L. King, *Harper's*, November 1967, 67.

26. Louis Armstrong, acetate discs of April 1950 interview for *The Record Changer*, Louis Armstrong House Museum.

27. Jay D. Smith and Len Guttridge, *Jack Teagarden: The Story of a Jazz Maverick* (London: Cassell, 1960), 75.

28. Kaiser Marshall, "When Armstrong Came to New York," *The Jazz Record* 52 (February 1947): 15.

29. Holmes, JOHP oral history, 1982.

30. Three years later, Ethel Waters delivered a note-perfect impersonation of Armstrong's vocal on her recording of the same song with Duke Ellington. But the effects are better felt when listening to Billie Holiday's 1936 recording of it, which is not an impersonation but features phrasing that would have been unthinkable without Armstrong's inspiration.

31. At this point, history differs as to what happened next. Every discography states that "I Can't Give You Anything but Love" was recorded on March 5, 1929, the same day as another tune, "Mahogany Hall Stomp." However, multiple musicians recalled the OKeh sessions being done in and around the Savoy engagement, which was March 2 and 3. And Charlie Holmes was adamant that "I Can't Give You Anything but Love" took up the entire session and the band had to get back to the Savoy for the second night and then returned to the studio the next day to record "Mahogany Hall Stomp." Though it differs from the discography, this is actually plausible. According to Condon, Rockwell had booked Eddie Lang for a session with Armstrong and the Luis Russell Orchestra but ended up using Lang for "Knockin' a Jug" instead and Lang wasn't available for the Russell date. Condon later joked that they "let me hold my banjo" on "I Can't Give You Anything but Love" but there is a clear banjo accompaniment throughout the record so they let him do more than "hold" it. But then on "Mahogany Hall Stomp," Lonnie Johnson is present throughout, soloing and providing counterpoint almost the entire time, something not heard on "I Can't Give You Anything but Love." Thus, the discographies might all be wrong and instead of a March 5, 1929, date for all, it seems more like "Knockin' a Jug" was recorded at 9 A.M. on March 3, "I Can't Give You Anything but Love" was recorded with Eddie Condon on banjo on the afternoon of March 3, and "Mahogany Hall Stomp" was recorded with Lonnie Johnson the following day, March 4, 1929.

32. Ad, *The Bee*, April 11, 1929, 9.

33. Ad, *Pittsburgh Courier*, April 13, 1929, 4. Perhaps the cleverest ad featured a fictional couple, "Ralph and Angie," offering their dialogue along with a drawing of the two characters. Ralph brags about this new recording of "I Can't Give You Anything but Love" and Angie responds, "Oh! That old thing . . . it's months old." "Wrong, my love!" says Ralph. "There have been others. But this is different. I have heard a hundred records just to find one that would delight the ears of our weary youths. And this one is a dazzle! Let me introduce you to Louis Armstrong and His Savoy Ballroom Five." Unconvinced, Angie agrees to listen but threatens, "But boy if it's a flop I'll hate you!" But after listening, she is won over. "Ralph darling," Angie offers. "I love you! I love you! I love. . . . 'I Can't Give You Anything but Love.' You say it's an Okeh record. Well, I always did say Okeh knows its rhythm! And I'm mad over Louis Armstrong's trumpet playing."

34. "Savoyisms," undated clipping found in scrapbook 1987.8.83, Louis Armstrong House Museum.

Chapter 2

1. Zutty Singleton, interviewed by Stanley Dance, Jazz Oral History Project, 1975.
2. "Louis Armstrong Electrifies," undated news clipping found in scrapbook 1987.8.83, Louis Armstrong House Museum.
3. Louis Armstrong, "The Goffin Notebooks," in *Louis Armstrong and His Own Words*, ed. Thomas Brothers (Oxford: Oxford University Press, 1999), 103.
4. Louis Armstrong, private conversation, c. March 1954, 1987.3.17, Louis Armstrong House Museum.
5. "It was all just ice and fog and snow," Singleton wrote, even though the trip was in May. "The falls were all frozen over. You could only hear the water gurgling underneath. So Louis said, 'Here we come all this way to see Niagara Falls and we're tired and hungry, and what happens? All we can do is hear 'em.'" Zutty Singleton, "Zutty First Saw Louis in Amateur Tent Show," *Down Beat*, July 14, 1950, 6.
6. "United States District Court. Southern District of New York. Louis Armstrong, Plaintiff, against Thomas G. Rockwell, Joseph N. Weber, et al., Defendants." Affidavit signed by Thomas G. Rockwell, August 26, 1931. 1996.50.1-05, Louis Armstrong House Museum.
7. Armstrong, "The Goffin Notebooks," 105.
8. Tape 1987.3.17, Louis Armstrong House Museum.
9. Armstrong, "The Goffin Notebooks," 105.
10. Tape 1987.3.17, Louis Armstrong House Museum. According to the CPI Inflation Calculator, $5,000 in May 1929 is the equivalent of $76,081.76 in February 2020.
11. Singleton, "Zutty First Saw Louis in Amateur Tent Show," 6.
12. Percival Outram, "Activities among Union Musicians," *New York Age*, June 8, 1929, 7.
13. Cootie Williams, Interviewed by Helen Oakley Dance, Jazz Oral History Project, Institute of Jazz Studies, Rutgers University, Smithsonian Institution, May 1976.
14. Louis Armstrong, acetate disc of April 1950 interview for *The Record Changer*, 2013.70.16, Louis Armstrong House Museum.
15. Mezzrow and Wolfe, *Really the Blues*, 225.
16. "Disk Reviews," *Variety*, January 16, 1929.
17. Connie's Inn and the Hudson Theater catered to white audiences, but Armstrong proved to be a sensation among black audiences in Harlem when he was booked as part of Addison Carey's "Move Along" revue at the Lafayette Theater, "America's Leading Colored Theater." According to the *New York Amsterdam News*, "The audience simply rose and cheered as this remarkable cornetist drew from his golden trumpet music such as has seldom been heard before here—rousing, snappy jazz and sweet, tender melody. Armstrong is certainly a genius." Observe, "At Harlem Theatres," *New York Amsterdam News*, June 26, 1929, 12.
18. Louis Armstrong and Zutty Singleton, tape-recorded conversation in February 1971, 2005.1.2209, Louis Armstrong House Museum.
19. Louis Armstrong, *Swing That Music* (London: Longmans, Green, and Co., 1936), 91.
20. Dave Peyton, "The Musical Bunch," *The Chicago Defender*, August 10, 1929, 7.
21. Barry Singer, *Black and Blue: The Life and Lyrics of Andy Razaf* (New York: Schirmer Books, 1992), 216–217.

22. On Ethel Waters's version, she actually doubled down on the song's female perspective, singing "Can't get a boyfriend," where Armstrong substituted, "Ain't got a friend."

23. Louis Armstrong with Richard Meryman, *Louis Armstrong: A Self-Portrait* (New York: The Eakins Press, 1971), 42.

24. Ralph Ellison, *Invisible Man* (New York: Random House, 1952), 8.

25. Peyton, "The Musical Bunch," August 10, 1929, 7.

26. Mezzrow with Wolfe, *Really the Blues*, 226–227. "Vipers" were marijuana smokers, a group that very much included Armstrong and Mezzrow, the latter becoming a famed dealer who sold it under Harlem's famed Tree of Hope. What was good for Armstrong became good for Harlem, and soon Armstrong's association with Mezzrow put marijuana on the map in New York.

27. "Armstrong Stirs the Nation Over Station W.C.F.L.," undated news clipping found in scrapbook 1987.8.83, Louis Armstrong House Museum.

28. Victoria Spivey, "The Louis Armstrong That I Know," *Record Research*, January 1963, 3.

29. Louis Armstrong, acetate disc of April 1950 interview for *The Record Changer*, 2013.70.16, Louis Armstrong House Museum.

30. Undated sheet music cover, found in scrapbook 1987.8.83, Louis Armstrong House Museum.

31. Walter Winchell, "On Broadway," *Scranton Republican*, December 2, 1929, 5.

32. Armstrong, "The Goffin Notebooks," 106.

33. Ibid.

34. Tape 1987.3.17, Louis Armstrong House Museum.

35. Mezzrow with Wolfe, *Really the Blues*, 252.

36. Tape 1987.3.17, Louis Armstrong House Museum.

37. Zutty Singleton and Marge Singleton, Interview with Stanley Dance, Jazz Oral History Project, 1975.

38. Louis Armstrong, acetate disc of April 1950 interview for *The Record Changer*, 2013.70.16, Louis Armstrong House Museum.

Chapter 3

1. Martin Williams, *Jazz Masters of New Orleans* (New York: Da Capo, 1978), 254.

2. Whitney Balliett, "The Blues Is a Slow Story," in *American Musicians II: Seventy-One Portraits in Jazz* (Jackson: University Press of Mississippi, 1986), 36.

3. Charlie Holmes, interviewed by Al Vollmer, Jazz Oral History Project, October 11, 1982.

4. Ibid. Holmes told this story as being "Mahogany Hall Stomp" but that song had nothing to do with Carmichael.

5. Billy Eckstine, interview with Steve Allen for BBC radio series, *Satchmo: The Wonderful World of Louis Armstrong*, c. 1973.

6. Schuller, *The Swing Era*, 165.

7. Dance, *The World of Earl Hines*, 147. Armstrong might not have been joking. The very next day, OKeh recorded "Song of the Islands" with a Hawaiian group, Kamala's Quartet; it's quite possible that they provided the background singing on Armstrong's recording. Also, Bernhard Behncke has argued that the band does not sound like the Russell band and admittedly, they do not, especially with the violins present. However, OKeh's records show

that Russell's recorded two numbers on January 24 without Armstrong, "Saratoga Shout" just before "Song of the Islands" and "Song of the Swanee" just after, so it makes sense to assume that they were set up for Armstrong's performance. But six days later, OKeh recorded the Stan Davis Hawaiian Ensemble's version of "Song of the Islands." It has not been possible to hear this version but one wonders if there's any similarities between their sound and arrangement of the song and Armstrong's.

8. Ibid, 225.

9. "C.G.B.," "New Acts Reviewed in New York," *Variety*, January 22, 1930. Found in scrapbook 1987.8.83, Louis Armstrong House Museum.

10. Conde G. Brewer, "Loew's State, New York," *The Billboard*, January 29, 1930. A slightly different version was signed "C.G.B." as "New Acts Reviewed in New York," *Variety*, January 22, 1930. Both are to be found in scrapbook 1987.8.83, Louis Armstrong House Museum.

11. "Loew's State Track," *Zit's Theatrical Newspaper*, January 29, 1930.

12. "Louis Armstrong Is Sensation in Home-Coming," *Chicago Defender*, February 15, 1930, 7.

13. Ad for Max's Suits and Overcoats, found in scrapbook 1987.8.83, Louis Armstrong House Museum.

14. Ad for Porter's Premier, *Chicago Bee*, found in scrapbook 1987.8.83, Louis Armstrong House Museum.

15. "Bud Billiken To Stage Party For Kiddies Feb. 15th," *Chicago Savoyager*, undated clipping found in scrapbook 1987.8.83, Louis Armstrong House Museum.

16. "J. H. Pleasure Banquets Elites," February 9, 1930, found in scrapbook 1987.8.83, Louis Armstrong House Museum.

17. Louis Armstrong, letter to Luis Russell, February 17, 1930, reprinted in Paul Kahn, *Call of the Freaks: Luis Russell & Louis Armstrong—Musical Pals*, master's thesis, Rutgers University-Newark, May 2018.

18. "What About It Folks?," undated news clipping found in scrapbook 1987.8.83, Louis Armstrong House Museum.

19. Walter Winchell, "Walter Winchell on Broadway," *New York Daily Mirror*, March 14, 1930, found in scrapbook 1987.8.83, Louis Armstrong House Museum.

20. "My Sweet" even displays a touch of Al Jolson in his vocal, which shouldn't be surprising since Armstrong was a fan and already displayed some of Jolson's influence on his 1926 "Big Butter and Egg Man" record. In a privately recorded conversation with friends in 1964, Armstrong asked, "How do you like Al Jolson's work? Wasn't he something? Goddamn, I love him!" Armstrong then named his three big favorites—"Al Jolson, Bill Robinson and Bing [Crosby]"—before adding, "There's something about Jolson, boy." Louis Armstrong, conversation with the Shoniker family, 1964, tape 2003.200.1, Louis Armstrong House Museum.

21. Bob Landry, "Disc Reviews," *Variety*, found in scrapbook 1987.8.83, Louis Armstrong House Museum.

22. Jones and Chilton, *Louis*, 266, 268.

23. "Mike" [Spike Hughes], "Armstrong's Best Ever," *The Melody Maker*, January 6, 1934, 5.

24. Levi H. Jolley, "Dance Halls," *Baltimore Afro-American*, May 3, 1930, 8.

25. Krin Gabbard, *Jammin' at the Margins: Jazz and the American Cinema* (Chicago: University of Illinois Press, 1996), 143.

26. Dance, *The World of Swing*, 82.

27. Sy Oliver, interview with Steve Allen for BBC radio series, *Satchmo: The Wonderful World of Louis Armstrong*, c. 1973.

28. Dance, *The World of Swing*, 79–80.

29. Undated clipping in *Variety*, found in scrapbook 1987.8.83, Louis Armstrong House Museum.

30. Advertisement in *Variety*, May 14, 1930, 44.

31. "United States District Court. Southern District of New York. Louis Armstrong, Plaintiff, against Thomas G. Rockwell, Joseph N. Weber, et al., Defendants." Affidavit signed by Thomas G. Rockwell, August 26, 1931. 1996.50.1-05, Louis Armstrong House Museum.

32. "United States District Court. Southern District of New York. Louis Armstrong, Plaintiff, against Thomas G. Rockwell, Joseph N. Weber, et al., Defendants." Affidavit signed by Louis Armstrong, July 9, 1931. 1996.50.1-06, Louis Armstrong House Museum.

33. "Farewell Party for Louis Armstrong," undated clipping found in scrapbook 1987.8.73, Louis Armstrong House Museum.

34. Armstrong, "The Goffin Notebooks," 107.

35. "San Francisco Radio Notes," *Inside Facts of Stage and Screen*, March 8, 1930.

36. Louis Armstrong, "The Satchmo Story," c. 1959, 1987.2.4, Louis Armstrong House Museum, 4.

Chapter 4

1. One such act caught "Johnny's fancy" in 1910 at Ramona Park in Grand Rapids, Michigan. It was called "Dunk the Coon" and *Variety* provided the details: "On the branch of a prop tree sat a 'coon.' Beneath him was a pool, and on the side of the tree trunk a small disk marked 'target.' Three balls allowed a customer. When one hits the target, the live 'coon' drops in the tank below. If the colored fellow doesn't drop during the first three balls thrown, the operator of the concession will sell three more, upon proper application." The article concluded, "Mr. Collins . . . thought so well of the amusement they have been secured the Eastern rights for parks and fairs." *Variety*, August 8, 1910, 6.

2. *Variety*, December 3, 1910, 5.

3. "Collins-Fischers Agency," *Variety*, July 19, 1912, 4.

4. "Collins Loses Franchise," *Variety*, November 14, 1928, 35.

5. Private tape made with George Avakian, October 24, 1953. Courtesy of David Ostwald and George Avakian.

6. "Johnny Collins on Coast," *Variety*, June 4, 1930, 50.

7. Louis Armstrong, "The Satchmo Story" (c. 1955 edition), 1987.2.117, 20, Louis Armstrong House Museum, 20. Louis Armstrong wrote two unpublished documents, with some overlapping stories, called "The Satchmo Story," one c. 1955, the other c. 1959. The California story is told in both with differing details in each. The dates of each specific manuscript will be referenced in the endnotes.

8. "Armstrong Ends Chicago Engagement at the Savoy," undated news clipping from 1931 found in scrapbook 1987.8.83, Louis Armstrong House Museum.

9. Armstrong, "The Satchmo Story" (c. 1959 edition), 4.

10. Armstrong, "The Satchmo Story" (c. 1955 edition), 20.

11. Armstrong, "The Satchmo Story" (c. 1959 edition), 5.

12. Armstrong, "The Satchmo Story" (c. 1955 edition), 20.

13. Armstrong, "The Satchmo Story" (c. 1955 edition), 20

14. There's controversy surrounding the first name of this obscure musician as many refer to him as "Leon" while others refer to him as "Vernon"; Lionel Hampton referred to him as both names at different times over the years. It's possible there was confusion with saxophonist Leon Herriford, who fronted the band.

15. Louis Armstrong, acetate disc of April 1950 interview for *The Record Changer*, 2013.70.1, Louis Armstrong House Museum.

16. Armstrong, "The Satchmo Story" (c. 1959 edition), 5.

17. Louis Armstrong, acetate disc of April 1950 interview for *The Record Changer*, 2013.70.27, Louis Armstrong House Museum.

18. Armstrong, "The Goffin Notebooks," 107.

19. Twenty-four years later, Armstrong wrote to Hampton, "You sure do need a car to leave Central Avenue to get to the Cotton Club and I sure did appreciate it!" Lionel Hampton, "Show Biz Buzzes," *Pittsburgh Courier*, January 9, 1954, 19.

20. Armstrong, "The Goffin Notebooks," 107.

21. Louis Armstrong, letter to unknown recipient, 1987.9.9, Louis Armstrong House Museum.

22. Armstrong, "The Goffin Notebooks," 107.

23. Louis Armstrong, Interview with Irwin Johnson on March 6, 1953, 1996.47.1, Louis Armstrong House Museum. When the record came out, the label only credited Jimmie Rogers "Singing with Orchestra." There was always speculation that it was Louis on trumpet. In 1962, the Jimmie Rodgers Society sent him a tape of "Blue Yodel Number 9" and remarked that the original recording ledger had a note, "Lillian on piano." Louis himself had forgotten about it until collector Joe Mares Jr. gave him a copy in 1952. Louis introduced the record on one of his tapes, saying, "Folks, this is Louis Armstrong. I'd like to interrupt through here and play a record of Jimmie Rodgers, the yodeler, with orchestra. I made a record with Jimmie, oh, about 20 years ago and I'm still looking for it." After listening, Armstrong says, "Well, well, well, can you beat that!? I was just talking about how I was looking for this record and it happened to be on the other side and the title is 'Blue Yodel Number 9 (Standing on the Corner),' Jimmie Rodgers, yodeler with guitar, strings and bass.' And the trumpet must be a surprise because I was looking for this record. Now, that knocked me out. . . . ump ump ump."

24. "Armstrong Is Hit in Debut at Sebastian's," *Los Angeles Evening Herald*, July 19, 1930, found in scrapbook 1987.8.83, Louis Armstrong House Museum. It's very possible that Armstrong and Hampton first made use of Hampton's vibraharp on "Song of the Islands." Before Armstrong came to California, Hampton said he used to play Armstrong's solo on that song on the vibes. Armstrong heard him do it and according to Hampton, "That knocked him out, and he said to me, 'When I sing, you play behind me like that.' " In Dance, *The World of Swing*, 268.

25. W. E. Oliver, "Louis Armstrong Sensation at Trumpet," *Los Angeles Evening Herald*, July 21, 1930, found in scrapbook 1987.8.83, Louis Armstrong House Museum.

26. "Brooks' Colored Revue," *Variety*, July 26, 1930.

27. Untitled clipping in *Los Angeles Evening Herald*, July 25, 1930, found in scrapbook 1987.8.83, Louis Armstrong House Museum.

28. Frankeye Marilyn Whitlock, "Coast Breezes," undated news clipping found in scrapbook 1987.8.83, Louis Armstrong House Museum.

29. Bill Coleman, Jazz Oral History Manuscript, 143.

30. Dance, *The World of Swing*, 270.

31. Peter Vacher, *Swingin' on Central Avenue: African American Jazz in Los Angeles* (Lanham, MD: Roman & Littlefield, 2015), 113.

32. Hampton, "Show Biz Buzzes," 19.

33. Louis Armstrong, letter to unknown recipient, 1987.9.9, Louis Armstrong House Museum.

34. Mezzrow and Wolfe, *Really the Blues*, 225.

35. Jones and Chilton, *Louis*, 131. For a more detailed look at both recordings, see http://dippermouth.blogspot.com/2015/08/85-years-of-confessin-and-if-i-could-be.html.

36. Buck Clayton, interview with Steve Allen for BBC radio series, *Satchmo: The Wonderful World of Louis Armstrong*, c. 1973. The impact of this solo on a generation of jazz musicians could still be felt decades later, when British writer Steve Voce played Armstrong's recording backstage at a concert featuring various Swing Era musicians in 1967. "Immediately a choir of Buck Clayton, Earle Warren, Vic Dickenson and Roy Eldridge began to sing the solos and the vocal along with the tape, not one of them had forgotten a note," Voce wrote. Steve Voce, *Jazz Journal*, May 1967.

37. Lawrence Brown, Jazz Oral History Project.

38. Jones and Chilton, *Louis*, 128.

39. Dance, *The World of Swing*, 270.

40. *Satchmo: The Wonderful World of Louis Armstrong*, Episode 4, BBC Radio, January 19, 1975.

41. *Satchmo: The Wonderful World of Louis Armstrong*, Episode 4, BBC Radio, January 19, 1975.

42. Cootie Williams, Jazz Oral History Project.

43. "Sebastian Signs New Musical Director For Cotton Club," *Los Angeles Evening Herald*, July 29, 1930, found in scrapbook 1987.8.83, Louis Armstrong House Museum.

44. "Hamer," *Inside Facts of Stage and Screen*, August 16, 1930.

45. Louis Armstrong, acetate disc of April 1950 interview for *The Record Changer*, 2013.70.1, Louis Armstrong House Museum.

46. Frankeye M. Whitlock, "Coast Breezes," *The Chicago Defender*, August 30, 1930, 5.

47. "United States District Court. Southern District of New York. Louis Armstrong, Plaintiff, against Thomas G. Rockwell, Joseph N. Weber, et al., Defendants." Affidavit signed by Louis Armstrong, July 9, 1931. 1996.50.1-06, Louis Armstrong House Museum.

48. Ibid.

49. Armstrong, "The Goffin Notebooks," 108.

50. "Armstrong in Flame," *Inside Facts of Stage and Screen*, September 13, 1930.

51. Jones and Chilton, *Louis*, 128.

Chapter 5

1. Vacher, *Swingin' on Central Avenue*, 111.

2. Louis Armstrong, letter to Max Jones, August 15, 1970, read out loud by Armstrong on tape 1987.3.424, Louis Armstrong House Museum.

3. Louis Armstrong, "The Satchmo Story" (c. 1959 edition), 1987.2.4, Louis Armstrong House Museum, 3.

4. Tape 1987.3.424, Louis Armstrong House Museum.

5. Vacher, *Swingin' on Central Avenue*, 54.

6. Tape 1987.3.424, Louis Armstrong House Museum. The detectives then told Armstrong he was ratted on by another "band leader—who probably smoked marijuana himself—who is playing just up the road from you. . . . But he was jealous because you were doing bigger business than him." Armstrong never broke the detective's confidentiality and revealed the name of the bandleader who ratted him out but it's quite possible that it was George Olsen. Olsen opened his own supper club in Culver City, the Plantation Cafe, in March 1930 and immediately attracted a plethora of Hollywood stars—the same stars who flocked to hear Armstrong at the Cotton Club just a few months later. In September, *Variety* ran a blurb that "Louis Armstrong, colored trumpet tooter at the Cotton Club is giving George Olsen a run for Culver City money." Two days later, another newspaper reported, "Louie at the Cotton club is drawing great ofay crowds while George Olsen and his orchestra, an ofay star unit, is struggling to keep with the cornetist." Armstrong never publicly admitted it was Olsen but one can imagine that Olsen did not appreciate being called out in the press as to losing business to Armstrong. Untitled news clipping with September 19, 1930, dateline, found in scrapbook 1987.8.83, Louis Armstrong House Museum.

7. Chappy Gardner, "Coronetist Held in Big Dope Catch," *Pittsburgh Courier*, December 6, 1930, 1.

8. Jones and Chilton, *Louis*, 129.

9. Armstrong also calls Hampton "Satchelmouth," pronouncing it "Satch-a-mouth" in a way that could possibly be misinterpreted as "Satch-a-mo'" to listeners unfamiliar with Armstrong's nicknames, leading credence to Armstrong's claim that he got the nickname "Satchmo" from Percy Brooks, who couldn't decipher "Satchelmouth" on his records.

10. Undated news clipping from San Francisco, found in scrapbook 1987.8.83, Louis Armstrong House Museum.

11. James Lincoln Collier, *Louis Armstrong: An American Genius* (New York: Oxford University Press, 1983), 179.

12. "Thomas G. 'Tommy' Rockwell," message board posting on June 9, 2008, at https://weeniecampbell.com/yabbse/index.php?topic=4982.0.

13. "Four Mills Brothers," *Variety*, October 27, 1931, 58.

14. "At the Odeon Theatre," *New York Age*, February 28, 1931, 6. "For Sixty Years the World's Most Famous Love Story," *The Tribune*, March 8, 1931, 14.

15. Harry Lovette, "Movie Lot Gossip," *Pittsburgh Courier*, February 7, 1931, 18.

16. Tape 1987.3.562, Louis Armstrong House Museum.

17. Walter Winchell, "On Broadway," *New York Daily Mirror*, undated news clipping found in scrapbook 1987.8.83, Louis Armstrong House Museum.

18. Jones and Chilton, 131.

19. "Smoking 'Reefers,' Dope Got Louis Armstrong, Negro Musician, 1 Mo.," *Variety*, March 25, 1931.

20. "Harlem's 'Deadly Reefer' Cigarettes Are Only Plain Hemp," *Afro-American*, April 25, 1931, 9.

21. Ibid.

22. "Hollywood," *Variety*, March 25, 1931, 67.

23. Tape 1987.3.424, Louis Armstrong House Museum.

24. Ibid.

25. Preston Jackson, *Trombone Man: Preston Jackson's Story as Told to Laurie Wright* (England: L. Wright, 2005), 96–97.

26. Armstrong, "The Goffin Notebooks," 109.

27. Ibid.

28. Ibid.

29. "Jail Musician for Blackmail of Armstrong," undated news clipping found in scrapbook 1987.8.83, Louis Armstrong House Museum.

30. "Song Writer for Thompson Held to Jury," undated news clipping found in scrapbook 1987.8.83, Louis Armstrong House Museum.

31. "United States District Court. Southern District of New York. Louis Armstrong, Plaintiff, against Thomas G. Rockwell, Joseph N. Weber, et al., Defendants." Affidavit signed by Louis Armstrong, July 9, 1931. 1996.50.1-06, Louis Armstrong House Museum.

32. Collier, *Louis Armstrong: An American Genius*, 225.

33. Armstrong, "The Goffin Notebooks," 110.

34. Tape 1987.3.254, Louis Armstrong House Museum.

35. Armstrong, "The Goffin Notebooks," 110. In his 1931 affidavit, Armstrong identified it as Connie but in a private conversation from c. 1951, he said it was George Immerman on the phone.

36. "United States District Court. Southern District of New York. Louis Armstrong, Plaintiff, against Thomas G. Rockwell, Joseph N. Weber, et al., Defendants." Affidavit signed by Louis Armstrong, July 9, 1931. 1996.50.1-06, Louis Armstrong House Museum.

37. Larry L. King, "Everybody's Louie," *Harper's*, November 1967, 68.

38. George James and Laurie Wright, "George James, no relation to Harry . . .," *Storyville 86*, December 1979–January 1980, 49.

39. Collier, *Louis Armstrong: An American Genius*, 225.

40. Tape 1987.3.254, Louis Armstrong House Museum.

41. Ibid.

42. Ibid.

43. "Gang Threats Make Cornet Player Tremble in Rhythm!," undated news clipping found in scrapbook 1987.8.83, Louis Armstrong House Museum.

44. Rudy Vallee, "Tuneful Topics," *Radio Digest*, Summer 1931, 53. In a later column, Vallee wrote that Armstrong's version of "*I Surrender Dear* usually sends those who listen to it for the first time into gales of laughter." Rudy Vallee, "Tuneful Topics," *Radio Digest*, December 1931, 94.

45. Lewis Porter, "Hear the Earliest Surviving Radio Broadcast by Duke Ellington, A Historic Find, in Deep Dive," October 4, 2018, http://www.wbgo.org/post/hear-earliest-surviving-radio-broadcast-duke-ellington-historic-find-deep-dive#stream/0. *Radio Doings*, February 1932, 28.

46. Leon Rene, "A Story of 'When It's Sleepytime Down South,'" found on the backside of a special edition of the sheet music of "When It's Sleepy Time Down South," published after Louis Armstrong's death in 1971.

47. Vallee, "Tuneful Topics," December 1931, 94.

48. Tape 1987.3.19, Louis Armstrong House Museum.

49. Eight days later, on April 28, Armstrong recorded another song aimed at his black audience, "Little Joe." This one was written by white writers Jule Styne and Ned Miller and was filled with what soon became unfashionable references to a "kinky-headed baby" and "papa's little colored sonny boy." But like Al Jolson's "Sonny Boy," the protagonist of the song is offering nothing but love to his black offspring trying to navigate the cruel, racist

world. "I will always love you til the judgement day," he sings. "Even though the white folks may think nothing of you, and they always chase you away." Armstrong's black audiences would have gotten the message in 1931, but the stereotypes in the lyrics eventually rendered it taboo and it remains little known to this day.

50. Club Madrid advertisement, *The Courier-Journal*, May 13, 1931, 22.
51. Untitled, undated news clipping found in scrapbook 1987.8.83, Louis Armstrong House Museum.
52. "United States District Court. Southern District of New York. Louis Armstrong, Plaintiff, against Thomas G. Rockwell, Joseph N. Weber, et al., Defendants." Affidavit signed by Louis Armstrong, July 9, 1931. 1996.50.1-06, Louis Armstrong House Museum.

Chapter 6

1. "Savoy Packed to Welcome Armstrong," undated news clipping found in scrapbook 1987.8.83, Louis Armstrong House Museum. First reference to, " 'Little' Joe Lindsay is traveling with 'Louie.' "
2. Club Madrid advertisement, *The Courier-Journal*, 22.
3. James and Wright, "George James, no relation to Harry . . .," 50. It wasn't without incident as trombonist Preston Jackson recalled Armstrong ran into "another little bit of trouble" there when a white woman began calling out, "Louis, Oh Sweet Louis!" "That being in prejudiced Louisville kind of set up Louis and the band," Jackson said. "So, at intermission Louis hid in the dressing room and this woman came looking for him. Finally, she said she did not like what Louis did; Paul Whiteman did not act that way." Jackson, *Trombone Man*, 101.
4. Zilner Randolph, Interview with Don DeMichael, Jazz Oral History Project, February 13, 1977.
5. Armstrong, "The Goffin Notebooks," 108.
6. "Plan Jubilee for Armstrong in N. Orleans," June 5, 1931, news clipping found in scrapbook 1987.8.5, Louis Armstrong House Museum.
7. Armstrong, "The Satchmo Story" (c. 1955 edition), 15.
8. "Crowd Struggles to See Cornetist," *New Orleans Times Picayune*, June 7, 1931, found in scrapbook 1987.8.5, Louis Armstrong House Museum.
9. "United States District Court. Southern District of New York. Louis Armstrong, Plaintiff, against Thomas G. Rockwell, Joseph N. Weber, et al., Defendants." Affidavit signed by Louis Armstrong, July 9, 1931. 1996.50.1-06, Louis Armstrong House Museum.
10. Faith Dawson, "Pops, on a 'Flight' from Chicago," *New Wave*, July 30, 2015. https://www2.tulane.edu/news/newwave/073015_satchmo-summerfest-new-orleans-raeburn.cfm?RenderForPrint=1. The information on Boasberg comes from Bruce Raeburn, longtime curator of the Hogan Jazz Archives. But according to the website http://www.marlowcasinochips.com/links/genetrimble/illegaloftheday/CipangoClubTX.pdf, the Suburban Gardens was owned by Joe W. Brown, who later took over the Las Vegas Horseshoe Club in the 1950s. Either way, it was a high-powered, well-connected figure from the world of gambling who owned the venue.
11. "United States District Court. Southern District of New York. Louis Armstrong, Plaintiff, against Thomas G. Rockwell, Joseph N. Weber, et al., Defendants." Affidavit signed by Louis Armstrong, July 9, 1931. 1996.50.1-06, Louis Armstrong House Museum.

12. Preston Jackson, *Satchmo: The Wonderful World of Louis Armstrong*, Episode Four, broadcast on BBC Radio, January 19, 1975.

13. Jackson, *Trombone Man*, 103.

14. "United States District Court. Southern District of New York. Louis Armstrong, Plaintiff, against Thomas G. Rockwell, Joseph N. Weber, et al., Defendants." Affidavit signed by Louis Armstrong, July 9, 1931. 1996.50.1-06, Louis Armstrong House Museum.

15. James and Wright, "George James, no relation to Harry...," 50–51.

16. Armstrong, "The Satchmo Story" (c. 1955 edition), 15.

17. Ibid., 16.

18. *The Dick Cavett Show*, July 29, 1970.

19. Ibid.

20. Armstrong, "The Satchmo Story" (c. 1955 edition), 16.

21. Ibid. The identity of the announcer as Charles Nelson was discovered by Swedish jazz historian Björn Bärnheim. Bärnheim also found a clipping stating, "Charles Nelson is back at Suburban Gardens as program director and announcer for radio periods." Clearly, Nelson was reinstated after being fired. Mel Washburn, "The Spotlight," *The Morning Tribune*, June 25, 1931, 16. Courtesy of the Björn Bärnheim Collection.

22. Armstrong, "The Satchmo Story" (c. 1955 edition), 17.

23. Ibid.

24. Mel Washburn, "The Spotlight," *The Morning Tribune,* found in scrapbook 1987.8.5, Louis Armstrong House Museum.

25. Mel Washburn, "The Spotlight," *The Morning Tribune*, June 9, 1931, found in scrapbook 1987.8.5, Louis Armstrong House Museum.

26. James and Wright, "George James, no relation to Harry...," 50.

27. Jackson, *Trombone Man*, 103.

28. "Armstrong, Wizard of the Cornet, Former Item Newsie; Used to Live at Waifs' Home," *New Orleans Item*, June 14, 1931, found in scrapbook 1987.8.5, Louis Armstrong House Museum.

29. Ibid.

30. Robert B. McElree, Letter to Louis Armstrong, June 11, 1931, found in scrapbook 1987.8.5, Louis Armstrong House Museum.

31. Armstrong, "The Satchmo Story" (c. 1955 edition), 19.

32. Zilner Randolph, JOHP interview.

33. Jones and Chilton, *Louis*, 149.

34. Ibid., 150.

35. Armstrong, "The Satchmo Story" (c. 1955 edition), 18.

36. James and Wright, "George James, no relation to Harry....," 51.

37. Jackson, *Trombone Man*, 106.

38. "Louis . . . by his friends," *Storyville 59* (June–July 1975): 182–183.

39. James and Wright, "George James, no relation to Harry...," 51.

40. Armstrong, "The Satchmo Story" (c. 1955 edition), 18.

41. Jackson, *Trombone Man*, 115–116.

42. Armstrong, "The Satchmo Story" (c. 1955 edition), 17.

43. Armstrong, "The Satchmo Story" (c. 1955 edition), 18.

44. "Lads That Louis Armstrong Dyked Up Are Whitewashed," undated news clipping found in scrapbook 1987.8.5, Louis Armstrong House Museum.

45. Armstrong, "The Satchmo Story" (c. 1955 edition), 18. Armstrong did get himself into hot water by promoting one of the Secret Nine's games on the radio and saying, "Yea folks, you must dig that game, because we're going to take 'em just like Grant took Richmond!" Armstrong recalled, "And my God, you'd thought that 'hell broke loose,' the way all the bosses came running up to the bandstand saying, 'Don't say that, don't say that because no one's allowed to say those words down South.'" "Brother did the letters pour in," said Randolph, necessitating an apology from Armstrong the following night.

46. "Louis Armstrong Back in New York," *Pittsburgh Courier,* August 8, 1931, 18.

47. Untitled news clipping found in scrapbook 1987.8.5, Louis Armstrong House Museum.

48. "Louis Armstrong, Band Feted by Zulu Club," undated news clipping found in scrapbook 1987.8.5, Louis Armstrong House Museum.

49. Emily C. Davis, "Louisiana State: New Orleans News," *Chicago Defender*, August 22, 1931, 17. Piron infamously put his name on the smash hit "I Wish I Could Shimmy Like My Sister Kate," which was originally composed by Armstrong as "Get Off Katie's Head" and sold to music publisher Clarence Williams for $50 in 1919.

50. "Thanks Unity for Musical Instruments," *Louisiana Weekly*, undated news clipping found in scrapbook 1987.8.5, Louis Armstrong House Museum.

51. *Louisiana Weekly* ad for August 31, 1931, dance, found in scrapbook 1987.8.5, Louis Armstrong House Museum.

52. "Louis Armstrong at Army Base," *Louisiana Weekly*, August 29, 1931, found in scrapbook 1987.8.5, Louis Armstrong House Museum.

53. Armstrong, "The Satchmo Story" (c. 1955 edition), 18.

54. Ibid., 17.

55. "Louie Armstrong Had No Place to Toot Horn; Crowds Followed Him," *Pittsburgh Courier*, September 19, 1931, A8.

56. Armstrong, "The Satchmo Story" (c. 1955 edition), 17.

57. Randolph, JOHP interview.

58. Jackson, *Trombone Man*, 103.

59. "Louie Armstrong Had No Place to Toot Horn."

60. "No One Wants to Talk about the Big Dance," *Louisiana Weekly*, September 26, 1931, found in scrapbook 1987.8.5, Louis Armstrong House Museum.

61. Tape 2016.91.8, Louis Armstrong House Museum.

Chapter 7

1. Armstrong, "The Satchmo Story" (c. 1955 edition), 18.

2. "Large Crowd Hears Louis Armstrong," *Houston Chronicle*, September 5, 1931, found in scrapbook 1987.8.5, Louis Armstrong House Museum. On Labor Day, Armstrong promised to play "The Peanut Vendor" "and all of his 'hits'" during a five-hour dance in Galveston, further testament to the popularity of Armstrong's Cuban specialty at this time. *Galveston Voice*, September 5, 1931, found in scrapbook 1987.8.5, Louis Armstrong House Museum.

3. Arnold Rampersad, *Ralph Ellison: A Biography* (New York: Alfred A. Knopf, 2007), 29.

4. Ralph Ellison, *Living with Music: Ralph Ellison's Jazz Writings*, ed. Robert G. O'Meally (New York: Modern Library, 2001), 28–29. Ellison placed this encounter in 1929 but there's no record of Armstrong appearing in Oklahoma City until 1931.

5. Jackson, *Trombone Man*, 107.

6. Larry L. King, "Everybody's Louie," *Harper's*, November 1967, 66–67.

7. Charles L. Black, "My World with Louis Armstrong," *Yale Law Review* 69, no. 1 (Autumn 1979): 3. Black was certain that Louis played a dance at the Driskill Hotel between October 11–15, 1931, and that he was there on October 12. However, Armstrong was definitely in St. Louis that week and nothing could found regarding Armstrong at the Driskill. He definitely played a dance at the University of Texas at Austin on September 26 and might have played more dates, possibly including at the Driskill, that week.

8. Ibid., 4.

9. W. Ardee, "Armstrong, Fetchit and Robinson Go Vaude, 'Pearly Gates' Flops Hard," *Philadelphia Tribune*, September 10, 1931, 7.

10. "Armstrong Goes Vaude," *Variety*, September 8, 1931.

11. "United States District Court. Southern District of New York. Louis Armstrong, Plaintiff, against Thomas G. Rockwell, Joseph N. Weber, et al., Defendants." 1996.50.1-08, Louis Armstrong House Museum.

12. "Ed Sullivan Sees Broadway," *New York Evening Graphic*, October 9, 1931, found in scrapbook 1987.8.5, Louis Armstrong House Museum.

13. Paul Whiteman, signed affidavit, September 22, 1931, found in scrapbook 1987.8.5, Louis Armstrong House Museum.

14. "Ed Sullivan Sees Broadway," *New York Evening Graphic*, October 9, 1931, found in scrapbook 1987.8.5, Louis Armstrong House Museum.

15. Mezzrow and Wolfe, *Really the Blues*, 249.

16. "Darktown Stage Troupe to Face Judge Instead of Arkansas Audience," undated news clipping found in scrapbook 1987.8.5, Louis Armstrong House Museum.

17. Mezzrow and Wolfe, *Really the Blues*, 249.

18. Jones and Chilton, *Louis*, 239.

19. Preston Jackson, Interview in *Satchmo: The Life of Louis Armstrong*, BBC 2 Radio series, broadcast January 14, 1975.

20. "Darktown Stage Troupe to Face Judge Instead of Arkansas Audience."

21. James and Wright, "George James, no relation to Harry . . .," 51.

22. "Darktown Stage Troupe to Face Judge Instead of Arkansas Audience."

23. Ibid.

24. Preston Jackson, Interview in *Satchmo: The Life of Louis Armstrong*, BBC 2 Radio series, broadcast January 14, 1975.

25. Jackson, *Trombone Man*, 109.

26. Randolph, JOHP interview.

27. Jones and Chilton, *Louis*, 239.

28. James and Wright, "George James, no relation to Harry . . .," 51.

29. King, "Everybody's Louie," 67.

30. James and Wright, "George James, no relation to Harry . . .," 51.

31. Randolph, JOHP interview.

32. Tubby Hall was the "Salmon Canope," Mike McKendrick was the "Princess Salad," and the leader was immortalized with "Fried Chicken A la Armstrong." All information taken from various advertisements and programs found in scrapbook 1987.8.5, Louis Armstrong House Museum.

33. James and Wright, "George James, no relation to Harry . . .," 51.

34. Jackson, *Trombone Man*, 109.

35. Jones and Chilton, *Louis*, 239–240.

36. Untitled news clipping found in scrapbook 1987.8.5, Louis Armstrong House Museum.

37. "$2,250 for Armstrong," *Variety*, October 6, 1931, 35.

38. Jackson, *Trombone Man*, 110.

39. "Lou Armstrong Says Gangsters Pester Him," *Baltimore Afro-American*, October 17, 1931, 10.

40. Tod Raper, "'Iron Lip Louis' Heads Stage Bill," undated news clipping found in scrapbook 1987.8.5, Louis Armstrong House Museum.

41. W. S. C., "'My Sin' Is Fair Picture—Louis Armstrong and Jim McWilliams Head Palace Vaudeville Bill," *Columbus Citizen*, October 19, 1931, found in scrapbook 1987.8.5, Louis Armstrong House Museum.

42. Harry Edison, interview with Steve Allen for BBC Radio 2 documentary series, *Satchmo: The Life of Louis Armstrong*, 1974.

43. Jackson, *Trombone Man*, 111.

44. Levi Jolley, "Louis Armstrong's Ex-Manager Takes Receipts at Dance," *Afro-American*, July 13, 1935, 8.

45. "Hittin' High Notes with Walter Barnes Jr.," undated news clipping found in scrapbook 1987.8.5, Louis Armstrong House Museum.

46. Stanley Dance, *The World of Earl Hines*, 148.

47. Ibid.

48. Carpenter took the day off school on November 3 and attended Armstrong's session, but was disappointed when Armstrong didn't record his composition. After recording it on November 5, Armstrong sent Carpenter a telegram, "Recorded your little tune today. Hope you like it." Carpenter was embarrassed. "He gave me a another of the several lectures he gave me along the way, about being so quick to jump to conclusions, and how I should be more patient, because I had a long way to go, being just a little youngster not out of my teens," Carpenter said. "This was typical of Louis, and I learned an awful lot from him and that good old mother wit he had." Ibid.

Chapter 8

1. Jack Bradley, "A Symposium on Louis Armstrong," *Saturday Review*, July 4, 1970. This quote comes from the cassette containing the entire original, unedited interview, Jack Bradley Collection, 2005.1.2184, Louis Armstrong House Museum.

2. Erskine Hawkins, interviewed by Leonard Goines for the Jazz Oral History Project, Institute of Jazz Studies, February 6, 1983.

3. Archie Bell, "Armstrong's [headline missing letters] Big Success at Palace," *Cleveland News*, November 9, 1931, clipping found in scrapbook 1987.8.5, Louis Armstrong House Museum. Bell also reported that during pianist Jim McWilliams's act, "he assured the audience that the boys in the colored band behave themselves and act like gentlemen. Of course they do. Can you imagine Louis Armstrong assuring an audience that Jim McWilliams knows how to conduct himself and behaves in a seemly manner? Yet as much sense to one as the other."

4. "Minute Review," *La Vie Cleveland*, November 14, 1931, clipping found in scrapbook 1987.8.5, Louis Armstrong House Museum.

5. Walter Winchell, "On Broadway," *Akron Beacon Journal*, November 14, 1931, 13.

6. Tape 1987.3.255, Louis Armstrong House Museum.

7. Tape 1987.3.424, Louis Armstrong House Museum.

8. "Trumpeter of Hot Chocolates Plays Royal," *Afro-American*, December 12, 1931.

9. Tape 1987.3.424, Louis Armstrong House Museum.

10. "Disc Leaders in 1931," *Variety*, December 29, 1931, 41.

11. Contract between RCA Victor Company, Inc. and John J. Collins and Louis Armstrong, December 23, 1931, found at 2013.20.1-01, Louis Armstrong House Museum.

12. "Hound Musician," *Baltimore Afro-American*, January 9, 1932, 1.

13. John Hammond, "Introducing John Hammond," *Melody Maker*, February 1932.

14. Armstrong also had to do something he tried to avoid at all costs: cancel engagements. Collins took out a notice that Armstrong would be in court and would have to reschedule appearances in Norfolk, Newport News, Richmond, Washington, DC, Baltimore, and Wilmington. "NOTICE!!," *Baltimore Afro-American*, January 16, 1932, 9.

15. "Armstrong, in Suit, Says He's Not Unique," *Baltimore Afro-American*, January 16, 1932, 16.

16. United States District Court Louis Armstrong, Plaintiff, vs. Thomas G. Rockwell, et al., Defendants, transcription of examination of Eli Oberstein on January 11, 1932, 1996.50.1-11, Louis Armstrong House Museum.

17. Ibid.

18. "Trumpeter Fights Band: Louis Armstrong's Talent Not Unique, Managers Contend," *New York Amsterdam News*, January 13, 1932, 1.

19. "L. Armstrong Wins Case against Manager: But Gangland Still Worries Cornetist," *Chicago Defender*, January 23, 1932, 5.

20. James and Wright, "George James, no relation to Harry . . .," 52–53.

21. Nearly every discography has said that Armstrong's January 25 and 27 sessions took place in Chicago but all surviving press shows him clearly in New York City in January.

22. Dempsey J. Travis, *An Autobiography of Black Jazz* (Chicago: Urban Research Institute, 1983), 222.

23. Ibid., 222.

24. "Here Come the 'Scat' Singers," *Fort Lauderdale News*, February 8, 1932, 4.

25. Gilbert Swan, "In New York with Gilbert Swan," *Muncie Evening Press*, February 1, 1932, 4.

26. "Cardinal Denounces Crooners as Whiners Defiling the Air," *New York Times*, January 11, 1932, 21.

27. *Omnibus*, aired on BBC TV on July 6, 1971.

28. Robert G. O'Meally, "Checking Our Balances: Louis Armstrong, Ralph Ellison, and Betty Boop," in *Uptown Conversation: The New Jazz Studies* (New York: Columbia University Press, 2004), 290–291.

29. Ad for Crystal Ballroom, *Lowell Sun*, February 10, 1932.

30. Jackson, *Trombone Man*, 113.

31. John Hammond, "The Decline of Earl Hines," *Melody Maker*, April 1932.

32. "Lafayette Theatre," *New York Age*, February 27, 1932, 6.

33. John Chilton, *Roy Eldridge: Little Jazz Giant* (London: Continuum, 2002), 50.

34. Bill Crow, *Jazz Anecdotes* (New York: Oxford University Press, 1990), 211.

35. Ira Gitler, *Swing to Bop* (New York: Oxford University Press, 1985), 47.

36. Armstrong also gave him a gift: a tin of Ansatz Creme, a special lip salve made in Germany that Armstrong had been using since discovering it in a music shop in Upper Darby, Pennsylvania, in 1929. Armstrong swore by it but it didn't have the same effect on Eldridge,

who said, "I put that shit on my lip, and I couldn't play for a week! It was good for him, but it didn't work for me *no* kind of way." Crow, *Jazz Anecdotes*, 212.

37. "Music USA," Voice of America radio broadcast, November 1958, Tape 2011.20.661, Louis Armstrong House Museum, Gosta Hagglof Collection.

38. Jones and Chilton, *Louis*, 154.

39. The Rambler, "Harlem Rambles," *Afro-American*, March 5, 1932, 9.

40. James and Wright, "George James, no relation to Harry . . .," 53.

41. Ibid.

42. Randolph, JOHP interview.

43. James and Wright, "George James, no relation to Harry . . .," 53.

44. Armstrong, "The Satchmo Story" (c. 1955 edition), 18.

45. "Louis Armstrong Goes Back to Cotton Club; May Retire," *Chicago Defender*, April 9, 1932, 5. Cook left for New Orleans after the party and disappeared from Armstrong's story after his eventful year as his bodyguard.

46. "Louis Armstrong and Band Back on Coast," *Chicago Defender*, April 16, 1932, 5. The reunion with Lawrence Brown was short-lived. Johnny Collins, whom Brown called "a very peculiar man," called a mandatory rehearsal for Easter Sunday, March 27, and Brown balked, going to spend the holiday with his mother and father instead. Brown was so fed up, he put in his notice. That week, Duke Ellington's manager, Irving Mills, came to the Cotton Club and heard Brown play his feature on "Trees" and signed him up to join the Ellington band. Having said that, it is unclear exactly when Armstrong arrived in California but news reports make it appear to be early April, meaning Brown's Easter Sunday recollection would be wrong. It's possible the rehearsal was called for another Sunday in April and Brown misremembered it decades later. Brown, JOHP interview.

47. Armstrong, "The Satchmo Story" (c. 1955 edition), 19.

48. Ibid.

49. Ibid.

50. Louis Armstrong, as told to David Duchs, "Daddy, How the Country Has Changed!," *Ebony*, May 1961, 84.

51. "Battle of Press Agents," *Evening News*, April 5, 1932, 2.

52. Floyd J. Snelson Jr., "Newsy Newsettes," *Pittsburgh Courier*, April 9, 1932, 16.

53. "March Music Survey," *Variety*, April 19, 1932, 61.

54. "April Music Survey," *Variety*, May 17, 1932, 52. Later that year, Columbia developed a new "Royal Blue" record and made a special promotional "Profit Making Plan" record aimed at dealers to let them know about it. At one point on the recording, the announcer listed the top names on the Columbia roster: Eddie Cantor, Rudy Vallee, Harry Richman, Ted Lewis, Kate Smith, Ruth Etting, Ben Selvin, Roger Wolfe Kahn, and Louis Armstrong, the last of whom being the only African American mentioned. https://www.youtube.com/watch?v=d7fQb6-LofU.

55. "Okeh Vs. Victor: Disc Companies in Suit over Louis Armstrong," *Variety*, May 31, 1932, 61.

56. "May Music Survey," *Variety*, June 21, 1932, 60.

57. "Black Rascal," *Time*, June 13, 1932.

58. "Dance Band News: Louis Armstrong Coming to London," *The Melody Maker*, Jul 1932.

Chapter 9

1. "On the Wax," *Rhythm*, January 1932, 52.
2. Edgar Jackson, "Hot Dance Bands," *The Gramophone*, November 1930, 293.
3. Edgar Jackson, "Hot Rhythm Records," *The Gramophone*, May 1931, 596.
4. Edgar Jackson, "Hot Rhythm Records," *The Gramophone*, July 1931, 62.
5. Review of "Dinah" and "Chinatown, My Chinatown," *Melody Maker*, April 1931.
6. "I wanted him to take an aeroplane for part of the journey," Collins told a reporter, "but he wouldn't do it. He's scared of going up in the air." Armstrong was quoted as replying, "Aw, aeroplanes are jus' too bad!" "Prank That Made a Man's Career," undated news clipping found in scrapbook 1987.8.6, Louis Armstrong House Museum.
7. Louis Armstrong, "Greetings to Britain!," *Rhythm*, August 1932, 27–28.
8. Dan S. Ingman, "England's Welcome to Louis Armstrong," *Melody Maker*, August 1932.
9. Tape 1987.3.176, Louis Armstrong House Museum.
10. Jones and Chilton, *Louis*, 49.
11. Ingman, "England's Welcome to Louis Armstrong."
12. Tom Driberg, "Talk of London," *Daily Express*, July 20, 1932, clipping found in scrapbook 1987.8.6, Louis Armstrong House Museum.
13. Gonella interview.
14. Ibid. Gonella also sprang into action and helped Armstrong retrieve his suit from the cleaners as the rest of his luggage remained at Paddington Station. Often when mentioning Gonella, Armstrong added the detail about him helping to get his pants pressed before the reception!
15. Gibson Young, "Radio Views: Consecrating an Abbey," *Daily Express*, August 10, 1932, clipping found in scrapbook 1987.8.6, Louis Armstrong House Museum.
16. Private tape made with George Avakian, November 1, 1953. Courtesy of David Ostwald and George Avakian.
17. Edgar Jackson, "Hot Dance Bands: Louis Armstrong at the Palladium—and Four New Records to Mark the Occasion," *The Gramophone*, August 1932, 111.
18. Tape 1987.3.176, Louis Armstrong House Museum.
19. Gonella interview.
20. "The Palladium," *Variety*, July 28, 1932, clipping found in scrapbook 1987.8.6, Louis Armstrong House Museum.
21. "English Like King Cornetist but Can't Say Why," *Atlanta Daily World*, August 11, 1932, 2A.
22. Leonard Feather, interview with Steve Allen for BBC 2 radio documentary series, *Satchmo: The Life of Louis Armstrong*, c. 1973.
23. Gonella interview.
24. Ibid.
25. Spike Hughes (as "Mike"), "Armstrong—in the 'Flesh'," *Melody Maker*, August 1932.
26. Ingman, "England's Welcome to Louis Armstrong."
27. Jackson, "Louis Armstrong at the Palladium."
28. Jones and Chilton, *Louis*, 146.
29. Gonella BBC interview. Gonella seems to have been prone to exaggeration, saying at one point "Everybody had gone home!" Numerous articles referenced walkouts but not close to "everybody had gone home." "Even at the Palladium, where he was topping the bills, I saw a handful of elderly members of the audience get up and leave the theatre in high dudgeon,"

Melody Maker reported, adding, "But Louis, even misunderstood as an artiste, is so much of a sensation—for after all only one such miracle can be born in any epoch—that his work should not be withheld because it is over the heads of so many. Louis packed the Palladium and thereby confounded the prophets, who thought his admirers could be counted in scores only." "Armstrong and the B.B.C.," *Melody Maker*, August 1932.

30. Driberg, "Talk of London."
31. "Trumpeter, What Are You Sounding Now? (Nobody Seems to Know)," *Sunday Mail*, August 14, 1932, clipping found in scrapbook 1987.8.6, Louis Armstrong House Museum.
32. Hannen Swaffer, "Storm over Negro Trumpeter," *Daily Herald*, July 22, 1932, clipping found in scrapbook 1987.8.6, Louis Armstrong House Museum.
33. Hannen Swaffer, "I Heard Yesterday," *Daily Herald*, July 25, 1932, clipping found in scrapbook 1987.8.6, Louis Armstrong House Museum.
34. Ibid.
35. Gonella interview.
36. "London Reports," *Variety, Music, Stage and Film News*, July 29, 1932, clipping found in scrapbook 1987.8.6, Louis Armstrong House Museum.
37. Jones and Chilton, *Louis*, 218.
38. Selmer advertisement, *Rhythm*, September 1932, 24.
39. William Smallwood, "Armstrong Liked London; Nearly Lost in a Soupy Fog," *Afro-American*, December 17, 1932, 9.
40. Untitled, undated clipping found in scrapbook 1987.8.6, Louis Armstrong House Museum.
41. "Bass Clef," "In Defiance of Nature—Louis Armstrong & His Trumpet—A Criticism," assumed to be *Daily Record*, August 1932, undated clipping found in scrapbook 1987.8.6, Louis Armstrong House Museum.
42. Louis Armstrong, letter to "Mabel," September 17, 1932, Louis Armstrong House Museum, 2002.32.1. People assumed Louis and Alpha were married and Armstrong didn't do anything to change their minds. "And these English people are just wild about Alpha," he wrote. "They admire the way she looks after me, etc. She is so kind and sweet to me. The people admire seeing us together, we get loads of invitations."
43. Ibid.
44. Louis Armstrong, Letter to Mezz Mezzrow, September 18, 1932, Louis Armstrong House Museum, 1998.48.1.
45. Ibid.
46. Gonella interview.
47. Jones and Chilton, *Louis*, 176.
48. Angus Scott, "They Really Manage," undated clipping found in scrapbook 1987.8.6, Louis Armstrong House Museum.
49. "King of the Trumpets," undated clipping found in scrapbook 1987.8.6, Louis Armstrong House Museum.
50. Jones and Chilton, *Louis*, 162.
51. "New Rhythm Style Series Nos. 17 and 18 Respectively," undated news clipping found in scrapbook 1987.8.6, Louis Armstrong House Museum.
52. Spike Hughes and Dan Ingman (as "Mike and Pick Up"), Review of "Them There Eyes" and "When You're Smiling," *Melody Maker*, October 1932, 843.
53. "What I Think of Louis Armstrong," *Melody Maker*, October 1932.

54. Dudley Leslie, *Evening News and Evening Mail*, July 22, 1932, untitled clipping found in scrapbook 1987.8.6, Louis Armstrong House Museum.

Chapter 10

1. Feather BBC 2 interview.
2. A sampling: "English Like King Cornetist but Can't Say Why" was the headline in the *Atlanta Daily World* on August 11. "Louis Armstrong Clicking Abroad" reported the *Pittsburgh Courier* on August 20. On September 4, the *Chicago Defender* published "Louis Armstrong Draws Praise of European Critics." And on October 22, the *Baltimore Afro-American* told its readers "Louis Armstrong Takes London by Storm."
3. Smallwood, "Armstrong Liked London; Nearly Lost in a Soupy Fog."
4. Bill Mather, "Harlem Hi-lights—According to Mather," *Melody Maker*, December 1932.
5. Tape 1987.3.255, Louis Armstrong House Museum.
6. Mather, "Harlem Hi-lights—According to Mather."
7. Tape 1987.3.255, Louis Armstrong House Museum. Armstrong told the story on one of his private reel-to-reel tapes with Thompson present. Thompson then launched into "All of Me," singing it exactly as Armstrong did in 1932.
8. Letter to Johnny Collins from J. Clerdman, November 16, 1932, 2013.20.1-02, Louis Armstrong House Museum.
9. "Pearl," *Philadelphia Inquirer*, December 4, 1932, 74.
10. "At the Lafayette," *New York Age*, December 3, 1932, 6.
11. Mezzrow and Wolfe, *Really the Blues*, 271.
12. Louis Jordan, interview with Steve Allen for BBC 2 radio documentary series *Satchmo: The Life of Louis Armstrong*, c. 1973.
13. Mezzrow and Wolfe, *Really the Blues*, 273–276. Mezzrow mistakenly wrote in *Really the Blues* that it was New Year's Eve but an ad in the *Baltimore Sun* on December 22, 1932, showed that Armstrong was playing a "Christmas Eve Dance" on December 24 and was out of Baltimore by New Year's Eve.
14. Hilda See, "Critic Finds L. Armstrong Here 'To Rest'—King of Trumpeters in No Mood for Work," *Chicago Defender*, January 21, 1933, 5.
15. Walter Winchell, "On Broadway," *Akron Beacon Journal*, January 24, 1933, 15. John Edgar Weir, "Music in the Movies," *New Movie Magazine*, May 1933, 66.
16. Teddy Wilson, interviewed by Milt Hinton for the Jazz Oral History Project, JHOP 119.4.1–119.4.2, September 1979.
17. "Roses for Satchmo," *Downbeat*, July 1970, 17.
18. Randolph, JOHP interview.
19. Wilson, JOHP interview.
20. Mike Pinfold, *Louis Armstrong: His Life and Times* (Staplehurst, UK: Spellmount Ltd., 1987), 59.
21. Whitney Balliett, "The Center of the Note," July 8, 1974, 41.
22. Johnson, JOHP interview.
23. Dance, *The World of Earl Hines*, 212.
24. Johnson, JOHP interview.
25. Tape 1987.3.188, Louis Armstrong House Museum.

26. Johnson, JOHP interview. Johnson wasn't joking. When released in the fall, John Edgar Weir selected "Sweet Sue" as one of "The Month's Biggest Hits" in the *New Movie Magazine*! "It's an old-timer that Louis plays for us this time, 'Sweet Sue,' and he features a chorus that he terms the 'Vipers' Language,' sung by Bud [*sic*] Johnson, with an even more viperish obbligato by Louis himself," Weir wrote. "It you like Louis you'll go for this one." John Edgar Weir, "Music in the Movies," *New Movie Magazine*, October 1933, 64.

27. Johnson, JOHP interview.

28. Armstrong owned multiple copies of the disc and after dubbing "Laughin' Louie" to tape in 1950s, followed it with "The OKeh Laughing Record," saying, "And now I shall play the other recording that gave us the idea of this silly thing." Armstrong was laughing when the record ended, saying, "Now isn't that the maddest thing you wanna hear? That cat had me rolling, man!" Tape 1987.3.461, Louis Armstrong House Museum.

29. Ibid. To hear it in a silent movie context, it can be heard played by a violin at 1:08:46 on the original score of the 1938 *Charlie Chaplin Festival*.

30. Dance, *The World of Earl Hines*, 185.

31. Dan Morgenstern, "Pops in Perspective," *Jazz Journal*, May 1962, 6.

32. "Louis Armstrong, Wonder-master of the Trumpet, Dead," *Kingston Daily Gleaner*, May 1, 1933, 17.

33. Edgar Jackson, "Hot Dance Bands: Louis Armstrong Not Guilty—and Very Much Alive," *The Gramophone*, May 1933, 485.

34. Eric (Von) Wilkinson, "Gallivanting about Brooklyn," *New York Age*, April 8, 1933, 3.

35. Walter Winchell, "Saint Louis Boos!," *Reading Times*, April 5, 1933, 6.

36. Louis Armstrong, letter to Henry "Red" Allen, April 20, 1933, 2005.38.6, Louis Armstrong House Museum.

37. "The Armstrong Comedy," *Rhythm*, May 1933, 15. Armstrong laughed off the rumors of his death, but around the same time, he discovered legendary New Orleans cornetist Freddie Keppard was ailing in Chicago, suffering from tuberculosis. Budd Johnson remembered Armstrong telling the band's bus driver to go out of their way so he could pay his last respects. "And here was a name I knew, but I'd never met the man," Johnson recalled. "And Louis took us all up there to see Freddie Keppard and he was like on his deathbed." Keppard died on July 15 at the age of 44.

38. "Louis Armstrong Band on Tour," *Pittsburgh Courier*, May 13, 1933, 5.

39. Dance, *The World of Earl Hines*, 212.

40. Walter Winchell, "On Broadway," *Scranton Republican*, May 19, 1933, 5.

41. Smallwood, "Armstrong Liked London; Nearly Lost in a Soupy Fog."

42. Louis Armstrong, letter to "Gate" (addresses recipient as "George" but without last name), April 5, 1933. Accessed at http://www.profilesinhistory.com/flipbooks/Historical-Documents-Auction-54/files/data/search.xml.

43. "Armstrong's Band Here to Rest a While," *Chicago Defender*, June 24, 1933, 5.

44. Ellington was a sensation at the Palladium but encountered some similar responses to his music as Armstrong. Hannen Swaffer was once again called in to provide the extreme reactions, printing a letter from a friend who had to "rush out" four times and summed up the experience by writing, "No, it won't do for white men. . . . It might suit the cotton fields, but not Lancashire cotton mill workers." Swaffer also reported on Ellington's audiences at

the Palladium. "On Monday night twenty people walked out while Duke Ellington was playing," he wrote, adding, "On Wednesday night only sixteen walked out. On Thursday night they tell me, the number was reduced to twelve. The walk-outs are dying off. Louis Armstrong wore them down a few weeks ago. After that they will stand anything." Hannen Swaffer, "Hannen Swaffer Listens to the Soul of a Negro," *Pittsburgh Courier*, July 15, 1933, 13.

45. John Hammond, "An Innocent Abroad," *Melody Maker*, August 12, 1933, 3.
46. Private tape made with George Avakian, November 1, 1953. Courtesy of David Ostwald and George Avakian.
47. Ibid.

Chapter 11

1. Edgar Jackson, "Louis Armstrong Is Here Again!," *The Gramophone*, August 1933, 107.
2. "Amazing Reception for Armstrong," *Melody Maker*, August 5, 1933, 1–2.
3. John Hammond, "An Innocent Still Abroad," *Melody Maker*, August 19, 1933, 3.
4. Ibid.
5. "Armstrong's Iron Lips Let Him Down," *Melody Maker*, August 26, 1933, 1.
6. "Louis Armstrong's Magnificent Come Back," *Melody Maker*, September 16, 1933, 1.
7. Selmer advertisement, *Melody Maker*, September 9, 1933, 5.
8. "Louis Armstrong Makes Up His Mind," *Melody Maker*, September 30, 1933, 13.
9. Armstrong with Meryman, *A Self-Portrait*, 45.
10. Johnny Collins, letter to F. C. Erdman, October 16, 1933, and F. C. Erdman, letter to Johnny Collins, 2013.20.1-03, Louis Armstrong House Museum. Thanks to Vince Giordano for documents related to RCA Victor.
11. "Louis Armstrong Makes Up His Mind."
12. Ivan H. Browning, "Louis Armstrong Is Rage in Denmark," December 2, 1933, 16.
13. The first half consisted of "Them There Eyes," "I've Got the World on a String," "Dinah," "On the Sunny Side of the Street," and "St. Louis Blues." After intermission, Armstrong played "That's My Home," "I Cover the Waterfront," "I Gotta Right to Sing the Blues," "Rockin' Chair," "Chinatown, My Chinatown," and "Tiger Rag," coming back for encores of "You Rascal You" and "Hobo, You Can't Ride This Train." Gösta Hägglöf, Liner notes to *Louis Armstrong in Scandinavia 1933–1952*.
14. Gösta Hägglöf, Liner notes to *Louis Armstrong in Scandinavia 1933–1952* (Storyville 101 8348, 2005), 2–3.
15. Hägglöf, *Louis Armstrong in Scandinavia 1933–1952*, 4–5.
16. "Louis jazzar och ler," undated Swedish news clipping found in the Gösta Hägglöf Collection, Louis Armstrong House Museum, 2011.22.3-16. Armstrong's October 28 concert was even partially recorded, some of the first live concert recordings to have ever survived, finding him taking extra choruses on a wild "Chinatown," giving "You Rascal You" a relaxed reading and performing a magical rendition of "On the Sunny Side of the Street" a full year before his first studio recording of it. It is commercially available on the Storyville CD, *Louis Armstrong in Scandinavia 1933–1952*.
17. "5000 Københavnere modtog Manden med Sølvtrompeten," undated Danish news clipping found in the Gösta Hägglöf Collection, Louis Armstrong House Museum, 2011.22.3-01.

18. Untitled Swedish news clipping from October 21, 1933, found in the Gösta Hägglöf Collection, Louis Armstrong House Museum, 2011.22.3-07.
19. "Louis Armstrong's Split Lip Compels a Rest," *Melody Maker*, January 6, 1932, 2.
20. Armstrong, *A Self-Portrait*, 39.
21. "Louis Armstrong's Split Lip Compels a Rest."
22. "Chatter," *Variety*, January 9, 1934, 53.
23. Bettie Edwards [Leonard Feather], "Louis—A Study in Brown," *Melody Maker*, January 27, 1934, 22.
24. Leonard Feather, "Armstrong through the Ages: A Discographical Survey," *Melody Maker*, June 9, 1934, 8, 11.
25. Leonard Feather, "No Future for Hot Music Declares Reginald Foresythe in an Interview with Leonard Feather," *Melody Maker*, January 6, 1934, 22.
26. Leonard Feather, "The Four Best Records for the South Pole!," *Melody Maker*, February 17, 1934, 15.
27. Louis Armstrong, acetate disc of April 1950 interview for *The Record Changer*, 2013.70.27, Louis Armstrong House Museum.
28. Feather, "A Study in Brown," 22.
29. "Armstrong Tears Up Collins Wire: 'Never, Never!,'" *Melody Maker*, March 17, 1934, 3.
30. Robert Goffin, "Jazzmen's Greatest Kicks," *Esquire* 22 (August 1944), 142. Dan Morgenstern story from correspondence with the author, February 25, 2020.
31. Scott DeVeaux, *The Birth of Bebop: A Social and Musical History* (Berkely: University of California Press, 1997), 73. Townley, "Reminiscing with Cootie," 172.
32. "Hawk Coming to Partner Louis," *Melody Maker*, March 24, 1934, 1.
33. "Hawkins' Fine Welcome to England," *Melody Maker*, April 7, 1934, 1.
34. "Louis Quits, Concert Wrecked," *Melody Maker*, April 14, 1934, 1.
35. Percy Mathison Brooks, "More Than Fair Play for Louis Armstrong," *Melody Maker*, May 5, 1934, 8.
36. Ibid.
37. "Fair Play for Louis," *Tune Times*, May 1934, 1.
38. "The Real Lowdown on Louis Armstrong," *Tune Times*, May 1934, 1.
39. "Louis Armstrong's Story of Walkout: 'No Jealousy,' Says Ace of Musicians," *Chicago Defender*, May 5, 1934, 9.
40. Hugues Panassie, "Louis Armstrong at the Salle Pleyel (1946)," reprinted in *The Louis Armstrong Companion*, ed. Joshua Berrett (New York: Schirmer Books, 1999), 63.
41. Tape 1987.3.424, Louis Armstrong House Museum.
42. "Hawkins' Triumph," *Melody Maker*, April 21, 1934, 1.
43. Writer John Edgar Weir was even certain that it was Armstrong himself on the recording. John Edgar Weir, "Music in the Movies," *New Movie Magazine*, May 1934, 60.
44. Cleveland Allen, "East Hears Louis Armstrong Seeks Divorce from His Wife," *Chicago Defender*, April 28, 1934, 8.
45. Howard Rye, "Visiting Firemen 2: Louis Armstrong," *Storyville 89*, June–July 1980, 187.
46. "Louis Sailing Home: Swan Song Played after Year of Triumph," June 30, 1934, 1.
47. Arthur Briggs, interviewed by James Lincoln Collier, Jazz Oral History Project, February 26, 1982.
48. Jones and Chilton, *Louis*, 184.
49. Tape 1987.3.424, Louis Armstrong House Museum.
50. Briggs, JOHP interview.

51. N. J. Canetti, letter to RCA Victor Co. Inc., September 5, 1934, Louis Armstrong House Museum, 2013.20.1-04.

52. Inter-office memo at RCA Victor, September 20, 1934, Louis Armstrong House Museum, 2013.20.1-04.

53. RCA Victor letter to N. J. Canetti, September 20, 1934, Louis Armstrong House Museum, 2013.20.1-04.

54. Correspondence between Johnny Collins and Eli Oberstein, both dated October 11, 1934, Louis Armstrong House Museum, 2013.20.1-04.

55. Tape 1987.3.176, Louis Armstrong House Museum.

56. Panassie, "Louis Armstrong at the Salle Pleyel (1946), 64.

57. Edgar Wiggins, "Louis Armstrong Adds to Laurels by Stellar Performances at Parisian Hall," *Philadelphia Tribune*, November 29, 1934, 10.

58. Wiggins, "Louis Armstrong Adds to Laurels by Stellar Performances at Parisian Hall."

59. Edgar Wiggins, "Montmartre: The Truth about Armstrong-Canetti Split," *Philadelphia Tribune*, February 14, 1935, 13.

60. Edgar Wiggins, "Louis Armstrong Splits with French Mgr.; Returns Home," *Philadelphia Tribune*, January 31, 1935, 13.

61. "Grave Trouble for Armstrong," *The Melody Maker*, January 26, 1935, 1.

62. Wiggins, "Louis Armstrong Splits with French Mgr.; Returns Home," 13.

63. N. J. Canetti, "Armstrong Flees to U.S.A.," *Melody Maker*, February 2, 1935, 1. *Melody Maker* also stuck an interesting "Editor's Note" at the end of Canetti's article saying that just before Canetti signed Armstrong, Armstrong had already committed to having British variety agent Audrey Thacker represent him for a year. Clearly, Armstrong said "yes" to anyone interested in being his manager and didn't worry about any ramifications.

64. "Armstrong's Return Surprises His Friends," *New York Amsterdam News*, February 2, 1935, 10.

65. Ibid.

66. Armstrong, "The Satchmo Story" (c. 1955 edition), 12.

67. Mezzrow and Wolfe, *Really the Blues*, 288–289.

68. "Theatre Riled by Armstrong: Fails to Appear Here—Union Trouble and Sore Lip Blamed," *New York Amsterdam News*, February 23, 1935, 1.

69. "Theatre Riled by Armstrong," 1.

70. "N. Y. Turns Out to See Louis Armstrong at Apollo Theatre; He Stays in Chicago," *Chicago Defender*, February 23, 1935, 8.

71. Armstrong with Meryman, *A Self-Portrait*, 45.

72. Mezzrow and Wolfe, *Really the Blues*, 289.

73. Randolph, JOHP interview. Randolph only could remember the drummer's surname, Gable.

74. Tape 1987.3.188, Louis Armstrong House Museum.

75. "Is He Through?," *Afro-American*, April 20, 1935, 9.

76. Private tape made with George Avakian, November 1, 1953. Courtesy of David Ostwald and George Avakian.

77. Edgar A. Wiggins (as "The Street-Wolf of Paris"), "Montmartre," *Philadelphia Tribune*, May 2, 1935, 11.

78. Dance, *The World of Earl Hines*, 212.

Chapter 12

1. George Tucker, "Manhattan," *Daily News-Journal*, February 25, 1942, 2.
2. "Miss Elaine Harless Introduced to Society," *Chicago Tribune*, December 1913, 10.
3. Leonard Feather, "Satchmo Remembers the Big Magaffa," *Los Angeles Times*, June 22, 1969, 44.
4. "Diploma Mill for Physicians Laid to Doctors," *Chicago Tribune*, April 1916, 17.
5. "Took to Sidewalk; Arrested," *Chicago Star Publication*, August 26, 1916, 5.
6. Ad, *Chicago Tribune*, June 23, 1918, 67.
7. Ad, *Chicago Tribune*, December 19, 1918, 26.
8. "Glenwood and Rosedale Flats Sold for $120,000," *Chicago Tribune*, December 23, 1923, 14.
9. "Rev. Williamson Assails Police and 'Vice Graft,'" *Chicago Tribune*, September 18, 1922, 3.
10. Jack Schiffman, *Uptown: The Story of Harlem's Apollo Theatre* (New York: Cowles Book Company, 1971), 163.
11. Ad, *Chicago Tribune*, August 10, 1924, 87.
12. Studs Terkel, *And They All Sang: Adventures of an Eclectic Disc Jockey* (New York: The New Press, 2011), 148.
13. Louis Armstrong, letter to Slim Evans, incorrectly dated "September 31st, 1967," Louis Armstrong House Museum, 2008.1.32.<<AU: sometimes these numbers are before Louis Armstrong House Museum and more often before. Does it make a difference? If so, please search and transpose.>>
14. Ibid.
15. "'Black and Tan' Resorts Raided by Schoemaker" *Chicago Tribune*, December 26, 1926, 1.
16. "Judge Attacks Sunset Cabaret, Fining Owners," January 12, 1927, 14.
17. Anderson, "Louis Armstrong and Joe Glaser Part 1," 127.
18. "Child Attacker Finally Tried; Gets 10 Years," *Chicago Tribune*, February 8, 1928, 1.
19. "Tells of $5,000 Offer by Glaser to Drop Charges," *Chicago Tribune*, February 24, 1928, 7.
20. "Court Refuses Glaser's Move for New Trial," *Chicago Tribune*, February 26, 1928, 22.
21. "Glaser, Married to Girl Accuser, Refused Mercy," *Chicago Tribune*, March 2, 1928, 7.
22. "Fight Manager in Toils Again," *Decatur Evening Herald*, March 6, 1928, 1.
23. "Glaser Saved from Prison by Supreme Court," *Chicago Tribune*, June 21, 1929, 4.
24. "Glaser Sued for $10,000," *Des Moines Register*, January 29, 1930, 1.
25. Glaser's later associate Ernie Anderson had a theory: "By that time, Joe Glaser was a firm member of the Al Capone organization. As such he was entitled to the services of the legal arm of the Capone mob in the person of the brilliant young Sidney Korshak, who studied in Chicago's DePaul law school. The delays and Joe Glaser's marriage to the young victim were all part of Sidney Korshak's legal strategy. In the end he beat the rap and Joe Glaser did not serve his ten-year sentence in Joliet Penitentiary." This theory does not hold up, though, as Korshak was 20 at the time of Glaser's arrest and by the time he received his law degree from DePaul in 1930, Glaser was already a free man. Glaser and Korshak would have a connection later, but it most likely did not exist in 1929. Anderson, "Louis Armstrong and Joe Glaser Part 1," 126–127.
26. "Joe Glaser Is Ordered to Pay Alimony to Wife," *Chicago Tribune*, January 27, 1931, 2.
27. "Frolics Will Open with N. Y. Cast," *Chicago Defender*, March 10, 1934, 5.
28. Earl J. Morris, "Chicago Benefit Show for the Regal," *Pittsburgh Courier*, June 2, 1934, A9.
29. Earl J. Morris," "Floor Show at Sunset Thrills," *Pittsburgh Courier*, July 14, 1938, A8.

30. "Vote to Indict Joe Glaser in Liquor Robbery," *Chicago Tribune*, April 9, 1935, 5.
31. Tommy Fitzgerald, "Lena, Here, Seeks Bout for Levinsky: Ferguson Hopes to Sign King for Go this Month," *Courier-Journal*, May 1, 1935, 18.
32. "Manager Joe Glaser on Louis," *Life*, April 15, 1966.
33. At the time of that interview in 1975, Anderson said it was a "very modest" amount and didn't feel comfortable disclosing it. Later in life, Anderson said the figure was $1,000 a week. Others have said $500. Armstrong himself once alluded to making $75 a night in 1937, equaling $525, which lends credence to the more modest $500 figure, especially if Glaser had to keep making regular payments to Lil, Tommy Rockwell, and Johnny Collins. Because there was no contract, the exact figure has remained a mystery, but suffice it to say, it was a decent amount of money in Depression-hobbled 1935 (even $500 equals roughly $9,300 in 2020 money). Ernie Anderson, interview in *Satchmo: The Life of Louis Armstrong* BBC 2 radio series, episode five, broadcast January 26, 1975.
34. Tape 1987.3.254, Louis Armstrong House Museum.
35. Randolph, JOHP interview.
36. Collier, *Louis Armstrong: An American Genius*, 274.
37. "Louis Armstrong O. K. Again; Gets Band Back," *Pittsburgh Courier*, June 29, 1935, 22.
38. Sec Taylor, "Sittin' In with the Athlete," *Des Moines Register*, September 1, 1935, 11.
39. Jolley, "Louis Armstrong's Ex-Manager Takes Receipts at Dance," 8.
40. Ishmael Northcross, "Armstrong Eyes Symphonic Jazz as Real Hope of Music," *Pittsburgh Courier*, July 13, 1935, 16.
41. "'My Chops Was Beat,' Says Louie, 'But I'm Dyin' to Swing Again,'" *Down Beat*, June 1935, 1, 8.
42. R. Edwin S. Hinchcliffe, "'Red' Allen," *Swing Music*, May 1935, 56.
43. "'My Chops Was Beat,'" 8.
44. Start, "Louis Armstrong," 59.
45. Armstrong and Duchs, "'Daddy, How This Country Has Changed," 81–82.
46. Jolley, "Louis Armstrong's Ex-Manager Takes Receipts at Dance," 8.
47. Ibid.
48. Armstrong and Meryman, *A Self-Portrait*, 40–41.
49. Rollo S. Vest, "Armstrong Headed to Detroit," *Pittsburgh Courier*, July 13, 1935, 16.
50. "Louis Armstrong Back with Rockwell-O'Keefe," July 17, 1935. This spelled the end of Al Travers's short-lived tenure as Armstrong's "manager." As Travers had already helped book Armstrong's southern tour, he was still getting inquiries for the trumpeter's services, leading Glaser to put a notice in all the black newspapers, "That on and after August 20, 1935, Al A. Travers or his representative Ed Strong, are no longer associated or connected with Joseph Glaser or Louis Armstrong and his band in any capacity whatsoever. . . . Joseph Glaser is now associated with Rockwell and O'Keefe." "Travers Out with Armstrong Joe Glaser Warns Promoters," *Pittsburgh Courier*, August 24, 1935, A6.
51. Northcross, "Armstrong Eyes Symphonic Jazz as Real Hope of Music," 16.
52. "Louis Armstrong Will Play in 'Home Town,'" *Pittsburgh Courier*, July 13, 1935, 16. Armstrong biographers Laurence Bergreen and Scott Allen Nollen reported that Armstrong charged admission for the first three performances at the Golden Dragon and then played the rest of the week with free admission. This is based on a misreading of a Golden Dragon flyer that has become ubiquitous on the Internet. The flyer is for the week of July 21–27 but clearly shows Armstrong only played three shows over the first two days

of the week. The "Rhapsodians Orchestra" took over on Tuesday with the flyer announcing free admission for their midweek performances, but not for Armstrong.

53. Randolph, JOHP interview.

54. Allan McMillan, "Hi Hattin' in Harlem," *Chicago Defender*, September 7, 1935, 8.

55. "Louis Armstrong Is Sensation at the Howard: Stand in Aisles to Cheer 'King of Trumpeters,'" *Pittsburgh Courier*, August 21, 1935, 17.

56. The *Esquire* story was a bit problematic. Hermann Deutsch wrote a short story simply called "Louis Armstrong," using the 1931 Suburban Gardens as the backdrop for the "semi-fiction" tale of Armstrong playing for white fans while his black audience watched from the levee. That wasn't the problematic part; that was true. Where Deutsch erred was by writing the entire 1,650 word story in dialect, with lines like, "Black folks can't go to de club where de white folks steppin' to music Louis Armstrong playin'. Nossuh my Jesus! Black folks got to sit out here on de levee in de dark, feets a-tappin' in de grass." It was painful—reader Elmer Green wrote to the editor the following month, "Your articles were fine with the exception of one on Louis Armstrong. Tell Hymie we speak English and read it." Herman Deutsch, "Louis Armstrong," *Esquire*, October 1935, 70.

57. "'Trumpet King' Crashes Fortune, Esquire and Vanity Fair," *Pittsburgh Courier*, October 26, 1935, 19.

58. Edison, BBC interview with Steve Allen.

59. For the definitive background information on Kapp, Crosby, and the formation of Decca Records, see Gary Giddins, *Bing Crosby: A Pocketful of Dreams, The Early Years 1903–1940* (Boston: Little, Brown and Company, 2001), 365–378.

60. "Composer Discloses Story behind 'Old Man Mose Is Dead,'" *Courier-Journal*, November 18, 1938, 30.

61. Randolph, JOHP interview.

62. Percival Outram, "Among Union Musicians," *New York Age*, October 5, 1935, 4.

63. Leslie Velie, "Vocal Boy Makes Good," *Collier's*, December 13, 1947.

64. Giddins, *Bing Crosby*, 366.

65. Michael Steinman, "'A Truly Loving Person: Dan Morgenstern Remembers Louis Armstrong," May 24, 2019, https://jazzlives.wordpress.com/2019/05/30/a-truly-loving-person-dan-morgenstern-remembers-louis-armstrong-may-24-2019/

66. Giddins, *Bing Crosby*, 367.

67. Tape 1987.3.181, Louis Armstrong House Museum.

68. Dan Morgenstern, Liner notes to *The Complete Louis Armstrong Decca Sessions (1935–1946)*, (Mosaic Records 243, 2009), 4.

69. Charlie Holmes, interview with Steve Allen for BBC 2 radio documentary series, *Satchmo: The Life of Louis Armstrong*, c. 1973.

70. Percival Outram, "Among Union Musicians," *New York Age*, November 9, 1935, 4.

71. Kahn, *Call of the Freaks*, 186–187.

72. Cahn interview, January 26, 1975.

73. "Swing Stuff: Armstrong Returns," *Variety*, November 6, 1935.

74. Connie Immerman Is Again Hitting on High: Latest 'Chocolates of 1936' off to Wonderful Start on the Main Stem," *New York Amsterdam News*, November 2, 1935, 13.

75. *Variety* was listening and reported on Armstrong's broadcasts, writing after one, "In one trumpet chorus of 'Dinah,' Louis Armstrong managed to work in licks from 'Stars and Stripes Forever,' 'The Prisoner's Song,' 'Lady Be Good' and 'Johnny Get Your Gun.'" Never

mind that Armstrong had been unleashing quotes on "Dinah" for five years; the world had finally caught up with him thanks to the popularity of swing. "Swing Stuff," *Variety*, December 25, 1935, 38.

76. "Disc Reviews," *Variety*, November 20, 1935, 52.

77. Leonard G. Feather, "A Year of Music: A Survey of 1935 in Jazz," *The Era*, January 1, 1936.

78. "Swing Stuff: Armstrong Revival," *Variety*, December 4, 1935, 41.

79. Walter Winchell, "On Broadway," *Wilkes-Barre Times Leader, The Evening News*, February 7, 1936, 33.

80. Black, "The Music Box Review," 150.

81. Jack Schiffman, *Uptown: The Story of Harlem's Apollo Theatre* (New York: Cowles Book Company, 1971), 50.

82. Adam Clayton Powell Jr., "The Soapbox," *New York Amsterdam News*, February 22, 1936, 12.

83. Floyd J. Calvin, "Five Broadway Spots Set High Record for Race Performers," *New York Age*, December 7, 1935, 4.

84. Floyd J. Calvin, "'Selling Personality' Back of Band Maestros' Popularity," *Pittsburgh Courier*, November 9, 1935, 11.

85. Leonard Feather, "Breakfast Dance," *Melody Maker*, January 11, 1936.

86. "Holds Louis Armstrong's Trunk, Music," *Chicago Defender*, November 16, 1936, 9.

87. "Armstrong and Ex-Boss Spat," *Chicago Defender*, October 12, 1935, 9. Interestingly, Edgar A. Wiggins, who defended Armstrong against Canetti in the black press, turned on Armstrong in early 1936, writing that Armstrong never reimbursed him for his voyage from Paris to Aveyron to meet with Hugues Panassie. "My sole object of writing this article is to give a sidelight on a great personality in private life," Wiggins wrote about Armstrong's lack of gratitude. In some ways, it's no wonder Armstrong didn't return to France until 1948. Edgar A. Wiggins, "Hands across the Ocean," *Philadelphia Tribune*, March 12, 1936, 15.

Chapter 13

1. "Louis Armstrong Started Newest Who-ho-ho Popular Song Hit," *Baltimore Afro-American*, January 25, 1936, 6.

2. Holmes, BBC interview.

3. "Louis Armstrong Doing Book as Swing, Jam Bands Increase," *Billboard*, January 18, 1936, 12.

4. Peter Carr, *Jimmy Archey: The Little Giant of the Trombone* (New Orleans: Jazzology Press, 1999), 59.

5. Nels Nelson, "'He Loved Life,'" *Philadelphia Daily News*, July 7, 1971, 5.

6. Helen M. Oakley, "Goodman's Playing Defies Adequate Description," *Down Beat*, August 1935, 4..

7. Julian B. Bach, "Inspiration Was Satchmo," *Down Beat*, September 1, 1941, found in scrapbook 1987.8.11, Louis Armstrong House Museum.

8. "'Berigan Can't Do No Wrong,' Says Armstrong," *Down Beat*, September 1, 1941, found in scrapbook 1987.8.11, Louis Armstrong House Museum.

9. Edgar Jackson, "Swing Music Reviewed," *The Gramophone*, May 1936, 526.

10. Porter Roberts, "Praise and Criticism," *Pittsburgh Courier*, April 11, 1936, 19.

11. "Joe Glaser Denies Report of White Orchestra for 'Louie,'" *Pittsburgh Courier*, April 18, 1936, A6.

12. Allan McMillan, "Chappie Willette [*sic*] Tells How Songs Are Made Popular," *Chicago Defender*, February 8, 1936, 8. For more on Willet, see John Wriggle, *Blue Rhythm Fantasy: Big Band Jazz Arranging in the Swing Era* (Champaign: University of Illinois Press, 2016).

13. Glaser's new billing was appropriate but not quite original. Benny Goodman's drummer Gene Krupa was billed as "The King of Swing" in *Down Beat*'s December 1935–January 1936 issue but by March 1936, the magazine was using it to describe Goodman himself. Both Armstrong and Goodman continued using the moniker for much of 1936 until Glaser finally blinked and began billing his client as "The Trumpet King of Swing" in June (though sporadic references to Armstrong as solely "The King of Swing" continued into 1937). Jack Egan, "Onyx Club Is Port of Missing Musicians," *Down Beat*, February 1936, 4.

14. *New York Age*, March 14, 1936.

15. "Louis Armstrong Goes to Boston," 17.

16. George Frazier, "Critic Scores 'Goops' Who Interpret Casa Loma: Armstrong Is Playing Commercial 'Junk,'" *Down Beat*, April 1936, 1, 15.

17. Eric A. C. Ballard, "I Come from a Musical Family/Somebody Stole My Break," *Rhythm Record Review*, August 2, 1936.

18. Eric A. C. Ballard, "Ev'ntide/Lyin to Myself," *Rhythm Record Review*, September 5, 1936.

19. "Fletcher's Men Jam with Zutty and His Boys at Three Deuces," *Down Beat*, March 1936, 9.

20. "Swing Stuff: On the Wax," *Variety*, April 29, 1936, 48.

21. Andrew Wolf, "Three American Originals," *New York Sun*, July 3, 2008. https://www.nysun.com/opinion/three-american-originals/81196/.

22. "All Star Jam at Imperial, N. Y.; 17 Orchestras Swing It for 3 Hours," *Variety*, May 27, 1936, 44.

23. "Sobol Calls Louie Armstrong 'King of Swing': Noted Columnist, Walter Winchell, Rave about Louie," *Pittsburgh Courier*, June 6, 1936, A7.

24. John Hammond, "N. Y. Swing Concert Proved Headache—Too Hard to Commercialize on Jam Music," *Down Beat*, June 1936, 6.

25. George Frazier, "Satchelmo's Band Is Worlds Worst; Norvo Excels," *Down Beat*, June 1936, 2.

26. "Goodman-Casa Loma & Lunceford Best Swing Bands," *Down Beat*, July 1936, 12.

27. "Vaudeville Reviews," *Billboard,* June 6, 1936, 17.

28. "Louis Armstrong Polls Big Vote on Broadway," *Afro-American*, June 6, 1936, 11.

29. Walter Winchell, "On Broadway," *Wilkes-Barre Times Leader, The Evening News*, June 1, 1936.

30. Jack Stinnett, "A New Yorker at Large," *Montana Standard*, June 22, 1936, 6.

31. "Louis Armstrong Beats Jesse Owens at Record-Breaking," *Pittsburgh Courier*, July 25, 1936, 17.

32. Leonard Feather (as "Rophone"), "Ellington Still on High," *Melody Maker*, September 19, 1936, 4.

33. Leonard Feather, "On Tour with Armstrong," *Melody Maker*, September 12, 1936, 2.

34. Leonard Feather, "Swinging Down the Mississippi," *Melody Maker*, September 26, 1936, 13.

35. Feather could not understand the appeal of Woods to the black audience. "The worse he sang it, the more frantic the reception; two repeat choruses and an encore hardly seemed enough," he said.

36. Ibid., 5.

37. Leonard Feather, "Harlem's Dark Secrets: Feather Forecast and News," *Melody Maker*, undated clipping found in Leonard Feather scrapbook, 1938. For his part, Feather found it "quite impossible to judge" the Basie band because of the rough atmosphere of the venue. "People who have heard Basie on the air inform me that the band is really terrific, but for the life of me I could make no decision," he said.

38. Leonard Feather, "Swinging in Kansas City," October 3, 1936, 2–3.

39. G. M. (Leonard Feather as "Geoffrey Marne"), "Satch'Mo," *Rhythm*, September 1936, 37.

40. Giddins, *Bing Crosby: A Pocketful of Dreams*, 419.

41. Bernice Patton, "Louie ' "Scats" to Town' in New Picture," *Pittsburgh Courier*, August 29, 1936, 17.

42. Thompson helped Armstrong memorize his lines at the Dunbar Hotel, playing the role of Crosby. Armstrong reminisced of Thompson, "And this son-of-a-bitch delivers a line to me, 'Well, look here you [motherfucker]!' We'd go out there the next morning, I'm straight, man." Tape 1987.3.255, Louis Armstrong House Museum.

43. Buckner, *Satchmo: The Life and Times of Louis Armstrong*, January 26, 1975.

44. Leonard Feather (as "Rophone"), "Norvo and Bailey an Unbeatable Combination," *Melody Maker*, January 9, 1937.

45. Joe Glaser, "Race Artists Bring Profits," *Billboard*, September 23, 1939, 36–37.

46. Robert Paul Smith, "A Guide to Le Jazz Hot," *Brooklyn Daily Eagle*, August 23, 1936, 10C.

47. Louis Armstrong, *Swing That Music* (London: Longmans, Green and Co., 1936).

48. Robert L. Nelson, "On Wings of Swing," *New York Age*, November 14, 1936, 8.

49. John Hammond, "Count Basie Band Makes Chicago Debut," *Down Beat*, November 1936, 4.

50. "Reviews of New Films: Pennies from Heaven," *The Film Daily*, November 16, 1936, 7.

51. Henry Sutherland, "Preview Parade," *Tampa Tribune*, November 22, 1936, 13.

52. Bernice Patton, "Armstrong 'Steals' Bing Crosby's Picture," *Pittsburgh Courier*, November 21, 1936, 17.

53. In his year-end column, Roberts delivered a "Bouquets of Praise" to Armstrong but his list of "Brick Bats of Criticism" was especially pointed, taking on musicians, actors, and even fellow *Courier* columnist Allan McMillan. Examples of some of the brickbats he tossed: "At Langston Hughes for putting across the white man's propaganda in his writings. At Fletcher Henderson for catering to white musicians with his arrangements. At Chick Webb for cutting Benny Goodman in on 'Stomping At the Savoy.'" The list continued for quite a long time. Porter Roberts, "Praise and Criticism," *Pittsburgh Courier*, December 26, 1937, 17.

54. Porter Roberts, "Praise and Criticism," *Pittsburgh Courier*, January 16, 1937, 19.

55. Porter Roberts, "Praise and Criticism," *New Journal and Guide*, April 3, 1937, 18.

56. Marion Marshall, "Raps Louis Armstrong in 'Pennies from Heaven,'" *Atlanta Daily World*, March 29, 1937, 2.

57. Alfred A. Duckett, "Radio-Stage-Screen: Our Way of Thinking," *New York Age*, April 3, 1937, 9.

58. Marion Marshall, "Taken to Task," *New York Age*, April 24, 1937, 9.

59. Alfred A. Duckett, "Radio-Stage-Screen: Holding Our Ground," *New York Age*, May 1, 1937, 9. Such debates were common in the African American press in the 1930s. "Anyone who reads the editorial pages of black American newspapers in the 1930s can indeed find—on the subject of *Amos 'n' Andy* and on many other topics—petty jealousies, eclectic concatenations of ideas, and internal contradictions sometimes bordering on incoherence," Melvin Patrick Ely wrote in his social history of *Amos 'n' Andy*. "Yet the reader also finds a ferment, a searching and candid intensity that could be fruitful even in its disorder and its abrasiveness. This debate was ultimately about self-definition, and thus about worldview as well." Melvin Patrick Ely, *The Adventures of Amos 'n' Andy: A Social History of an American Phenomenon* (Charlottesville: University Press of Virginia, 2001), 248.
60. Louis Armstrong, letter to unknown recipient, 1987.9.9, Louis Armstrong House Museum.
61. Tape 2003.200.1, Louis Armstrong House Museum.

Chapter 14

1. K. K. Hansen, "Casa Loma 'Goop' Goes to Town on Critic," *Down Beat*, May 1936, 4.
2. "Louis Armstrong Undergoes Operation: Old Satchmo Must Stay In Several Weeks," *Chicago Defender*, January 23, 1937, 2. Armstrong was going through a spell of calling the 21-year-old Clarence his "cousin," writing to a friend, "He used to call me 'papa until recently I had to stop him because his voice became too heavy, and it made me seem that I was an old man..Ha..Ha..Never no old man, No Suh." Louis Armstrong, letter to J. H. Reese, January 29, 1937.
3. Louis Armstrong, letter to J. H. Reese, January 29, 1937.
4. Jones and Chilton, *Louis*, 164.
5. Chilton, *Ride, Red, Ride*, 96.
6. Holmes, BBC interview.
7. Billy Rowe, "Billy Rowe's Note Book," *Pittsburgh Courier*, April 6, 1947, 18.
8. Allan McMillan, "Amazing Popularity of Louis Armstrong Nets 'Swing King' 10,000 Fan Letters," *Pittsburgh Courier*, March 20, 1937, 18.
9. Edgar Jackson, "Swing Music Reviewed," *The Gramophone*, June 1937, 28.
10. Harry Mills, interview with Steve Allen for BBC 2 Radio documentary series *Satchmo: The Life and Times of Louis Armstrong*, c. 1973.
11. Billy Rowe, "Louis Armstrong Breaks All Box Office Records in Philly prior to Start of Commercial," *Pittsburgh Courier*, April 10, 1937, 19.
12. "Main Street with Ol' Scoops Daly," *Radio Daily*, March 25, 1937, 4.
13. Louis Armstrong, letter to "George," April 5, 1933, http://www.invaluable.com/auction-lot/armstrong,-louis.-autograph-letter-signed-louis-216-c-9c330bfdca. "That those who loved and took pride in black music and humor often enjoyed *Amos 'n' Andy* reminds us how tricky it can be to define black consciousness, black militancy, and the relationship between the two," Melvin Patrick Ely has written. Ely, *The Adventures of Amos 'n' Andy*, 193.
14. Billy Rowe, "Louis Armstrong, His Orchestra Sign to Headline Coast-to-Coast Commercial Business Concern," *Pittsburgh Courier*, April 3, 1937, 19.
15. "Premiere," *Oakland Tribune*, April 9, 1937, 12.
16. "Air Parade in Review: Louis Armstrong," *Radio Daily*, April 12, 1937, 6.
17. Land, "Radio Reviews," *Variety*, April 14, 1937, 38.

18. Billy Rowe, "Billy Rowe Gives His Criticisms of Armstrong's Debut," *Pittsburgh Courier*, April 17, 1937, 18.

19. "Editorial: Whose Commercial Was It? Armstrong's or Cohen's!," *Pittsburgh Courier*, April 17, 1937, 18.

20. "Armstrong Show Reviewed," *New York Amsterdam News*, April 17, 1937, 16.

21. "Would Boycott Satchmo Program," *Philadelphia Tribune*, April 15, 1937, 16.

22. Frank Marshall Davis (as Franklin Frank), "Things Theatrical: Rev. Satchelmouth and Brother Cook," *Galveston Guide*, April 17, 1937, 2. Davis gave the example of the African American team of Miller and Lyles, who were given a show on CBS in an attempt to compete with *Amos 'n' Andy* and their white actors doing black dialect. It didn't work. "Our black wolves helped haul them down from that high porch," Davis wrote.

23. Davis, "Things Theatrical," 2.

24. Earl J. Morris, "In Grand Town," *Pittsburgh Courier*, April 17, 1937, 18.

25. "Trumpet King Clicks on Commercial Radio Program," *Baltimore Afro-American*, April 17, 1937, 5.

26. Billy Rowe, "Armstrong Heads to Paramount," *Pittsburgh Courier*, April 17, 1937, 18.

27. E. Robertson, "Armstrong's Band Wows Patrons of Paramount Theatre," *New York Amsterdam News*, April 24, 1937.

28. Billy Rowe, "Armstrong Breaks All Records at Paramount," 19.

29. "Radio Reviews: Follow Up Comment," *Variety*, April 28, 1937, 40.

30. Richard M. Greenwood, "Radio," *Journal and Courier*, May 6, 1937, 29.

31. Frank Marshall Davis (as Franklyn Frank), "Commentators Using 'Sinister Propaganda' to Drive Armstrong Off the Air," May 15, 1937, 19.

32. Frank Marshall Davis (as Franklyn Frank), "Things Theatrical: Notes on Satchmo," *Philadelphia Tribune*, May 20, 1937, 13.

33. "Lloyd's Insures Louis Armstrong Delivery in New York," *Variety*, May 12, 1937, 29. Paramount also insured that Armstrong get to Hollywood early on Saturday morning so he could put in a full day's work, but a dust storm in Kansas City caused a five-hour delay and Armstrong didn't land until 2 P.M., costing the studio $5,000 immediately. Billy Rowe, "Plane Delay Cost Lloyds $5,000 on Louie Armstrong," *Pittsburgh Courier*, June 12, 1937.

34. Bernice Patton, " 'Wanted Louie to Work with Me,' Martha Raye: Famed Film Star Raves about Work of Trumpet King," *Pittsburgh Courier*, June 12, 1937, 21.

35. Joe McElhaney, *Vincente Minnelli: The Art of Entertainment* (Detroit: Wayne State University Press, 2009), 435.

36. "Armstrong Series Ending," *Radio Daily*, June 7, 1937, 6.

37. Billy Rowe, "Armstrong's Radio Engagement Ends June 25," *Pittsburgh Courier*, June 19, 1937, 20.

38. Porter Roberts, "Praise and Criticism," *Pittsburgh Courier*, June 23, 1937, 23. Armstrong never spoke out against criticism from Roberts and other members of his race, but it did affect his friend and contemporary Fats Waller, who threatened to quit the music business after a steady stream of complaints from Roberts. Waller said that much harm was being done to black bandleaders by the "destructive pokes that are issued and fall into the hands of promoters of the other race in different sections of the country. What I can't understand is why the campaign to place the paper in the hands of white people for them to see the personal jibes of such critics who offer nothing constructive." He added, "Let

these critics travel some and they will know that they are flaying the wrong individuals when they jump us." J. T. Duncan, "Fats Waller to Quit as Orchestra Leader," *Pittsburgh Courier*, August 21, 1937, 21.

39. Billy Rowe, "Billy Rowe Places Blame for Armstrong's Failure on Air at Door of Program's Sponsor," *Pittsburgh Courier*, July 10, 1937, 21.

40. Land, "Radio Reviews: Rudy Vallee Hour," July 14, 1937, 14.

41. Louis Armstrong, letter to Leonard Feather, September 18, 1941, Louis Armstrong House Museum, 1987.9.10.

42. Earl J. Morris, "Earl J. Morris in Grand Town Day and Night," *Pittsburgh Courier*, July 3, 1937, 20.

Chapter 15

1. That doesn't mean they weren't subject to the Kapp treatment; on July 7, they had two pop tunes waiting for them, "Smarty" and "Listen My Children and You Shall Hear," but Kapp also allowed them to record two instrumentals, "John's Idea" and "One O'Clock Jump," the latter becoming a Swing Era anthem and Basie's eternal theme song (and the recipient of a two-star review in *Melody Maker* from Leonard Feather as "Rophone").

2. "Benny Goodman Tops Paramount Band Poll," *Variety*, August 11, 1937.

3. Walter Winchell, "On Broadway," *Wilkes-Barre Times Leader, The Evening News*, August 5, 1937, 25.

4. Abel Green, "Film Reviews: Artists and Models," *Variety*, August 4, 1937, 18.

5. "Dixie's Deep-South Blast over 'A&M's' Raye-Armstrong Bit," *Variety*, September 15, 1937, 2.

6. "Will Probe Ban on Mixed Movie," *Pittsburgh Courier*, January 15, 1938, 1, 4.

7. "Martha Raye 'Goes Colored' and the South Raises 'Cain,'" *Pittsburgh Courier*, January 1, 1937, 18. The *Independent* responded, "It is clear that Mr. Rush advocates Negro performers displaying their art only on company with other Negro performers on the assumption that the mixing of blacks and whites tends to degrade the white race. From the events taking place in the world today, Negroes could hardly degrade the white race more than they are degrading themselves—among those events being the rape of Ethiopia and the wanton slaughter of women and children at Guernios."

8. Bernice Patton, "Hollywood Tattle," *Pittsburgh Courier*, August 21, 1937, 21.

9. "Louis Armstrong Starts to Build Money 'Nest Egg,' Pays on $75,000 Annuity," *Pittsburgh Courier*, July 24, 1937, 21.

10. Tape 1987.3.254, Louis Armstrong House Museum.

11. Holmes, BBC interview.

12. Holmes, JOHP interview.

13. Armstrong and Meryman, *A Self-Portrait*, 46.

14. Louis Armstrong, acetate disc of April 1950 interview for *The Record Changer*, 2013.70.6, Louis Armstrong House Museum.

15. Louis Armstrong, acetate disc of April 1950 interview for *The Record Changer*, 2013.70.7, Louis Armstrong House Museum.

16. Ibid.

17. Armstrong and Meryman, *A Self Portrait*, 48.

18. Frank Marshall Davis, "ANP Presents '37 All-American Swing Band," *Pittsburgh Courier*, February 5, 1938, 21.

19. Porter Roberts, "Praise and Criticism," *Pittsburgh Courier*, December 18, 1937, 21.

20. Sallye Bell in the Associated Negro Press praised Armstrong's appearance on Crosby's show, writing, "If you heard the broadcast, you will recall that when Bing introduced Louis—rather when he announced him, for who needs an introduction to Ol' Satchmo?—there was not even the slightest shade of a difference in his manner as compared to when he announced Connie Boswell and the other guest artists. . . . Hats off, then, to Bing Crosby and the Kraft Music Hall for bringing us such a treat—and if we want to give our fan mail campaign a good start in the New Year, let's drop a letter or card to our local station through whose facilities the program came to us and let them know how much we appreciate it. . . . Let them hear from you, and you'll be on the road to hearing more and more of our Negro stars on these major programs." Sallye Bell, "In New Mae West Flicker," *Pittsburgh Courier*, January 8, 1938, 20.

21. Tape 1987.3.475, Louis Armstrong House Museum.

22. Holmes, JOHP interview.

23. Leonard Feather (as "Rophone"), "Vocal Mixture for Record Fans," *Melody Maker*, September 24, 1938.

24. Edgar Jackson, "Swing Music Reviewed," *The Gramophone*, October 1938, 213.

25. Roger Catlin, "To Really Appreciate Louis Armstrong's Trumpet, You Gotta Play It. Just Ask Wynton Marsalis," Smithsonian.com, May 23, 2016, https://www.smithsonianmag.com/smithsonian-institution/to-really-appreciate-louis-armstrongs-trumpet-you-gotta-play-it-180959184/?no-ist.

26. Nicholas Payton, Instagram post, January 18, 2019.

27. Though the Decca record now credited Louis as the composer, leading to an ugly spat between the two. Louis eventually let Lil keep the songwriter credit so she could collect royalties, telling friends, "She needs it more than I do," but he never stopped claiming publicly that he was the one who composed it.

28. "Satchmo Revisited," *Down Beat*, January 8, 1959, 15.

29. "Incorporations," *Motion Picture Herald*, October 30, 1937, 68.

30. "Rockwell-O'Keefe to Expand Band Dep't: Glaser Will Be 'Key Man' of New Broadway Set-Up," *Pittsburgh Courier*, March 19, 1938, 20.

31. "Armstrong's Loew's State Contracts Makes Him Highest Paid Attraction," *Pittsburgh Courier*, March 12, 1938, 20.

32. Armstrong and Meryman, *A Self-Portrait*, 49.

33. Louis Armstrong, acetate disc of April 1950 interview for *The Record Changer*, 2013.70.9, Louis Armstrong House Museum.

34. "Satchmo Is Soloist as King Joe Dies," *Baltimore Afro-American*, April 23, 1938, 10.

35. Louis Armstrong, acetate disc of April 1950 interview for *The Record Changer*, 2013.70.9, Louis Armstrong House Museum.

36. Roderick O. Williams, "Records in Review," *Brooklyn Daily Eagle*, 28. "The Week's Best Records," *Billboard*, August 6, 1938, 68. Walter Winchell, "On Broadway," *Cincinnati Enquirer*, August 10, 1938, 8.

37. Leonard Feather (as "Rophone), "Hot Records Reviewed," *Melody Maker*, November 19, 1938.

38. Billy Rowe, "What Happened to Louis Armstrong in Bing Crosby's Latest Picture," *Pittsburgh Courier*, June 11, 1938, 21.

39. Earl J. Morris, "Earl J. Morris in Grand Town Day and Night," *Pittsburgh Courier*, July 9, 1938, 20.

40. Earl J. Morris, "Tells Why Louie Didn't Appear in Crosby Picture," *Pittsburgh Courier*, July 16, 1938, 21.

41. Earl J. Morris, "Earl J. Morris in Grand Town Day and Night," *Pittsburgh Courier*, July 16, 1938, 21. Such prints have apparently not survived and "The Trumpet Player's Lament" remains lost to this day.

42. Earl J. Morris, "American Whites, Negroes Being Shoved into Background in Movies by Jewish Film Owners," *Pittsburgh Courier*, August 27, 1938, 20.

43. "Tiny Bradshaw and Peters Sisters on New Apollo Bill," *New York Age*, June 25, 1938, 7.

44. Marita Berg, "The Nazis Take On Degenerate Music," *DW*, May 24, 2013, https://www.dw.com/en/the-nazis-take-on-degenerate-music/a-16834697.

45. Unpublished quotes from a conversation between Mick Carlon and Heinz Praeger in 1992. Courtesy of Mick Carlon.

Chapter 16

1. "Joe Glaser's Change," *Variety*, July 20, 1938, 39.

2. Roderick O. Williams, "Records in Review," *Brooklyn Daily Eagle*, May 22, 1938, 37.

3. Harry James, "Jammin' with James," *Metronome*, August 1938.

4. Private tape made with George Avakian, November 1, 1953. Courtesy of David Ostwald and George Avakian.

5. Louis Armstrong, letter to Elmer Lewis, August 18, 1938, Louis Armstrong House Museum, 2015.17.2.

6. Tape 2003.200.1, Louis Armstrong House Museum. Armstrong's battles with Jeepers Creepers even made it into Jimmie Fidler's popular gossip column, Fidler describing the horse "rearing and plunging in vicious form" one day, quoting Armstrong as saying, "I'se going to apply for mah Social Security. I'se aged enough this morning to be eligible." Jimmie Fidler, "With Jimmie Fidler in Hollywood," *Quad-City Times*, October 7, 1938, 10.

7. "Behind the Make-Up," *Wilkes-Barre Record*, September 17, 1938, 6.

8. Armstrong even enjoyed making the cast and crew laugh on set. When filming the final scene where Jeepers Creepers wins the climactic race and receives a garland of flowers, the horse was supposed to lean over and kiss Armstrong but instead, Armstrong bent over and kissed the horse first, which, according to one report, "broke up the cast and necessitated remaking the film." "5,000 Loss," *Amarillo Globe-Times*, January 5, 1939, 9.

9. Collier, *Louis Armstrong: An American Genius*, 282. It's a conspiracy theory but the brouhaha over "Struttin' with Some Barbecue" might have led to Lil's decision as she was not pleased to see her ex-husband's name listed as composer on a song she was originally credited with composing. The record would have been released in mid-1938 and Lil did sue Louis over the issue at some point, which is perhaps why she was in a spiteful mood in the fall of 1938.

10. John R. Williams, "Armstrong Romance Ends in Wedding Bells," *Pittsburgh Courier*, October 22, 1938, 20. Armstrong's public statement on Alpha seemed to echo his private letters of the 1930s, in which he almost always found time to praise his sweetheart, as seen in a 1933 letter to Red Allen in which Armstrong bragged, "She's the sweetest thing in 'All this world. I'll never 'die as long as 'Alpha And I stay together. She's so sweet to me. WE

LOVE EACH OTHER." But in the same letter to Allen, Armstrong showed that he hadn't lost his wandering eye, inquiring about a chorus girl at Small's Paradise in Harlem, saying, "She doesn't 'even 'know it 'herself, 'that I 'have "Fresh Love" for 'her'. Ha. Ha. Oh how I'll 'watch that 'Gal. Is she still down THERE? Find out for 'me wilya WILL, YOU? Ha. Ha." Louis Armstrong, letter to Henry "Red" Allen, April 20, 1933.

11. Louis Armstrong, "Why I Like Dark Women," *Ebony*, August 1954, 65.
12. "Notes—Louis Armstrong—Blue Note," November 29, 1953, 5. Historic New Orleans Collection M35 536, Armstrong, F31.
13. Hank Cherry, "Bunk Johnson: History Is Bunk," *OffBeat Magazine*, June 1, 2010, www.off-beat.com/articles/bunk-johnson-history-is-bunk/.
14. Billy Rowe, "Armstrong's Magnetism, Personality Top Whiteman's Carnegie Hall Concert," *Pittsburgh Courier*, December 31, 1938, 17.
15. Roscoe Williams, "Hollywood Previews: Going Places," *Motion Picture Daily*, December 21, 1938, 8.
16. Philip K. Scheur, "Dick Powell Steeplechase Rider in New Song Farce," *Los Angeles Times*, January 2, 1939, 10.
17. Frank S. Nugent, " 'Going Places' at the Strand," *New York Times*, January 7, 1939, 6.
18. Joe Glaser Inc. ad, *Variety*, January 18, 1939, 56.
19. Porter Roberts, "Praise and Criticism," *Pittsburgh Courier*, January 7, 1939, 20.
20. Earl J. Morris, "Earl Morris Tells Who to Thank in Hollywood," *Pittsburgh Courier*, January 14, 1939, 11.
21. Louis Armstrong, "Louis Armstrong + The Jewish Family in New Orleans, La., 1907," Louis Armstrong House Museum, 1987.2.1, 55. But Armstrong also learned that sharing a bill with Robinson had its own challenges. At the Strand one night, Armstrong was playing "The Skeleton in the Closet" and "just as I was getting ready to hit that high note," Armstrong wrote, Robinson interrupted him on stage and said, "Wait a minute, Satchmo, just one minute!" Armstrong stopped playing, writing that "a gush of wind came from my mouth because I was getting ready to hit that High Ass note." As Armstrong and his band wondered, "What tha Fuck's his Story now?" Robinson walked across the stage and gave a photo to a little girl in the audience because she reminded him of Shirley Temple! "No one else in the world could HAVE gotten away with that shit but the great Bill(Bojangles) Robinson. . . . Nobody else would have the nerve anyway . . . tee heeeee" Louis Armstrong, "Forward" [*sic*] to unpublished joke book, c. 1943, Louis Armstrong House Museum, 1987.2.20, 2–3.
22. Tape 1987.3.248, Louis Armstrong House Museum. Ruby Braff would listen to Armstrong's Decca recordings with the trumpeter when he visited him at his Corona, Queens, home in the 1950s and remembered Armstrong often exclaiming, "There's that Catlett again! Seems like he was on every swinging record I ever made." Michael Steinman, "Sidney Catlett at 100," January 16, 2010, https://jazzlives.wordpress.com/2010/01/16/sidney-catlett-at-100/.
23. Louis Armstrong, "Forward" [*sic*] to unpublished joke book, c. 1943, Louis Armstrong House Museum, 1987.2.20, 3.
24. "Is Hot Jazz Cooling Off?," *Daily Mail*, January 20, 1939, 6.
25. Edgar Jackson, "Swing Music Reviewed," *The Gramophone*, October 1937, 214.
26. Edgar Jackson, "Swing Music Reviewed," *The Gramophone*, September 1939, 167.
27. "Says 'Swinging Spiritual' Is Disgrace to Race," *Pittsburgh Courier*, March 11, 1939, 15.

28. "Baptist Reverend Asks for Pardon," *Pittsburgh Courier*, March 25, 1939, 14.

29. Isabel M. Thompson, "Armstrong Defends 'Saints' Record," *Pittsburgh Courier*, April 8, 1939, 21.

30. Onah Spencer, "Satchmo' Big Again; Catlett Won't Leave," *Down Beat*, August 1939.

31. "CRA-Joe Glaser Combine," *Billboard*, June 17, 1939, 13.

32. Tape 1987.3.254, Louis Armstrong House Museum. As Armstrong settled into the Cotton Club, Walter Winchell even got a dig in at Connie Immerman. "A dozen years ago Louis Armstrong got $20 weekly trumpeting at Connie's Inn," Winchell wrote. "Now Louis gets $1,750 a week at the Cotton Club, where Connie is the head waiter." Walter Winchell, "On Broadway," *Cincinnati Enquirer*, October 16, 1939, 18.

33. "Cotton Club News," *New York Times*, October 29, 1939, 2.

34. Robinson not only taught Armstrong about the stage, but also about food. Growing up poor, Armstrong admitted, "It was a long time before I had a steak. . . . But when I came up here and played in the Cotton Club on the bill with Bill Robinson, I noticed after he got back he got dressed and went out in the room and he was eating. I was talking to him and I said, 'What is that you're eating, what kind of steak?' He said, 'Filet mignon.' From then on I had to have filet mignon, if Bill Robinson had one!" Bob Rusch, "Louis Armstrong Interview," *Cadence*, January 1986, 8. Original interview took place on February 7, 1969.

35. Louis Armstrong, letter to William Russell, October 3, 1939, the Historic New Orleans Collection, MSS 536, Louis Armstrong, f. 2, 92-48-L.

36. Louis Armstrong, letter to Hoyt Kline, October 22, 1939, Historic New Orleans Collection M33 536, L. Armstrong, f. 4.

37. "Looks at Books," *Pittsburgh Courier*, November 25, 1939, 7.

38. "On the Beat," *Variety*, September 6, 1939, 34.

39. "'He's Promised to Me," Two Producers Say; Satchmo Says Nothing," *Afro-American*, November 4, 1939, 14.

40. Louis Sobol, "The Voice of New York," *The Press Democrat*, November 19, 1939, 16.

41. Tape 1987.3.454, Louis Armstrong House Museum.

42. "Billing Battle," *Variety*, November 15, 1939.

43. "Armstrong, Goodman to Get Same Billing," *Pittsburgh Courier*, November 18, 1939, 20.

44. The original opening night *Playbill* can be viewed at http://www.playbill.com/production/swingin-the-dream-center-theatre-vault-0000012011.

45. Floyd G. Snelson, "Harlem," *New York Age*, November 25, 1939, 4.

46. Tape 1987.3.237, Louis Armstrong House Museum.

47. Ibid.

48. George Ross, "Broadway," *Pittsburgh Press*, November 27, 1939, 9.

49. Dorothy Kilgallen, *Miami News*, December 1, 1939, 19.

50. Arthur Pollock, "Shakespeare Gets Swung at Center," *Brooklyn Daily Eagle*, November 30, 1939, 11.

51. "'Swingin' the Dream' Review," *Billboard*, December 9, 1939, 16.

52. Philip Carter, "Plenty of Swing in 'Dream' but Acting Is at Premium," *New York Amsterdam News*, December 9, 1939.

53. Brooks Atkinson, "Swinging Shakespeare's 'Dream' with Benny Goodman, Louis Armstrong and Maxine Sullivan," *New York Times*, November 30, 1939, 24.

54. William G. Nunn, "'Swingin' the Dream' Has Something . . . but What!," *Pittsburgh Courier*, December 9, 1939, 20.

55. The revue was originally due to co-star Stepin Fetchit, but Fetchit proved to be a handful; his lazy on-screen comic persona was becoming out of favor with black audiences and his reckless offstage behavior kept him in the headlines for all the wrong reasons. Unlike Bill Robinson, Fetchit didn't want to be "slumming" in an all-vaudeville bill and insisted on production numbers with the Cotton Club dancers. On his second night, he missed his cue by ten minutes and soon after, walked off abruptly, not to return.

56. Paul Denis, "Cotton Club New Show Good; Armstrong, Sullivan Featured," *Billboard*, December 9, 1939, 18.

57. Nunn, "Swingin' the Dream' Has Something . . . but What!," 20.

58. "Brady Play Date Advanced," *Los Angeles Times*, December 7, 1939, 12.

59. Joseph Dorfman, "Not Enough Armstrong," *Science and Society*, undated clipping found in Institute of Jazz Studies clippings file.

60. "Benny Goodman and Sextet Leave 'Dream,'" *Afro-American*, December 9, 1939, 13.

61. "'Swingin' the Dream' at End of Run: Play Needed More Financial Backing," *Afro-American*, December 16, 1939, 14.

62. Billy Rowe, "'Swingin' the Dream' Loses Its Swing: Closes," *Pittsburgh Courier*, December 16, 1939, 21.

63. George Ross, "In New York," *Chester Times*, December 20, 1939, 9.

64. George R. Dempsey, "Reviewing the Records," *Oshkosh Northwestern*, January 24, 1940, 8.

65. "The Biggest Money Making Stars of 1939," *Motion Picture Herald*, December 23, 1939, 13–15.

66. "Louis Armstrong Is Sued for Love Balm," *Afro-American*, November 25, 1939, 1.

67. "Better after Operation," *Pittsburgh Courier*, December 30, 1939, 20.

Chapter 17

1. Lucille later claimed to have graduated high school but only left behind a diploma from June 25, 1929, stating that she "completed satisfactorily the studies prescribed for the Industrial Course in the Junior High School of the City of New York and is entitled to admission to the second year in this course in the High Schools." In interviews, she said she started working at 15, which would be 1929, the year of the Stock Market crash. See diploma at 1987.15.34, Louis Armstrong House Museum.

2. Carolyn A. Bowers, "Lucille—The Woman behind the Great Satchmo," *Buenos Aires Herald*, May 17, 1971, 5.

3. Armstrong, "Why I Like Dark Women," 61.

4. Untitled, undated news clipping from 1935, found at 1987.8.36-03, Louis Armstrong House Museum.

5. Clare Doctor, "The Road Is Home to Mrs. Satchmo," *Long Island Press*, March 7, 1965, 37.

6. "From Chorus to Star," undated news clipping from 1936, found at 1987.8.36, Louis Armstrong House Museum.

7. Doctor, "The Road Is Home to Mrs. Satchmo," 37.

8. Billy Rowe, "Billy Rowe's Harlem Note Book," *Pittsburgh Courier*, May 15, 1937, 12, and December 4, 1937, 21.

9. Armstrong, "Why I Like Dark Women," 61.

10. Louis Armstrong, "Open Letter to Fans," 1970, Louis Armstrong House Museum, 1987.2.8, 14–19.

11. Tape 1987.3.481, Louis Armstrong House Museum.

12. Untitled, undated manuscript, Louis Armstrong House Museum, 1987.2.6, 2–6.

13. Louis Armstrong, letter to Elmer Lewis, July 16, 1940, 2015.17.2.

14. Paul Ross, "New Decade Spells Death for Jitterbug Stuff; Public Prefers Sweet Melody, Survey Shows," *Great Falls Tribune*, February 20, 1940, 7.

15. Barry Ulanov, "Swing Band Review," *Metronome*, March 1940, 19, 31.

16. "Armstrong Gets Rid of Eight Men," *Pittsburgh Courier*, May 11, 1940, 21.

17. Foster with Stoddard, *Pops Foster*, 165–166.

18. Charlie Holmes, JOHP interview, October 9, 1982.

19. Holmes, BBC interview.

20. Chilton, *Ride, Red, Ride*, 111.

21. "Satchmo's Raids Hawkins' Band," *Down Beat*, June 15, 1940. Upon reading a report that he had "blitzkrieged" Hawkins's orchestra, Armstrong, referring to his new band as "a solid sender," wrote a column in the *Tattler* to address the accusation, writing, "There's no such thing as a blitzkrieg (or whatever that dern word is) . . . anyway, there's no such thing in music." Louis Armstrong, "Special Jive," *Tattler*, July 19, 1940, 17.

22. Onah Spencer, "New Armstrong Band Is His Best Yet, Says Spencer," *Down Beat*, July 1, 1940, 15.

23. Tape 1987.3.424, Louis Armstrong House Museum.

24. Sidney Bechet, *Treat It Gentle* (New York: Da Capo Press, 1978), 176.

25. John Chilton, *Sidney Bechet: The Wizard of Jazz* (New York: Da Capo Press, 1996), 129.

26. Ibid., 128.

27. Bechet, *Treat It Gentle*, 175–176.

28. Frank Marshall Davis, "New Orleans Jazz Album Proves Oldsters' Worth," *Baltimore Afro-American*, October 5, 1940, 14.

29. Edgar Jackson, "Decca's 'New Orleans Jazz Album' Reviewed," *Melody Maker*, September 13, 1941, 3.

30. Daniel Richman, "On the Records," *Billboard*, October 5, 1940, 12.

31. George Avakian, interviewed by Ann Sneed, National Museum of American History, September 28, 1993, https://americanhistory.si.edu/sites/default/files/file-uploader/Avakian_Goegre_Interview_Transcription%20%282%29.pdf.

32. "Patter off the Platter," *Radio Varieties*, November 1940, 2.

33. Mark Barron, "Anderson's Bible Play," *Cincinnati Enquirer*, October 13, 1940, 3.

34. "On the Lighter Side," *Tampa Tribune*, February 2, 1941, 43.

35. Robert White, "Record Turn Table," *Arizona Daily Star*, December 8, 1940, 28.

36. Paul Eduard Miller, "Musical Blasphemies," *Music and Rhythm*, January 1941.

37. "Gold," "Variety House Reviews: Oriental, Chi.," *Variety*, February 19, 1941, 47.

38. "On the Record," *Tampa Tribune*, June 15, 1941, 41.

39. Frank Marshall Davis, "Rating the Records," *Atlanta Daily World*, June 2, 1941, 2.

40. "Hot Jazz," *Des Moines Register*, May 18, 1941, 8.

41. M. Oakley Christoph, "Strictly Off the Record," *Hartford Courant*, May 18, 1941, 23.

42. "Louis Armstrong," *Down Beat*, June 1, 1941, clipping found in scrapbook 1987.8.11, Louis Armstrong House Museum.

43. "DISCussions," *Metronome*, September 1941, clipping found in scrapbook 1987.8.11, Louis Armstrong House Museum.

44. Original autographed artifact can be found at 1987.3.1535, Louis Armstrong House Museum.
45. George Avakian, interviewed by Ann Sneed, National Museum of American History, September 28, 1993, https://americanhistory.si.edu/sites/default/files/file-uploader/ Avakian_Goegre_Interview_Transcription%20%282%29.pdf.
46. Martin Mack, "Armstrong, Sweet and Hot," *New Masses*, August 12, 1941.
47. Howard Taubman, "Records: Mozart Feast," *New York Times*, August 3, 1941, 6x. Don Woodrum, "Reviewing the Records," *Honolulu Star-Bulletin*, July 19, 1941, 35.
48. Peter Dana, " 'Satchmo' Rated Master Showman," *New Journal and Guide*, June 7, 1941, 15.

Chapter 18

1. Armstrong, letter to Leonard Feather, August 5, 1941.
2. Zilner Randolph, JOHP interview.
3. Louis Armstrong, letter to Leonard Feather, September 18, 1941.
4. Charlie Emge, "Orson Welles Jazz Movie Will Star Louis Armstrong," *Down Beat*, August 15, 1941.
5. Edgar T. Rouzeau, "Stardust," *Journal & Guide*, September 6, 1941.
6. Bill Newton, "Celebrating the Silver Jubilee of Louis Armstrong's Trumpet," *Daily Worker*, November 13, 1941.
7. Louis Armstrong, letter to Leonard Feather, September 18, 1941.
8. "Lil Armstrong Snubbed by Hollywood," *Down Beat*, October 1, 1941.
9. "Billie Holiday to Play Role of Bessie Smith in Armstrong Film," *Pittsburgh Courier*, October 18, 1941, 20.
10. "Inside Stuff—Orchestras," *Variety*, September 10, 1941, 32.
11. "Louis Film Director Slaps at Duke," *Metronome*, November 1941, clipping found in scrapbook 1987.8.11, Louis Armstrong House Museum.
12. "RKO Filming of Louis Armstrong Postponed," *Pittsburgh Courier*, October 25, 1941, 21.
13. Louis Armstrong, "60-year-old 'Bunk' Johnson, Louis' Tutor, Sits in the Band," *Down Beat*, August 15, 1941.
14. Armstrong, "60-year-old Bunk Johnson."
15. Kenny Clarke, Jazz Oral History Project interview with Helen Oakley Dance, Institute of Jazz Studies, Rutgers University, September 1, 1977.
16. Mike Hennessey, *Klook: The Story of Kenny Clarke* (London: Quartet Books, 1990), 33.
17. Harold Turner, "Offshoots," *Pensacola News Journal*, August 29, 1941, 4.
18. Louis Armstrong, letter to Leonard Feather, October 1, 1941.
19. Ibid.
20. Clarke, JOHP interview.
21. Leonard Feather [as Geoffrey Marne], "The Waxworks," *Swing Magazine*, December 1941, 34.
22. D. Leon Wolff, "Louis Armstrong Stopped Being God in 1932," *Music and Rhythm*, August 1941, IJS clippings file.
23. Leonard Feather, " 'I Never Tried to Be God,' Cries Louis," *Music and Rhythm*, September 1941, 9, , clipping found in scrapbook 1987.8.11, Louis Armstrong House Museum.
24. Ibid.

25. Coincidently, on December 7, the *Hartford Courant* published a blurb reading, "A letter from England to Louis Armstrong reveals that seven Armstrong fan clubs, of which Louis became president during his visits to Britain, are still active, some holding their sessions in air-raid shelters." M. Oakley Christoph, "Strictly Off the Record," *Hartford Courant*, December 7, 1941, 27.

26. "U. S. People Keeping Calm, Satchmo Says," *Winnipeg Free Press*, December 10, 1941, 5.

27. Billy Rowe, "Billy Rowe's Notebook," *Pittsburgh Courier*, December 13, 1941, 20.

28. "Facing the Music," *Radio and Television Mirror*, August 1942, 78.

29. "Glaser Shifts Brown, Other Orchs to MCA for Booking, but Keeps Control," *Variety*, December 31, 1941, 39.

30. Bob Musel, "On Broadway," *Herald Tribune*, January 19, 1942, 9.

31. Louis Armstrong, letter to Walter Winchell, January 19, 1942, 2008.1.60, Louis Armstrong House Museum.

32. Walter Winchell, "On Broadway: The Love Letters of a New Yorker," *Muncie Evening Press*, January 22, 1942, 5.

33. Billy Rowe, "Billy Rowe's Notebook," *Pittsburgh Courier*, January 31, 1942, 21.

34. "Louis Armstrong's Wife Wants Freedom: Asks $250 Alimony $5000 Counsel Fee in Separation Suit," *Philadelphia Tribune*, February 7, 1942, 15.

35. Billy Rowe, "Billy Rowe's Notebook," *Pittsburgh Courier*, February 7, 1942, 20.

36. "Negroes Pre-Dominate in New All-Star Band," *Pittsburgh Courier*, January 10, 1942, 19.

37. "Courier All-American—$1,000,000 In Talent," *Pittsburgh Courier*, February 7, 1942, 20.

38. Ted Yates, "Hail Louis Armstrong's Band as Finest He's Had in Years," *Philadelphia Tribune*, February 28, 1942, 15.

39. Armstrong also never recorded it in the studio but as late as a 1944 Eddie Condon broadcast from Town Hall, when vocalist Liza Morrow told Condon she was going to perform this song, Condon replied, "That's the favorite song of Louie Armstrong's, isn't it?" Clearly, it was one of Armstrong's regular features in this period, further proof that the studio records don't tell the complete story.

40. Joe Glaser, "Why Operators Are Getting Better Records," *Billboard* supplement, September 27, 1941, 16.

41. "A Tough Fight Looms," *Variety*, June 17, 1942, 41.

42. "Metro's 'Cabin in the Sky' May Pave the Way for More Negro Films," *Variety*, April 8, 1942, 22.

43. Peter Suskind, "Stardust: 'Satchmo' Picture Off List," *New Journal and Guide*, May 30, 1942, 17.

44. Walter Winchell, "On Broadway," *Bradford Evening Star*, March 3, 1942, 3.

45. Walter Winchell, "On Broadway," *Akron Beacon Journal*, March 18, 1942, 15.

46. Louis Armstrong, letter to Walter Winchell, May 31, 1942.

47. "Movie Machine Reviews," *Billboard*, July 4, 1942, 69.

48. Pinfold, *Louis Armstrong*, 96. "Man, he was cute, but do you know what? Pops lost so much power," Galbreath said. "He never realized the reason was this self-imposed diet." Finally, Galbreath said "someone struck on the idea that Satch would stand in the spotlight with the horn to his lips and I'd stand in the back and do the blowing. And that's what we did! Imagine this!" Armstrong relied on his singing and his talented variety revue to fool the critics, as *Billboard* reviewed him at the Orpheum and gave him a positive notice, only referring to him as "vocalizing" on numbers like "Exactly Like You," "Cash for Your Trash,"

and "Blues in the Night," before finally playing a little "hot trumpet"—or was it Galbreath—before an extended drum feature for Catlett on "Blues for the Second Line." Sam Abbott, "Night Clubs—Vaudeville," *Billboard*, May 9, 1942, 21.

49. "Louis Armstrong Breaks Record at Regal Theater: July 4th Attendance Greatest in History," *Chicago Defender*, July 11, 1942, 23.

50. "Glaser Says Bands Will Weather Crisis," *Baltimore Afro-American*, July 28, 1942, 10.

51. Simmons, JOHP interview.

52. Ibid.

Chapter 19

1. "Hollywood Goes Glaser!" advertisement, *Variety*, August 26, 1942, 42.

2. "Inside Stuff—Orchestras," *Variety*, September 16, 1942, 41.

3. "[A]ccording to managers of Negro groups, the past four or six weeks has seen a sharp stepping up of induction orders among the personnel of their properties and the supply of good colored men isn't equal to the demand," *Variety* reported in September. "Colored Bands Hit by Draft for 1st Time," *Variety*, September 16, 1942, 41.

4. Louis Armstrong, letter to William Russell, September 25, 1942, Historic New Orleans Collection M35 536, L. Armstrong, f. 7.

5. Armstrong, "Why I Like Dark Women," 68.

6. George Wein, interview with Louis Armstrong, July 23, 1970, https://www.cv.org/louis-armstrong/unknown-july-23-1970.html.

7. Armstrong, "Why I Like Dark Women," 68.

8. "Funeral services for Mrs. Alpha Smith Armstrong, 53, former wife of musician Louis Armstrong, will be conducted at 11 a.m. Friday in the Chapel of the Spaulding Mortuary, Santa Monica," the *Los Angeles Times* reported on January 6, 1960. "Mrs. Armstrong died Monday after a brief illness. She lived at 709 N Roxbury Dr., Beverly Hills." "Mrs. Alpha Armstrong," *Los Angeles Times*, January 6, 1960, part 3, 2.

9. Lucille Armstrong, *Satchmo: The Life and Times of Louis Armstrong*, BBC Radio 2 documentary, episode 7, February 9, 1975.

10. "Kahn," "House Reviews: Apollo, N. Y.," *Variety*, November 4, 1942, 47.

11. H. P. Goldstein, "Query for Negro Readers," *Pittsburgh Courier*, July 1, 1944, 13.

12. Louis Armstrong, letter to Leonard Feather, October 1, 1941, Louis Armstrong House Museum, 1987.9.10.

13. Armstrong, "Joke Book," 2. Armstrong began writing this joke book in November 1942, referencing his current engagement at the Lyric Theater in Bridgeport, Connecticut. The first two are presumed lost, though Armstrong told Leonard Feather he gave one away to Pvt. George Grow and the troops at Fort Barrancas in 1941.

14. Armstrong, "Joke Book," 3. Armstrong called their time together in Chicago in 1920s "awful glorious days," explaining, "Why I call them glorious days also—is because although they were tough as hell—we did manage to get together almost everyday and rehearse and play to suit our damn selves and not some Jerk Arranger, or some little Ol pimple'ly face Youngster(Hep'Cat) trying to tell us how we should play our instruments . . . Nay Nay . . . we would'nt stand for in those days . . . Maybe thats why we nearly starved to death . . . haw haw haw. . . . Huh?" Armstrong was noticeably losing patience with "pimply-faced youngsters" telling him how he should be playing in the early 1940s. Ibid., 3.

15. Ibid., 2–3.
16. "Charles Mingus' Destiny," *Coda*, February/March 1986, 12.
17. Carlo Alberto Martins, "Mingus: 'Louis Was an Uncle Tom,' " *Jazz Journal International*, October 1977, 20.
18. "Charles Mingus," Facebook post, October 27, 2014. There is a sense of mystery about how long Mingus's tenure in Armstrong's band actually lasted. Most assume he left right before the band toured the south, which would be November–December 1942, meshing with Mingus's own remembrance of being with the band for "two or three months." But Mingus also mentioned joining in Los Angeles, heading north into Canada and then venting while still in Canada about his unwillingness to play the south. "It was on the ferry boat going to Canada that somebody said we were going to the South, and I gave them my views. I wasn't going to take any shit from anybody in the South. So Louis decided it was best that I leave the band." Since Canada was so early in Mingus's tenure, it's possible he lasted two to three weeks rather than months. For more, see Brian Priestley, *Mingus: A Critical Biography* (New York: Da Capo Press, 1982), 19.
19. "Army Jim Crow Laid to Louis Armstrong," *Baltimore Afro-American*, January 9, 1943, 1.
20. Lucille Armstrong, interview in Sweden, January 1959, Tape 2011.20.671, Louis Armstrong House Museum.
21. Harrison Carroll, "Behind the Scenes in Hollywood," *Jackson Sun*, January 29, 1943, 4.
22. "Trumpet King Plays at Duncan Air Field," *Pittsburgh Courier*, January 9, 1943, 20.
23. Paul Denis, "The Negro Makes Advances," *Billboard*, January 2, 1943, 28.
24. Tape 1987.3.176, Louis Armstrong House Museum.
25. Armstrong was still working on his joke book and devoted an entire page to the lyrics to "Ain't It the Truth," writing at the end, "P.S. AIN'T IT THE TRUTH' is the song I recorded in the film 'CABIN IN THE SKIES. But-they-No-Release . . . Why? . . Be 'Damned if I know. . . . Tee Hee." Armstrong, "Joke Book," 69.
26. "The Box Office Slant: Cabin in the Sky," *Showmen's Trade Review*, February 13, 1943, 10.
27. Leo Roa, "Success of 'Cabin in the Sky' Will Help Negroes in Films," *New York Age*, February 13, 1943, 10.
28. Fats Baker, "They Done Him Wrong," *The Jazz Record*, June 15, 1943, 6.
29. Leonard Feather, "Sunny California Section: Feather on the Wing," *Metronome*, undated news clipping.
30. Lucille Armstrong, interview with Steve Allen, c. 1974.
31. Louis Armstrong House Closing Statement, March 3, 1943, 2002.140.1, Louis Armstrong House Museum.
32. Leonard Feather, "Sunny California Section: Feather on the Wing," *Metronome*, undated clipping, 1943, 21.
33. "Alcazar Revue Is Continuing," *Oakland Tribune*, April 19, 1943, 12.
34. Jazz critics were tough on Woods, but audiences loved him and it's unfortunate that he never got an opportunity to record on his own during his time with Armstrong. Armstrong remembered him fondly on a tape he made in the 1950s. When a friend remarked that he thought Woods was only a "blues singer," Armstrong responded, "Everything, everything, no. 'Without a Song,' 'Jeannie with the Light Brown Hair,' 'Empty Saddles'—Sonny Woods sang 'Empty Saddles' in the Apollo and shit, thunderous applause. My God, that boy could sing. Before Eckstine and all of them." Tape 1987.3.269, Louis Armstrong House Museum.

35. "Louis Armstrong Available on Swing Back from Coast," *Pittsburgh Courier*, July 10, 1943, 10.

36. "Glaser's Stable of Orks Running into Big Dough," *Billboard*, May 1, 1943, 20. In July, *Billboard* published a story, "Glaser, Inc., Big Business" about how "Glaser is beginning to think like an agency." The Sherman Hotel in Chicago needed a name band, so Glaser offered them Les Brown—but only if they also took Jan Savitt and Teddy Powell." "Glaser, Inc., Big Business," *Billboard*, July 24, 1943, 18.

37. "MCA Pays Glaser $100,000 for 50% of Agcy; Can Buy Rest in 2 Yrs.," *Variety*, October 13, 1943, 35.

38. "Glaser-Stein, Inc.," *Variety*, December 15, 1943, 40.

39. Lucille Armstrong, interview with Steve Allen, c. 1973.

40. Armstrong, untitled manuscript, 1987.2.6, 51–53.

41. Lucille Armstrong, interview with Steve Allen, c. 1973.

42. Armstrong, untitled manuscript, 1987.2.6, 53.

43. Lucille Armstrong, interview with Steve Allen, c. 1973.

44. "Armstrong Big $40,000 N. Y.," *Variety*, November 3, 34.

45. Joe Evans, Christopher Brooks, *Follow Your Heart: Moving with the Giants of Jazz, Swing, and Rhythm and Blues* (Champaign: University of Illinois Press, 2010), 66.

46. "On the Stand," *Billboard*, November 27, 1943, 15.

Chapter 20

1. Robert Goffin, "Esquire's All-American Band," *Esquire*, February 1943, 74.

2. Izzy Rowe, "'Ace' Negro Musicians Sweep Esquire Mag's Jazz Band Poll," *Pittsburgh Courier*, January 8, 1944, 15.

3. One month after the *Esquire* concert, on February 16, Hawkins would record for Apollo Records, surrounding himself with young lions Dizzy Gillespie, Leo Parker, Don Byas, Oscar Pettiford, and Max Roach. One of the selections recorded, Gillespie's composition "Woody 'n' You," would later be called the first "bebop" record.

4. Chilton, *Roy Eldridge*, 137.

5. Ibid., 137–138.

6. "Sedate 'Met' Invaded by Jazz—Hep-Cats Howl for Bond Drive," *Argus-Leader*, January 19, 1944, 1. In the black press, Dan Burley was not impressed and seemed to predict the eventual rise of Jazz at Lincoln Center almost 60 years later. "I for one didn't go for it," Burley wrote. "The idea in the first place didn't hit me as being just right since I frankly feel that Swing Music has made enough money in the years it has been high in public favor off recordings, radio, night clubs, etc., to build its own Metropolitan House of Jazz right here in New York or elsewhere to provide the ultimate goal of jazz and swingsters as the Metropolitan Opera provides for the future Tibbetts, Flagstads, Melchiors, Pons and others." Dan Burley, "Jazz Concert at the Met out of Place," *New York Amsterdam News*, January 29, 1944, 10A.

7. Elliott Grennard, "'All American Jazz Band' Concert at Met Is Just Another Jam Session," *Billboard*, January 29, 1944, 13.

8. Barry Ulanov, "Esquire's Metropolitan Concert: From Bake to Bailey," *Metronome*, February 1944, 6.

9. Jazzbo Brown, "The Esquire Farce," *The Record Changer*, March 1944, ., 23.

10. Leonard Feather, "Armstrong—Teagarden 'Date' At Super New York Jazz Show," *Melody Maker*, March 18, 1944,

11. "Louis and Letters," *Metronome*, April 1945, 17.

12. Louis Armstrong, letter to Robert Goffin, July 19, 1944, IJS clippings file.

13. "Editorial: A tale of two trumpets or how high was the jumpin' at the Met?,'" *Esquire*, April 1944, 6.

14. Harry Faulkener, "Louis Armstrong Talks on Jazz and Harry James," *New Journal and Guide*, January 22, 1944, B18.

15. "Joe Glaser Sets Up ABC Coast Office," *Billboard*, January 22, 1944, 13.

16. Teddy McRae, Jazz Oral History Project interview with Ron Welburn, Institute of Jazz Studies, Rutgers University, JOHP 71.4.1–71.4.2, October 6, 1981.

17. Teddy McRae, Jazz Oral History Project interview with Ron Welburn, Institute of Jazz Studies, Rutgers University, JOHP 71.4.3, October 13, 1981.

18. Armstrong was happy to let the younger musicians blow, though some of them, like iron-lipped Andres Merenguito, better known as "Fats Ford," already had plenty of confidence. "In my big band, whenever we had a new man coming in on first, I liked to try and make him feel at home—have a nice talk before he played his first date with us," Armstrong recalled. "Never forget the night that Fats Ford joined, he came into the room and we shook hands. 'Well Louis,' he says, 'I want you to know that I start out on top F.' Wump! But he could play all right." Chilton and Jones, *Louis*, 242.

19. Teddy McRae, Jazz Oral History Project interview with Ron Welburn, Institute of Jazz Studies, Rutgers University, JOHP 71.4.3, October 13, 1981.

20. Teddy McRae, Jazz Oral History Project interview with Ron Welburn, Institute of Jazz Studies, Rutgers University, JOHP 71.4.3 October 13, 1981.

21. "WM Claims Results with Combos Used Like Big Bands," *Billboard*, April 22, 1944, 22.

22. Maxine Gordon, *Sophisticated Giant: The Life and Legacy of Dexter Gordon* (Oakland: University of California Press, 2018), 44–45.

23. Milt Gabler Oral History, Louis Armstrong House Museum, 1994.19.3.

24. Gordon, *Sophisticated Giant*, 44–50.

25. Associated Booking Corporation ad, *Pittsburgh Courier*, August 5, 1944, 13.

26. "Hollywood's Cash Quells Qualms of Broadway," *Salt Lake Tribune*, July 16, 1944, 45.

27. Dorothy Kilgallen, "Voice of Broadway," *The Mercury*, March 29, 1945, 4.

28. Lucille Armstrong, interview with Steve Allen, c. 1973.

29. There was so much star-studded talent, Cafe Zanzibar management came up with a stunt to have the public vote on who should get top billing, with the final vote going to Robinson.

30. Simmons, JOHP interview.

31. George T. Simon, "Simon Says . . .," *Metronome*, January 1945, 38.

32. Ibid.

33. Ibid.

34. Ibid.

35. Tape 1987.3.268, Louis Armstrong House Museum.

Chapter 21

1. Joe Glaser Inc., ad, *Variety*, January 3, 1945, 146.

2. Paul Secon, "More $$ for Negro Musickers," *Billboard*, February 3, 1945, 13, 15.

3. William Russell, "New Orleans—August 1944," *The Record Changer*, September 1944, 4.

4. Ibid., 6.

5. Alyn Shipton, *Groovin' High: The Life of Dizzy Gillespie* (New York: Oxford University Press, 2001), 131–132.

6. Dizzy Gillespie and Al Fraser, *To Be or Not . . . to Bop* (New York: Doubleday, 1979), 204.

7. "[Billy Eckstine] had no respect for Leonard Feather and basically thought he was an asshole who was a thorn in his side and a forced necessary evil in his life and the lives of black musicians of his generation," Ed Eckstein, Billy's son, said. "He hawked his 'sad-sass, corny tunes' that [Billy] refused to record, but humored him nonetheless because he had seven mouths to feed and the power of Leonard's pen could hinder the process of he and others he loved and respected from getting gigs." Cary Ginell, *Mr. B: The Music and Life of Billy Eckstine* (Milwaukee: Hal Leonard Books, 2013), 64.

8. Hugues Panassie, "Presenting Mr. Feather," *The Record Changer*, January 1947, 12–13.

9. Chilton, *Sidney Bechet*, 161.

10. "Donn.," "Radio Reviews: All American Jazz Concert," *Variety*, January 24, 1945, 30.

11. Nesuhi Ertegun, "Esquire 1945," *The Record Changer*, February 1945, 3–4.

12. Teddy McRae, Jazz Oral History Project interview with Ron Welburn, Institute of Jazz Studies, Rutgers University, JOHP 71.4.1–71.4.2, October 6, 1981.

13. Paul Ross, "Vaudeville Reviews: Roxy, New York," *Billboard*, February 3, 1945, 27.

14. Harold Timberlake, "This, That," *New York Age*, March 3, 1945, 7.

15. Louis Armstrong, letter to Joe Lindsey, February 27, 1945, http://www.invaluable.com/auction-lot/music.-armstrong,-louis-satchmo.-two-page-typ-325-c-e1lceeochd.

16. "Jose.," "House Reviews: Apollo, N. Y.," *Variety*, April 25, 1945, 46.

17. "Merr.," "House Reviews: Apollo, N. Y.," *Variety*, December 27, 1944, 35.

18. "Satchmo' Scores—Louis Armstrong Sets Tour; Waxes 'I Wonder,'" *Pittsburgh Courier*, March 17, 1945, 13.

19. Charles Menees, "The Record Makers," *St. Louis Post-Dispatch*, March 14, 1945, 27.

20. Leonard Feather, "Stage Show Reviews," *Metronome*, undated news clipping from 1945, Louis Armstrong House Museum, 2017.99.156.

21. Barry Ulanov and Leonard Feather, "Editorial: Louis!," *Metronome*, April 1945, 6.

22. Barry Ulanov, "Louis and Jazz," *Metronome*, April 1945, 33.

23. Ibid., 20–21.

24. Ibid., 33.

25. "Editorial," 6.

26. Ulanov, "Louis and Jazz," 33.

27. Leonard Feather, "Sweet and Hot," *Modern Screen*, June 1945, 95.

28. "Moldy Fig," "The Sound and the Fury," *Esquire*, March 1945, 10.

29. Paul Wachtel, "The Sound and the Fury," *Esquire*, May 1945, 10.

30. Sam Platt, "The Sound and the Fury," *Esquire*, June 1945, 10.

31. The uproar over the original "Moldy Fig" letter continued into August, when *Esquire* published a letter by Cpl. H. F. Overton, stationed in Germany, who wrote, "The unfortunate truth is that this fellow Moldy Fig (and he really is moldy—with age) is merely the victim of a non-progressive mind which has obviously set upon the time honored but slightly out-of-date New Orleans style as the only real jazz." Overton was a pianist who was learning to play jazz while in the service. He eventually attended Juilliard and became a professional musician using his full name, Hall Overton, recording with Stan Getz, presiding over the famous "loft scene" in Manhattan in the 1950s and most famously, writing

arrangements for Thelonious Monk compositions that Monk recorded at concerts at Town Hall and Philharmonic Hall. Clearly, Overton was no moldy fig. Cpl. H. F. Overton, "The Sound and the Fury," *Esquire*, August 1945, 141.

32. Jean Gleason, "Bunk Storms 52nd Street," *The Record Changer*, April 1945.
33. Louis Armstrong, letter to Robert Nutt, May 9, 1945, Eddie Condon Collection, New York Public Library.
34. Ibid.
35. Armstrong, letter to Joe Lindsey.
36. Louis Armstrong, letter to Lil Hardin, June 1, 1945, 2017.46.1, Louis Armstrong House Museum.
37. Ibid.
38. Dolores Calvin, "Mrs. 'Satchmo' Is Career Girl for Husband's Wants," *Chicago Defender*, June 2, 1945, 17.
39. Lawrence F. Lamar, "Louis Armstrong Faces Trouble with 4th Wife: 'Satchmo' Admits Marital Rift; Says He's Through with Marriage, but May Love Again," *New York Amsterdam News*, September 15, 1945, A1.
40. Louis Armstrong, letter to Joe Glaser, August 2, 1955, 2008.1.43, Louis Armstrong House Museum.
41. Barbara Coleman Fox, "Life with Satchmo," *Evening Bulletin*, October 20, 1964, 56.
42. Walter Winchell, "On Broadway," *Cincinnati Enquirer*, October 24, 1945, 3.
43. Gillespie, *To Be or Not . . . to Bop*, 223.
44. Ibid., 229–230.
45. The same went for Louis Jordan, who the previous year broadcast a tune titled "Re-Bop," but it was actually a slightly smoothed-out version of Charlie Parker's composition "Red Cross." Jordan's dalliance with bop was a brief one. As late as 1948, he said of bebop, "Man, I love it," but added, "We've got seven or eight bebop numbers in the book right now, but you can't put them over on the stage. Not now. Maybe in a couple of years when people get educated to it." Jordan's longtime trumpeter Aaron Izenhall said, "Louis himself liked bop, and he was crazy about Charlie Parker, but he didn't want it in his band. His motto, which he often said, was: 'Keep it simple.' He wanted music that a working man could relax to." John Chilton *Let the Good Times Roll: The Story of Louis Jordan and His Music* (Ann Arbor: The University of Michigan Press, 1994), 143, 145.
46. Will Davidson, "Recordially Yours," *Chicago Tribune*, July 22, 1945, 50.
47. Leonard Feather, "Jazz Is Where You Find It," *Esquire*, October 1945, 128.
48. Leonard Feather, "On Musical Fascism," *Metronome*, September 1945, 16.
49. Frederic Ramsey Jr., "We Shall Walk through the Streets of the City," *The Record Changer*, December 1945, 7.
50. Gillespie, *To Be or Not . . . to Bop!*, 231
51. Ibid., 243.
52. "Brog.," "House Reviews: Orpheum, L. A.," *Variety*, September 19, 1945, 49.
53. "Armstrong at Randevu," *Salt Lake Tribune*, November 3, 1945, 16.

Chapter 22

1. Leonard Feather, *The Jazz Years* (New York: Da Capo Press, 1987), 106.
2. Arvell Shaw, interview for *Ken Burns' Jazz*, http://www.pbs.org/jazz/about/pdfs/ShawA.pdf.

3. Louis Armstrong, letter to Frances Church, March 10, 1946, IJS clippings file.

4. Ibid.

5. Robert Sylvester, "Warring Jazz Cults in a New Scramble; Condon vs. Herman," *New York Daily News*, April 2, 1946, 33.

6. "Louis Armstrong to Record 12 Sides for RCA Victor Record," *New York Age*, March 30, 1946, 4.

7. In April 1946, Feather had written another critical piece for *Esquire*, "What Happened to Benny Goodman?," in which he took the "King of Swing" to task for "living in the glorious past" and having an "indifference to keeping up with modern trends." Feather wrote that "the current spectacular type of jazz calls for an eight- or nine-piece brass section" and that Goodman's five-piece brass section sounded "puny and thin by comparison." Leonard Feather, "What Happened to Benny Goodman?," *Esquire*, April 1946, 100.

8. Armstrong didn't necessarily like the sounds, as related in a story by reed player Sam "Leroy" Parkins, who heard Armstrong's big band at a dance in Lexington, Kentucky, in the spring of 1945. "A very clear statement about his loathing for modern music, coming at him like a tornado," Parkins wrote. Parkins remembered Armstrong playing a song in the key of F and at the close instead of playing the traditional "dominant" C chord, the arrangement substituted a more "modernized" G-flat 7th chord. "Louis slashes an angry C triad right across it, making him play at least two 'wrong' notes, and Louis was incapable of playing wrong notes," Parkins wrote, describing it as the musical equivalent of Armstrong saying, "That for your godamned modernism!" Michael Steinman, "Louis and 'That Modern Malice,'" *Jazz Lives*, January 19, 2009, https://jazzlives.wordpress.com/2009/01/19/louis-and-that-modern-malice/.

9. "New Orleans' Own Louis Armstrong," *The Negro Soul*, April 1946, 37.

10. "Louis Armstrong Believes Present Band Best of All," *Baltimore Afro-American*, May 18, 1946, 20.

11. "Reverend Satchelmouth," *Time*, April 29, 1946, 47.

12. "Album Reviews," *Billboard*, June 29, 1946, 32.

13. "Most-Played Juke Box Race Records," *Billboard*, July 6, 1946, 31.

14. The only bandleaders on the various charts were the likes of Les Brown, Sammy Kaye, and Freddy Martin. Guy Lombardo was still there with his recording of "The Gypsy" while the Tex Beneke–Glenn Miller Orchestra was represented by its take on "Hey! Ba-Ba-Re-Bop."

15. "Did Atomic Bomb Double on Bikini (Pacific) and the Road (U. S. A.)?," *Billboard*, July 13, 1946, 16, 22–23.

16. Joe Glaser, letter to Joe Garland, July 25, 1946, Louis Armstrong House Museum, 1987.13.992.

17. Earl Wilson, "Earl Wilson," *Miami News*, July 31, 1946, 31.

18. Billy Rowe, "'New Orleans' Film Based on Armstrong's Life," *Pittsburgh Courier*, August 3, 1946, 18.

19. "Jules Levey Crew in New Orleans for Jazz Pic," *Variety*, August 28, 1946, 15.

20. "Joe Glaser, Stein Set for Coast Huddle on ABC Buy of MCA's 50%," *Variety*, August 28, 1946, 44.

21. The reaction of the men assembled shouldn't have been that much of a surprise. None of these musicians were especially interested in looking backwards. Bigard spent 15 years

with Duke Ellington. When Ory was rediscovered, he joined Bigard's small swing group with Charles Mingus on bass. Singleton had been part of Roy Eldridge's band in the 1930s and even recorded with Charlie Parker and Dizzy Gillespie on a Slim Gaillard date in 1945. Armstrong admired Bunk Johnson but he hadn't played regularly in that New Orleans style in about 20 years. Leonard Feather, "Satchmo To-Day," *Melody Maker*, December 7, 1946, 7.

22. Feather, "Satchmo To-Day," 7.
23. Phil Schaap, WKCR broadcast, July 4, 2017, http://www.philschaapjazz.com/radio/2017_07_04_BB_Louis_Armstrong_I_117th.mp3.
24. Feather, "Satchmo To-Day," 7.
25. John Szwed, *Billie Holiday: The Musician and the Myth* (New York: Penguin, 2016) 61.
26. Billie Holiday with William Dufty, *Lady Sings the Blues* (New York: Doubleday, 1956), 142.
27. Ibid., 144.
28. Louis Armstrong, letter to Madeleine Berard, November 25, 1946, Louis Armstrong House Museum, 1987.9.6.
29. George Avakian, "Records—Old and New," *Jazz Record*, March 1947, 5.
30. William C. Love, "Collector's Corner, *Jazz Record*, April 1947, 15.
31. Will Davidson, "Recordially Yours," *Chicago Tribune*, March 16, 1947, 131.
32. Ibid., 77.
33. Gilbert S. McKean, "The Diz and Bebop," *Esquire*, October 1947, 214.
34. Hyland Harris, *Joe Harris: Bebop Journeyman, An Oral History*, Rutgers University-Newark master's thesis, 2009, 96–97.
35. "Pittsburgh Courier All-American Band for 1947," *Pittsburgh Courier*, February 22, 1947, 19.
36. "Louis Sidran, "Esquire's All-American Jazz Band, 1947," *Esquire*, February 1947, 45.
37. Louis Armstrong, letter to *Melody Maker*, December 21, 1946, Louis Armstrong House Museum, 1987.9.10.
38. "Louis Armstrong on 'Re Bop,'" in Lewis Porter, *Jazz: A Century of Change* (New York: Schirmer Books, 1997), 182.
39. All "Blindfold Tests" in this chapter were originally published in *Metronome* and can be found in a scrapbook Leonard Feather compiled that is available on the Digital Collections website of the University of Idaho at https://digital.lib.uidaho.edu/digital/collection/lfc/id/6956/rec/29.
40. "Tomm.," "House Reviews: Apollo, N. Y.," *Variety*, January 22, 1947, 55.
41. Louis Armstrong, letter to Leonard Feather, December 5, 1946.
42. Herm., "Armstrong, Perennial Artist and Showman, Clicks at Carnegie, N. Y.," *Variety*, February 12, 1947, 36.
43. Michael Levin, "Louis Is Superb in Carnegie Hall Concert," *Down Beat*, February 26, 1947, 2.
44. Ben Richardson, "Louis Armstrong Runs Gamut of Musical Kicks, Says Rev," *People's Voice*, February 22, 1947, 24.
45. Billy Rowe, "Armstrong Ace-High in Carnegie Concert," *Pittsburgh Courier*, March 1, 1947, 18.
46. Levin, "Louis Is Superb in Carnegie Hall Concert," 2.
47. Arvell Shaw, interview with Phil Schaap, 1980, Louis Armstrong House Museum, 2005.1.2156.

Chapter 23

1. "Jazz Crix Bolt Esky Affiliation," *Billboard*, February 8, 1947, 14.
2. "Musicians Resign from Esky Jazz Book Board," *Pittsburgh Courier*, April 5, 1947, 16.
3. Louis Armstrong, acetate disc of April 1950 interview for *The Record Changer*, 2013.70.21, Louis Armstrong House Museum. On top of that, Armstrong was supposed to be presented with his two Gold Awards from *Esquire* at the Carnegie Hall concert but it never happened. "I still don't get my Oscar until I get sick with ulcers," Armstrong said in 1950, "and Ernie come to see me, I say, 'You didn't even send my award to me!' He did, 'They didn't?' Now, next day I get the award." Lucille Armstrong added, "The box was open and the trumpet was broken." Armstrong said, "It was down in somebody's basement. And if I don't ask for it, I don't get it. They don't present it to me at the Carnegie Hall like they should have, like they planned to do." The broken award still exists at the Louis Armstrong House Museum.
4. Anderson, "Joe Glaser & Louis Armstrong Part 1: The Early Days," 131. In this document and in other interviews from the 1990s, Anderson claimed that this conversation took place backstage at the Earle Theatre with Armstrong and Bobby Hackett. However, Armstrong began playing the Earle on May 9 and the May 17 Town Hall concert was already in the *New York Daily News* on May 11. Because Armstrong himself vividly remembered in 1950 that Anderson visited him while he was convalescing from ulcers, it is my opinion that all of the Town Hall discussions and negotiations took place in March. Anderson and Hackett might have indeed visited Armstrong at the Earle to go over the plans during the week before the show.
5. Ibid., 131–133.
6. John Lucas, "Jazz on Records," *The Record Changer*, June 1947, 11.
7. Ad, *Motion Picture Daily*, April 25, 1947, 6–7.
8. Theresa Loeb, "Film Fare Fine for Jazz Fans," *Oakland Tribune*, June 20, 1947, 15.
9. Donald Kirkley, " 'New Orleans' on Screen," *Baltimore Sun*, July 26, 1947, 8.
10. " 'New Orleans' Opens at Winter Garden; Negro Actors Get Prominent Roles," *New York Age*, June 28, 1947, 1.
11. Billy Rowe, "Billy Rowe's Notebook," *Pittsburgh Courier*, May 24, 1947, 16.
12. Edwin Schallert, "Jazz Highlights Lame Story in 'New Orleans,' " *Los Angeles Times*, June 18, 1947, 11.
13. Rudi Blesh, *Shining Trumpets* (New York: Alfred A. Knopf, 1946), 260–261.
14. Bob Arthur, "Jazzorama," *Jazz Record*, June 1947, 19–20.
15. Ibid.
16. The Earle engagement ended with Holiday being arrested and sent to prison for a narcotics violation; Joe Glaser, exasperated with her heroin addiction, cooperated with the Federal Narcotics Bureau to send her away. For a detailed telling of the incident, see Donald Clarke's *Billie Holiday: Wishing on the Moon* (Hachette Books, 2009).
17. "Dozen Songs on Earle Bill," *Philadelphia Inquirer*, May 10, 1947, 6.
18. "Shal.," "House Reviews: Earle, Philly," May 14, 1947, 50.
19. Sidney Bechet was also hired to perform and was featured in all the advertisements for the concert but on the day of the show, Anderson learned that Bechet was too sick to perform and needed to back out. Anderson recalled, "I later learned that he had showed up on time for his job [at Jimmy Ryan's] and I can only assume that he felt our concert date was too hot

to handle." Bechet had clearly not forgotten the 1945 *Esquire* concert fiasco. Anderson, "Joe Glaser & Louis Armstrong Part 1: The Early Days," 133.

20. Robert Sylvester, "Ol' Satch and Horn in Best Jazz Concert of Town Hall Series," *New York Daily News*, May 19, 1947, 31.

21. "Back O'Town Blues" also included a completely spontaneous moment when a particularly talkative member of the audience elicited a sharp, "Shut up, boy" from Armstrong, breaking up the entire audience. Armstrong wasn't one to tamper with a routine that worked; in future versions, he set his own musicians up as hecklers, winning some extra laughs during his blues choruses.

22. Art Hodes, "I Ran Into . . .," *Jazz Record*, August 1947, 4.

23. Anderson, "Joe Glaser & Louis Armstrong Part 1: The Early Days," 133.

24. Feather had nothing to do with the Town Hall concert so he didn't write about it; in fact, Ernie Anderson was squarely on the opposite side of Feather in the jazz wars and went so far as inviting Feather's nemesis Art Hodes to say a few words during Armstrong's intermission at Town Hall. A recording doesn't survive but writing in the *New York Daily News*, Robert Sylvester said Anderson and Robbins made a "mistake," writing, "This time they sent Art Hodes out on the stage to interrupt the music with a long and inarticulate tirade against the opposition jazz cults. Art, who usually has more sense, ended with a long eulogy of Robbins and then couldn't remember Robbins' name." Sylvester, "Ol' Satch and Horn in Best Jazz Concert of Town Hall Series," 31.

25. "House Reviews, Apollo, N. Y.," *Variety*, June 15, 1947, 49. Gillespie might have finally won over the *Variety* writers, but longtime supporters such as Barry Ulanov wished Gillespie would tone it down. Ulanov was "annoyed" about Gillespie's use of quotes, such as inserting "Jingle Bells" during the "lovely coda" at the end of "I Can't Get Started" and sensed a "bitterness [ripping] through much of what he does," warning that Gillespie should give "the over-frantic clowning, which proceeds from the bitterness, more than casual thought." Barry Ulanov, "Band Reviews: Dizzy Gillespie," *Metronome*, September 1947, 22.

26. "House Reviews: Earle Theatre, Philly," *Variety*, June 15, 1947, 49.

27. John Chilton, *Let the Good Times Roll: The Story of Louis Jordan and His Music* (Ann Arbor: University of Michigan Press, 1994), 144–145.

28. Ibid., 145.

29. "House Reviews: Apollo, N. Y.," *Variety*, July 9, 1947, 18.

30. Tape 1987.3.176, Louis Armstrong House Museum.

31. Dorothy Kilgallen, "Voice of Broadway," *Record-Argus*, August 18, 1947, 4.

32. "Satchmo Comes Back," *Time*, September 1, 1947.

33. "Kap.," "Band Reviews: Louis Armstrong Orch, Billy Berg's, Hollywood," *Variety*, August 20, 1947.

34. John Lucas, "Louis, Born with Jazz, Still Its King--—And Success on Coast Today Is Proof," *Down Beat*, August 27, 1947.

35. Herman Hill, "Satchmo Smash Hit at Berg's," *Pittsburgh Courier*, August 23, 1947, 17.

36. "Satchmo Socko," *Billboard*, August 30, 1947, 21.

37. "Satchmo Comes Back," *Time*, September 1, 1947, 32.

38. Hugues Panassie, "Louis Armstrong off Stage," *Jazz Journal*, May 1956, 3.

39. Albert S. Otto, "Dixieland Jubilee," *The Record Changer*, January 1949, 7.

40. "Satchmo Comes Back," 32.

41. Gilbert S. McKean, "The Diz and the Bebop," *Esquire*, October 1947, 214.

42. Roy W. Stephens, "Writer Raps Armstrong for Criticism of Trend," *Baltimore Afro-American*, November 15, 1947, 6.

43. George T. Simon, "Bebop's the Easy Out, Claims Louis," *Metronome*, March 1948, 14–15.

44. "'Diz' Calls 'Satchmo' Reactionary," *Philadelphia Tribune*, January 4, 1949, 12.

45. "Louis the First," *Time*, February 21, 1949, 55–56.

46. Ted Hallock, "Dizzy's New Idea Would Help Interpret Arrangers," *Down Beat*, July 1, 1949, 13.

47. "Bird Wrong; Bop Must Get a Beat: Diz," *Down Beat*, October 7, 1949.

48. "Charlie Parker with Strings," *Billboard*, April 1, 1950, 44.

49. Allen Krebs, "Louis Armstrong, the Jazz Trumpeter and Singer, Dies in His Home at 71," *New York Times*, July 7, 1971, 41.

50. Orrin Keepnews, "Lemme Take This Chorus," *The Record Changer*, April 1948, p. 4.

51. This and all succeeding quotes from this evening are taken from a series of 16 acetate discs containing the complete surviving two and a half hours of audio as recorded by Keepnews and Grauer on this evening in 1950. They originally used a tape recorder belonging to Boris Rose but since tape recorders were not yet common, had a dub made onto acetate discs. A copy was given to Paul Bacon, who designed the cover of this issue of *The Record Changer*. After Bacon's death, the 16 discs were acquired by Stan King, who donated them to the Louis Armstrong House Museum in 2014. Certain portions made it into the finished issue, but usually in edited form. These quotes are transcribed from the original discs.

52. Feather, *The Jazz Years*, 298–300. Barry Ulanov, on the other hand, wrote, "What we fought for was right and the way we fought was right, too, I am still persuaded. We were up against extraordinarily thick heads and tin ears. . . . How could we help but snarl and mock and be appalled by those self-appointed guardians of the 'real jazz' who were working overtime to attack a genius [Parker] and the superb music he was bringing into being?"

53. In the 1950s, trombonist Jim Beebe, a young white musician from Chicago most at home in traditional jazz settings, went to see trumpeter Bob Scobey's Dixieland group at the Blackhawk in Chicago and was stunned to see Miles Davis sitting in with the band. During the break, Beebe went up to Davis and "stammered out something to the effect that I couldn't believe that he was there playing with Scobey as I had it in my mind from what I read that stylistically they could never play together and they must dislike each other." Davis looked at him and said, "You've been reading that asshole Leonard Feather, haven't you?" "I nodded and Miles neatly and briefly explained that the divisions in jazz were artificial and promoted by writers like Feather," Beebe recalled, adding, "This little exchange with Miles changed forever the way I looked at jazz and music in general." Jim Beebe, "Leonard Feather (An Encounter with Miles Davis)," at http://leeharrismusic.net/leonard_feather.htm.

54. Dizzy Gillespie with Ralph Ginzburg, "Jazz Is Too Good for Americans," *Esquire*, June 1957, 55.

55. Gillespie, *To Be or Not . . . to Bop!*, 295–296.

56. Dizzy Gillespie, "Louis Armstrong 1900–1971," *New York Times*, July 18, 1971.

57. James Stewart Thayer, "Armstrong Heads Dizzy's List," *Seattle Times*, February 14, 1982, E5.

Epilogue

1. "Louis the First," *Time*, 56.
2. Trummy Young, Jazz Oral History Project interview with Patricia Willard, September 17, 1976, Institute of Jazz Studies, Rutgers University.
3. Tape 1987.3.254, Louis Armstrong House Museum.
4. Private tape made with George Avakian, November 1, 1953. Courtesy of David Ostwald and George Avakian.
5. Tape 1987.3.17, Louis Armstrong House Museum.
6. Patrick Scott, "The Hot Miss Lil," *Toronto Globe and Mail,* September 18, 1965.
7. Gilbert Millstein, "Africa Harks to Satch's Horn," *New York Times Magazine*, November 24, 1960.
8. Tape 1987.3.424, Louis Armstrong House Museum.
9. Chris Albertson, "Lil Hardin Armstrong—A Fond Remembrance," *Stereo Review*, September 25, 1971, 67.
10. Carolyn Carter-Kennedy, *The Lucille Armstrong Story: A Lady With a Vision* (Bloomington, Indiana: iUniverse, 2010), 44.
11. Zutty and Marge Singleton, JOHP interview.
12. Ibid.
13. Patrick Scott, "A Tired Old Pal Remembers Satchmo," *Toronto Globe and Mail*, July 1971 (undated news clipping), Louis Armstrong House Museum, 2003.80.77.
14. Stanley Crouch, "Wherever He Went Joy Was Sure to Follow," *New York Times*, March 12, 2000, 200–201.
15. Robert G. O'Meally, "Checking Our Balances: Louis Armstrong, Ralph Ellison, and Betty Boop," in *Uptown Conversation*, ed. Robert G. O'Meally, Brent Hayes Edwards, and Farah Jasmine Griffin (New York: Columbia University Press, 2004), 280.
16. Untitled Swedish news clipping from October 21, 1933, found in the Gösta Hägglöf Collection, Louis Armstrong House Museum, 2011.22.3-07.

Index

Figures are indicated by *f* following the page number

For the benefit of digital users, indexed terms that span two pages (e.g., 52–53) may, on occasion, appear on only one of those pages.